Instructor's Manual
to Accompany

THE WESTERN HUMANITIES
Third Edition

Roy T. Matthews
F. DeWitt Platt
Michigan State University

Mayfield Publishing Company
Mountain View, California
London • Toronto

International Standard Book Number: 1-55934-967-0

Manufactured in the United States of America
10   9   8   7   6   5   4   3   2   1

Mayfield Publishing Company
1280 Villa Street
Mountain View, California 94041

PREFACE

The third edition of this manual has been revised and expanded based on suggestions of instructors who used the second edition of *The Western Humanities* and the accompanying Instructor's Manual.

The organization of this manual reflects the same emphases that characterize *The Western Humanities;* that is, approximately one-third of each chapter's content focuses on political, social, and economic trends—material history—and the remaining two-thirds or so on the artistic, literary, musical, and intellectual developments—cultural history. We have followed these ratios, especially in preparing the examination questions.

This manual includes for each chapter teaching strategies and suggestions, test items, film and music suggestions, and a detailed outline revised to accompany the third edition of *The Western Humanities.* The unique teaching device adopted in the manual's second edition—a list of significant developments in non-Western cultures that parallel the events described in the main textbook—has been reorganized, expanded, and updated. Instructors can draw on these data about non-Western historical and cultural developments in order to relate Western events to a global setting.

Personal Perspective Background, a new section in this manual, offers further information about those persons and events showcased in the Personal Perspectives—an innovative feature added to each chapter in the third edition of *The Western Humanities.* Each Personal Perspective reflects its era by presenting one or more unique voices commenting on a range of happenings, such as personal calamities, public crises, social changes, religious upheavals, humorous events, and impressions of foreigners. This new section will help instructors to interpret the passages in the main text for their students.

Three different types of sample tests are included in the manual: identification, discussion/essay, and multiple-choice questions. All have been thoroughly revised to reflect the additions and changes in the textbook. In addition, five comparative, multiple-choice questions have been added at the end of Chapters 7, 14, and 21; each set of five questions covers the previous seven chapters. These comparative questions will enable instructors to prepare tests that cover more than a single chapter. These latter questions also complement the already-existing discussion/essay questions, which require students to draw on themes or topics from individual chapters.

A list of film and music selections that are intended to supplement the classroom lectures is provided in each chapter of the manual. The recommended films have been produced in the past twenty years and have proven their usefulness as teaching devices. Because ancient music has virtually disappeared, the music selections begin only with Chapter 9, The High Middle Ages; these selections are meant to augment the music listed in the textbook.

The list of recommended books for students has been extensively revised in the manual. Instead of the two categories used in the second edition—Secondary Sources and Suggestions for Further Reading—there is now a single heading: Suggestions for Further Reading. Books selected for the bibliography have been chosen based on one or more of the following criteria: the book reflects recent scholarship; an older book, if still influential, continues to be listed; the book offers more advanced information that the textbook; the list of books in each chapter offers balanced coverage of the period's arts, history, literature, philosophy, and religion. We have examined and annotated each selection, and we are fully aware that our list is merely an introduction to vast areas of learning whose scholarship continues to grow at a rapid rate.

Listening Guides following the chapter-by-chapter material can be duplicated for students to use if the instructor incorporates music into the classroom. In the Appendix, biographical data on new persons included in the third edition of *The Western Humanities* have been added to the existing listing of major cultural figures highlighting differences in class, sex, and religious beliefs.

Accompanying the Instructor's Manual and the textbook are additional teaching aids: computerized testing for Macintosh and IBM-compatible computers; 100 art slides; 25 map slides; tape cassette and compact disc recordings of music; and videotapes. If used on a regular basis in the classroom, these teaching aids will enhance the quality of instruction.

Available packaged with the textbook, at a nominal cost to the student, is *Music in the Western Tradition,* which discusses many of the music selections available with the textbook in more detail than is possible for us to do here. This supplement introduces students to basic musical concepts, key developments of musical history and selected compositions, and approaches to writing about music.

For information on how to obtain these items, contact your Mayfield representative or call (800) 433-1279.

CONTENTS

TEACHING STRATEGIES FOR THE WESTERN HUMANITIES

A key feature in this Instructor's Manual is the section in each chapter called Teaching Strategies and Suggestions. We are motivated to offer these teaching suggestions by two interrelated classroom ideals: First, we believe that university and college students should have a working knowledge of the basic vocabulary, major milestones, and general history of the Western arts and humanities; and, second, we believe that students should use that information to help them think critically—the goal of education at every level. These educational principles reinforce the message of our textbook, *The Western Humanities*, since it is based on these same ideals.

Presented with the challenge of offering advice to instructors who adopt our textbook, and ruminating on the knowledge we have gained through years of university teaching, we recommend the following five general teaching strategies and seven specific lecture suggestions. Although not an exhaustive list, these strategies and suggestions represent basic approaches to teaching and are flexible enough to be adaptable to many different settings. For this reason we have organized the *Teaching Strategies and Suggestions* sections around these basic approaches, suggesting their use in various combinations depending on each chapter's demands. Instructors, of course, may develop their own teaching strategies and suggestions, since not all pedagogical methods will work in the same way for each person.

FIVE BASIC TEACHING STRATEGIES

1. *Standard Lecture.* The Standard Lecture teaching strategy is the oldest and most frequently used teaching tool in the world. It involves a single instructor, with or without teaching aids, who gives a lecture that conveys a large quantity of information to note-taking students. When well done, the Standard Lecture method can be extremely effective; when done poorly, it is a deadening experience. We believe that the Standard Lecture strategy is best when done with the following teaching aids: a well-thought-out outline made available to students before the lecture (projected on a screen, written on a blackboard, or distributed in a handout); adequate time for students to ask questions or request clarification about the lecture; a summary at the lecture's end to drive home the vital points; and the instructor's vigor in varying voice level, using appropriate gestures, writing on the blackboard or using an overhead projector, and moving about the classroom.

    We envision that the Standard Lecture strategy will be the one used most frequently by instructors who adopt *The Western Humanities*. It is ideal for topics that lend themselves to a direct approach—specifically historical issues, such as the rise of Rome or the causes of the Crusades. The Standard Lecture approach is also flexible enough to add new instructional ingredients, and our suggestions for the next two strategies are variations of this basic method.

2. *Slide Lecture.* A variation on the Standard Lecture approach, the Slide Lecture strategy is centered on the presentation of slides of art and architecture with running commentary by the instructor. This particular model is the preferred method for introducing the visual arts of a specific historical era, such as the Hellenic style of ancient Greece. Instructors will want eventually to amass their own art slide collections. In the meantime the slides in the auxiliary materials accompanying *The Western Humanities* provide the beginning of a collection, since five slides of key artistic works are included for each chapter. With these five slides, instructors can

illustrate the leading characteristics of each artistic style, and when juxtaposed with slides from another period, can demonstrate differences between styles. For maximum educational benefit, instructors should provide students with slide lists, giving the name of each artist or architect and the full title and date of each work of art or building under review. The slide lists serve both as reminders of the art viewed and as writing areas for students to record lecture notes.

3. *Music Lecture.* Another variation on the Standard Lecture approach, the Music Lecture strategy is excellent for illustrating musical styles as well as significant monuments of Western music. A set of key musical recordings, with helpful notes, is provided to instructors in the auxiliary materials accompanying *The Western Humanities.* With these materials, instructors can play recordings in class and provide students with handouts that set forth the composer and title of each selection along with general instructions for listening.

4. *Discussion.* The Discussion strategy is just what its name implies, a class conducted by the discussion method. This strategy works best when the class is limited to twenty-five or fewer students so that there can be maximum interaction between the discussion leader and the students. If the class is too large, the discussion fails to engage most of the students, and they end up being bored or hostile. In those instances when the classroom size is favorable, we recommend that discussion questions be based on the *Teaching Objectives* section of the Instructor's Manual. Even in larger classes, ten or fifteen minutes of discussion can provide variety and be illuminating to students. Particularly helpful in such settings is the use of open-ended questions that cause students to think for themselves. For example, when teaching Greek civilization, the instructor might ask, "Which is the more beautiful style of art: the Hellenic or the Hellenistic?" Because there is no "correct" answer, this question allows many students to express their opinions. While encouraging a democracy of opinions, a good discussion leader will ask students to back up their points of view with sound reasoning based on specific works of art.

5. *Film.* The Film strategy is a teaching technique in which the instructor presents a film on a certain topic. For the Film strategy to work best, films must be used as teaching aids and not simply be treated as ends in themselves. At a minimum, this means that the instructor should "frame" each film by giving it an introduction that explains what it is about and a conclusion that places its message into the context of the course being taught. The Film strategy is especially good for dealing with the arts and architecture and for presenting sweeping surveys of a historical period. Only high-quality and well-made films should be shown; otherwise, this technique is counterproductive of sound educational goals because it leads students to ridicule what they view and to judge a poorly made film to be a waste of learning time.

SEVEN SPECIFIC LECTURE SUGGESTIONS

1. *The Diffusion Model.* If the classroom topic involves the interaction of two societies or cultures, then the Diffusion model is probably the best way to organize that part of the lecture. Such an organization involves an identification of the cultural ideas, values, and techniques that pass from one society to another and an elaboration of the ways in which the things borrowed are assimilated into the receiving culture. This is a highly valuable lecture-organizing technique for instructors to master, since nearly every chapter of *The Western Humanities* touches on cultural interaction in some way, particularly regarding the enduring influence of Greece and Rome on later phases of Western culture.

2. *The Pattern of Change.* The Pattern of Change organizing device is a convenient way to deal with the many different types of change that recur in Eastern culture, such as moving from relatively simple to more complex ideas, from an original to an imitative artistic style, from a pure to an eclectic artistic style, or from unadorned to richly ornamented architectural works. A good lecture topic that would lend itself to the Pattern of Change model is the shift in the Middle Ages from the Romanesque to the Gothic style, a shift that retained many ingredients of the plain

Romanesque style while laying the foundation for a soaring Gothic style that went through several complex and elaborate phases.

3. *The Spirit of the Age.* "The Spirit of the Age" is a phrase borrowed from the thought of the German thinker G. F. W. Hegel, who believed that every historic period had a distinct spirit—*zeitgeist*—that was expressed unconsciously in its achievements, both cultural and material. Although controversial, Hegel's theory is a useful way to help students understand the traits that distinguish one age from another. Instructors interested in adopting this approach to their lectures may consult the introductory paragraphs and each chapter legacy of *The Western Humanities*, for these sections are often compatible with Hegel's point of view.

4. *Case Study.* The Case Study method is an excellent tool for drawing lessons from history. In this approach, the instructor focuses on a well-defined historic incident or set of events that permit comparisons with later developments. For example, a lecture on the collapse of the Roman republic or the Roman Empire would provide the instructor with a Case Study that touches on contemporary issues; students could be asked to assess parallels between Rome and the United States in the areas of involvement in world affairs, the rise of popular spectacles, and the upsurge in urban violence.

5. *Comparison/Contrast.* The Comparison/Contrast model is a teaching tool that is part of many lecture models, such as the Diffusion or the Patterns of Change models, but it can also stand on its own. Highly flexible, the Comparison/Contrast method can be used in situations where there are strong similarities and differences, as in art (Impressionism and Post-Impressionism), in culture (fifth-century B.C. Athens and fifteenth-century Florence), and in politics (seventeenth-century England and France).

6. *Historical Overview.* The Historical Overview is a method of surveying a vast sweep of history, usually illustrated with a time line that can be projected on a screen. Instructors who adopt *The Western Humanities* have been provided with twenty-six time lines that list decisive dates of historical events along with significant cultural achievements. Though limited in its use, the Historical Overview can be quite effective at the beginning of a course or at any major point in the course when a new phase of history is introduced, such as in a survey course when the instructor moves from the Middle Ages to the Renaissance.

7. *Reflections/Connections.* The Reflections/Connections approach is based on the notion that a civilization's creative works are closely linked to its political, social, and economic institutions. This means that the arts and humanities are not produced in a vacuum, but rather mirror the dominant values of a society. This Reflections/Connections model can be used throughout the book. For example, this model can be used to treat the Late Middle Ages, when the rise of capitalism and its secular spirit was reflected in Chaucer's descriptions of middle-class pilgrims in *The Canterbury Tales*.

PREHISTORY AND NEAR
EASTERN CIVILIZATIONS

TEACHING STRATEGIES AND SUGGESTIONS

The instructor can approach the topic of prehistory and early culture through the Historical Overview model and use the Comparison/Contrast model to explain the differences between culture and civilization. An important point to emphasize is that human creativity is a basic human activity that predates the rise of civilization.

Using the Historical Overview, the instructor can easily survey Mesopotamian and Egyptian civilizations in separate lectures. Having explained the major phases of these earliest Western civilizations, the instructor can then shift to the Comparison/Contrast model and lay out their similarities and differences. The instructor can also use the Patterns of Change model to explain the evolution of each of these civilizations from its earliest beginning to its height of power. Another model the instructor can use is the Reflections/Connections model. For example, a lecture on the Sumerian civilization and *The Epic of Gilgamesh* would show how the two are connected and also demonstrate that the themes of the epic are common to most human concerns.

LECTURE OUTLINE

Non-Western Events

I. Prehistory and Early Cultures
   A. Definitions of culture and civilization
   B. The time frame
      1. Origins of human life and culture
         a) Old Stone Age and New Stone Age
            (1) Artistic developments
            (2) Other achievements
         b) The Neolithic period
            (1) Artistic developments
            (2) Other achievements
      2. Rise of civilizations

II. The Civilizations of the Tigris and Euphrates River Valley: Mesopotamia
   A. The Sumerian, Akkadian, and Babylonian kingdoms
      1. Historical overview of the three kingdoms
      2. Economic, social, and political developments

4000–3000 B.C.
In Africa, beginning of Sahara, as a result of overworking the soil and overgrazing; in the Sahara Desert, more than 30,000 rock engravings and paintings, half of which are in the region known as Tassili; varied styles, scale, and subject matter, such as human beings, alone and in groups with other human beings or animals, figures of elephants, rhinoceroses, hippopotamuses, buffalo, camels, horses, sheep, and domestic cattle along with weapons carried by human

B. The Cradle of Civilization
   1. Writing
   2. Religion
   3. Literature
      a) Epics, tales, and legends
      b) *The Epic of Gilgamesh*
      c) *The Exaltation of Inanna*
   4. Law
      a) The Code of Hammurabi
      b) Judicial system
   5. Art and architecture
      a) Carvings
      b) The ziggurat

beings, such as axes, throwing sticks, bows, javelins, and swords; dating of figures is controversial, starting perhaps about 5500 B.C. and continuing until about 100 B.C.; in about 4000 B.C., pastoral life with pottery, polished stone axes, grindstones, and arrowheads, as well as domestication of cattle, sheep, and goats

In Andean culture, Lithic period, 10,000 to 3000 B.C.; village culture; domestication of maize, potatoes, chilies, gourds, beans, and cotton, and the first works of art in America, two gourds decorated with masks; domestication of llama and alpaca; longest continuous textile record in the world, starting with fibers in Guitarrero cave, 10,000 B.C.

In Australia, rock paintings

In southwest Asia, first use of bronze hard enough to hold an edge, 3600 B.C.

In Caribbean, settlement of islands by colonists from the Yucatán

In China, multicolored ceramics, made in Russia, reach China

In Japan, Jomon culture, about 4000 B.C.–about 300 B.C.; handmade pottery with rope pattern designs; circular and rectangular huts, with the floor in a pit

In Mesoamerica, thriving village culture and domestication of maize and cotton; trade with southwestern North America

In North America, maritime Archaic Indian settlements in northern Labrador; use of harpoons, large boats, and burial mounds

III. The Civilization of the Nile River Valley:
Egypt
  A. Prehistory to 3000 B.C.
    1. Characteristics
    2. Upper and Lower Egypt
    3. Neolithic developments
  B. Continuity and change over three
     thousand years, 3100–525 B.C.
    1. Survey of Egypt's dynasties
    2. Common threads in politics,
       economics, and society
  C. A quest for eternal cultural values
    1. Religion
        a) The theocratic state
        b) The pharaoh's defining role
        c) The abortive Amarna revolution
        d) The promise of immortality
    2. Writing and literature
        a) Hieroglyphics
        b) Literary genres of the Old
             Kingdom, the First Intermediate
             Period, and the Middle
             Kingdom
        c) The rich heritage of the New
             Kingdom
             (1) *Hymn to Aten*
             (2) Love lyrics, model letters,
                 wisdom literature, and
                 fairy tales
    3. Architecture
        a) The pyramid
             (1) The earliest version
             (2) The true pyramid
        b) The funerary temple
    4. Sculpture, painting, and minor arts
        a) Colossal sculpture: the Sphinx
        b) Sculptures in the round
        c) Portrait sculptures
        d) The break in tradition: Amarna
        e) The artistic canon
        f) Tomb sculpture

3000–2000 B.C.
In Afghanistan, large cities of
  Mundigak and Shahr-i-
Sokhta on the Hilmand
  River, about 2500 B.C.;
  influence reached the
  Arabian peninsula; less
  complex than the Indus
  River cultures
In Andean culture, Pre-
  Ceramic period, 3000–1800
  B.C.; at Huaca Prieta, on
  Peru's coast, fishnets,
  textiles, and cotton scraps
  with polychrome patterns
  and zigzag edges;
  monumental architecture
  and sculpture, and jaguar,
  snake, and bird imagery;
  Kotosh, a ceremonial site
  built of stone and earth,
  including the Crossed
  Hands temple, about 2450
  B.C.; metallurgy begins
  about 3000 B.C.
In China, the potter's wheel
  in about 3000 B.C.; silk
  weaving by about 2700
  B.C.; meeting houses in
  villages; Banshan (painted)
  pottery around 2500 B.C.;
  zenith of Lungshan (black)
  pottery, 2500–2000 B.C.;
  Lungshan villages, built on
  hills and surrounded by
  walls of pounded earth;
  yang and yin philosophy
  of nature is begun by the
  legendary ruler Fu Hsi, in
  about 2800 B.C.; the
  principles of herbal medicine
  and acupuncture,
  originated by the
  legendary ruler, Shen
  Nung, in about 2700 B.C.;
  Nei Ching, the most ancient
  medical text, by the ruler
  Huang Ti in 2595 B.C.;
  civilization begins with the
  Xia (about 2200–1750 B.C.);
  tithe system with annual
  distribution of fields; first
  bamboo musical pipe;

equinoxes and solstices determined; the making of bronze, before 2000 B.C.; architecture, moving slowly from simple to more complex forms, usually made of wood and based on the pavilion

In China and India, start of regular astronomical observations

In Europe, in Norway, rock carvings depict skiing

In India, Indus River Civilization, about 2500–1750 B.C.; development of urban grain-growing culture on the Indus River; Harappa and Mohenjo Daro are two main cities; cities are laid out on a grid, with dwelling units made uniform according to social class of inhabitants, built of baked bricks but with ample use of wood; caravan resting places at street crossings, grain silos, public baths, drainage canals, and sewerage systems; economy based on agriculture, on the growing of cotton and flax; trade over a vast area; proto-Dravidian script that remains untranslated

In Turkemenistan, the large cities of Namazzatepe and other centers on the Tedzent River, about 2500 B.C.; less complex than the Indus River cultures

In Southeast Asia, the making of bronze, by 2500 B.C.

2000–1500 B.C.

In Andean culture, Pre-Ceramic period, 3000–1800 B.C.; Initial period, 1800–1000 B.C.; two basic architectural styles emerge, U-shaped pyramids on the coast and sunken circular courts in the highlands; the

U-shaped style at Huaca la Florida, Rimac Valley, about 2000 B.C.; the sunken circular format at Moxeke; Sechín Alto, the largest ceremonial center in the Americas, from about 1700 to 500 B.C.; the beginning of state formation in South America, 1700 B.C.

In China, Xia (about 2200–1750 B.C.), Shang (about 1750–1100 B.C.), and Zhou (about 1100–771 B.C. in the West and 1100–256 B.C. in the East) dynasties; the Shang isthe first dynasty for which archeological evidence exists; writing system, practice of divination, walled cities, bronze technology, and use of horse-drawn chariots; first city, around 1900 B.C. at Erlitou on the Yellow River; jadeworking, pottery, bronze tools, weapons, and vessels; in North China, use of *hangtu*, or rammed earth technique for building; first of seven periods for Chinese literature

In Europe, in England, the building of Stonehenge

In India, Indus River Civilization, about 2500–1750 B.C.; ended by ecological change and migrations; Aryan Migration, about 1750–1000 B.C.; migration into northwest India of nomadic tribes from Iranian plateau; beginning of Indo-European language; four basic elements known: earth, air, fire, and water

In Mesoamerica, Formative period, 2000–200 B.C.; earliest village settlements were at Las Charcas in

Guatemala and El Arbolillo and Zacatenco in Mexico, about 2000 B.C.; domestication of chilies, tomatoes, cacao, beans, squashes, and tobacco; pottery with geometric designs; "pretty lady" type figurines from the village of Tlatilco, Mexico; rise of Olmec culture, the "jaguar people," in about 1500 B.C.; the Olmecs, originating along the rivers of the tropical Gulf Coast, are the "mother culture" from which the theocratic cultures of the Classic period derived; beginning of Mayan culture, before 1500 B.C.

In North America, cultivation of gourds, sunflowers, and marsh elder; first mound complex, Poverty Point, Louisiana, about 1600–1700 B.C.; red jasper beads; from Maine to Labrador, trade in burial goods, especially ramah chert, a translucent stone; in Great Lakes region, copperworking

In Pacific Islands, colonization by Lapita people, about 1600 B.C.

1500–1000 B.C.

In Africa, Ethiopia becomes an independent power; the arrival of Libyan horsemen disrupts pastoral life, as represented in the Saharan rock paintings and engravings, 1200 B.C.; horses and war chariots allow Libyans to cross the Sahara, as represented in the art though the artists themselves don't appear to be horse-owning

In Andean culture, use of terraces dates from about 1200 B.C.

In China, Shang (about 1750–

1100 B.C.) and Zhou (about 1100–771 B.C. in the West and about 1100–256 B.C. in the East) dynasties; under the Zhou dynasty, a hierarchical political and social system; power held by aristocratic families as lords of their domains; Chinese "feudalism" depended on ancestral cults; Shang and Zhou dynasties create long-lasting building and structural prototypes; first Chinese dictionary; silk fabrics; elaborate bronze sculptures; Shang capitals successively at Erlitou, Zhengzhou, and Anyang; urban planning at Anyang, including chessboard pattern layout and royal tombs; slavery and human sacrifice practiced; cowrie shells for currency; jade for trade; Fu Hao's Shaft Tomb; ivory objects with turquoise inlays; introduction of soybeans from Manchuria, about 1200 B.C.

In India, Aryan Migration, about 1750–1000 B.C.; the beginning of the Upanishad tradition, literary works speculating about the world system; the first oral versions of the Rig Veda, "songs of spiritual knowledge," composed in Sanskrit and eventually numbering ten books and 1,028 hymns; introduction of ironworking, before 1000 B.C.

In North America, in Lovelock Cave, Nevada, duck decoys, dating to 1500 B.C.; in Great Lakes region, trade with Gulf of Mexico

IV. Heirs to the Mesopotamian and Egyptian empires, after 1000 B.C.
   A. The Hittites
   B. The Assyrians
   C. The Medes and the Persians
      1. Persian art
      2. The religion of Zoroaster

V. The Legacy of Near Eastern Civilization

LEARNING OBJECTIVES

To learn:

1. The difference between *culture* and *civilization*

2. The great age of the earth and the relatively recent nature of human development

3. The distinction between *prehistory* and *history*

4. The stages of early human development

5. The earliest forms of artistic expression

6. How agriculture brought about the Neolithic period and the significance of this cultural period

7. How the discovery of metalworking led to the Bronze Age, which in turn produced the first civilizations in the West

8. The leading characteristics and major historical periods of the three civilizations that arose in Mesopotamia and the Egyptian civilization that began in the Nile river valley

9. The interaction between geography and cultural development in Mesopotamia and the Nile river valley

10. How Mesopotamia's and Egypt's cultural developments were each an outgrowth of specific political, economic, and social settings

11. Contrasts between Mesopotamian and Egyptian civilizations

12. The defining role played by religion in Mesopotamia's and Egypt's civilizations

13. Historic "firsts" achieved in Mesopotamia or Egypt or both that became legacies for later Western developments: writing, music, musical instruments, musical forms (such as hymns), astronomy, medicine, sound engineering principles rooted in mathematics, a law code, religious ideas, mathematical and geometrical knowledge, the 365-day, 12-month calendar, town life, town planning, standard weights and measures, literary genres, the column with capitals, the pyramid, post-and-lintel construction, sculpture in the round, portrait sculptures, relief sculptures, sculptural and painting techniques, and an aesthetic canon for artists

SUGGESTIONS FOR FILMS

Ancient Egypt: Digging Up Her Rich Past. Time-Life, 51 min., color.

Ancient Mesopotamia. Coronet, 10 min., color.

Dr. Leakey and the Dawn of Man. Films, Inc., 27 min., color.

Egypt—The Gift of the Nile. Centron Educational Films, 29 min., color.

The Mysteries of the Great Pyramid. Wolper Productions, 50 min., color.

Persia: The Sudden Empire. Time-Life, 30 min., color.

Prehistoric Man in Europe. International Film Bureau, 23 min., color.

Yesterday's World: The Missing City Gates. NET, 29 min., color. (On ancient Assyria)

SUGGESTIONS FOR FURTHER READING

General

Achtemeier, P., ed. *Harper's Bible Dictionary.* San Francisco: Harper & Row, 1985. One of the best one-volume dictionaries for students who want biblical information quickly.

Duby, G., and Perrot, M., general editors. *A History of Women in the West.* 5 vols. Vol. I: *From Ancient Goddesses to Christian Saints,* edited by P. S. Pantel, and translated by A. Goldhammer. Vol. II: *Silences of the Middle Ages,* edited by C. Klapisch-Zuber. Vol. III: *Renaissance and Enlightenment Paradoxes,* edited by N. Z. Davis and A. Farge. Vol. IV: *Emerging Feminism from Revolution to World War,* edited by G. Fraisse and M. Perrot. Vol. V: *Toward a Cultural Identity in the Twentieth Century,* edited by F. Thebaud. Cambridge: Belknap Press of Harvard University Press, 1994. An Italian publication in origin, with two general editors from France, and volume editors from various countries; each volume is a series of essays by leading feminist scholars; the standard work for the history of women and gender.

Lerner, G. *The Creation of Feminist Consciousness.* New York: Oxford University Press, 1993. Volume 2 of Lerner's history of women; organized thematically on topics such as "self-authorization" and "authorization through creativity," Lerner explores the various ways that recorded history has shaped the consciousness of Western women, from the Middle Ages to 1870.

Morehead, P. D. *The New International Dictionary of Music.* Harmondsworth, England: Meridian, a division of Penguin, 1992. Handy, authoritative information on a wide range of musical topics, including composers, musical instruments, and musical styles and terms.

Nuttgens, P. *Simon and Schuster's Pocket Guide to Architecture.* New York: Simon & Schuster, 1991. A useful guide to styles of architecture, mainly in the West.

Pannekoek, A. *A History of Astronomy.* New York: Dover, 1989. First published in Dutch in 1951, this work is still especially good on the astronomy of the ancient world and of the Scientific Revolution of the seventeenth century.

Rosenstiel, L. *Schirmer History of Music.* New York: Schirmer, 1982. The finest guide for those who can read music; comprehensive.

Salzberg, H. W. *From Caveman to Chemist: Circumstances and Achievements.* Washington, D.C.: American Chemical Society, 1991. A useful history of chemistry, which incidentally touches on technology, from the earliest times to the twentieth century.

Prehistory

Barber, E. W. *Women's Work. The First 20,000 Years. Women, Cloth, and Society in Early Times.* New York: Norton, 1994. An innovative work that reconstructs the history of a largely perishable commodity—cloth—and the women and societies that made it; covers prehistory to the Industrial Revolution.

Bilsborough, A. *Human Evolution.* London: Blackie Academic & Professional, 1992. A well-written introduction to the study of human development up to the beginning of civilization; a unique feature of this work is the focus on hominids with respect to contrasts between and within groupings.

Chauvet, J.-M., et al. *Dawn of Art: The Chauvet Cave: The Oldest Known Paintings in the World.* New York: Abrams, 1996. Striking photographs of the earliest known paintings, accompanied by an informative but not interpretive text.

Dahlberg, F., ed. *Woman, the Gatherer.* New Haven: Yale University Press, 1981. Six essays in support of the thesis that woman's social and economic role was more important in early societies than previously assumed.

Ehrenberg, M. *Women in Prehistory.* London: British Museum, 1989. An excellent study that summarizes the latest research on the earliest women.

Gamble, C. *Timewalkers: The Prehistory of Global Colonization.* Stroud, England: Alan Sutton, 1993. An innovative work of cultural archeology that deals with the often-overlooked question of the near-global distribution of the human race at the dawn of history.

Landau, M. *Narratives of Human Evolution.* New Haven: Yale University Press, 1991. Drawing on literary theory but operating in the discipline of paleoanthropology, this controversial study proposes that modern theories of human evolution are akin to good folk tales or heroic myths.

Leakey, R. E. *The Origin of Humankind.* New York: Basic Books, 1994. Written by the son of one of the most famous families working today in anthropology, whose findings regarding the origins of humans have generated many debates.

Mesopotamia

Black, J., and Green, A. *Gods, Demons and Symbols of Ancient Mesopotamia. An Illustrated Dictionary.* Austin: University of Texas Press, 1992. An invaluable handbook for things Mesopotamian; many helpful illustrations, provided by T. Rickards, and photographs.

Collon, D. *Ancient Near Eastern Art.* Berkeley: University of California Press, 1995. A survey of the art of pre-Islamic Turkey, Syria, Lebanon, Israel, Palestine, Jordan, Iraq, Iran, and the Arabian peninsula; handsomely illustrated with works from the British Museum.

Cook, J. M. *The Persian Empire.* New York: Schocken, 1983. The best recent introduction to Persian civilization that makes careful use of new archeological discoveries.

Kramer, S. N. *History Begins at Sumer: Thirty-Nine Firsts in Man's Recorded History.* 3rd rev. ed. Philadelphia: University of Pennsylvania Press, 1981. A collection of Sumerian texts, translated by the century's greatest Sumerian scholar; first published in 1956.

Lerner, G. *The Creation of Patriarchy.* New York: Oxford University Press, 1986. A theoretical work that challenges the traditional history of the various cultures of the ancient Near East; while denying that matriarchy ever existed, Lerner maintains that women's relatively independent status and role in early Mesopotamia was forever altered by the establishment of patriarchy, a collective act by men with enduring consequences for women.

Macqueen, J. G. *The Hittites and Their Contemporaries in Asia Minor.* Rev. ed. London: Thames and Hudson, 1986. Uses textual and archeological sources to create historical narrative and analysis of the Hittites.

Oates, J. *Babylon.* Rev. ed. London: Thames and Hudson, 1986. Taking advantage of the latest Mesopotamian archeology, this up-to-date survey covers the region's history through the Neo-Babylonian period; well-chosen illustrations.

Reade, J. *Mesopotamia.* Cambridge: Harvard University Press, 1991. A brief history of Mesopotamia to about 1500 B.C., told mainly with art and artifacts from the British Museum collection.

Saggs, H. W. F. *Civilization Before Greece and Rome.* New Haven: Yale University Press, 1989. A thoughtful overview of ancient Near Eastern and Egyptian civilizations.

Egypt

Davis, W. *The Canonical Tradition in Ancient Egyptian Art.* Cambridge: Cambridge University Press, 1989. A well-reasoned defense of the essential role played by the idea of an artistic canon in Egyptian art.

Grimal, N. *A History of Ancient Egypt.* Translated by I. Shaw. Oxford: Oxford University Press, 1992. A comprehensive cultural history of ancient Egypt by a leading French Egyptologist; published in France in 1988.

James, T. G. H. *Ancient Egypt: The Land and Its Legacy.* Austin: University of Texas Press, 1988. A popular history of Egypt focusing on social, literary, and artistic matters; profusely illustrated.

Robins, G. *Women in Ancient Egypt.* Cambridge: Harvard University Press, 1993. A careful study of the position of women in ancient Egypt, based on surviving texts, inscriptions, and representations on funerary and votive monuments.

————. *Proportion and Style in Ancient Egyptian Art.* Austin: University of Texas Press, 1994. A well-documented monograph on the Egyptian practice of laying out paintings and relief sculptures on a squared grid; treats male and female images, contrary to previous studies that focus on masculine imagery.

Schafer, H. *Principles of Egyptian Art.* Edited and with an epilogue by E. Brunner-Traut; translated and edited with an introduction by J. Baines; foreword by E. H. Gombrich. Oxford: Humanities Press, 1986. A classic of Egyptology, this work sets forth the widely accepted thesis that Egyptian art is based on mental images held by the artists, rather than on the appearance of physical objects; thus, an unbridgeable gulf exists between the Egyptian and the Greek artistic method; the German edition dates from 1919.

Smith, W. S. *The Art and Architecture of Ancient Egypt.* Rev. ed. New York: Penguin, 1981. The most comprehensive guide to Egyptian art and architecture; many illustrations and drawings.

Stead, M. *Egyptian Life.* London: British Museum, 1989. A short survey of everyday life in ancient Egypt; richly illustrated with objects from the superb collection of the British Museum.

Wilson, A. *Culture of Ancient Egypt.* Chicago: University of Chicago Press, 1956. The classic in the field, though it must be supplemented with works based on recent discoveries and research in Egyptian studies.

IDENTIFICATIONS

culture	stele
civilization	post-and-lintel construction
Paleolithic	ziggurat
Neolithic	hieroglyphs
pictogram	theocracy
ideogram	genre
phonogram	hymn
cuneiform	monotheism
polytheism	portico
anthropomorphism	regalia
pantheism	canon

PERSONAL PERSPECTIVE BACKGROUND

A Sumerian Father-Son Dispute

This Personal Perspective demonstrates the French saying, "The more things change, the more they remain the same." Almost 5,000 years dawn between this incident and our time, but it could easily have happened today. It's about the generation gap: A father is angry because his son is "hanging out" in the streets.

Egypt: The Dispute of a Man with His Soul

In this Personal Perspective, a man lists a veritable catalogue of social ills: decline in family values ("brothers are mean"), social anomie ("friends of today do not love"), rampant greed ("everyone robs his comrade's good"), and crime ("the land is left to evildoers"). Given such chaos, he claims that death is as welcome for him as recovery is for a sick man. (For additional information, consult *The Western Humanities* and *Readings in the Western Humanities*.)

DISCUSSION/ESSAY QUESTIONS

1. Compare and contrast the Paleolithic and Neolithic cultures, noting material inventions, social orders, and artistic efforts.
2. Define the Neolithic revolution. What was its importance in the development of material institutions and the arts of early civilizations?
3. What were some of the changes occurring in social structures about the time of the Bronze Age, and how did these changes affect the status of men and women?
4. In what ways did geography expand and constrain the development of Mesopotamian and Egyptian civilizations?
5. Discuss the common characteristics of the religions practiced by the Sumerians, Akkadians, and Babylonians.
6. Discuss the themes and characters in *The Epic of Gilgamesh*.
7. Identify Enheduanna, and discuss her contributions to Mesopotamian culture.
8. What were the general characteristics of Mesopotamian art? How did the ziggurat manifest these characteristics?
9. Discuss the role women played in Egyptian government.
10. Describe the Egyptian religious system. How did Egypt's religion affect developments in art, architecture, and literature?
11. Why is the pyramid the supreme symbol of Egyptian civilization?
12. Define the Amarna revolution. What was the significance of the Amarna revolution for Egypt, in both art and history?
13. Compare and contrast the evolution of Sumerian cuneiform writing and Egyptian writing in terms of their uses and stages of change and style.
14. What were the legacies of Mesopotamian and Egyptian civilization to the West?
15. How did Persian civilization differ from that of the Assyrians whom they conquered? What was the most enduring achievement of Persian civilization?

MULTIPLE-CHOICE QUESTIONS

1. The term *culture* usually refers to all of the following EXCEPT:
   a. the sum of all human endeavors
   b. the political, social, and economic institutions of a people
   * c. insensitivity to other people (p. 1)
   d. a people's values and beliefs

2. One of the primary traits of civilization is:
   * a. writing (p. 1)
     b. farming
     c. worshiping deities
     d. hunting

3. The earliest primate ancestors of present-day humans probably originated in:
     a. eastern Europe
     b. eastern India
   * c. eastern Africa (p. 1)
     d. western China

4. The term *Paleolithic* is another name for the:
     a. New Stone Age
     b. Bronze Age
   * c. Old Stone Age (p. 2)
     d. Iron Age

5. *Homo sapiens,* or human beings, evolved into their present form in about:
     a. 500,000 B.C.
   * b. 200,000 B.C. (p. 2)
     c. 10,000 B.C.
     d. 3000 B.C.

6. Surviving evidence from the Upper Paleolithic period shows paintings of:
     a. human forms on canvas
   * b. animals on the walls of caves (p. 3)
     c. scenes of everyday life on walls of houses
     d. abstract designs on rocks

7. How may the Figurine of Willendorf be described?
     a. It may have been used as a fertility symbol.
     b. Such figures appeared in more than one Paleolithic culture.
     c. Its emphasized features may be symbolic of creativity.
   * d. all of the above (pp. 3–4)

8. Human beings in the early Neolithic period began to:
     a. establish large cities
     b. support the arts
   * c. plow the earth and sow seeds (p. 4)
     d. build complex social structures based on commerce

9. As a consequence of the coming of the Neolithic period:
     a. The domestication of wild animals declined.
     b. Villages lost population.
   * c. Communities grew and became more complex. (p. 4)
     d. Human beings stopped worshiping their deities.

10. The two geographical areas where civilizations first arose in the Near East were located:
      a. on the islands of the eastern Mediterranean and in Egypt
    * b. in the Tigris-Euphrates river valley and in the Nile river valley (p. 4)
      c. in southern Greece and in Egypt
      d. in the Tigris-Euphrates river valley and in southern Africa

11. The arc of land that swings through some of the most productive land in the Near East is called:
    a. the Womb of Civilization
    b. the Breadbasket of the World
  * c. the Fertile Crescent (p. 5)
    d. the Bountiful Valley

12. The three successive civilizations that flourished in the Tigris-Euphrates area, in chronological order, were:
    a. Akkadian, Babylonian, Sumerian
    b. Sumerian, Babylonian, Akkadian
  * c. Sumerian, Akkadian, Babylonian (p. 5)
    d. Babylonian, Sumerian, Akkadian

13. The first and greatest leader of the Akkadians was:
    a. Gilgamesh
    b. Moses
    c. Hammurabi
  * d. Sargon (p. 6)

14. The lawgiver for the Babylonians was:
    a. Moses
  * b. Hammurabi (p. 6)
    c. Enlil
    d. Gilgamesh

15. The social order in many ancient cultures began to change in the:
    a. Paleolithic period
    b. New Stone Age
  * c. Bronze Age (p. 6)
    d. Iron Age

16. Some of the social changes occurring in the Bronze Age included:
    a. the tribe or clan replacing the family
    b. acceptance of the right of the young to marry whom they wished
  * c. a more limited role for women (p. 6)
    d. an easing of the divorce laws and customs for men and women

17. The Babylonian law code can be described as a:
    a. humane code that took into consideration human mistakes
    b. relativistic code subject to many interpretations
    c. code created by a committee of lawyers
  * d. code based on retaliation (p. 10)

18. A famous literary episode in Sumer describes the generational conflict between a father and son over:
    a. taking out the garbage
  * b. studying in school (Personal Perspective)
    c. disobeying one's mother
    d. drinking too much

19. One of the earliest surviving written epics is the:
    a. Epic of Sargon
    * b. Epic of Gilgamesh (p. 8)
    c. Epic of Moses
    d. Epic of Achilles

20. This epic (Question 19) touches on which of the following themes?
    * a. the power of the gods over mortals (p. 9)
    b. the issue of free will
    c. the role of slaves in society
    d. the rights of free citizens

21. The hero in the epic (Question 19) can be described as:
    a. a man full of self-confidence all of his life
    * b. a person who learns that humans are mortal (p. 9)
    c. an individual who outwits the gods
    d. all of the above

22. Within the epic (Question 19) is another tale that:
    a. recounts the deeds of a noble warrior
    b. explains the origins of the deities
    * c. tells about a great flood (p. 9)
    d. praises the power of human beings

23. As is often the case in epics, the main character:
    * a. takes on characteristics of a superhuman being (p. 8)
    b. is transformed into another person
    c. finds peace and happiness in this life
    d. discovers that one can do whatever one desires in life

24. The earliest known literary figure was:
    a. Gilgamesh
    b. Homer
    c. Sappho
    * d. Enheduanna (p. 9)

25. *The Exaltation of Inanna* recounts the:
    * a. elevation of Inanna to supremacy among the gods (p. 10)
    b. exploits of Inanna and Gilgamesh
    c. love affair between Inanna and Sargon
    d. crowning of Inanna as ruler of her people

26. Mesopotamian religion may NOT be described as:
    a. polytheistic, or having many deities
    b. anthropomorphic, or having deities that possess human characteristics
    c. pantheistic, or having deities found throughout nature
    * d. ethical, or having deities that behave in moral ways toward their human subjects (p. 8)

27. The central architectural feature of a Mesopotamian city usually was:
    * a. a temple (p. 12)
    b. the city hall
    c. the palace of the king
    d. the marketplace

28. The proper name of the architectural work in Question 27 is:
    a. basilica
    b. cathedral
    c. mosque
  * d. ziggurat (p. 12)

29. The basic type of construction for buildings in Mesopotamia was:
    a. vaulted ceiling and columns
    b. arches and columns
  * c. post-and-lintel (p. 11)
    d. flying buttresses and arches

30. In Mesopotamian religion:
    a. Priests had very little power.
    b. The people believed that the deities never interfered with human effort.
    c. There was only one god.
  * d. The flooding of the lands helped define the faith. (pp. 7–8)

31. Geography influenced Egyptian culture in all these ways EXCEPT:
  * a. Heavy rainfall made Upper Egypt the breadbasket of the country. (pp. 12–13)
    b. Isolated by deserts on either side, Egypt was little influenced by neighboring cultures.
    c. The Nile's periodic flooding made civilized life possible in Egypt.
    d. Proximity to the Mediterranean made Lower Egypt more cosmopolitan than Upper Egypt.

32. The first king of Egypt was:
    a. Hatshepsut
    b. Djoser
  * c. Menes (p. 13)
    d. Kheops

33. All of the following can be considered to have been permanent features of Egyptian civilization EXCEPT:
    a. rulers who claimed to be divinities
    b. the construction of elaborate royal tombs
  * c. the constant threat from outside invaders (pp. 13–15)
    d. the control of foreign trade by the rulers

34. Scholars think that the appearance of a female ruler in Egypt:
    a. represented a change in social attitudes toward women in society
  * b. signaled a political crisis (p. 15)
    c. occurred during periods of prosperity and peace
    d. was a normal event, as men and women shared political power

35. Which of the following does NOT apply to Egypt's New Kingdom?
    a. For the first time in its history, Egypt tried a religious experiment.
    b. For the first time in its history, Egyptian art underwent a short-lived revolution.
    c. Egypt became a great power, dividing the Near East with the Assyrians and the Hittites.
  * d. The New Kingdom experimented with new economic policies. (pp. 15, 20)

36. One of the few women to become pharaoh in her own right was:
  * a. Hatshepsut (p. 15)
    b. Menes
    c. Ti
    d. Nefertiti

37. Egyptian religion was characterized by all of the following EXCEPT:
    a. the belief in immortality
    b. the worship of the ruler
*   c. a single national deity for the state (p. 16)
    d. polytheism

38. Which pharaoh brought about the Amarna revolution?
*   a. Akhenaten (p. 16)
    b. Menes
    c. Hatshepsut
    d. Amenemhat

39. Which was an aspect of the Amarna revolution in Egypt?
    a. Egyptian art became more rigid and formalized.
    b. Egyptian religion took a permanent new direction.
    c. A polytheistic system of religion emerged.
*   d. Aten was raised to a new level above the other deities. (pp. 15, 20)

40. The most famous work of Egyptian literature is:
    a. *The Epic of Gilgamesh*
    b. *An Argument Between a Man Contemplating Suicide and His Soul*
*   c. the *Story of Sinuhe* (p. 16)
    d. the *Hymn to Aten*

41. A uniquely pessimistic work in Egyptian literature is
    a. *The Story of Sinuhe*
    b. *Hymn to Aten*
*   c. *The Dispute of a Man with His Soul* (Personal Perspective)
    d. *Exaltation of Inanna*

42. The model for the Step Pyramid of King Djoser was:
    a. an original Egyptian design
*   b. borrowed from the Mesopotamian ziggurat (caption for Fig. 1.12)
    c. a variation of the earlier pure pyramid design
    d. adopted from a Chinese design

43. In Egypt, the building of pyramids occurred:
    a. throughout Egyptian history
*   b. only in the Old Kingdom (pp. 17–18)
    c. during the Amarna revolution
    d. only in the Middle Kingdom

44. What was the cultural significance of the Egyptian pyramid?
    a. It was a representation of the God Re.
    b. It was a merely decorative device for the rulers.
*   c. It seemed to embody a constant and eternal order. (pp. 16–18)
    d. It signified that the Egyptians were not interested in life after death.

45. All of the following are aspects of Hatshepsut's temple EXCEPT:
*   a. Its central shrine is in the pure pyramid shape. (pp. 18–19)
    b. It is built with post-and-lintel style of construction.
    c. It uses columns with decorated capitals.
    d. Its colonnaded courtyards lead to a hidden sanctuary in a cliff.

46. Which does NOT apply to the Great Sphinx?
    a. It represents a mythical creature, part human and part animal.
  * b. It is carved from Libyan stone that was transported to the Giza site. (p. 19)
    c. Its original purpose was to guard the nearby pyramid group.
    d. Its face depicts Khephren, the ruler who commissioned it.

47. The classical Egyptian style of sculpture did NOT include this trait:
    a. left leg forward
    b. fists clenched
  * c. complete nudity (pp. 19–20)
    d. unemotional countenance

48. This female pharaoh built a temple at Deir el Bahri, near Luxor:
  * a. Hatshepsut (p. 19)
    b. Nefertiti
    c. Mykerinus
    d. Akhenaten

49. Egypt's outstanding contribution in relief sculpture was the:
    a. ability to depict figures facing straight ahead
    b. development of the principles of perspective
  * c. invention of a canon of proportions for depicting the human figure (p. 23)
    d. creation of a vast repertory of poses for portraying human actions

50. The only excavated royal tomb that was discovered relatively intact was the tomb of:
    a. Hatshepsut
    b. Djoser
    c. Akhenaten
  * d. Tutankhamen (p. 23)

51. What new subject was introduced into sculpture during the Amarna revolution?
  * a. intimate scenes of court life (p. 20 and caption for Fig. 1.17)
    b. royal portraits
    c. banqueting scenes
    d. all of the above

52. Persian art was characterized by:
    a. violent and savage images
    b. abstract and nonfigurative shapes
  * c. contemplative themes with less action (p. 24)
    d. all of the above

53. Which was NOT an aspect of the Zoroastrian religion?
    a. It taught that the universe was engaged in a cosmic struggle between good and evil.
  * b. It originated in Assyrian culture. (p. 24)
    c. It advocated puritanical behavior as a way to gain favor in the afterlife.
    d. It prophesied a Last Judgment.

54. Egypt's legacy to the West did NOT include:
    a. a solar calendar of 360 days, divided into twelve 30-day months, plus five holidays
  * b. the novel (p. 25)
    c. the decorated column
    d. medical learning and knowledge of drugs

55. Mesopotamia's legacy to the West did NOT include:
*   a. the dome (p. 25)
    b. a mathematical system based on 60
    c. standard weights and measures
    d. writing

2

AEGEAN CIVILIZATION
The Minoans, the Mycenaeans,
and the Greeks of the Archaic Age

TEACHING STRATEGIES AND SUGGESTIONS

A good approach to Aegean civilization is for the instructor to begin with a lecture that combines elements of the Historical Overview with the Diffusion model. In this opening presentation the teacher should provide a clear survey of early events in the Aegean area from about 2000 to 479 B.C.; clarify the influences operating on Archaic Greece from the Near East, Crete, and Mycenae; and set forth the basic differences between Archaic Greece and earlier civilizations. The instructor should then focus on Archaic Greece, identifying its leading characteristics and stressing the primary role played by religion in shaping culture. To give a well-rounded view of this earliest stage of Greek civilization, the instructor can use four different strategies: the Slide Lecture model to set forth the artistic achievements; the Reflections/Connections model to establish the linkages between cultural and material history; the Comparison/Contrast method to deal with the dominant literary forms of epic and lyric poetry; and the Spirit of the Age approach to show the unity amid the artistic and literary diversity. The instructor can also employ the Case Study method to deal with the rise of philosophy/science, one of the most enduring legacies of this remarkable age. And above all else, the instructor should show how the Archaic Greeks laid the foundation for the humanities, since the evolution of the humanistic tradition is a leading theme for the rest of *The Western Humanities*.

LECTURE OUTLINE

Non-Western Events

I. Introduction and Overview
   A. Brief contrast of Greek civilization
      with that of Mesopotamia and Egypt
      1. Human-centered versus
         god-centered
      2. Protagoras: "Man is the measure of
         all things"
   B. The Greek foundation of Western
      civilization
   C. Greek borrowings from the Near East

II. Prelude: Minoan Civilization, 3000–1300 B.C.
   A. The source of the term *Minoan*
   B. Characteristics of Minoan civilization

C. Its outstanding architectural creation:
   the palace at Knossos
   1. Layout
   2. Decorative plan
D. Cretan script, Linear A and B
E. Religion
   1. Worship of a mother goddess
   2. The bull cult
F. Commerce
G. Mythology and its later impact on
   Greece

III. Beginnings: Mycenaean Civilization,
   1900–1100 B.C.
   A. A source of legends for Greece
   B. Power center: Mycenae and the
      Peloponnesus
   C. Political, social, and economic
      structure
   D. The chief symbol of this militaristic
      civilization: the fortress-palace
      1. Ashlar construction
      2. The Lion Gate, Mycenae
   E. Religion
      1. Worship of divinities
      2. Burial practices
      3. Contribution to later Greek
         practice of worship of heroes
   F. The Trojan War
      1. The realities of the war
      2. The inspiration for Homer's *Iliad* and
         Odyssey
   G. Mycenae and the Homeric tradition

IV. Interlude: The Dark Ages, 1100–800 B.C.
   A. The collapse of one form of civilized
      order
   B. The emergence of a new civilized order

1000–800 B.C.

In Andean culture, Initial period, 1800–1000 B.C.; Early Horizon period, 1000–200 B.C.; the Chavín aesthetic develops and influences art, architecture, textiles, and styles throughout the area; the aesthetic takes its name from the cult center Chavín de Huantar, with its buildings and related sculpture, about 900–200 B.C.; uses both the U-shaped and sunken court types of architecture along with imagery of jaguars, snakes, and other animal-human composites; Chavín art included ceramic vessels, often with stirrup-spout form, obsidian- and goldwork, including face masks, pectorals, headgear, and jewelry

In China, western Zhou dynasty (about 1100–771 B.C.) and eastern Zhou dynasty (about 1100–256 B.C.); sun's height measured in relation to incline of polar axis; Beijing founded; brush-and-ink painting begins; treatise on fish cultivation, 850 B.C.

In India, Brahmanism, about 900 B.C.; early Hinduism identified with sacrificial rituals, belief in karma and reincarnation, and division of society into four classes (*varnas*); Atmanism, about 900 B.C.

In Japan, Jomon culture, about 4000–about 300 B.C.

In Mesoamerica, Formative period, 2000–200 B.C.; fine pottery and votive figurines at Santa Cruz near Cuernavaca, between 1000 and 500 B.C.; Olmec culture, 1500–100 B.C., with its characteristic pyramids, portraiture, and mirrors; perhaps 1,000 people at San Lorenzo site, inhabited about 1200 to 900 B.C.; focused on worship of a jaguar deity; jade is the most prized element; other centers at La Venta, Tres Zapotes, and Cerro de las Mesas, all temple-cities; the Las Limas youth holding a rain god, the most famous of Olmec greenstone sculptures

In North America, in California, Pinto Indians build huts; the Adena people, 1000–100 B.C.

V. The Archaic Age, 800–479 B.C.
   A. Historical overview: Age of innovation and experimentation
   B. The origin of *Hellas* and *Hellene*
   C. Political, economic, and social structures
      1. The rise of the polis
         a) The acropolis
         b) The agora
         c) The goal of the polis
      2. The shift from monarchy to oligarchy
         a) Exemplary leadership, civil idealism, and cultural and artistic patronage
         b) New military tactics
         c) Overseas expansion and colonization
            (1) The coasts of Spain and North Africa, and the Black Sea area
            (2) Southern Italy and Sicily: *Magna Graecia*
            (3) Social developments
            (4) The rise of tyrants
      3. The shift from oligarchy to democracy
         a) The rights of male citizens
         b) Few rights for women
         c) The hard lot of foreigners and slaves
   D. The Greek polis: Sparta and Athens
      1. Sparta, the symbol of Dorian civilization
         a) Origins of oligarchic rule
         b) Limited cultural achievements
      2. Athens, the symbol of Ionian civilization
         a) Origins of democratic rule
            (1) Mounting social problems
            (2) Solon's reforms
            (3) Cleisthenes' democratic constitution
         b) Inauguration of the Hellenic Age
   E. The Persian Wars
      1. The threat from Persia
         a) The war against Darius
         b) The war against Xerxes
      2. The consequences of a Greek victory for the West
   F. The emergence of Greek genius: the mastery of form

along the Ohio River practice mound building

800–700 B.C.
In Africa, rise of Nubian Kingdom of Kush (modern Sudan), 750 B.C.; temples of Jebel Barkal and Musawarat es-Sofra
In China, baked clay roof tiles; order provided by the Zhou dynasty breaks down into rivalry among semiautonomous states; astronomers now understand planetary movements; Spring and Autumn period, 722–481 B.C.
In Europe, Celts move into England
In India, medicine is freed from priestly control
In Mesoamerica, Olmecs build La Venta, between 800 and 300 B.C., the earliest example of a temple-city; giant basalt heads, possibly of rulers; stone stelae and altars and the 260-day calendar; jade mosaics, figurines, masks, disks, and jewelry; anthropomorphic stone axes; Olmec pyramid in the Mayan city of Uaxactún; Mezcala (in Guerrero) figurines and masks that share traits with Olmec art; beginning of Zapotec culture, near Oaxaca
In North America, in Alaska, Arctic pottery
In Vietnam, first evidence of boat building in southeast Asia

700–600 B.C.
In China, Spring and Autumn period, 722–481 B.C., a time of rivalry among

1. The role of the muses in artistic creativity
2. Religion
   a) Olympian and chthonic deities
   b) The concept of *hubris*
3. Epic poetry
   a) The *Iliad*
   b) The *Odyssey*
   c) The role of Homer in Greek civilization
4. Lyric poetry
   a) The solo lyric
   b) The poems of Sappho
5. Natural philosophy
   a) The emergence of philosophy/science
   b) The Milesian school: Thales
   c) The Sicilian school: Pythagoras
   d) The originator of dialectical reasoning: Heraclitus
6. The supreme architectural achievement of the Greeks: the temple
   a) Post-beam-triangle construction
   b) The principal parts
   c) The Doric-style temple
7. Sculpture
   a) The chief sculptural forms of this period
      (1) Kouros and Kore
      (2) Characteristics
      (3) Influence from Egypt and Greek innovations
   b) The shift from the Archaic to the Hellenic style

VI. The Legacy of Archaic Greek Civilization

semiautonomous states; beginning of second period of Chinese literature, to 200 B.C.; Lao-tzu, philosopher, author of *The Book of Dao*; first metal coinage (bronze); city planning, divided into "inner" and "outer" areas set the standard for the next 2,500 years; a government minister teaches peasants crop rotation

In India, the Vedas completed

In North America, southeast Indians cultivate vegetable gardens

600–500 B.C.

In Africa, ironworking introduced to the kingdom of Kush, the first in sub-Saharan Africa; Kush's capital, Meroe, becomes an ironworking center

In Burma, Shwe Dagon Pagoda

In China, Spring and Autumn period, 722–481 B.C., a time of rivalry among semiautonomous states; *Book of Songs*, lyric verses, the first poetry in China; Kung Fu-Tse (Confucius), philosopher, 551–479 B.C., author or editor of the "Five Ching," or Canonical Books; iron and ironworking begins

In Himalaya region, in Nepal, birth of Gautama Buddha at Kapilavastu, capital of the Licchavi dynasty, 570 B.C.

In India, Brahmanism, about 900 B.C.; Siddhartha (550–480 B.C.), the founder of Buddhism; "Ramayana," Hindu poem, about 500 B.C.; Indian vina, the ancestor of hollow string musical instruments; Mahavira Jina

(Vardhamana), the first
known rebel against
India's caste system,
founds Jainism
In Japan, Jomon culture,
about 4000–about 300 B.C.;
huts with floors at ground
level; rice introduced from
China, about 500 B.C.
In Mesoamerica, the first
surviving paintings in
America, cave art at
Oxtotitlán and
Juxtlahuaca, in Gurrero
In Persia, first coin with
image of ruler
In Siberia, wooden wagons
that could be dismantled
and carried by packhorses
In South America, in
Colombia, hammered
goldwork, the finest in
the Americas

500–479 B.C.
In Ecuador, Jama Coaque
figurines, 500 B.C.–A.D. 500
In Europe, in England, Celts
overrun the British Isles,
about 450 B.C.
In India, surgeon Susrata
performs cataract
operations
In North America, in Utah,
rock art
In Middle East, Hanno the
Carthaginian travels down
the west coast of Africa

LEARNING OBJECTIVES

To learn:

1. How Greek civilization borrowed from Near Eastern civilizations

2. How the Greeks laid the foundation of Western civilization

3. The cultural contributions of the Minoans, the makers of the first high civilization in what became the Greek area

4. The cultural contributions of the Mycenaeans, the makers of the first high civilization on the Greek peninsula

5. The origin of the Dorians and the Ionians and the significance of these cultural terms for Greek civilization

6. The significance of the Dark Ages

7. The characteristics and major forms of cultural expression of Archaic Greece

8. The meaning of *polis* and the central role it played in Greek civilization

9. The evolution of the polis, from monarchy to oligarchy to democracy

10. The significance of Sparta and Athens, symbols respectively of Dorian and Ionian civilization

11. How the Athenian victory over Persia laid the groundwork for the Athenian dominance of Greece

12. How religion helped to shape Greek culture, especially the muses, the Olympian gods and goddesses, and the chthonic deities

13. The epic tradition as established by Homer in the *Iliad* and the *Odyssey*

14. The lyric poetic tradition as expressed in the verses of Sappho

15. The early history of natural philosophy and the contributions of Thales, Pythagoras, and Heraclitus

16. To recognize visually the Doric style of temple building and to identify its components, decorative details, and aesthetic principles

17. To recognize visually the Archaic style in sculpture and to identify its distinguishing characteristics, with special reference to kouros and kore statuary

18. To recognize visually the changes taking place in Archaic-style sculpture that were leading to Hellenic-style sculpture and to identify significant changes in this transition period

19. Historic "firsts" achieved in Archaic Greece that became legacies for later Western developments: the polis, epic poetry, lyric poetry, the post-beam-triangle temple, the kore and kouros sculptures, black-figure–style vase painting, natural philosophy, and the humanities

SUGGESTIONS FOR FILMS

The Aegean Age. Coronet, 14 min., color.

The Glory That Was Greece: The Age of Civil War. Time-Life, 36 min., black and white. (On the Persian Wars)

The Glory That Was Greece: The Age of Minos. Time-Life, 36 min., black and white.

The Greek Myths. Encyclopedia Britannica, 54 min., color.

The Greek Temple. Universal Education and Visual Arts, 54 min., color.

The Search for Ulysses. Carousel Films, 53 min.

SUGGESTIONS FOR FURTHER READING

Beye, C. R. *Ancient Greek Literature and Society*. Ithaca, N.Y.: Cornell University Press, 1989. 2nd ed. Excellent treatment of early Greek writings with special emphasis on their public nature. Expanded to reflect latest research.

Boardman, J., et al. *The Oxford History of Classical Art*. Oxford: Oxford University Press, 1993. Serves as the companion to *The Oxford History of the Classical World*. It covers the arts from Pre-classical Greece to the diffusion of classical art. Profusely illustrated with many diagrams and drawings; each artistic period is covered by a leading art historian.

————. *The Oxford History of the Classical World*. Oxford: Oxford University Press, 1986. An outstanding collection of essays by leading scholars on Greek and Roman history.

Brilliant, R. *Art of the Ancient Greeks*. New York: McGraw-Hill, 1973. A standard treatment that is still useful but superseded by more recent scholarship. Well illustrated with many details on the works of art.

Burkert, W. *Greek Religion*. Translated by J. Raffon. Cambridge: Harvard University Press, 1985. A detailed survey that relies on the most recent scholarship and evidence that will challenge the student.

Carpenter, T. H. *Art and Myth in Ancient Greece*. London: Thames and Hudson, 1991. For the serious student who wants to explore how Greek myths appear in the surviving Greek art, primarily on vases and in sculpture.

Charbonneaux, J., et al. *Archaic Greek Art, 620–480 B.C.* Translated by J. Emmons and R. Allen. London: Thames and Hudson, 1971. The text and illustrations on painting and pottery are most instructive.

Fantham, E., et al. *Women in the Classical World: Image and Text*. New York: Oxford University Press, 1994. A sourcebook on the changing roles and status of women that includes primary sources and essays.

Finley, M. I. *Early Greece: The Bronze and Archaic Age*. New York: Norton, 1981. A sound overview by this well-known scholar who has written extensively on Greek life.

Graves, R. *The Greek Myths*. Garden City, N.Y.: Doubleday, 1981. Perhaps the most thorough treatment of the myths in modern scholarship.

Guthrie, W. K. C. *The Greeks and Their Gods*. Boston: Beacon Press, 1954. This is still the most clearly written survey on one of the central themes in Greek culture—the origins and evolution of Greek religion and its relationship to Greek philosophy.

————. *Greek Philosophers: From Thales to Aristotle*. New York: Harper & Row, 1960. Although somewhat outdated, this remains one of the most clearly written introductions to a complex topic; easily understood by the beginning student.

Hampe, R., and Simon, E. *The Birth of Greek Art: From the Mycenean to the Archaic Period*. New York: Oxford University Press, 1981. All branches of art are covered, dating from 1600 to 600 B.C. Fully illustrated with numerous color plates, detailed photographs, and an extensive bibliography.

Higgins, R. A. *Minoan and Mycenaean Art*. Rev. ed. London: Thames and Hudson, 1981. Revised from the 1967 edition, this brief survey includes all the arts, from architecture and jewelry to vases and weapons.

Lawrence, A. W. *Greek Architecture*. New York: Penguin, 1983. A survey of Greek architecture from the Neolithic period to the Roman conquest.

Martin, T. R. *Ancient Greece: From Prehistoric to Hellenistic Times*. New Haven: Yale University Press, 1996. Political, social, and cultural history are integrated into this overview of ancient Greece. The book is a "hard copy" of the electronic database *Perseus* project.

Norberg-Schulz, C. *Meaning in Western Architecture.* London: Studio Vista, 1975. Analyzes a key architectural monument in each great age of Western architecture, such as the Parthenon in fifth-century B.C. Greece.

Pomeroy, S. *Goddesses, Whores, Wives, and Slaves: Women in Classical Antiquity.* New York: Schocken Books, 1975. A survey of the roles of women in their public and private lives and their images in literature, from Homeric to Roman times.

Richter, G. A. *Korai.* London: Phaidon, 1968. *Kouroi.* Rev. ed. London: Phaidon, 1970. The definitive studies of this type of Greek statuary; extensively illustrated

Romilly, J. de. *A Short History of Greek Literature.* Translated by L. Doherty. Chicago: University of Chicago Press, 1985. A brief, authoritative survey of Greek writings from Homer, in about 800 B.C., through the Greek-speaking Roman emperor Julian, in the fourth century A.D.

IDENTIFICATIONS

frieze	pediment
fresco	entablature
ashlar	cornice
shaft graves	stylobate
oligarchy	cella '
muse	Doric
Olympian deities	capital
chthonic deities	triglyph
hubris	metope
epic poetry	relief
bard	entasis
Homeric epithet	fluting
lyre	kouros
lyric poetry	kore
post-beam-triangle	Archaic
construction	humanities
architrave	

PERSONAL PERSPECTIVE BACKGROUND

Hesiod, "On the Dignity of Work"

Of Hesiod's life, little is known. He seems to have been a peasant from Boeotia ("cow land"), a polis near Attica. Early in his life, he quarreled with his brother Perses, and he himself worked a small and infertile plot of land. He is the first Greek poet to say "I," the first to write about himself and his own life. He advises his brother Perses to work hard and manage his property carefully. This is the first notice in the West of the "gospel of work," what in modern times is usually called "the Puritan work ethic." (See *The Western Humanities* and *Readings in the Western Humanities* for more information on Hesiod's *Works and Days.*)

Sappho, "He Seems to Be a God"

Sappho pioneered the personal lyric genre. Her literary style is direct and concrete, as is seen in the Personal Perspective. The emotional intensity is remarkable: "My tongue sticks to my dry mouth . . . my aching ears roar . . . Chill sweat slides down my body. . . ." No wonder that for centuries Sappho was quoted and imitated by other poets. Sappho lived among young girls to whom she taught the art of writing poetry, and it was women whom she loved. (See *The Western Humanities* and *Readings in the Western Humanities* for additional information.)

DISCUSSION/ESSAY QUESTIONS

1. Discuss the Greek "vision of humanity" and show how this vision made the Greeks different from the Mesopotamians and the Egyptians.
2. Explain the relationship of Archaic sculpture to Egyptian art. How did Archaic sculpture differ from Egyptian art?
3. Discuss the discoveries of Sir Arthur Evans at Knossos regarding Minoan civilization and describe some of the characteristics of this civilization.
4. What were the achievements of Minoan civilization? Discuss the impact of Minoan civilization on Archaic Greece.
5. What is meant by a feudal system? Describe Mycenaean feudal society.
6. What were the achievements of Mycenaean civilization? Discuss the impact of Mycenaean civilization on Archaic Greece.
7. Summarize the leading aspects of Greek religion and show how religion helped to shape cultural developments.
8. Select a work of Archaic sculpture and show how it expresses the Archaic style of art.
9. In what ways did Archaic Greece lay the foundations for Western civilization?
10. Define *polis*. Why was the development of the polis one of the most important contributions of Greek civilization?
11. What was the significance of Homer for Greek civilization?
12. Discuss the traits of Greek religion during the Archaic Age, and assess Homer's role in explaining religion to the Greeks.
13. Compare and contrast epic poetry with lyric poetry. What different audiences would be attracted to each of these poetic genres?
14. Compare and contrast *The Epic of Gilgamesh* and Homer's *Iliad*, noting characters, narrative, and themes.
15. Show how Protagoras's statement that "Man is the measure of all things" was realized in Archaic Greek civilization.
16. Explain briefly the philosophies of Thales, Pythagoras, and Heraclitus. Why were their accomplishments so momentous?
17. Describe a typical Doric temple, and name and identify its chief features.
18. Explain the differences between Athens and Sparta. What cultural features did they have in common?
19. Define "the humanities." What role did the humanities play in the life of Archaic Greece?
20. What were the legacies of Archaic Greece to later Western civilization?

MULTIPLE-CHOICE QUESTIONS

1. Which is NOT an aspect of Minoan civilization?
   a. It was named for the legendary king Minos.
   b. Its major center was Knossos.
   * c. Its cities were ringed with massive walls (pp. 27–29)
   d. Its leading nobles lived in palaces.

2. Minoan religion was NOT characterized by:
   a. numerous minor household goddesses
   b. a female figure representative of the source of life and creation
   c. statues of female deities whose exact roles are unknown
   * d. belief in eternal life (p. 29)

3. Minoan art reveals the following Cretan religious practice:
   a. worship of a god of thunder
   b. human sacrifices
 * c. worship of a mother goddess (p. 29 and caption for Fig. 2.2)
   d. belief in a deity who resides within each human subject

4. Minoan civilization eventually fell to the:
   a. Egyptians
   b. Etruscans
 * c. Mycenaeans (p. 29)
   d. Dorians

5. Mycenaean civilization was centered:
 * a. on the Peloponnesus (p. 31)
   b. in northern Greece
   c. on the Greek islands
   d. on Crete

6. Which was NOT an achievement of Mycenaean civilization?
   a. decorative daggers and weapons
 * b. imaginative literature (pp. 31–32)
   c. strong bureaucracies
   d. shaft graves

7. Mycenaean civilization transmitted which legacy to Archaic Greece?
   a. fortress-palaces
   b. ashlar-style construction
 * c. legends and myths of gods and heroes (pp. 32, 34)
   d. imaginative literature

8. Mycenaean art was noted for:
   a. life-size statues
   b. elaborate stone friezes on temples
  *c. gold-decorated funerary objects (p. 32 and caption for Fig. 2.7)
   d. polychrome floor mosaics

9. Homer's writings drew on legends of:
   a. Egyptian civilization
   b. Minoan civilization
 * c. Mycenaean civilization (p. 34)
   d. Etruscan civilization

10. All of the following occurred in the Greek Dark Ages EXCEPT the:
    a. adoption of Iron Age technology
    b. migration of Greek-speaking peoples to the coast of Asia Minor
    c. fragmentation of the Greek world
  * d. triumph of the Mycenaeans (p. 34)

11. Who is the originator of the epic literary tradition?
  * a. Homer (p. 39)
    b. Hesiod
    c. Sappho
    d. Archilocus

12. Greeks of the Archaic Age were NOT bound together by a:
    a. common language
    * b. unified state (p. 34)
    c. shared tradition of heroic stories and folk tales
    d. standard set of myths and religious practices

13. Which was NOT one of the three major Greek tribes?
    a. the Ionians
    b. the Dorians
    c. the Aeolians
    * d. the Corinthians (p. 34)

14. The Archaic Greeks called their land:
    * a. Hellas (p. 34)
    b. Peloponnesus
    c. Morea
    d. Greece

15. A typical polis did NOT include a:
    * a. forbidden area restricted to priests and rulers (p. 34)
    b. central gathering place for business and socializing
    c. sanctuary for temples and shrines
    d. citadel where the rulers lived

16. An agora is a(n):
    a. theater
    * b. open area that serves as a marketplace and city center (p. 34)
    c. military organization
    d. devotee of the god Dionysus

17. Which is the correct sequence to describe governmental shifts in a typical polis during the Archaic Age?
    * a. oligarchy to tyranny to democracy (pp. 34–35)
    b. democracy to tyranny to oligarchy
    c. oligarchy to democracy to tyranny
    d. tyranny to democracy to oligarchy

18. In the Archaic Greek experience, a tyrant was a person:
    * a. given extraordinary power to solve specific problems (p. 35)
    b. who usually represented a foreign power
    c. whom the Greeks came to trust above all others
    d. who claimed to rule by divine right

19. All of these had happened by the end of the Archaic Age EXCEPT:
    a. Greek colonies dotted the coasts of Spain, North Africa, the Black Sea and southern Russia, and Sicily and southern Italy.
    b. Foot soldiers had replaced warriors in horse-drawn chariots.
    c. Most adult male property owners enjoyed citizenship rights.
    * d. Women joined their husbands in carrying out public duties. (pp. 34–35)

20. Which is NOT an aspect of ancient Sparta? The Spartans:
    * a. welcomed foreigners into their midst (p. 36)
    b. prided themselves on their hierarchical social system
    c. restricted the accumulation of wealth by citizens
    d. valued social order and military might

21. The rest of Greece admired Sparta for its:
    a. artistic creativity
    b. contributions to philosophy
    * c. military might (p. 36)
    d. all of the above

22. The significance of the Persian Wars was that they:
    a. meant the triumph of the East over the West
    b. ended the Golden Age of Greece
    * c. allowed Greek democratic institutions and humanistic values to continue to develop
       (p. 37)
    d. led Greece to experience a century of peace

23. A major victory of the Persians during the Persian Wars was at the battle of:
    * a. Thermopylae (p. 37)
    b. Marathon
    c. Salamis
    d. Plataea

24. Which is NOT a correct pairing of a muse with her area of creativity?
    * a. Thalia   painting (p. 37)
    b. Calliope   epic poetry
    c. Clio   history
    d. Terpsichore   dance and song

25. The Olympian deities had all of these aspects EXCEPT:
    a. They lived in the sky or on mountain tops.
    b. They were associated with the Homeric heroes.
    * c. They originated among the peasants and lower social orders. (pp. 37–38)
    d. The Greeks endowed them with bodies and individual personalities.

26. Greek religion taught the faithful to avoid the sin of *hubris,* or:
    a. greed
    * b. pride (p. 38)
    c. sexual immorality
    d. murder

27. Which is NOT a correct pairing of an Olympian deity and his or her duty?
    a. Zeus   king of the gods and goddesses
    * b. Athena   goddess of love (p. 38)
    c. Artemis   virgin goddess who aided women
    d. Hermes   god of merchants and thieves

28. Chthonic religious cults had all of these aspects EXCEPT:
    a. They were called mystery cults.
    b. They originally were intended to invoke the powers of the earth to ensure a successful planting and a rich harvest.
    c. They later claimed to promise immortality to worshipers.
  * d. They began among the aristocratic population. (p. 38)

29. The cultural institution that grew out of the worship of Dionysus was the:
    a. library
    b. academy
    c. church
  * d. theater (p. 39)

30. A bard may be identified as a:
    a. person who bartered in the Greek agora
  * b. poet who sang verses of an epic while strumming a stringed instrument (p. 39)
    c. Greek thinker interested in philosophy
    d. composer of Greek lyric poems

31. The hero of the *Iliad* is:
    a. Odysseus
    b. Menelaus
  * c. Achilles (p. 39)
    d. Hector

32. Which of the following applies to the *Odyssey?*
    a. It tells about the battles of the Minoan civilization.
  * b. It focuses on Odysseus's efforts to return home. (p. 39)
    c. It reveals how women are often unfaithful to their husbands.
    d. It recounts the defeat of the Greeks by the Trojans.

33. Homer influenced Greek civilization by:
    a. giving texture to the Greek language
    b. acting as a theologian of the Greek religion
    c. serving as a moral guide
  * d. all of the above (p. 40)

34. Which was NOT an aspect of lyric poetry?
  * a. Its richest period occurred before the time of Homer. (p. 40)
    b. It expressed an author's personal, private thoughts.
    c. It reflected the rising democratic spirit of the Archaic Age.
    d. Its inspiration was credited to the muse Euterpe.

35. Hesiod is the author of:
    a. *Iliad*
    b. *Odyssey*
  * c. *Works and Days* (Personal Perspective)
    d. *Epic of Gilgamesh*

36. The author, in *Works and Days,* tells his brother to:
    a. relax and enjoy life
  * b. find the meaning of life in work (Personal Perspective)
    c. sacrifice to the gods to ensure a bountiful harvest
    d. be true to himself

37. Sappho's lyric poetry was mainly on the subject of:
    a. victorious athletes
  * b. passionate love in all of its aspects (p. 41)
    c. political and social problems
    d. nature

38. What aspect of love does Sappho describe in the poem "He Seems to Be a God"?
    a. ecstasy
    b. contentment
    c. hatred
  * d. jealousy (Personal Perspective)

39. Who was the first philosopher/scientist?
  * a. Thales (p. 42)
    b. Pythagoras
    c. Heraclitus
    d. Democritus

40. Pythagoras was author of which scientific theory?
    a. the notion that the basic stuff of nature is water
    b. the concept of atomism
    c. the view of the four elements, earth, air, fire, and water
  * d. the belief that everything is based on numbers (p. 42)

41. The philosopher Heraclitus:
    a. was a materialist like Thales
    b. followed idealism like Pythagoras
  * c. established the first dialectical form of reasoning (p. 42)
    d. found truth in a stable universe

42. All of the following characterize the philosopher/scientist of Archaic Greece EXCEPT:
    a. belief in the regularity of the universe
    b. belief that human reason can understand the natural order
  * c. belief that the deities control human events (p. 42)
    d. belief that there is a basic matter in nature

43. Which was NOT part of the impact of Greece's first philosophers?
    a. They described the physical world as the result of natural causes and effects.
    b. They questioned the role, power, and existence of the Greek deities.
    c. They established a body of knowledge that came to be identified as natural philosophy.
  * d. They pioneered the first ethical philosophies. (p. 42)

44. Which is NOT an aspect of Greek post-beam-triangle construction?
    a. It greatly influenced later Western architecture.
    b. The term refers to the way the columns and horizontal beams intersect.
    c. It was used throughout the history of Greek temple building.
  * d. It usually included a dome. (p. 43)

45. Typical Greek temple architecture did NOT have this feature:
    a. post-beam-triangle construction
    b. a cornice
  * c. arches (p. 43)
    d. a cella

46. All of these features are unique to the Doric temple style EXCEPT:
    a. columns with undecorated capitals
 * b. a pediment with sculptures (pp. 43–44)
    c. triglyphs
    d. metopes

47. The beauty of the Temple of Aphaia, Aegina, is the result of all of the following EXCEPT:
    a. fluting on the columns
    b. mathematical proportions
    c. refined details
 * d. stylistic unity of its statues (p. 44 and caption for Fig. 2.14)

48. An Egyptian influence on Archaic Greek sculpture was:
    a. open body stance and balance
    b. shifting of bodily weight onto one leg
 * c. left foot forward movement (pp. 45–46)
    d. emotions recorded on faces

49. Unlike the Egyptian style, the Archaic style was characterized by:
 * a. slight smile on the face (pp. 45–46, 48)
    b. female and male nudes
    c. distortion of the musculature
    d. free movement of the body

50. A frequent subject in Archaic Greek sculpture was:
    a. portrait busts
 * b. youths and maidens (p. 45)
    c. scenes of everyday life
    d. all of the above

51. The Ptoon Kouros is a statue of a:
    a. winged god
    b. creature with an animal's body and a man's face
 * c. standing youth (caption for Fig. 2.16 and p. 46)
    d. kneeling archer

52. In the Archaic style, how did a statue of a kore differ from a statue of a kouros?
    a. A kore was given an archaic smile.
 * b. A kore was portrayed clothed. (p. 46)
    c. A kore was portrayed with stylized hair.
    d. all of the above

53. What change occurred in Archaic sculpture at the end of the period?
    a. Faces became more emotional.
 * b. Realistic tension was now depicted in the body. (p. 48)
    c. Frontality was introduced.
    d. all of the above

54. The humanities are the:
    a. things that human beings do in any culture
    b. beliefs that arise out of religious worship
 * c. original artistic and literary forms of the Greeks (p. 49)
    d. attitudes and practices that make human beings more sympathetic to others

55. The Archaic Greeks laid the foundation for Western civilization by:
    a.   creating the concept of monotheism
  * b.   originating the spirit of scientific inquiry (pp. 27, 42, 50)
    c.   organizing a model for world government
    d.   establishing the decimal system

3

CLASSICAL GREEK CIVILIZATION
The Hellenic Age

TEACHING STRATEGIES AND SUGGESTIONS

The instructor can introduce this chapter with the Comparison/Contrast model, noting similarities and differences between the Archaic and Hellenic Greek civilizations with emphasis on the political, economic, and social institutions. The instructor can use the Historic Overview approach to set forth the principal historic divisions and then give a more detailed analysis of the causes of the Peloponnesian War. Thucydides' account of the war could be effectively used along with an explanation of the changing "climate of opinion" in late fifth-century B.C. Athens. The instructor could connect these events with Greek philosophy just before the time of Socrates.

The teacher should utilize the Reflections/Connections model to discuss Greek theater and its relationship to the arts and civic institutions. Having the students read one or two tragedies will introduce them to Greek values and ideals. Two or more hours of Standard Lecture on Greek philosophy are essential to lay the foundation of the major schools of Western thought whose influences come down to the present day. Arguably, this will be the most important set of lectures of the entire term. The instructor can adopt the Comparison/Contrast model for treating Platonism and Aristotelianism; the discussion of these systems of thought must be in simple enough terms so that students will be able to recognize them when they resurface in later philosophy.

A variety of approaches may be used in dealing with Greek architecture and sculpture. The Reflections/Connections model will enable students to relate Greek values to the visual arts. The Diffusion method can illustrate the changes that occurred in Hellenic art as compared with Archaic art. This method can also illustrate the influence of the Greek Classical style on later revivals of this style, in particular as found in the United States in the late eighteenth century. The Case Study approach will permit the instructor to note how America's leaders looked to Greece (and to Republican Rome) for inspiration regarding political systems and architecture.

A summary lecture, using the Spirit of the Age model, should identify the most significant legacies of Hellenic Greece and the common artistic and moral values that were expressed in those achievements.

LECTURE OUTLINE

Non-Western Events

I. Geography and Historical Overview

II. General Characteristics of Hellenic Civilization
    A. Competitiveness
    B. Religious

C. High regard for moderation
   1. Dionysus
   2. Apollo

III. Domestic and Foreign Affairs:
   War, Peace, and the Triumph of Macedonia
   A. Economic changes
   B. The Delian League
      1. A mutual defense organization
      2. The central role of Athens
   C. Wars in Greece and with Persia and the
      Thirty Years' Peace
      1. Instability in Greece
      2. The Hellenic Age of Athens
      3. The connection of Athenian imperialism
         and cultural exuberance
      4. The Age of Pericles
         a) Cultural zenith
         b) Fear of Athens among other city-states
   D. The Peloponnesian War
      1. Its origins
      2. The death of Pericles
      3. The Sicilian expedition
      4. The defeat of Athens by Sparta
   E. Spartan and Theban hegemony and the
      triumph of Macedonia
      1. Shifting fortunes in Greece
      2. Conquest of Greece by Philip of
         Macedonia
      3. The reign of Alexander the Great
         a) Alexander's dream
         b) Alexander's sudden death

IV. The Perfection of the Tradition:
   The Glory of Hellenic Greece
   A. Brief overview of Athens in the Hellenic
      Age
      1. Definition of Classic
      2. Definition of Classicism
   B. Theater: Tragedy
      1. Its origins
      2. Features of the Tragic Theater
         a) The actors and chorus
         b) The physical theater
         c) The staging of the plays
         d) The structure of the Great Dionysia
      3. Tragic Drama
         a) Essence of Greek tragedy
            (1) The moral nature of tragedy
            (2) The source of the plots
            (3) The issues treated in
                the plays
            (4) Aristotle's theory of tragedy

479–323 B.C.
In China, eastern Zhou
   dynasty, about 771–256
   B.C.; the Warring States
   period, 403–221 B.C.
In India, Alexander the Great
   invades, 326 B.C.;
   Chandragupta Maurya
   reconquers North India
   from Alexander's general
   and founds the Mauryan
   Empire, 319 B.C.
In Mesoamerica, Formative
   period, 2000–200 B.C.; in
   Cuicuilco, near
   Cuernavaca, a round,
   stepped pyramid, about
   450 to 100 B.C.; Olmec
   influence on figurines at
   Tlapacoya

                b)   Aeschylus and the *Oresteia*
                c)   Sophocles
                     (1) *Antigone*
                     (2) *Oedipus the King*
                     (3) *Oedipus at Colonus*
                d)   Euripides
                     (1) *The Trojan Women*
                     (2) *The Bacchae*
   C. Theater: Comedy
        1. Nature of Greek comedy
                a)   Characteristics
                b)   Comedy and democratic values
        2. Aristophanes
                a)   Old Comedy
                b)   *Lysistrata*
   D. Music
        1. Role in Greek society
                a)   Music as one of the humanities
                b)   A partially reconstructed legacy
                     (1) The diatonic system of
                          Pythagoras
                     (2) The series of scales, called
                          modes
        2. Music's dependent status
   E. History
        1. Herodotus, the founder of secular
            history
                a)   The *Histories*
                b)   The methodology
        2. Thucydides, the founder of scientific
            history
                a)   *History of the Peloponnesian War*
                b)   The methodology
   F. Natural Philosophy
        1. Historic overview
        2. The Pre-Socratics
                a)   The School of Elea
                     (1) Parmenides
                     (2) Empedocles
                b)   Atomism
                c)   Anaxagoras
        3. The Sophists
                a)   Source of the name
                b)   Their teachings
                c)   Their influence
        4. The Socratic revolution
                a)   Comparison with Sophists
                b)   The life and teachings of
                     Socrates
                     (1) The Socratic method
                     (2) The teaching that "Virtue
                          is Knowledge"

                (3)   The revolutionary nature
                      of his thinking
                (4)   The death of Socrates
        5. Plato
            a)   The influence of Socrates
            b)   The author of Western idealism
            c)   Platonism
                (1)   The doctrine of the Forms,
                      or Ideas
                (2)   Platonic dualism
                (3)   The Form (Idea) of the Good
            d)   The originator of political
                 philosophy—the *Republic*
        6. Aristotle
            a)   The influence of Plato
            b)   Emphasis on empiricism
            c)   Aristotelianism
                (1)   The indivisibility of Form
                      and Matter
                (2)   Focus on purpose
                (3)   The First Cause
                (4)   The ethical ideal of
                      moderation: a sound mind
                      in a sound body
                (5)   Political theory based on
                      research
            d)   His enduring influence
    G. Architecture
        1. Sanctuaries
            a)   Apollo's shrine at Delphi
            b)   The effect of the rise of the polis
        2. The temple: The perfection of the form
            a)   The style of western Greece
                (1)   Characteristics
                (2)   The Second Temple of Hera
                      at Poseidonia
            b)   The style of eastern Greece
                (1)   Characteristics
                (2)   The Parthenon
            c)   The Ionic temple
                (1)   Characteristics
                (2)   The Erechtheum
    H. Sculpture
        1. The Severe style
            a)   Characteristics
            b)   *Kritios Boy*
            c)   *Birth of Aphrodite*
        2. The High Classical style
            a)   Characteristics
            b)   *Poseidon*, or *Zeus*
            c)   The *Doryphoros*
            d)   The Parthenon sculptures

LEARNING OBJECTIVES

To learn:

1. The general characteristics of Hellenic civilization

2. The Greek examples and images of balance and harmony

3. The causes, phases, and results of the Peloponnesian War

4. The reasons for and results of the coming of the Macedonians

5. The definitions of Classic, Classical, and Classicism

6. The origins and characteristics of Greek drama, the names of the major playwrights and their contributions

7. The origins and characteristics of Greek comedy, the name of the chief comic playwright and his contributions

8. The origins and moral purpose of Greek music

9. The writing techniques and contributions of the first Greek historians

10. The leading thinkers, their contributions, and the phases of philosophy in Hellenic Greece

11. The characteristics of the Ionic order of Greek architecture and its similarities and differences from the Doric order

12. The characteristics of Greek Hellenic sculpture, its various phases, and examples of sculptural works from each phase

13. The historic "firsts" of Hellenic civilization that became part of the Western tradition: humanism; a school curriculum based on humanistic studies; Classicism; the literary genres of tragedy, comedy, and dialogue; written secular history; the Ionic temple; the open-air theater; the Hellenic art style; the idea of democracy; the skeptical spirit rooted in scientific knowledge; and Platonism, Aristotelianism, and Atomism

14. The role of Hellenic civilization in transmitting the heritage of Archaic Greece: redirecting philosophy away from the study of nature and into humanistic inquiry, redefining sculpture along more realistic lines, and elaborating the basic temple form

SUGGESTIONS FOR FILMS

The Acropolis of Athens. Media Guide, 26 min., color.

Athens: The Golden Age. Encyclopedia Britannica, 30 min., color.

The Greek Temple. Universal Education and Visual Arts, 54 min., color.

Plato's Apology—The Life and Teachings of Socrates. Encyclopedia Britannica, 30 min., color.

SUGGESTIONS FOR FURTHER READING

Barnes, J. *Aristotle.* Oxford: Oxford University Press. A lively and incisive introduction to Aristotle and his thought; presented within the context of his own times and of the modern world.

Biers, W. R. *The Archaeology of Greece: An Introduction.* Ithaca, N.Y.: Cornell University Press, 1996. 2nd ed. An authoritative overview of the key monuments of Greek archeology, set forth in successive chapters that blend historical and artistic summaries, covering the periods from the Bronze Age through Hellenistic times; profusely illustrated with painting, sculpture, architecture, coins, and inscriptions.

Boardman, J. *Greek Art.* London: Thames and Hudson. Rev. ed. 1985. An excellent introduction by one of the world's leading authorities on Classical art.

———. *Greek Sculpture: The Classical Period: A Handbook.* London: Thames and Hudson, 1985. *Greek Sculpture: The Late Classical Period and Sculpture in Colonies and Overseas.* New York: Thames and Hudson, 1995. Accessible and well-written, this two-volume work is an excellent guide for the beginning student.

Davies, J. K. *Democracy and Classical Greece.* 2nd ed. New York: Humanities Press, 1993. Based on current research; covers both Athens and Sparta .

Fine, J. V. A. *The Ancient Greeks: A Critical History.* In this thoughtful volume on Greek cultural history, the late Professor Fine of Princeton lays out the nature and the ambiguities of the historical evidence; ranges from Archaic times to 323 B.C.

Frost, F. J. *Greek Society.* Rev. ed. Lexington, Mass.: Heath, 1987. Explores Greek social and economic institutions, focusing on class structure and representative figures from each class.

Goldhill, S. *Reading Greek Tragedy.* Cambridge: Cambridge University Press, 1986. A critical study of texts of Greek tragedy, relying on modern literary theory; for advanced students.

Green, J. R. *Theatre in Ancient Greek Society.* A multidimensional study that juxtaposes the audience's views of Greek theater with that of literary scholars and also includes archeological evidence of tragedy and comedy.

Irwin, T. H. *Classical Thought.* Oxford: Oxford University Press, 1989. A short and informative guide to the major thinkers of Classical Greece.

Lacey, W. K. *The Family in Classical Greece.* Ithaca, N.Y.: Cornell University Press, 1984. A pioneering study that focuses on the family in the Archaic and Classical periods, especially in Athens.

Ley, G. *A Short Introduction to the Ancient Greek Theater.* Chicago: University of Chicago Press, 1991. A brief work that is concerned almost exclusively with the original staging of the Greek plays.

Mikalson, J. D. *Athenian Popular Religion.* Chapel Hill: University of North Carolina Press, 1983. This innovative work ignores the philosophic and religious beliefs of Greece's literary masters in order to focus on the views of ordinary Athenian townspeople; based on an analysis of religious rituals, myths, cult figures, orations, and inscriptions from 405 to 323 B.C.

Rowe, C. J. *Plato.* Brighton: Harvester, 1984. An authoritative study of Plato in the context of his own time and of the modern world.

Winkler, J. J., and Zeitlin, F. I., eds. *Nothing To Do With Dionysos? Athenian Drama in Its Social Context.* Princeton: Princeton University Press, 1990. These sixteen revisionist essays on Athens' Dionysian theater downplay the role of the wine god cult and instead emphasize the entire social context of the festivals; particularly noteworthy is S. Goldhill's essay entitled "The Great Dionysia and Civic Ideology."

IDENTIFICATIONS

Hellenic	modes
maenad	idealism
Classic (Classical)	Platonism
Classicism	Ionic
tragedy	Severe style
chorus	High Classical style
orchestra	Fourth Century style
skene	contrapposto
satyr-play	Praxitelean curve
Old Comedy	humanism

PERSONAL PERSPECTIVE BACKGROUND

Xenophon, Secrets of a Successful Marriage

The *Oeconomicus,* from which the Personal Perspective is taken, is in the form of a dialogue dealing with the training of a young wife to be mistress of a house. The wife is portrayed as pliable and eager to please, and, as a female scholar recently wrote, "[she] seems charming if one is not too confirmed a feminist." Unusual for its time is Xenophon's insistence, via Ischomachus, that husbands and wives are equally gifted with traits that lead to virtue.

DISCUSSION/ESSAY QUESTIONS

1. Describe the Greek political and economic situation at the beginning of the Hellenic Age. What changes take place during this period, and how do they impact on the culture?
2. Discuss the general characteristics of Hellenic civilization.
3. What were causes of the Peloponnesian War, and what were its results?
4. What were some causes of the rise of Macedonia as a world empire? Evaluate the career of Alexander the Great.
5. Define Classicism, and illustrate how Greek tragedy embodies it.
6. Discuss the features of Greek tragedy and explain how they were manifested in Sophocles' *Antigone.*
7. Explain the religious outlook of each of the three major Greek tragic playwrights, and show how the outlook of each is reflected in his plays.
8. Compare and contrast the works and techniques of Herodotus and Thucydides.
9. Who were the Pre-Socratics? Note the contributions to philosophy of two of the schools of pre-Socratic thinkers.
10. Discuss the pivotal role of Socrates in the history of Greek and, consequently, Western philosophy.
11. Compare and contrast Plato's and Aristotle's approaches to truth, and note their basic contributions to Western philosophy.

12. What is meant by the High Classical style? Discuss at least two examples of this style as found in Greek sculpture.
13. How did the Greeks define humanism? How was this concept manifested in Greek tragedy and in Aristotle's writings on ethics?

MULTIPLE-CHOICE QUESTIONS

1. One of the ideals the Greeks strived for was a:
   a. unified Greek state
   b. uniform religion with one major deity
 * c. balance or moderation in life (p. 51)
   d. recognition in life that all human beings are equal

2. Life for the Greeks in the Hellenic Era can be described as a(n):
   a. tranquil period marked by a century or more of peace
 * b. time when the old religions were questioned (p. 51)
   c. age of cooperation among all Greek city-states
   d. period of economic stagnation

3. To the Greeks, these two gods manifest the extremes of moderation and excess:
 * a. Apollo and Dionysus (p. 51)
   b. Zeus and Hera
   c. Apollo and Athena
   d. Mars and Aphrodite

4. At the height of its power Athens was dominated by:
   a. Quales
   b. Leonidas
   c. Philip
 * d. Pericles (p. 55)

5. The Age of Pericles was characterized by:
   a. a retreat from Athens' policy of imperial control
   b. a lessening of political democracy in Athens
 * c. an outburst in the arts and literature in Athens (p. 55)
   d. the establishment of a communal economy in Athens

6. The primary cause of the Peloponnesian War was:
   a. the rise of Sparta
 * b. Athens' growing domination over the other city-states (p. 55)
   c. the emergence of Thebes
   d. the threat from Philip of Macedonia

7. What event provoked the outbreak of the Peloponnesian War?
   a. Athens attacked her longtime enemy Sparta.
   b. Corinth was conquered by the Thebans.
 * c. Athens sent troops to aid the Corcyrians. (p. 55)
   d. Sparta called for help against the Athenians.

8. The Peloponnesian War was noteworthy for:
    a.   its disruptive influence on Spartan political affairs
    b.   its quick and decisive outcome
    c.   the triumph of Athens over the other city-states
  * d.   the weakening of Greece that made it an easy prey for outsiders (p. 55)

9. Which fourth-century leader had a dream that he would conquer the known world?
  * a.   Alexander the Great (p. 56)
    b.   Charles of Macedonia
    c.   Attila the Hun
    d.   Pericles the Conqueror

10. The dream of Alexander the Great was to:
  * a.   Create a united world based on Greek and Persian culture. (p. 56)
    b.   Set up an international league of city-states.
    c.   Destroy all cultures except the Greek culture.
    d.   Fuse African and Macedonian civilizations.

11. The essence of Classicism is to:
    a . Have everyone conform to a uniform way of thinking
  * b.   Strive toward a perfection, an ideal form (p. 57)
    c.   Have a balanced view of public and private life
    d.   Preserve the best of the past

12. According to tradition, the first playwright to introduce an actor with whom a chorus could interact was:
    a.   Aeschylus
    b.   Aristophanes
  * c.   Thespis (p. 57)
    d.   Sophocles

13. Greek drama had this feature:
    a.   The plays were full of on-stage action.
  * b.   The themes often dealt with serious moral issues. (p. 58)
    c.   Most of the dramas were based on current political events.
    d.   The plays had many characters and elaborate scenery.

14. This Greek philosopher wrote a book on tragedy:
    a.   Plato
    b.   Socrates
  * c.   Aristotle (p. 58)
    d.   Pythagoras

15. The *Oresteia* trilogy involved:
    a.   three individuals caught in a planned single murder
    b.   three short stories
  * c.   many moral issues (pp. 58–59)
    d.   a romantic tale of love

16. In Sophocles, *Antigone*, Antigone opposes Creon because:
  * a . Creon places the state's law above the divine. (p. 59)
    b.   Creon plans to revenge the murder of his parents.
    c.   Creon wants Antigone to be his wife.
    d.   Creon plans an invasion of the city of Athens.

17. Euripides wrote plays that can be described as:
    a. satiric studies of Greek manners
    b. always having a happy ending
    c. dealing with the lives of ordinary Greek citizens
  * d. often skeptical about religion (p. 60)

18. Greek Old Comedy can be described as:
    a. relatively unpopular with Greek audiences
    b. developed before tragedy
  * c. showing political criticism (p. 61)
    d. expressed through clever and subtle dialogue

19. The most famous and most successful comic playwright was:
    a. Aristotle
    b. Agisthenes
  * c. Aristophanes (p. 61)
    d. Aeschylus

20. The most important legacy of Greek comedy was:
  * a. Old Comedy (p. 61)
    b. New Comedy
    c. burlesque style
    d. New Satire

21. This Greek philosopher contributed to the development of music theory:
    a. Protagoras
  * b. Pythagoras (p. 62)
    c. Pericles
    d. Anaxagoras

22. The Greeks believed that music:
    a. was entertaining and fun
  * b. served ethical and educational functions (p. 62)
    c. was basically expressive and emotional
    d. was simply the product of human creativity and innovation

23. The two founders of Greek historical writing were:
    a. Empedocles and Pythagoras
    b. Sophocles and Euripides
  * c. Herodotus and Thucydides (p. 65)
    d. Plattus and Matthedides

24. Herodotus and Thucydides shared equally a:
    a. belief in historical cause and effect
    b. desire to be fair to all parties
  * c. willingness to accept any source as the truth (p. 62)
    d. belief that history teaches lessons

25. Empedocles attempted to unify materialism and idealism by claiming that:
    a. Everything is made up of atoms.
  * b. The basic four elements are affected by love and strife. (p. 63)
    c. The world is static and never changes.
    d. Water is the basic ingredient of all things.

26. The Greek thinker who developed the Atomic theory was:
  * a. Democritus (p. 63)
    b. Empedocles
    c. Parmenides
    d. Pythagoras

27. The Sophists could be described in all of the following ways EXCEPT:
    a. teachers who claimed that they could make their students successful
    b. critics of pre-Socratic philosophy
  * c. counselors on personal and private morals (pp. 63–64)
    d. experts in rhetoric, or the use of language

28. The Greek philosopher who is reputed to have said "Man is the measure of all things" was:
    a. Pythagoras
  * b. Protagoras (p. 63)
    c. Plato
    d. Socrates

29. Socrates criticized the Sophists for their:
    a. inability to present a reasoned argument
    b. beliefs in the Olympian deities
  * c. rejection of an enduring moral order in the universe (p. 64)
    d. all of the above

30. What Socrates meant by "Virtue is Knowledge" was that:
    a. Everyone who does good will be rewarded in heaven.
  * b. If one knows what is good, that person will not commit evil acts. (p. 64)
    c. Everyone will reach understanding if they have faith.
    d. Being virtuous is all one needs to exist.

31. Socrates was accused of:
    a. aiding Athens' enemies during the Peloponnesian War
  * b. corrupting the youth of Athens (p. 65)
    c. refusing to swear loyalty to the Athenian government
    d. not paying his debts

32. The Socratic method of teaching can be described as a:
    a. step-by-step memorization process to learn terms
  * b. step-by-step system of asking and answering questions (pp. 64–65)
    c. progression of theories based on numbers
    d. line of argument that refutes all basic values

33. Socrates' most famous pupil was:
    a. Aristotle
    b. Alcibiades
    c. Zeno
  * d. Plato (p. 65)

34. Plato's most important contribution to Western philosophy was his:
    a. theory of numbers
  * b. founding of the school of idealism (p. 65)
    c. establishment of the Academy
    d. legacy of a new set of deities

35. In the *Republic,* Plato created:
    a.   an ideal society under a government run by soldiers
  * b.   an ideal society run by philosopher-kings (p. 65)
    c.   a capitalist economic system
    d.   a utopian land of peace and plenty

36. Xenophon reasoned that married women's responsibilities included all of the following EXCEPT:
    a.   to manage the husband's estate
    b.   to bear children
  * c.   to submit to the husband's will in all things (p. 66)
    d.   to carry out domestic chores

37. Unlike Plato, Aristotle:
    a.   ignored the way that the world operated
    b.   thought that the senses were to be ignored
  * c.   argued that knowledge is derived from studying the material world (p. 66)
    d.   was not interested in politics

38. Aristotle has influenced Western thought in all of the following ways EXCEPT:
    a.   He was considered to have the most comprehensive mind of the ancient world.
  * b.   His ethical writings became the prevailing moral code of the West. (p. 67)
    c.   His writings formed the core of much of Classical learning.
    d.   His ideas were later accepted as authoritative by the Catholic Church.

39. Greek Classical art concerned itself with:
    a.   arranging proportions that would be unique for each figure and situation
  * b.   striving to create balance and harmony (p. 67)
    c.   seeking to render the human figure in stylized ways
    d.   creating a sense of dynamism and emotionalism

40. In general terms Hellenic Greek architecture:
    a.   created an asymmetrical type of building
    b.   tended to be without any decoration
  * c.   expressed the ideals of Greek art (p. 67)
    d.   concentrated on secular rather than religious buildings

41. Athens' major religious shrines were located:
    a.   in the agora
    b.   outside the city's walls
  * c.   on the Acropolis (pp. 67–70)
    d.   around the city's burial grounds

42. The two architects responsible for the building of Athens' temples in the mid–fifth century were:
  * a.   Ictinus and Callicrates (p. 67)
    b.   Pericles and Alcibiades
    c.   Aeschylus and Euripides
    d.   Myron and Praxiteles

43. The central temple on the Acropolis was the:
    a.   Erechtheum
  * b.   Parthenon (pp. 67, 69, and caption for Fig. 3.15)
    c.   Pantheon
    d.   Athena Nike

44. The Parthenon has become one of the most important architectural landmarks in the West for all of the following reasons EXCEPT:
    a. It embodies the ideals of Greek architecture.
    b. It represents the zenith of Greek architecture.
    c. It became the model for ideal proportions and symmetrical harmony.
*   d. It inspired Gothic art. (pp. 67, 69, and caption for Fig. 3.15)

45. Doric and Ionic architecture shared this quality:
    a. The buildings in both orders used equal amounts of decoration.
*   b. Both orders used columns that were usually fluted. (p. 70)
    c. Both orders used columns topped with a double scroll or the horns of a ram.
    d. Both orders used columns of the same height and the same slenderness.

46. A comparison of the Doric and Ionic orders of columns reveals that:
    a. The Ionic is more decorated than the Doric.
    b. Most of the early temples were built with Doric columns.
    c. The Ionic column has a capital that looks like a double scroll or the horns of a ram.
*   d. all of the above (p. 70)

47. Which temple on the Acropolis was dedicated to Athena, Poseidon, and the legendary ruler who introduced the horse to Athens?
    a. Athena Nike
    b. Propylaea
*   c. Erechtheum (p. 70)
    d. Pantheon

48. The architect of the Erechtheum was:
    a. Ictinus
*   b. Mnesicles (p. 70)
    c. Praxiteles
    d. Myron

49. The three phases of sculpture, in chronological order, as they evolved during the Hellenic Age were:
*   a. Severe, High Classical, and Fourth Century (p. 70)
    b. Severe, Fourth Century, and High Classical
    c. High Classical, Severe, and Fourth Century
    d. Severe, High Classical, and Baroque

50. Greek sculptors carved the human form in a graceful pose known as the:
    a. three-point stance
*   b. *contrapposto* (p. 70)
    c. *sfumato*
    d. flat-footed pose

51. Statues carved during the Hellenic Age often:
    a. were distorted in body proportions
    b. revealed human feelings and emotions
*   c. stood in the inner sanctums of temples (pp. 73–74)
    d. reflected the faces of real persons

52. Which statement is NOT correct for the Ludovisi Throne?
    * a. It was originally part of the Parthenon frieze. (pp. 70, 73 and caption for Fig. 3.19)
    b. Its central panel depicts the birth of Aphrodite.
    c. It is one of the first depictions of naked women in large-scale Greek sculpture.
    d. The softly curving lines of the central figure deviate from the Severe style.

53. The High Classical sculptural style attempted to:
    a. accept repose as a normal state for the carved object
    b. create a sense of vast motion
    * c. show motion in a static medium (p. 73)
    d. demonstrate that emotion should dominate a work of art

54. The sculptor who supervised the carvings that decorated the Parthenon was:
    a. Praxiteles
    b. Ictinus
    * c. Phidias (p. 74)
    d. Mnesicles

55. The frieze that decorated the Parthenon:
    a. depicted a procession of Greek deities
    b. was carved in high relief
    c. has been lost and we only have copies of it
    * d. included humans, animals, and deities (p. 74)

4

CLASSICAL GREEK CIVILIZATION
The Hellenistic Age

TEACHING STRATEGIES AND SUGGESTIONS

The instructor should begin the study of Hellenistic civilization with a Historic Overview that sets forth the imperial dream of Alexander the Great, the general trajectory of history after his death, and the general characteristics of the culture and society that now developed. The best introductory approach to cultural achievements in this volatile age is with the Reflections/Connections model, showing how art, literature, and philosophy reflected changes in material history. Special attention should be paid to the rise of enormous cities that caused a change in consciousness, which, in turn, had an impact on art, philosophy, religion, and propaganda. A related development was the rise of Hellenistic Classicism, rooted in Hellenic forms but emotional, violence-loving, and playful. The instructor can use a combination of five strategies when treating the rich diversity of Hellenistic civilization: The Diffusion model can show the impact of Persian, Egyptian, and Babylonian cultures on the Greek tradition; the Patterns of Change approach can illustrate the shift from the pure Hellenic to the eclectic Hellenistic style; the Comparison/Contrast method is excellent for analyzing the premier Hellenistic philosophies; the Spirit of the Age technique can demonstrate the harmony amid the cultural confusion; and the Case Study approach will enable the instructor to apply lessons from Hellenistic civilization to today's similarly multicultural and multiracial world.

LECTURE OUTLINE

Non-Western Events

I. The Hellenistic World
   A. Meaning of "Hellenistic"
   B. The legacy of Alexander the Great
   C. Brief summary of key Hellenistic concepts
   D. Overview of Hellenistic politics, society, and economics
      1. The class system
      2. The role and status of women

II. The Stages of Hellenistic History
   A. The end of the empire and the rise of the states
      1. The shattering of Alexander's dream, 323–307 B.C.

323–146 B.C.
In Africa, the founding of the settlement of Jenne-jeno on the Niger delta in modern Mali, about 250 B.C., which

2. The era of the successor states, 307–215 B.C.
   a) Freedom of movement of Greeks and barbarians
   b) Common *koine* language
   c) The Macedonian kingdom
   d) The Seleucid kingdom
      (1) Parthia and Bactria
      (2) Pergamum
   e) The Ptolemaic kingdom
      (1) Alexandria as the capital
      (2) Its agricultural and commercial riches
3. The arrival and triumph of Rome
   a) The fall of Macedonia, 146 B.C.
   b) The fall of the Seleucid kingdom, 65 B.C.
   c) The gift of Pergamum
   d) The fall of the Ptolemaic kingdom, 31 B.C.

III. The Cities of Hellenistic Civilization
   A. Alexander's vision of the city
   B. Pergamum
      1. The capital of the Pergamum kingdom
      2. Artistic and intellectual center
   C. Alexandria in Egypt
      1. The capital of the Ptolemaic kingdom
      2. The largest city of the Hellenistic world
      3. An unmatched cultural center
         a) The world's first museum
         b) The largest library of the ancient world

IV. The Elaboration of the Greek Tradition: The Spread of Classicism to the Hellenistic World
   A. Hellenistic cultural style and Classicism
   B. Drama and literature
      1. New Comedy
         a) Definition
         b) Menander, the leading exponent
            (1) The comedy of manners
            (2) *The Woman of Samos*
            (3) His later influence
      2. Alexandrianism—the Hellenistic literary style
         a) Important genres
         b) Characteristics
      3. Theocritus
         a) The pastoral

by A.D. 800 had become one of West Africa's first urban centers
In Andean culture, Early Horizon period, 1000–200 B.C.; Early Intermediate period, 200 B.C.–A.D. 500
In Europe, in Britain, invasion of La Tene people, about 250 B.C.
In China, the philosophers Mencius, 372–289 B.C., and Hsun-tse, 315–235 B.C., develop the ideas of Confucius; the religious teacher Mo-Ti, about 441 to about 376 B.C., rejects Confucianism; the death of Sun-tsi, 233 B.C., marks end of classical philosophy in China
In Himalayan region, in Kashmir, founding of Gonandiya dynasty, about 500 B.C. to A.D. 622; Kashmir was part of Mauryan Empire after 319 B.C.; later part of the Kushan Empire; in Nepal, memorial column to Emperor Asoka of India's Mauryan dynasty, fourth century B.C.; Buddhist monuments, including the Piprahva stupa and the Chabahil complex with its Carumati stupa, at Patan, third century B.C.
In India, Chandragupta Maurya founds the Mauryan Empire in North India, 319 B.C.; Mauryan rule extended to south by grandson Asoka; Mauryan culture, 319–185 B.C.; the Indian epic "Mahabharata" being written (perhaps to A.D. 350); rainfall is measured; the emperor Asoka establishes India's first hospitals and herbal gardens, placing both under Buddhist control, in

about 260 B.C.; erects 40-foot-high columns inscribed with his laws, about 250 B.C.; raising of stambas, free-standing pillars topped by a capital supporting symbolic animals or inanimate figures, a device adapted from Persian culture; the stamba evolved into the amalaka, the cushion-shaped capital that is characteristic of Indian architecture; beginning of rock-cut architecture; the cave of Sudama containing a chaitya (sanctuary) cut from rock, about 256 B.C.; major texts of Hindu tradition are now in place; codification of laws, grammar, science, arts; gods Shiva and Vishnu are major figures; spread of Sanskritic culture to South India; Shunga dynasty replaces Mauryan dynasty, 185–30 B.C.

In Japan, Jomon culture, about 4000 to about 300 B.C.; Yayoi culture, about 300 B.C. to about A.D. 300; metals and wheel-turned pottery

In Mesoamerica, Formative period, 2000–200 B.C.

D. Architecture
    1. The defining role of religion
        a) The altar
        b) The temple
    2. The Corinthian temple
        a) Characteristics of the Corinthian column and temple
        b) The Corinthian column as a symbol of Hellenistic influence
        c) The Olympieum in Athens
            (1) History
            (2) Description
    3. The altar
        a) General changes to altars in the Hellenistic period
        b) The altar of Zeus at Pergamum
            (1) Description
            (2) Its role in the beautification of Pergamum
            (3) The idea of a "new" Athens

E. Sculpture
    1. Comparison with Hellenic style
    2. *Gaul and Wife*
        a) Why it was created
        b) Description
        c) Characteristics
    3. *Boy Struggling with a Goose*
        a) Description
        b) A genre subject
    4. *Old Market Woman*
        a) Description
        b) A genre subject
    5. Pergamum altar frieze
        a) Subject and description
        b) Characteristics
        c) Moral purpose of the art
    6. *Aphrodite of Melos*
        a) Subject and description
        b) Characteristics
    7. *Aphrodite of Cyrene*
        a) The nude female as an artistic specialty
        b) Characteristics
    8. *Horse and Jockey*
        a) Subject and description
        b) Characteristics
        c) Contrast with the Hellenic style

F. Rhodes: Late Hellenistic style
    1. The persistence of Rhodes as a center of Hellenistic culture, until the early Christian era

2. The Rhodian style
  a) *Melpomene, or Polyhymnia*
    (1) Subject and description
    (2) Characteristics
    (3) Hellenistic representation of
      women
  b) *The Laocoön Group*
    (1) Subject and description
    (2) Characteristics
    (3) Later influence of this
      sculptural group

V. The Legacy of the Hellenistic World

LEARNING OBJECTIVES

To learn:

1. That Hellenistic society was one of the first world-states to be organized on multiracial lines

2. The role of Alexander in giving a vision to Hellenistic civilization

3. A brief summary of Hellenistic economics and society

4. A comparison of Hellenistic women with those of Hellenic Greece

5. The two historic stages of Hellenistic civilization

6. The major Hellenistic successor states to Alexander the Great's unified empire, their leading cultural characteristics, and how each state eventually fell to Rome

7. The two largest Hellenistic cities, Pergamum and Alexandria, and their chief contributions to the civilization of this age

8. How Hellenistic artists and writers adopted the Hellenic style and modified it into Hellenistic Classicism

9. How Menander developed New Comedy and the ways it differed from the Old Comedy of the Hellenic period

10. The characteristics of Alexandrianism, the unique literary style of the Hellenistic Age

11. The contributions and enduring influence of Theocritus, the chief writer of the Hellenistic period

12. The principles of the main Hellenistic philosophies (Cynicism, Skepticism, Epicureanism, and Stoicism), their leading spokespersons, and how they differed from one another

13. The teachings of the Hellenistic mystery cults and the belief in Fate

14. How Hellenistic religions and philosophies reflected the then-prevailing climate of opinion, especially in the cities

15. The characteristics of the Corinthian temple, as seen in the Olympieum, Athens

16. How today the Corinthian style is a symbol of Hellenistic influence

17. To describe and recognize the altar of Zeus at Pergamum

18. How Hellenistic rulers wanted to identify with Greek culture and to create cities that were "new" versions of Athens

19. The identifying characteristics of Hellenistic sculpture

20. To recognize visually key examples of Hellenistic sculpture

21. How Hellenistic sculpture differs from Hellenic sculpture

22. Historic "firsts" of Hellenistic civilization that became part of the Western tradition: the union of Greek culture and politics for propaganda purposes; the concept of a capital city as a "new Athens"; the Corinthian temple; the literary forms of the pastoral and the idyll; the Alexandrian literary style; the earliest museum; a multiracial and multiethnic empire; the Hellenistic art style, including new images of women; and the philosophies of Cynicism, Skepticism, Epicureanism, and Stoicism

23. The role of Hellenistic civilization in transmitting the heritage of earlier civilizations: redefining Classicism to meet new needs, adopting the humanities as the curriculum in the schools, preserving the chief texts of Greek literature in Alexandria, expanding Greek science, making libraries into primary institutions in the large cities, and adopting the Near Eastern idea of a ruler-god

SUGGESTIONS FOR FILMS

Alexander the Great and the Hellenistic Age. Coronet, 14 min., color.

Aristotle's Ethics—The Theory of Happiness. Encyclopedia Britannica, 30 min., color.

The Search for Alexander the Great: The Young Lion; The Young Conqueror; Lord of Asia; The Last March. Time-Life, each segment 60 min., color.

You Are There: The Triumph of Alexander the Great. McGraw-Hill, 26 min., black and white.

SUGGESTIONS FOR FURTHER READING

Burkert, W. *Ancient Mystery Cults*. Cambridge: Harvard University Press, 1987. Four lectures on the structure, functions, and beliefs of the mystery cults; for the serious student.

Charbonneaux, J., et al. *Hellenistic Art, 330–50 B.C.* New York: Braziller, 1973. In the splendid "The Arts of Mankind" series, this volume maintains the high standards of text and visuals found in the other works. Architecture, painting, and sculpture are examined in separate essays with many illustrations.

Grant, M. *From Alexander to Cleopatra: The Hellenistic World*. London: Weidenfeld and Nicolson, 1982. A clearly written survey that explores all aspects of the Hellenistic world that one should study for its own unique characteristics and contributions.

Green, P. *Alexander of Macedon, 356–323 B.C.* New York: Praeger, 1970. Among many biographies, this is a well-researched and lively but critical and sometimes controversial account of one of history's most famous personalities.

Kristeller, P. O. *Greek Philosophers of the Hellenistic Age.* New York: Columbia University Press, 1993. Eight lucid and factual lectures that focus on Epicureanism, Stoicism, and Skepticism, their founders, and those who spread these schools of thought across the ancient world.

Long, A. A. *Hellenistic Philosophy: Stoics, Epicureans, Sceptics.* London: Duckworth, 1986. A general appraisal and analysis of the three philosophies.

Pollitt, J. J. *Art in the Hellenistic Age.* Cambridge: Cambridge University Press, 1986. An excellent recent survey by a leading authority; richly illustrated.

Rist, A. *The Poems of Theocritus.* Chapel Hill: University of North Carolina Press, 1978. One of the best studies of the finest poet of the Hellenistic Age.

Samuel, A. E. *The Promise of the West: The Greek World, Rome and Judaism.* New York: Routledge, 1988. An ambitious affirmation of the spirit of humanity, how it evolved, and how it still affects Western civilization today. A synthesis of thought and culture that will challenge and enlighten the reader.

Smith, R. R. R. *Hellenistic Sculpture.* London: Thames and Hudson, 1991. Hellenistic statuary is examined from a thematic approach placed in both a historical and geographical context. The book uses the latest discoveries and is full of black-and-white photographs.

Tarn, W. W., and Griffith, G. T. *Hellenistic Civilization.* Rev. ed. New York: New American Library, 1961. Superseded by more recent scholarship but still a useful introduction for the beginning student.

Wallbank, F. W. *The Hellenistic World.* Cambridge: Harvard University Press, 1982. Another sound and methodical survey of a turbulent but important period of ancient history.

IDENTIFICATIONS

Hellenistic
koine
New Comedy
comedy of manners
Alexandrianism
pastoral
idyll
Cynicism
autarky

Skepticism
Epicureanism
ataraxia
Stoicism
logos
Corinthian
podium
genre subject

PERSONAL PERSPECTIVE BACKGROUND

Theocritus, A Street Scene in Alexandria

This Personal Perspective is gently satirical in its treatment of Gorgo and Praxinoa, for these two ladies are from the provinces, the relatively small town of Syracuse, and they are eager to play tourist in the metropolis of Alexandria. Born in Syracuse himself, Theocritus was drawn to Alexandria to seek patronage for his poetry from the reigning Ptolemies. The poem also demonstrates the freedom upper- and middle-class women enjoyed during the Hellenistic period.

DISCUSSION/ESSAY QUESTIONS

1. In what ways did Hellenistic civilization differ from Hellenic civilization, and what were the causes for these differences?
2. Compare and contrast the role of women in Hellenic and Hellenistic society. Explain the reasons for their similarities and differences.
3. What was Alexander the Great's vision for the world-state that he founded? To what extent did the Hellenistic era's successor states embody Alexander's dream? Include both material and cultural aspects in your essay.
4. Identify the Hellenistic states that arose as a result of the partition of Alexander the Great's far-flung empire. What forces unified these states during the Hellenistic period? Explain the circumstances under which these states eventually fell to the rising Roman Empire.
5. Compare and contrast the two largest cities of the Hellenistic Age: Pergamum and Alexandria. Be specific as to the cultural contributions of each city.
6. How did the rise of the Hellenistic cities affect Hellenistic cultural and artistic developments?
7. Discuss the changes made to Classicism by Hellenistic writers and artists. What was retained from Greek Classicism and what became the hallmark of Hellenistic Classicism?
8. Define New Comedy. Which playwright dominated this literary genre? What impact did this playwright's works have on the Western theatrical tradition?
9. Compare and contrast Hellenic and Hellenistic comedy, noting playwrights, treatment of characters, and plots and themes.
10. Define Alexandrianism. Discuss this literary style in relation to the greatest writer of the Hellenistic period, Theocritus. What were the contributions of Theocritus to Western literature?
11. Why was the Hellenistic Age so rich in new philosophies and religions? What contradictory points of view emerged and why?
12. Identify the four philosophies that dominated the Hellenistic period, and compare and contrast their differing principles and goals. Indicate the relative long-term importance of each of these philosophies to the Western tradition.
13. Discuss Hellenistic religions with special focus on the belief in Fate and the mystery cults. Why were these religions so popular with the masses?
14. Describe a Corinthian-style temple, using the Olympieum in Athens as the model. Explain how the Olympieum mirrored the propaganda goals of the rulers who commissioned it.
15. What changes occurred in the design of altars during the Hellenistic Age? Describe the altar of Zeus at Pergamum. Why was this altar made into such a spectacular work of art?
16. Which work of Hellenistic sculpture epitomizes the Hellenistic style? Explain.
17. Discuss the influence of Hellenistic religion on Hellenistic culture, in particular architecture and sculpture.
18. *The Laocoön Group* is the most famous sculpture from the Hellenistic period. What makes this such a well-known work of art? Which sculptural school produced the *Laocoön*? Describe the artistic style of this famous sculptural group.
19. Choosing two examples of Hellenistic sculpture, show how these works reflect the values of Hellenistic civilization.
20. What was the legacy of the Hellenistic Age to the West? Discuss both material developments and cultural contributions. What was original, and what was simply a transmission of ideas, beliefs, and genres from earlier civilizations?

MULTIPLE-CHOICE QUESTIONS

1. Greek culture and society played what role in the Hellenistic world?
   * a. It furnished the Hellenistic world's commercial language. (p. 79)
   b. It supplied troops for the Hellenistic armies.
   c. It set the religious standards of Hellenistic society.
   d. Its city-state form of government became the Hellenistic ideal.

2. Near Eastern civilizations made all of the following contributions to Hellenistic civilization EXCEPT:
   a. the concept of a ruler-god
 * b. models of government that allowed the masses a significant voice (p. 79)
   c. new mystery cults that promised immortality
   d. new aesthetic techniques and forms in the arts

3. Which was NOT a characteristic of Hellenistic material civilization?
 * a. union into a single political state (p. 79)
   b. government by men who declared themselves deities
   c. multiracial and multiethnic populations
   d. huge metropolitan centers

4. Hellenistic women found new freedom in their ability to:
   a. conduct their own legal and economic affairs
   b. work in the liberal arts and professions
   c. make charitable bequests and erect impressive gravestones
 * d. all of the above (pp. 79–80)

5. What was Alexander's political dream?
   a. a world divided into rival, but friendly states, each pursuing its own direction
 * b. a world united into a single empire under a single ruler, dominated by its Greek and Persian peoples (p. 79)
   c. a world fragmented into small poleis (pl. of polis) that were guided by their citizens
   d. a world composed of a single ethnic group and governed as a constitutional monarchy

6. Hellenistic society can be described as a society:
   a. with few class distinctions
 * b. with enormous cities but whose economy was still rural (p. 79)
   c. in which one race dominated the rest
   d. that opposed materialism and individualism

7. What was the name of the colloquial Greek language that was spoken throughout the Hellenistic world, from Gaul to Syria?
   a. kouros
   b. kore
 * c. *koine* (p. 80)
   d. hubris

8. From the Seleucid kingdom, a Hellenistic state, emerged the new state of:
   a. Egypt
   b. Macedonia
 * c. Pergamum (p. 81)
   d. Greece

9. Which was the last Hellenistic state to fall to Rome?
 * a. Egypt (p. 82)
   b. Pergamum
   c. Macedonia
   d. the Seleucid kingdom

10. The last ruler of Egypt prior to its fall to Rome was:
*   a.   Cleopatra (p. 82)
     b.   Ptolemy Soter
     c.   Seleucus
     d.   Antigonus

11. What was Alexander's enduring legacy to the Hellenistic world?
     a.   his dream of a unified, single world-state
*   b.   his new image of the city (p. 82)
     c.   his ideal of a Greco-Oriental civilization
     d.   his goal to found a peaceful world community

12. Which was NOT an aspect of the brilliant city of Pergamum?
     a.   It was founded by the Attalid dynasty.
     b.   Its library was second in the number of volumes only to the one in Alexandria.
*   c.   It was the capital of the Seleucid kingdom. (p. 82)
     d.   Its most famous structure was the altar of Zeus, one of the seven wonders of the ancient world.

13. The largest city of the Hellenistic world was:
     a.   Pergamum
*   b.   Alexandria (p. 83)
     c.   Antioch
     d.   Athens

14. Which was NOT an aspect of the city of Alexandria?
*   a.   Its population was relatively homogeneous. (p. 83)
     b.   Its rulers built the first museum in the world.
     c.   Its library was the largest of antiquity.
     d.   Its scholars collected the classic texts of Greek civilization.

15. The *Nike of Samothrace* represents which trait of Hellenistic civilization?
*   a.   the ever-present threat of war (caption for Fig. 4.4)
     b.   the yawning gulf between rich and poor
     c.   the search for peace of mind
     d.   the class warfare

16. Unlike Hellenic Classicism, Hellenistic Classicism was characterized by:
     a.   balance and harmony
     b.   tranquility and restfulness
     c.   simplicity and restraint
*   d.   eroticism and everyday themes (pp. 83–85)

17. Hellenistic Classicism shared with Hellenic Classicism the ideal that:
*   a.   Art must serve moral purposes. (p. 84)
     b.   Art should be expressed in simple terms.
     c.   Art should be characterized by restraint.
     d.   all of the above

18. Which was NOT a characteristic of Hellenistic civilization?
     a.   New philosophies and religions abounded.
     b.   Grandiose architecture was the norm.
*   c.   Tragedies were preferred to comedies. (pp. 84–85, 91)
     d.   Exotic scholarship replaced imaginative literature.

19. Unlike Hellenic Comedy, Hellenistic Comedy was characterized by:
    a. the absence of masks
    b. focus on the chorus rather than the actors
  * c. realistic costumes for actors (pp. 84–85)
    d. politically motivated plots

20. New Comedy, the style of comic drama during the Hellenistic period, was characterized by:
  * a. gently satirical scenes from middle-class life (p. 85)
    b. casual obscenity
    c. political criticism
    d. all of the above

21. The favorite subject of New Comedy was:
    a. political satire
  * b. comic romances (p. 85)
    c. slapstick comedies
    d. burlesques of Greek tragedies

22. A defining characteristic of New Comedy was:
  * a. the support of the traditional social order (p. 85)
    b. a moral tale with a sad ending
    c. realistic characters
    d. comic scenes of low life

23. The originator of New Comedy was:
    a. Aristophanes
  * b. Menander (p. 85)
    c. Plautus
    d. Theocritus

24. Which aspect of Menander's *The Woman of Samos* is typical of New Comedy plays?
    a. It had a serious moral tone.
  * b. It was filled with absurd misunderstandings. (p. 85)
    c. It took place in one long act.
    d. Its plot was resolved through the intervention of a kindly priest.

25. New Comedy influenced:
    a. Racine's plays
    b. medieval morality plays
  * c. Shakespeare's comedies (p. 85)
    d. Goethe's *Faust*

26. Alexandrianism is:
  * a. the literary style of the writers in the city of Alexandria (p. 85)
    b. the political style of Alexander the Great
    c. the cultural style of the era of Alexander the Great
    d. all of the above

27. A characteristic of Alexandrianism is:
    a. simplicity
  * b. arid scholarship (p. 85)
    c. clarity
    d. all of the above

28. The dominant poet of the Hellenistic period was:
    a. Menander
    b. Euclid
    c. Aristarchus
  * d. Theocritus (p. 85)

29. Theocritus developed the new literary genre called the:
    a. epic
  * b. pastoral (p. 85)
    c. sonnet
    d. novel

30. The subject of Theocritus's *Idylls* was the:
    a. immoral lives of the rich
    b. perils of life in the city
    c. dilemmas of married life
  * d. lives of shepherds described in artificial ways (p. 85)

31. One of Theocritus's *Idylls* describes an Alexandrian street thus:
    a. filled with men, as women are kept in seclusion
  * b. bustling with men, women, and children (p. 85)
    c. deserted because of plague
    d. orderly because of the presence of troops

32. Hellenistic philosophies often encouraged a type of self-sufficiency called:
    a. moral relativism
    b. *arete*
  * c. *autarky* (pp. 85, 87–89)
    d. *hubris*

33. This philosophy denounced all religions and governments; shunned physical comfort; and taught that if one wanted nothing, then one could not lack anything:
  * a. Cynicism (p. 87)
    b. Skepticism
    c. Epicureanism
    d. Stoicism

34. This philosophy encouraged a philosophy of doubting, arguing that nothing could be known for certain:
    a. Cynicism
  * b. Skepticism (p. 87)
    c. Epicureanism
    d. Stoicism

35. This philosophy taught that the best life is lived withdrawn from the world, cultivating simple pleasures and avoiding fame, power, and wealth:
    a. Cynicism
    b. Skepticism
  * c. Epicureanism (pp. 87–89)
    d. Stoicism

36. This philosophy taught that the order of things cannot be changed and hence wisdom lies in doing one's duty, without complaining, and in a spirit of dedication:
    a. Cynicism
    b. Skepticism
    c. Epicureanism
  * d. Stoicism (p. 89)

37. A key principle of Stoicism was the:
  * a. identification of God with nature and reason (p. 89)
    b. belief in twin gods, a god of evil and a god of goodness
    c. belief in reincarnation
    d. assumption that the best way to live is separated from society

38. Epicureanism was partially based on:
    a. Thales' belief that all things are made of water
  * b. Democritus's atomism (pp. 88–89)
    c. Pythagoras's belief that all things are made of numbers
    d. Heraclitus's dialectical reasoning

39. Hellenistic women were attracted to Epicureanism because this philosophy:
    a. called for a strict separation between the sexes
    b. advocated sexual equality within society
  * c. promoted friendship and thus made the sexes equal (p. 88)
    d. urged that women pursue careers the same as men

40. One of the goals of Hellenistic philosophy was *ataraxia*, which can be defined as a:
  * a. sense of being above the cares of the world (p. 89)
    b. belief that salvation will be given in an afterlife
    c. feeling of belonging to a select group of saved souls
    d. conviction of being in the hands of Fate

41. In the Hellenistic period, which was NOT a part of the cult of Fate?
    a. the belief that Fate ruled the universe
    b. the idea that Fate could not be changed but could be guarded against
    c. the notion that astrology and magic could ward off Fate's worst aspects
  * d. the conviction that suicide was the best response to bad Fate (pp. 89–90)

42. All of these were facets of Mithraism EXCEPT:
    a. It was an offshoot of Zoroastrianism.
  * b. It was especially attractive to women. (p. 90)
    c. It had an emphasis on duty and loyalty.
    d. It originated in Persia.

43. Hellenistic temples were characterized by their:
    a. small sizes
    b. plain decorations
  * c. columns with decorated capitals (p. 91)
    d. raised platforms and many-stepped entrances

44. During the Hellenistic period, temples were altered so that:
    a. Space was made inside to seat the congregation of worshipers.
  * b. Their grandeur enhanced the earthly majesty of the ruler who built them. (p. 91)
    c. No statues of gods or goddesses would be placed inside.
    d. all of the above

45. This Hellenistic sculpture depicts a genre subject:
    a. *Aphrodite of Cyrene*
    b. *Gaul and Wife*
 * c. *Old Market Woman* (pp. 93, 95, and caption for Fig. 4.13)
    d. *The Laocoön Group*

46. Hellenistic sculpture usually depicted:
    a. serenity
    b. order and symmetry
    c. idealized emotion
 * d. realism (p. 93)

47. Genre art is usually art that:
    a. includes famous persons, such as a ruler
    b. is often associated with religious themes and images
 * c. portrays scenes from everyday life (p. 95)
    d. delivers a moral lesson

48. Which of these Hellenistic sculptures represents a muse?
 * a. *Melpomene,* or *Polyhymnia* (caption for Fig. 4.18 and pp. 96, 98)
    b. *Aphrodite of Cyrene*
    c. *The Laocoön Group*
    d. *Nike of Samothrace*

49. Which of the following was NOT a new subject in Hellenistic art?
    a. children at play
    b. female nudity
 * c. family portraits (pp. 93–98)
    d. genre scenes

50. The Hellenistic *Aphrodite of Melos* and the Hellenic *Hermes with the Infant Dionysus* share all of the following EXCEPT:
    a. exaggerated contrapposto
    b. sensuous modeling of the bodies
 * c. a mystical representation of the divine (pp. 95–96)
    d. a countenance with an unmistakable gaze

51. This sculpture was produced by the sculptural school of Rhodes:
    a. *Gaul with Wife*
    b. *Aphrodite of Melos*
 * c. *The Laocoön Group* (p. 98)
    d. *Old Market Woman*

52. All of these are aspects of *The Laocoön Group* EXCEPT:
 * a. It was based on a story in Homer's *Odyssey.* (p. 98)
    b. When rediscovered by Michelangelo, it helped to launch the Baroque style.
    c. It depicts the violent struggles of three athletic males.
    d. The face of Laocoön is contorted in deep anguish.

53. All are legacies of Hellenistic civilization EXCEPT:
 * a. the practice of democracy (p. 99)
    b. the idea of a "new Athens"
    c. a multiracial society
    d. state support of the arts

54. A typical Hellenistic city included:
    a. a cooperative feeling among all classes
    b. an efficient government
    c. a combination of rural and urban economies
  * d. a library and a school of philosophy (p. 99)

55. The eventual conquerors of the Hellenistic kingdoms were the:
    a. Carthaginians
    b. Etruscans
  * c. Romans (p. 99)
    d. Germans

5

ROMAN CIVILIZATION
The Pre-Christian Centuries

TEACHING STRATEGIES AND SUGGESTIONS

The instructor can use every one of the teaching strategies with this chapter. An introductory lecture, combining the Historical Overview model with the Diffusion approach, can present a brief survey of the 1,200 years of Roman history and show the evolutionary development of Rome from a small city-state to master of the world to an empire in shambles. The Diffusion model can also be employed to discuss how Rome conquered Greece but became, in the end, conquered by Greek ideals and art. The instructor can drive this point home with a Slide Lecture, showing Roman art and architecture's dependence on Greek styles and models.

An especially useful method for presenting Roman culture is the Reflections/Connections approach, relating political, economic, and social changes to shifting Roman values as manifested in sculpture, architecture, and history. The Patterns of Change technique blended with a Slide Lecture can then show the evolution of Roman styles of architecture. With the aid of the Spirit of the Age strategy, the instructor can provide a brief summary of Roman cultural achievements that stresses the unity underneath this complex civilization.

A good conclusion to the Roman unit can be achieved by presenting Roman civilization as a Case Study of a society that self-destructs, not once but twice in its history, although with different outcomes each time. First, at the end of the Late Republic, Augustus saves Rome from collapse by transforming the republic into an empire; and, second, during the Late Empire, none of the emperors, despite heroic and innovative efforts, can halt Rome's long and slow slide into oblivion. A Discussion approach is also appropriate when considering the causes of Rome's decline and fall.

LECTURE OUTLINE

Non-Western Events

I.   Historical Overview

II. The Colossus of the Mediterranean World
    A. General characteristics of Roman
        civilization
        1. Contrast with Greeks
        2. The Roman character
            a) The agrarian tradition
            b) The sanctity of the family
            c) Religious values
    B. The Etruscan and Greek connections
        1. The Etruscans
            a) A people with a high culture
            b) Their legacy to Rome

2. The Greeks of the Hellenistic Age
   a) A people with a high culture
   b) Their legacy to Rome
C. Rome in the Age of Kings, 753–509 B.C.
   1. Impact on Roman institutions
   2. The first appearance of class
      struggle in Rome
D. The Roman Republic, 509–31 B.C.
   1. The Early Republic, 509–264 B.C.
      a) The domestic crisis
         (1) Struggle between patricians
             and plebeians
         (2) The emergence of the Senate to
             leadership
      b) The foreign crisis
         (1) The threat of nearby peoples
         (2) Conquest of the Italian
             peninsula
         (3) Rome's genius at dealing with
             conquered people
   2. The Middle Republic, 264–133 B.C.
      a) The assimilation of Italy into
         the Roman orbit
      b) The challenge of Carthage
         (1) The issues making for war
         (2) The three Punic Wars
         (3) Ultimate Roman victory
      c) The conquest of the Hellenistic
         world
   3. The Late Republic, 133–31 B.C.
      a) Oligarchy
      b) The problem of the equestrian
         order
      c) The changing nature of the masses
         (1) Landless citizens, slaves, and
             foreigners
         (2) "Bread and circuses"
      d) Julius Caesar's lofty vision and
         failed reforms
      e) Civil war
E. Growing autocracy: Imperial
   Rome, 31 B.C.–A.D. 284
   1. Historical overview
   2. *Pax Romana*, 31 B.C.–A.D. 193
      a) Keeping the peace
      b) The key role of Egypt
      c) The spread of Roman civilization
      d) The growing economy
   3. Civil wars, A.D. 193–284
      a) The problem with choosing new
         emperors
      b) The Barrack Emperors
      c) Other imperial problems

753 B.C.–A.D. 284
In Afghanistan, in the Khulm
   Valley, the rock-cut
   monastery of Haibak,
   fourth to fifth century A.D.
In Africa, earliest sculptural
   tradition outside Egypt
   appears in Nigeria, Nok
   sculpture, 500 B.C. to A.D.
   500; Nok figures are typical
   of West African art, with
   tubular head set at an angle
   on a tubular neck, and
   bodily proportions typical
   of African art—large head
   and short legs; at Naga in
   Nubia, the Lion Temple,
   A.D. 1
In Andean culture, Early
   Horizon period, 1000–200
   B.C.; Early Intermediate
   period, 200 B.C.–A.D. 500;
   the Paracas people of the
   southern coast of Peru, 200
   B.C.–A.D. 200; Paracas
   textiles, ceramics, and
   goldwork; the Nasca
   people of the southern
   coast of Peru flourish,
   200 B.C.–A.D. 200; Nasca
   lines carved in rock, so
   large they are only visible
   from the air; the Nasca also
   develop wind musical
   instruments, such as
   panpipes; Nasca ceramics,
   the high point of artistry
   in clay in the Americas,
   characterized by bulbous
   shapes and slightly three-
   dimensional details; the
   Moche people and empire
   of the northern coast
   flourish, the first
   identifiable state of the
   Andes, first to eighth
   century A.D.; Moche's
   finest art is the Sipán burial
   ground with lavish gold
   treasures, A.D. 290; Moche
   architecture is best seen at

III. The Style of Pre-Christian Rome:
From Greek Imitation to Roman Grandeur
A. Foundation in Hellenistic Culture
B. Roman religion
1. Native cults and beliefs
2. Its syncretistic nature
   a) The gods and goddesses of Greece
   b) Innovative cults in the post–Punic War period
   c) Emperor worship
C. Language, literature, and drama
1. The Latin language
2. The first literary period, 250–31 B.C.
   a) Characteristics
   b) The birth of Roman theater: Roman comedy
      (1) Plautus
      (2) Terence
   c) Roman poetry
      (1) Lucretius's *On the Nature of Things*
      (2) Catullus's "small" epics, epigrams, and love poems
   d) Cicero, the greatest writer of the age
      (1) Philosophy
      (2) Oratory
      (3) Letters
3. The second literary period: The Golden Age, 31 B.C.–A.D. 14
   a) Characteristics
   b) Vergil
      (1) Pastorals: *Eclogues* and *Georgics*
      (2) Epic: the *Aeneid*
   c) Horace
      (1) Odes
      (2) Letters in verse
   d) Ovid and the *Metamorphoses*
4. The third literary period: The Silver Age, A.D. 145–200
   a) Characteristics
   b) Seneca and Roman tragedy
   c) Juvenal and satire
   d) Tacitus's *Annals* and *Histories*
      (1) Heir to the Greek tradition
      (2) History with a moral purpose
D. Philosophy
1. Characteristics of Roman thought
2. Stoicism
   a) Seneca
      (1) The *Letters on Morality*
      (2) His influence

Cerro Blanco, in the Palace of Huaca del Sol, a pyramid and stepped building, first century A.D.; Sacrificial Scene, a mural of a human sacrifice, at Pañamarca; Moche ceramic vessels with stirrup-spout and anthropomorphic forms

In China, Eastern Zhou dynasty, 771–256 B.C. and Spring and Autumn period, 722–481 B.C.; Warring States period, 403–221 B.C.; Zhuang Zhou, 369–286 B.C., a thinker who expounded on Lao-tzu's Daoism; first important Chinese poet, Ch'ü Yüan, 343–277 B.C.; Qin [Ch'ín] dynasty, 255–206 B.C.; union of the whole of China under Qin [or Ch'in] Shi Huangdi, as the first emperor and the country named after him, 221–206 B.C.; Qin's state is also called "the Celestial Empire"; enlightened yet harsh rule; standardization of weights and measures and of gauges for chariot wheels, 221 B.C.; the building of the Great Wall to keep out nomadic tribes, 215 B.C.; Qin Shi Huangdi's burial pit contains thousands of life-size terra-cotta models of soldiers; bookburning of dissident writers and some scholars are buried alive, in 212 B.C.; Western Han dynasty, 202 B.C.–A.D. 9 and Eastern Han, A.D. 25–220; new political order; Confucianism established as orthodoxy and civil service examinations begin, after A.D. 6; Han power extends to Korea and

b) Epictetus
   (1) Background
   (2) *Discourses* and *Handbook*
c) Marcus Aurelius
   (1) Background
   (2) *Meditations*

3. Neo-Platonism
  a) Origins in Platonism
  b) Plotinus

E. Law
  1. Rome's most original contribution
  2. The idea of natural law
  3. The evolution of Roman law
    a) The Twelve Tables
    b) The role of the praetors
    c) The *jurisconsults*
    d) The legal codifications of the second and third centuries A.D.

F. The visual arts
  1. Uses and influences
    a) Roman practicality
    b) Etruscan and Greek influences
  2. Architecture
    a) Materials and style
      (1) Changing types of building materials
      (2) The temple, the chief Roman architectural form
      (3) Innovations: rounded arch, barrel vault, groined vault, and dome
    b) The prototype of the Roman temple: the Maison Carrée
      (1) Features and characteristics
      (2) Influence
    c) The round temple: the Pantheon
      (1) Features and characteristics
      (2) Influence
    d) Urban planning: the forum
    e) The triumphal arch
      (1) A symbol of empire
      (2) Characteristics
    f) Amphitheaters
      (1) The Colosseum
      (2) Its relation to the realities of Roman life
    g) Provincial town centers
    h) Bridges and aqueducts
  3. Sculpture
    a) Tastes of artists and patrons
    b) First phase, third to first century B.C.

Vietnam; lacquer bowls, silk hangings and clothing, and writing on bamboo on the newly invented paper; China's earliest datable stone tomb sculpture; use of tall towers in the capital, Changan; artistic realism in Han sculpture; the tomb at Pei Cha Ts'un in Shantung, about A.D. 220; trade with Rome—Chinese ship apricots and peaches and receive grapes, pomegranates, and and walnuts in return, after 140 B.C.; Chinese ships reach India, the sailors having discovered the magnetic properties of lodestone, about 100 B.C.; the sundial is invented in about 30 B.C.; third period of Chinese literature begins in 200 B.C.; Ying Shao, compiler of popular tales, second century A.D.; Sima Qian's *Records of the Historian,* a political, social, and cultural history of early China, second to first century B.C.; Hu Shin makes dictionary of 10,000 characters, 149 B.C.; compilation of Confucian texts, later known as the Thirteen Classics, though the final form does not appear until about A.D. 932; these texts, such as *The Doctrine of the Mean,* the *Analects,* and *The Great Learning,* were used to train generations of Chinese civil servants and rulers in precepts believed to come from Confucius; Chinese octave (music) subdivided; Period of Disunity, or Six Dynasties, A.D. 220–581; fragmented empire; north dominated by invaders from the steppes, the south ruled by

Chinese dynasties; Buddhism spreads

In Himalayan region, in Kashmir, A.D. 200–622, monument inspired by Buddhism; the Harvan stupa; in Nepal, the rise of the Licchavi dynasty, to A.D. 585

In India, (see Chapter 4 for events to 146 B.C.) Shunga dynasty, 185–30 B.C.; invasions of North India by central Asian tribes: Bactrian Greeks, Sakas, and Kushans; the last named establish a dynasty, about A.D. 78–200; four monumental stone gateways added to the Great Stupa at Sanchi, late first century B.C.; two schools of Buddhist art, Mathura in central India, with its roots in folk art, and Gandhara in modern Pakistan, influenced by Greco-Roman styles, second century A.D.; the *Panchatantra*, a collection of 87 beast fables, written in Sanskrit, second century B.C., though many are B.C., though many are

In Japan, Jomon culture, about 4000 to about 300 B.C.; Yayoi culture, about 300 B.C.–A.D. 300; huts with floors raised on posts; Chinese influence seen in introduction of agriculture, especially rice by irrigation; establishment of the Yamato State, A.D. 200–1100

In Korea, Chinese immigrants found colony in the province of Lo-lang, near Pyongyang, in northwest Korea, about 108 B.C.; urban complex with an irregular form, built on a high platform in pounded

earth to support a
ceremonial hall, with a
necopolis nearby; Three
Kingdoms period, 57 B.C.–
A.D. 668; under Chinese
influence, Korean culture
came into its own; also,
Buddhist, Confucian, and
Daoist influences; the
three kingdoms are
Koguryo in the north,
Pakche in the southwest,
and Silla in the southeast;
the most advanced was the
Koguryo Kingdom, with
two capitals, T'ung-kou in
Manchuria and Pyongyang
in northwest Korea; "Tomb
of the Two Columns," based
on a Chinese prototype,
in Pyongyang

In Mesoamerica, Formative
period, 2000–200 B.C.;
Classic period, 200 B.C.–
A.D. 900; village art from
Chupícuaro, in western
Mexico, with its
"gingerbread figurines,"
after 500 B.C.; Jalisco
with its dancer
and large hollow
figurines; Colima with its
varied sculptures of
multiple human figures,
animals, and plants;
Nayarit with its Ixtlán
figurines showing
anecdotal realism;
Guerrero with its *art
brut* figurines; the use of
the 260-day and 365-day
calendars evolve after 200
B.C.; founding of
Teotihuacán, the first true
city in ancient America,
about A.D. 150 to 650 when
it was burned; at its height
it contained about 250,000
people and covered 6
square miles; it was
centered on the Pyramid
of the Sun and the Pyramid
of the Moon;
Teotihuacán became

the model for
Mesoamerica; the city's
arts included frescoes,
pictographic books,
pottery, clay figurines,
masks, and stone
sculptures; the wheel was
known but used only for
toys; the heyday of
Zapotec culture, A.D. 200–
600; Zapotecs found Monte
Albán, a temple-city (not
a true city) with numerous
buildings, including
perhaps an astronomical
observatory, ceremonial
stairways, ritual ball courts,
and a necropolis (city of
the dead); Monte Albán
art includes ritual ball
courts, murals, elaborate
inscriptions, pottery and
bowls representing birds,
fish, and jaguars, made of
gunmetal gray clay;
Mayan cities flourish in
southern Mesoamerica,
A.D. 200–600, from
Palenque in the west, up
into the Yucatán
peninsula and down
through Guatemala and
British Honduras to Copán;
Mayan culture included
complex writing system,
astronomy, and a counting
and calendar system that
used the zero; invention
of the corbelled arch;
Mayan observatories were
erected in most cities; the
city of Tikal had five
pyramids and a population
of 50,000 in the third and
fourth centuries A.D.;
Mayan art is realistic and
uses foreshortening and
group compositions in
realistic poses; four Mayan
books survive: (1) the
Dresden Codex, giving
mathematical and
astronomical tables, (2) the
Parisian Codex, listing

prophecies, (3) the Madrid Codex, consisting of ritual rules and observances, and (4) the Grolier Codex, a table setting forth the movements of the planet Venus, the basis of the Mayan calendar; the finest Mayan sculpture is at Palenque, in Mexico, at Yaxchilán and Piedras Negras on the Mexico-Guatemala border, and at Copán in Honduras; in Mexico, in the modern state of Veracruz, the culture called Remojadas flourished, A.D. 200–600; noted for its "smiling heads" clay figurines containing whistles and rattles; Veracruz culture also produced stone yokes, hachas (heads), and palmas (palm-shaped stones), vestments worn during ritual ball games

In North America, at Newark, Ohio, mounds oriented to lunar events, built by the Hopewell people, 100 B.C.–A.D. 400

In South Asia, richly decorated stupas (dome-shaped Buddhist monuments containing burials or relics)

In Sri Lanka, introduction of Buddhism, about 250 B.C. as a result of the visit of Mahinda, son of the Mauryan emperor; the stupa at Anuradhapura, third century B.C.

LEARNING OBJECTIVES

To learn:

1. The different phases of history in pre-Christian Rome and the major features of each phase

2. The geographic territories that made up the Roman Empire

3. The general characteristics of Roman civilization

4. The role played by religion in Roman life and culture

5. How women's role in Roman life differed from that of women in Greece

6. The influence of the Etruscans on Roman civilization

7. The influence of the Greeks on Roman civilization

8. The enduring features of Roman political life

9. The significance of the Punic Wars for Roman society and civilization

10. Rome's enlightened treatment of conquered peoples and the impact this had on Roman civilization

11. Rome as the heir of Hellenistic Greece

12. The cultural significance of Julius Caesar

13. The meaning of the *Pax Romana*

14. How Augustus saved the Roman state

15. Rome's three literary periods, including dates, characteristics, leading figures, literary genres, titles and descriptions of works

16. The characteristics of Roman Comedy

17. The principles of Roman Stoicism and Epicureanism, their leading advocates, and how they differed from both one another and the Greek originals

18. The beliefs of Neo-Platonism and its leading exponent

19. How Roman philosophy reflected Roman values and circumstances

20. The ideals of Roman law, the most original contribution of Rome

21. The innovations made by Roman architects

22. The identifying characteristics of the Roman temple, as seen in the Maison Carrée, Nîmes

23. The interrelationship between the arts and architecture and Rome's rulers

24. To recognize achievements in Roman architecture and the arts

25. The phases of Roman sculpture along with characteristic examples

26. The contributions of Roman music

27. Historic "firsts" of Roman civilization that became part of the Western tradition: the Latin language and its offspring, the Romance languages; Roman law; the educational ideal of the arts

and sciences; the architectural innovations based on the rounded arch, including barrel vaults, groined vaults, and domes; providing "bread and circuses" for citizens; and the Idea of Rome

28. The role of Roman civilization in transmitting the heritage of earlier civilizations: adding to Greek architecture to make the Greco-Roman style; redefining the Greek educational curriculum into the *trivium* and *quadrivium*; perpetuating Greek ideals and models in the arts, literature, and music; adopting the Hellenistic Age's political legacy of ruler-gods; preserving and expanding Hellenistic Greek science; continuing to make libraries primary institutions in major cities as had been done in Hellenistic Greece; and making the Hellenistic goal of a just and well-regulated society of multiethnic, multiracial citizens the guiding ideal of imperial Rome

SUGGESTIONS FOR FILMS

Buried Cities (Pompeii and Herculaneum). International Film Bureau, 14 min., color.

Julius Caesar—Rise of the Roman Empire. Encyclopedia Britannica, 22 min., color.

The Legacy of Rome. McGraw-Hill, 55 min., color.

Life in Ancient Rome. Encyclopedia Britannica, 14 min., color.

The Spirit of Rome. Encyclopedia Britannica, 29 min., color.

SUGGESTIONS FOR FURTHER READING

Adam, J. P. *Roman Building: Materials and Techniques.* Translated by A. Mathews. Bloomington: Indiana University Press, 1994. A technical analysis of techniques and materials used by the Romans for their buildings, monuments, and other structures.

Adkins, L., and Adkins, R. *Handbook to Life in Ancient Rome.* A remarkable compendium of facts covering the more than 1,200 years of Roman history; organized into chapters by topics, such as economy and industry, travel and trade, and everyday life.

Barton, C. A. *The Sorrows of the Ancient Romans. The Gladiator and the Monster.* Princeton: Princeton University Press, 1993. This striking work offers unique insights into the Roman character; it maps the "uncharted regions of the emotional life" of this ancient people, from 100 B.C. to A.D. 500.

Boren, H. C. *Roman Society: A Social, Economic, and Cultural History.* Lexington, Mass.: Heath, 1977. Discussion of cultural developments is integrated with analysis of social and economic changes.

Brendel, O. J. *Etruscan Art.* Harmondsworth: Penguin, 1978. A well-respected overview of Etruscan art.

Crawford, M. H. *The Roman Republic.* Cambridge: Harvard University Press, 1993. A history of the Roman Republic that balances history with an interpretive essay.

Elsner, J. *Art and the Roman Viewer. The Transformation of Art from the Pagan World to Christianity.* Cambridge: Cambridge University Press, 1995. A pioneering approach to art history, this interdisciplinary study focuses on the changing framework within which Roman viewers interpreted art so as to make it meaningful.

Fuhrmann, M. *Cicero and the Roman Republic.* Translated by W. E. Yuill. Oxford: Blackwell, 1992. An evenhanded biography of Cicero that places his literary achievements and political career within the historical context.

Gardner, J. F. *Being a Roman Citizen.* London: Routledge, 1993. A historical overview of Roman citizenship, under the republic and the empire, with the focus on the civil law and the legal capacities and disabilities of the citizenry.

Garnsey, P., and Saller, R. *The Roman Empire: Economy, Society, and Culture.* London: Duckworth, 1987. A well-respected, up-to-date introduction to the history of the Roman Empire.

MacMullen, R. *Enemies of the Roman Order: Treason, Unrest, and Alienation in the Empire.* Cambridge: Harvard University Press, 1993. This groundbreaking work challenges the prevailing view that the early Roman Empire successfully stifled political dissent.

Ogilvie, R. M. *Roman Literature and Society.* Harmondsworth: Penguin, 1980. A brief, informative summary of Latin literature within its social context.

Ramage, N. H., and Ramage, A. *Roman Art. Romulus to Constantine.* New York: Abrams, 1991. Based on the teaching and archeological careers of the two authors, this is a handy guidebook to Rome's art and architecture; with hundreds of illustrations, many of which are in color; floor plans for buildings.

Starr, C. G. *The Roman Empire, 27 B.C.–A.D. 476: A Story in Survival.* New York: Oxford University Press, 1982. A serviceable history that focuses primarily on political structures rather than on events.

Strong, D. E.; prepared for press by J. M. C. Toynbee. *Roman Art.* 2nd ed. Harmondsworth: Penguin, 1976. Revised and annotated by R. Ling. Another of the outstanding and authoritative volumes in the Pelican History of Art series.

IDENTIFICATIONS

syncretism	groined vault (cross vault)
satire	oculus
Neo-Platonism	forum
natural law	mural
voussoirs	mosaic
keystone	pantomime
vault	aulos
barrel vault	

PERSONAL PERSPECTIVE BACKGROUND

Ovid, My Last Night in Rome

When exiled to distant Tomi, on the Black Sea, at the order of Emperor Augustus, Ovid was among Rome's most distinguished writers. His erotic poems, collected under the title *Art of Love,* celebrated the capital's pleasure-loving society, a world in which he was at home. He often met with the great Vergil and called himself the friend of the country-dwelling Horace. Banishment from Rome was meant to hurt, and the Personal Perspective poignantly conveys Ovid's anguish over his fate. From Tomi, Ovid's pleas to the emperor for forgiveness (for what misstep remains obscure) were met by stony silence. Ovid died in exile, lamenting the carefree life he had enjoyed. (For more information on Ovid, see *The Western Humanities* and *Readings in the Western Humanities.*)

DISCUSSION/ESSAY QUESTIONS

1. In what ways did Rome's values account for its successful civilization?
2. How did the Etruscans and the Greeks affect the rise of Roman civilization?
3. Which factions of Roman society were involved in the Struggle of the Orders, and what were the results of this conflict?

4. When a civilization expands successfully, it often encounters new challenges and problems. What were some of Rome's problems as a result of its expansion, and how did these problems affect Roman values?

5. Discuss the expansion of Rome from about 250 to 31 B.C., and show how this expansion affected Roman society and values.

6. Discuss the central role that Julius Caesar played in the last years of the Roman Republic. Were his actions and contributions worthy of the attention history has paid to him? Why or why not?

7. What were the major problems confronting Augustus as emperor, and how did he solve these problems?

8. In what ways was Roman religion a product of syncretism, and how did other civilizations' religions affect the Roman ethos?

9. In what ways was Vergil the voice of the Golden Age of Roman literature?

10. Discuss characteristics and purposes of the epic, and show how epics from the Mesopotamian, Greek, and Roman civilizations reflect these traits.

11. Discuss the three major periods of Roman literature, setting forth their dates, characteristics, leading voices, and the major works. Take one work and show how it embodies the ideals of Roman civilization.

12. Compare and contrast Stoicism and Neo-Platonism, and note how each might appeal to the Roman character.

13. Describe the Roman temple, including its Greek and Etruscan roots. What special building techniques were developed by Roman architects?

14. Discuss the three major phases of Roman sculpture, identifying leading characteristics and giving an example from each phase. What was the relationship of Roman sculpture to that of Greece?

15. What roles did murals and mosaics play in the Roman arts?

16. How were Roman values evident in the writings of Roman literary figures and in Roman sculpture? Cite at least two examples from each area.

17. In what ways have the Romans influenced modern Western civilization?

MULTIPLE-CHOICE QUESTIONS

1. Generally speaking, the Romans could be characterized as:
   a. imaginative in the arts
   b. both deep and speculative thinkers
 * c. well-suited to adapt and borrow from other civilizations (p. 101)
   d. irresponsible

2. The ideal Roman was a(n):
   a. shrewd business type who amassed fortunes
   b. intellectual and philosophical type who spoke against sins
   c. artistic type with a keen and original imagination
 * d. farmer-soldier type who stood ready to protect his home (p. 101)

3. Roman values were identified with the following combination:
   a. business, medicine, law
 * b. farm, family, religion (pp. 101–103)
   c. multiculturalism, diversity, ethnicity
   d. leisure, entertainment, work

4. A people who influenced the Romans but whose history is not well documented were the:
   a. Greeks
   b. Phoenicians
 * c. Etruscans (pp. 103–104)
   d. Egyptians

5. The patricians of Early Republican Rome, like the Archaic Greeks, transformed their political system from:
   * a. a kingship to an oligarchy (p. 107)
   b. an oligarchy to a democracy
   c. a kingship to a democracy
   d. a theocracy to an oligarchy

6. The two major domestic groups who clashed over power in the Early Republic were the:
   a. plebeians and the equestrians
   * b. patricians and the plebeians (p. 107)
   c. equestrians and the patricians
   d. equestrians and the populares

7. One result of struggle between the patricians and the plebeians in the early years of the Roman Republic was:
   a. the installation of a city-state government
   b. overthrow of the patricians
   * c. sharing of the patricians' power with the plebeians (p. 107)
   d. abolition of the Roman Senate

8. Regardless of the political structure of the Roman Republic, the real location of power was the:
   a. army
   * b. Senate (pp. 107–108)
   c. college of priests
   d. emperor

9. By 264 B.C., the Romans had:
   a. conquered all of the Mediterranean lands
   b. moved their frontier into present-day France
   c. created a democratic government
   * d. brought all of the Italian peninsula under control (p. 107)

10. Rome's chief rival in the Mediterranean during the Middle Republic was:
    * a. Carthage (p. 107)
    b. Egypt
    c. Macedonia
    d. Judea

11. The leader of the Carthaginians during the Second Punic War was:
    a. Cato
    * b. Hannibal (p. 107)
    c. Scipio
    d. Hammurabi

12. Hannibal's military strategy to defeat the Romans was to:
    a. slaughter all the inhabitants of the Italian peninsula
    * b. scorch the earth and devastate the farms (p. 107)
    c. attack Rome and put it under siege
    d. bombard Rome from nearby ships

13. A new class that appeared on the scene in the Late Republic and demanded more political power was the:
    a. plebeian order
    b. farmer-soldier class
  * c. equestrian order (p. 107)
    d. patrician order

14. Which was NOT a cause of the collapse of the Roman Republic?
    a. the rise of the equestrian order
    b. the appearance of an urban underclass
    c. the decline of power among the rich families
  * d. the revolts in the provinces (pp. 107–108)

15. Which was NOT a characteristic of the Roman Republic?
    a. For 400 years it was led fairly effectively by the Senate.
  * b. Economic prosperity bred peaceful class relations. (p. 107)
    c. The army became a very successful fighting machine.
    d. By the Late Republic, Rome dominated the eastern Mediterranean.

16. Under Augustus Caesar, the Roman Empire:
    a. witnessed the abolition of the Senate
    b. returned to the old republican political traditions
    c. experienced years of domestic upheaval
  * d. moved along the path toward an absolute ruler (p. 108)

17. Under the *Pax Romana* all of the following occurred EXCEPT:
    a. The economy expanded during most of this period.
    b. The bureaucracy grew throughout the empire.
  * c. The power of the army drastically increased. (p. 108)
    d. The issue of ethnicity faded as most groups became Romanized.

18. One social group that gained more power under Augustus was the:
    a. urban poor
  * b. equestrian order (p. 108)
    c. patrician
    d. farmers

19. One of the important traits of Roman religion was that:
    a. It held firmly to its original practices and refused to accept new ones.
  * b. It accepted other cults, blending them into new ways of worship. (p. 111)
    c. It rejected the Greek deities.
    d. The Roman soldiers remained loyal to the old gods.

20. Roman religion, as a product of syncretism, meant that:
    a. The Romans refused to accept any other beliefs.
  * b. Roman religion was a blending of many faiths. (pp. 109–111)
    c. Roman religion evolved out of one ancient form.
    d. The Romans were always in search of a savior.

21. As Roman religion evolved, it came to be identified with:
    a. a message of social justice
  * b. the worship of the emperor (p. 111)
    c. a cult that worshiped trees and rocks
    d. a missionary impulse to spread the worship of Zeus

22. Which would NOT apply to Roman religion?
    * a.   Throughout Roman history religion was conducted by priests. (pp. 109–111)
      b.   Some of the Roman state gods came from the Etruscans.
      c.   Some of the Roman state deities were from the Greeks.
      d.   The Roman soldiers spread their own religion around the empire.

23. All of these characterized the Latin language EXCEPT:
      a.   Latin was well suited for documents and decrees.
    * b.   Latin's florid style lent itself to imaginative literature. (p. 111)
      c.   Latin became standardized early in the history of the republic.
      d.   Latin helped unify the various groups in the empire.

24. Roman writers and artists borrowed most from the:
      a.   Etruscans
      b.   Egyptians
      c.   Nubians
    * d.   Greeks (p. 111)

25. Which match between writer and literary genre is correct for the First Literary Period?
      a.   Plautus—lyric poetry
    * b.   Terence—comic plays (pp. 111–112)
      c.   Catullus—epic poems
      d.   Lucretius—drama

26. The most influential figure in the First Literary Period was:
      a.   Lucretius
      b.   Catullus
    * c.   Cicero (p. 112)
      d.   Vergil

27. Cicero was NOT a:
      a.   member of the equestrian class
      b.   student of Greek who translated Greek works into Latin
      c.   prolific writer whose works were read for centuries
    * d.   systematic philosopher (p. 112)

28. The three outstanding literary figures of the Golden Age of Roman literature were:
      a.   Vergil, Horace, and Seneca
    * b.   Vergil, Horace, and Ovid (pp. 112–113)
      c.   Lucretius, Catullus, and Cicero
      d.   Vergil, Ovid, and Juvenal

29. The most famous epic poet of Roman literature was:
      a.   Ovid
      b.   Horace
      c.   Homer
    * d.   Vergil (pp. 112–113)

30. Vergil wrote an epic poem about:
      a.   Achilles' efforts to win the battle of Troy
    * b.   the long voyage of Aeneas, a Trojan hero (pp. 112–113)
      c.   the exploits of Odysseus
      d.   the life of Augustus Caesar

31. The *Aeneid* was written to:
    a. Show that the Romans were direct descendants of the Greek gods.
    * b. Instill into the Romans the values of a great past. (p. 112)
    c. Mark the anniversary of the death of Julius Caesar.
    d. Win over the masses to the side of Augustus Caesar.

32. The Greek writer who had the most influence on Vergil was:
    a. Sophocles
    b. Hesiod
    * c. Homer (p. 112)
    d. Plato

33. Vergil's poems can be described as:
    * a. verses celebrating the rural values of old Rome (p. 112)
    b. attacks on Roman values
    c. satires of Roman customs
    d. comparisons of Rome with Greece, to Rome's detriment

34. The love poems of Ovid are remembered for their:
    a. tenderness toward women
    * b. overt sexuality (p. 113)
    c. efforts to raise the level of morality among the Romans
    d. sexual views, which anticipate Christian values

35. What is the subject of Ovid's poem *Tristia?*
    a. advice on how to seduce women
    b. stories about the transformation of people into other forms
    c. heroic exploits of Caesar Augustus
    * d. personal sadness consequent on exile (p. 113)

36. How does Rome's Silver Age of Literature differ from its Golden Age?
    a. The Silver Age was more original in its literary offerings.
    b. The Silver Age invented more new literary genres.
    * c. The Silver Age emphasized aesthetics rather than morals. (p. 114)
    d. The Silver Age was more likely to employ patriotic themes.

37. The Silver Age produced Rome's greatest historian:
    * a. Tacitus (p. 114)
    b. Ovid
    c. Suetonius
    d. Plutarch

38. Tacitus wrote his historical works to:
    a. Win favor from the emperors.
    * b. Trace the decline of political freedom in Rome. (p. 114)
    c. Celebrate the great achievements of the *Pax Romana.*
    d. Illustrate the rule of powerful and successful emperors.

39. The two most widespread philosophies during the Roman Empire were:
    a. Stoicism and Cynicism
    * b. Stoicism and Epicureanism (p. 114)
    c. Judaism and Stoicism
    d. Epicureanism and Cynicism

40. Which was NOT an Etruscan influence on Rome?
    a. the alphabet
    b. some features of architecture
    c. numbers
    * d. the solar calendar (pp. 103–104, 116)

41. Stoicism appealed to the Romans for all of these reasons EXCEPT:
    * a. the clarity of its abstract principles (pp. 114–116)
    b. its emphasis on day-to-day rules to live by
    c. its stress on duty and honor in one's work
    d. its compatibility with Rome's farmer-soldier ideal

42. Epictetus offered all of the following advice EXCEPT:
    a. Be patient in the face of trouble.
    b. Treat material things with indifference.
    * c. Enjoy the good things of life. (pp. 114–115)
    d. Accept one's destiny.

43. Marcus Aurelius wrote, in advice to himself to:
    * a. Accept with dignity his role in life. (pp. 115–116)
    b. Always strive to get ahead.
    c. Retreat from his civic duties.
    d. Be a loyal family man.

44. Neo-Platonism solved the problem of Platonic dualism by:
    a. appealing to Rome's state gods for assistance
    b. calling for worship of the emperor
    * c. using mystical insight to reach a new vision of truth (p. 116)
    d. supporting mystery cults

45. All of these describe Roman law EXCEPT:
    a. It was a product of the needs of the state.
    b. It came out of both Greek and Roman thought.
    c. It was identified with the concept of natural law.
    * d. It dealt exclusively with criminal law. (p. 116)

46. Which was NOT a Roman contribution to architecture?
    * a. the development of the Corinthian column and its order (pp. 116–117)
    b. innovations with the rounded arch (groined and barrel vaults and domes)
    c. the discovery of a mixture similar to modern concrete
    d. the combining of the practical with the decorative in public buildings

47. The Maison Carrée does NOT have this characteristic:
    a. Greek influence in its post-beam-triangle design
    b. Etruscan influence in its raised platform
    * c. lack of inner sanctum, or *cella* (p. 117)
    d. decorated with Corinthian columns

48. Roman urban planning and architecture:
    a. was of no consequence to urban dwellers
    b. failed to have an impact on later urban planners
    * c. first developed in Rome and spread throughout the Mediterranean (pp. 121–122)
    d. grew in a haphazard way from one town to another

49. What was the style of Roman portrait sculpture?
    a. impressionistic
 * b. realistic (pp. 123–127)
    c. abstract
    d. idealistic

50. Roman triumphal arches and victory columns:
 * a. are examples of art as propaganda (pp. 120, 127)
    b. were borrowed from Greek practice
    c. ceased to be used under the emperors
    d. were designed and executed by slave labor

51. Which is characteristic of the Late Roman Republican sculpture entitled *Republican Portrait of a Man:*
    a. appearance of optimism
 * b. a sense of unease (p. 124 and caption for Fig. 5.23)
    c. idealized features
    d. highly emotional

52. The last magnificent statue of a Roman ruler during the *Pax Romana* was:
    a. Augustus Caesar in the Prima Porta portrait
    b. Hadrian standing on a column
 * c. Marcus Aurelius on horseback (p. 127 and caption for Fig. 5.11)
    d. Titus in a carved relief on the Arch of Titus

53. A frequent subject of Roman painting was:
 * a. Greek and Roman myths (p. 129)
    b. still lifes
    c. the daily life of the emperor
    d. scenes taken from literature

54. Imperial Romans preferred which type of cultural event?
    a. tragedies
    b. comedies
 * c. pantomimes (p. 130)
    d. public readings

55. Which is NOT a Roman legacy to Western art and thought?
    a. its law and legal codes
 * b. its democratic ideas and practices (p. 131)
    c. its school curriculum of the sciences and the arts
    d. its building forms and techniques

6

JUDAISM AND
THE RISE OF CHRISTIANITY

TEACHING STRATEGIES AND SUGGESTIONS

The best introduction to Judaism is through a Historical Overview of the Hebrew people from the earliest times to the destruction of the Temple in A.D. 70, surveying cultural milestones and central religious beliefs. The instructor will also find the Reflections/Connections approach helpful, because Jewish religious ideas are so clearly rooted in history; for example, the Jewish belief that God controls history springs from the tradition that God liberated the Hebrew people from bondage in Egypt and gave them a land of their own. Of the central beliefs of Judaism the instructor should focus especially on the commandment to social justice, a belief first expressed by the Jewish prophets. Modern Western ideals of social justice have their roots in this Jewish belief; and no other ancient people, including the Mesopotamians, the Egyptians, the Greeks, and the Romans, had such a concern for the poor, the disadvantaged, and the downtrodden.

The instructor can then approach Christianity through a Historical Overview, laying out the major developments in this religion's evolution from the birth of Christ to A.D. 284. Because Christianity begins as a Jewish sect, the instructor could then use the Diffusion model to show how Jewish beliefs, traditions, and practices were assimilated into the Christian faith. Of central importance in this regard is the Jewish theme of the Suffering Servant (from Isaiah II) that early Christian writers adopted to explain Jesus' suffering and death on the cross. The instructor can also use a Slide Lecture to deal with the art of both Judaism and Christianity. The juxtaposing of the two artistic traditions will also illustrate dramatically how Judaism, because of its prohibition against graven images, differs from the more visually oriented Christian faith. In the Slide Lecture it is important to lay a good foundation for Christian art, since religious themes and ideas will dominate Western art until the coming of the Renaissance in 1400.

Another important topic in this chapter is the beginning of the stormy relationship between Christianity and humanism, the two traditions that make up the most enduring strands in Western civilization. The instructor can use the Comparison/Contrast strategy to deal with this topic, showing how the Christian faith and humanism are similar, yet different, and setting forth the issues that triggered disagreements between them. In addition, using the Reflections/Connections approach, the teacher can show how hostility between Christians and humanists reflected their differing value systems.

LECTURE OUTLINE

Non-Western Events

I. Historical Overview
    A. The uniqueness of the contribution
        of the Jews

(See Chapters 1 through 5
   for non-Western events.)

B. The influence of Judaism on
Christianity and Islam

II. Judaism
A. The people and their religion,
2000–1500 B.C.
1. Nomadic origins
2. Abraham
a) First introduction to Canaan
b) The covenant
c) The rite of circumcision
d) Belief in an ethical deity with
ethical principles for the
faithful
B. Egypt, exodus, and Moses, 1500–1000 B.C.
1. The Egyptian period
2. Moses
a) The exodus
b) Wandering on the Sinai peninsula
c) The Mosaic code
(1) Divinely given
(2) No distinction between
religious and secular
offenses
(3) The Ten Commandments
(4) The ideal: ethical
monotheism
(5) God or Yahweh
(6) Other religious practices
d) The conquest of Canaan
3. The Kingdom of Israel, 1000–926 B.C.
a) The reign of Saul
b) The reign of David
(1) Centralized government
(2) Economic changes
c) The reign of Solomon
(1) Peace with neighbors
(2) Expanded trade
(3) Building program in
Jerusalem
(4) Literature and the arts
4. The split of Israel into two kingdoms,
926–722 B.C.
a) The northern kingdom of Israel
and the southern kingdom of
Judah
b) The rise of prophets
(1) Full-fledged monotheism
(2) The demand for social
justice
5. The Babylonian Captivity and the
postexilic period, 722–540 B.C.
a) The destruction of Israel by
Assyria

        $b)$ The conquest of Judah by
        Babylonia

        $c)$ The Persian conquest
            (1)   Return to Jerusalem
            (2)   The Second Temple
            (3)   The beginning of the Diaspora

        $d)$ The renewed faith
            (1)   Zoroastrian influences
            (2)   Belief in the end of
                the world
            (3)   Belief in the apocalypse
            (4)   The notion of a Messiah

6. The Hellenistic and Roman periods,
    323 B.C.–A.D. 284

    $a)$ The Hellenistic threat to the
        Jewish way of life
    $b)$ The Maccabean Jewish state
    $c)$ The Roman conquest
        (1)   Various political strategies
            for governing
        (2)   The Third Temple
        (3)   The First Jewish War
        (4)   Destruction of the Temple
        (5)   The second Diaspora

C. Societal and Family Relationships
    1. Women's status in earlier times
    2. Women's changed status after the
        founding of the kingdom

D. The Bible
    1. Evolution of the scriptures
    2. The Septuagint
    3. The parts of the Hebrew Bible
        $a)$ The Law
            (1)   Its books and themes
            (2)   Canonization
        $b)$ The Prophets
            (1)   Its themes
            (2)   Canonization
        $c)$ The Writings
            (1)   Its themes
            (2)   Canonization
    4. Jewish literature outside the canon:
        the Apocrypha
    5. The Dead Sea Scrolls
    6. Key ideas of biblical Judaism

E. Early Jewish art and architecture
    1. The effect of the prohibition of
        graven images
    2. The Ark of the Covenant and other
        sacred objects
    3. Solomon's Temple
    4. The Second Temple

5. Hellenistic influences
   - *a)* The fortress-palace of John Hyrcanus
   - *b)* The tombs in the Kidron valley
6. Roman influences
   - *a)* Herod's fortress-palace at Masada
   - *b)* The Third Temple

III. Christianity, 4 B.C.–A.D. 284
   A. Historical overview
   B. The life of Jesus Christ and the New Testament
   1. Sources for the life of Jesus
      - *a)* Biographical summary
      - *b)* The Gospels
         (1) The synoptic Gospels of Mark, Matthew, and Luke
         (2) The Gospel of John
         (3) The reasons for the various versions
      - *c)* The Acts of the Apostles
         (1) Relation to Luke's Gospel
         (2) Its purpose
      - *d)* The seven epistles of Paul
         (1) Record of missionary activities
         (2) The first Christian theology
         (3) Interpretation of the life of Jesus
         (4) Teaching on the resurrection
      - *e)* The other seven epistles
      - *f)* The Book of Revelation
         (1) Its relation to Jewish apocalyptic literature
         (2) Its controversial nature
   2. The establishment of the Christian canon
   C. Christians and Jews
   1. Christian borrowings from Judaism
   2. Christian borrowings of Zoroastrian ideas, mediated through Judaism
      - *a)* Satan as a personification of evil
      - *b)* Good and bad demons who inhabit human bodies
      - *c)* Heaven and hell as the twin destinies of humanity
      - *d)* A divine savior who appears at the end of time
   3. Stormy relations between Jews and Christians
      - *a)* The Council of Jamnia, A.D. 90, as a turning point

   b) Causes of tensions between the
     two religions and their results
D. Christianity and Greco-Roman religions
  and philosophies
  1. Christian borrowings from the mystery
    cults
  2. Christian appropriations from
    Stoicism and Neo-Platonism
E. Christians in the Roman Empire
  1. Changing attitudes of Romans to
    Christians
    a) The early years
    b) The expansion of Christianity
      and its separation from
      Judaism
      (1) Localized, random
        persecution
      (2) Wide-ranging political
        assault in the mid–third
        century A.D.
  2. Christian borrowings from Roman
    culture
    a) The Latin language
    b) The Roman law
    c) The state administrative
      structure
    d) The imperial office
  3. Social patterns of conversion to
    the late second century A.D.
    a) Social classes
    b) Women
F. Early Christian literature
  1. Early Roman commentators on the
    Christian faith
    a) Celsus
    b) Galen
  2. The first Christian writers
    a) Tertullian
      (1) Key ideas
      (2) Uncompromising hostility
        to humanism
    b) Origen
      (1) Key ideas
      (2) Harmony with the humanistic
        legacy
    c) Vibia Perpetua
      (1) Historic setting
      (2) Willingness to die for
        one's beliefs
G. Early Christian art
  1. Confusion over the role of art
    in the early church
  2. The triumph of humanistic values
    in art

3. Art in the Roman catacombs
    a) The symbol of the good shepherd
    b) The symbol of a communion participant
    c) Christian appropriation of Jewish biblical figures

IV. The Legacy of Biblical Judaism and Early Christianity

LEARNING OBJECTIVES

To learn:

1. The milestones of Hebrew history from about 2000 B.C. to the destruction of the Third Temple in Jerusalem in A.D. 70

2. The close connection between Hebrew history and the beliefs and practices of Judaism

3. The key ideas of Judaism, including the covenant, Mosaic law, and ethical monotheism

4. The three different temples built by the Jews and the symbolic importance of the temple in the Jewish faith

5. The definition and significance of the Babylonian Captivity

6. The Zoroastrian ideas that became a part of Judaism after the Babylonian exile

7. The threat to Jewish civilization posed by the Hellenistic and Roman conquerors

8. The evolving role of women in Hebrew society

9. The parts of the Hebrew Bible, their dates of canonization, and their leading themes

10. The impact of the Second Commandment on Jewish art and architecture

11. The achievements of Jewish artists and architects of the biblical period

12. The origins of Christianity in Judaism

13. The sources for the life of Jesus Christ

14. The parts of the specifically Christian scriptures, their date of canonization, and their leading themes

15. The influence of Jewish ideas, beliefs, and practices on the early Christian church

16. The influence of Greco-Roman religions and philosophies and Roman civilization on Christian beliefs and organization

17. The changing attitude of the Roman authorities to the Christian religion

18. The appeal of Christianity to women

19. The attitudes of Roman writers to early Christianity

20. Tertullian's and Origen's differing views of Greco-Roman civilization and humanism

21. Women writers' impact on early Christianity

22. The nature of early Christian art, its themes, its symbols, and its artistic style

23. The historic "firsts" of biblical Judaism that became part of the Western tradition: monotheism; high moral standards for society; social justice for all, including the poor and the powerless; and a canon of scriptures

24. The historic "firsts" of early Christianity that became part of the Western tradition: a belief system that expressed uncompromising hostility to the prevailing culture and the secular state

25. The role of early Christianity in transmitting the heritage of Judaism and Greco-Roman humanism: redirecting Jewish monotheism to an international audience, regardless of racial and ethnic backgrounds; substituting Jesus' golden rule for Judaism's ethical teachings; perpetuating the commandment to give social justice to all; adopting the Jewish canon and enlarging it to include Christian writings; incorporating Greco-Roman subjects, themes, and styles into Christian art; and placing Greco-Roman philosophy in the service of religion

SUGGESTIONS FOR FILMS

The Bible as Literature: Part I—Saga and Story in the Old Testament. Encyclopedia Britannica, 26 min., color.

The Bible as Literature: Part II—History, Poetry, and Drama in the Old Testament. Encyclopedia Britannica, 24 min., color.

Christianity in World History—to 1000 A.D. Coronet, 14 min., color.

The Christians: Faith and Fear. McGraw-Hill, 39 min., color.

The Christians: A Peculiar People, 27 B.C.–A.D. 330. McGraw-Hill, 39 min., color.

Yesterday's Worlds: Treasures from the Land of the Bible. NET, 29 min., color.

SUGGESTIONS FOR FURTHER READING

Anderson, B. *Understanding the Old Testament.* 3rd ed. Englewood Cliffs, N.J.: Prentice-Hall, 1975. Narrates in a clear style the phases of Hebrew history while analyzing the books of the Old Testament associated with each historical period; still one of the best introductions to a complex topic.

Anderson, G. W. *The History and Religion of Ancient Israel.* London: Oxford University Press, 1966. Blends Jewish history, religion, and the debate over ancient sources to chronicle Judaism from its origins through the Exile and after.

Brown, P. *The World of Late Antiquity: A.D. 150–750.* New York: Harcourt, Jovanovich, 1971. By an outstanding scholar who presents a thoughtful account of the changes that accompanied the end of the Classical period.

Bultman, R. *Primitive Christianity in Its Contemporary Setting.* Translated by R. H. Fuller. Columbia, Ohio: World Publishing Company, 1970. Argues that Christianity was a syncretist religion that offered what many other competing religions provided but ultimately won more converts. Bultman's works set off many heated debates among biblical scholars.

Eilberg-Schwartz, H. *The Savage in Judaism: An Anthropology of Israelite Religion and Ancient Judaism.* Bloomington: Indiana University Press, 1990. A postmodern analysis of Judaism that compares it with "savage" religions.

Grant, R. *Early Christianity and Society. Seven Studies.* San Francisco: Harper & Row, 1977. Seven essays on Early Christianity, dealing with social and economic matters, such as Christian views on work, taxation, and private property.

Harris, S. *The New Testament: A Student's Introduction.* Mountain View, Calif.: Mayfield, 1988. A well-written introduction based on up-to-date research; includes color illustrations of paintings of biblical stories and events by Raphael, Tintoretto, and other great artists.

————. *Understanding the Bible: A Reader's Introduction.* 2nd ed. Mountain View, Calif.: Mayfield, 1985. A clear, easy-to-read survey of the Bible within its cultural, historical, and geographical contexts.

Harrison, R. K. *The Dead Sea Scrolls: An Introduction.* New York: Harper and Brothers, 1961. Described as an "interim report" and "concise guide," this brief work includes chapters on how the scrolls were discovered, what they contain, when they were written, what their relationships are to the Old Testament, and how the Qumran community and early Christianity might be linked. The book has been superseded by more recent studies of these highly controversial discoveries, but it still provides a sound introduction.

Hoffmann, R. J. *The Origins of Christianity: A Critical Introduction.* Buffalo, N.Y.: Prometheus Press, 1985. A collection of essays centering on four issues regarding the origins of Christianity: the religious and cultural background, the intellectual currents and themes, the Gospels, and the Jesus tradition, noting history, myth, and legend that offer different points of view. The essays, while requiring some knowledge of the topic, will challenge the inquisitive student.

Humphries, W. L. *Crisis and Story: Introduction to the Old Testament.* Mountain View, Calif.: Mayfield, 1990. A brief, nontechnical introduction that emphasizes the importance of narrative in the development of Jewish religious traditions and places them in their political and social context.

Johnson, P. *History of the Jews.* New York: Harper & Row, 1987. A sound recent survey that makes the Jewish story come alive for the general reader.

Lane Fox, R. *The Unauthorized Version. Truth and Fiction in the Bible.* New York: Knopf, 1992. A distinguished ancient historian looks at the Bible, assessing its authors, historical growth, and historical truth.

Lowrie, W. *Art in the Early Church.* Rev. ed. New York: Harper & Row, 1965. The groundbreaking study that first established early Christian art as a subject worthy of scholarly pursuit.

MacMullen, R. *Christianizing the Roman Empire (A.D. 100–400).* New Haven: Yale University Press, 1984. A judicious work of scholarship that documents the shift to Christianity in the late Roman Empire.

Milburn, R. L. P. *Early Christian Art and Architecture.* Aldershot, England: Scolar, 1988. Based on recent discoveries, this survey examines Christian art from its beginnings to mid–sixth century, including signs and symbols, the catacombs, house-churches, church buildings, mosaics, coins, and illustrated books. Many black-and-white illustrations and diagrams.

Roth, C. *Jewish Art: An Illustrated History.* Greenwich, Conn.: New York Graphic Society Publishers Ltd., 1961. Perhaps the best general survey on Jewish art and architecture—handsomely presented.

Shanks, H., ed. *Understanding the Dead Sea Scrolls: A Reader from the Biblical Archaeology Review.* New York: Random House, 1993. The controversies swirling around the Dead Sea Scrolls are clearly manifested in this collection of articles that examine not only their discovery, their content, and their relationships to the Bible, Judaism, and Christianity but also the debates and struggles between Jewish and Christian scholars.

IDENTIFICATIONS

covenant	canon
Diaspora	Gospels
eschatology	evangelists
apocalypse	theology
Messiah	liturgy
scripture	sarcophagus

PERSONAL PERSPECTIVE BACKGROUND

Flavius Josephus, The Destruction of the Temple at Jerusalem

Flavius Josephus, author of *History of the Jewish War,* is a controversial figure because he seemed to put personal safety before love of country. Cornered by Roman soldiers during the Jewish War, A.D. 66–70, Josephus made a suicide pact with his men rather than yield; but when only he and a colleague remained alive, he persuaded the other survivor to join him in surrender. He next escaped being sent to Rome in chains by ingratiating himself with the soon-to-be emperor (in 70) Vespasian. He then joined Vespasian's son Titus (emperor, in 79) in the siege of Jerusalem. When Titus's army surrounded the city, Josephus called upon the besieged to give up. The Jewish soldiers branded him a traitor and fought to the death. In his history, Josephus calculates that more than one million Jews perished during these struggles. The Roman historian Tacitus numbered the dead at about 600,000.

Vibia Perpetua, Account of Her Last Days Before Martyrdom

Vibia Perpetua, a young woman of distinguished birth and liberal education, was arrested during the campaign against Christians begun by the emperor in 202. She was a twenty-two-year-old married woman with a child. Perpetua's crime was that she was in the process of converting to Christianity, which was forbidden by imperial edict. A measure of her courage was that while in prison awaiting death, she was baptized into the banned faith. Perpetua's story survives in an account of the persecutions written by an anonymous contemporary. This writer claims that Perpetua's story was "written by her own hand, based on her impressions."

DISCUSSION/ESSAY QUESTIONS

1. In what ways did the Hebrews consider themselves different from the other tribes in the Middle East, and how did these differences affect the Hebrews' religious outlook?
2. Show how the beliefs, ideas, and practices of biblical Judaism reflect the early history of the Hebrew people.
3. Discuss the major historical periods of Hebrew history and note how each period influenced the evolution of Hebrew religion.
4. What was the significance of the development of monotheism by the Hebrew people?
5. Identify the key beliefs of Judaism, and indicate the ones that were later integrated into the Western tradition.
6. What impact ought the Second Commandment to have had on Jewish culture? How do you account for the existence of Jewish art and architecture in biblical times?
7. Discuss the evolving role of women in Hebrew society.

8. Compare and contrast the stages and evolution of the Jewish Bible and the Christian Bible, noting their various parts, subjects, and sources.
9. Discuss the borrowings of early Christianity from Judaism.
10. Compare and contrast Judaism and Christianity, using the following terms: covenant, law, messiah, social justice, and canon.
11. Identify the key beliefs of Christianity.
12. What impact did Greco-Roman religions and philosophy have on early Christianity?
13. Discuss the shifting nature of Christian-Roman relationships from the time of Jesus to 284, noting attitudes on both sides and their respective responses to each other.
14. Explain whether the early Christian church was hostile or friendly to the humanistic tradition of the Greco-Roman world.
15. Discuss the ways that Roman civilization helped to shape the early Christian faith and church.
16. Explain the appeal of Christianity to early women converts.
17. Contrast Tertullian's and Origen's responses to Greco-Roman culture.
18. Discuss the influence of women writers on early Christianity, in particular, Vibia Perpetua's influence.
19. Discuss the legacy of early Christianity to Western civilization.
20. Discuss early Christian art, its themes, its symbols, and its style. What was the relationship of Christian art to Greco-Roman styles of art?

MULTIPLE-CHOICE QUESTIONS

1. The beliefs of Judaism helped to shape the religion of Christianity and:
   a. Buddhism
 * b. Islam (p. 133)
   c. Zoroastrianism
   d. Shintoism

2. Christians refer to the Jewish Bible as the:
 * a. Old Testament (p. 133)
   b. New Testament
   c. Torah
   d. Pseudepigrapha

3. The Hebrew people in their early history were NOT:
   a. nomads without a homeland
   b. outsiders for periods of time in other cultures
 * c. famous for their literature and philosophy (p. 133)
   d. promised the land of Canaan

4. According to tradition the first patriarch to settle in Canaan was:
   a. Moses
 * b. Abraham (p. 133)
   c. Aaron
   d. Adam

5. In their early years, the Hebrews may NOT be described as a:
   a. wandering tribe, similar to their neighbors, in about 2000 B.C.
   b. patriarchal clan
   c. people who believed that a deity had chosen them as a special group
 * d. national people possessed of a homeland (pp. 133–135)

6. The word *covenant* means:
   a. promise
   b. life
 * c. agreement (p. 133)
   d. bargain

7. The outward sign of the covenant between God and the Hebrews was:
   a. special hair styles for men and women
 * b. the circumcision of all male children (p. 133)
   c. distinctive clothing worn by men and women
   d. unique hats for men and concealing garments for women

8. According to the Bible, Moses did NOT:
   a. lead the Hebrews in the exodus from Egypt
 * b. live to enter Canaan, the promised land (p. 135)
   c. receive a law code, including the Ten Commandments, from God
   d. mold his followers into a unified people under a strict ethical code

9. Which of the Ten Commandments had a negative impact on Jewish art?
   a. First Commandment
 * b. Second Commandment (p. 141)
   c. Third Commandment
   d. Fourth Commandment

10. What made Jewish law different from other ancient law codes?
    a. It claimed to be received from a deity.
    b. It was presented in writing.
  * c. It made no distinction between religious and secular offenses. (p. 134)
    d. It was a vengeance code, an "eye for an eye and a tooth for a tooth."

11. The Ten Commandments did NOT condemn:
  * a. child abuse (p. 135)
    b. theft
    c. disrespect toward parents
    d. murder

12. Which was NOT a Hebrew name for God?
    a. YHWH
  * b. Allah (p. 135)
    c. Yahweh
    d. Adonai

13. The Hebrews scored what literary achievement during the reign of Solomon?
  * a. the first historical writings (p. 135)
    b. the first written tragedies
    c. the first written epics
    d. the first novels

14. The three kings of the Kingdom of Israel were:
    a. Abraham, Isaac, Jacob
    b. Elijah, Elisha, Elihu
  * c. Saul, David, Solomon (p. 135)
    d. Moses, Aaron, Joshua

15. How did the Hebrew historians differ from the Greek historians?
  * a. The Hebrew writers made God the central force in human history, unlike the secular-minded Greek authors. (p. 135)
    b. The Hebrew writers composed oral works, unlike the Greek authors, who wrote on scrolls.
    c. The Hebrew writers wrote history in poetic forms, unlike the Greek authors, who composed in prose.
    d. The Hebrew writers wrote scientific history; the Greek authors wrote religious history.

16. The two civilizations that gravely threatened the ancient Jews were the:
    a. Hellenic and Persian
  * b. Hellenistic and Roman (pp. 136–137)
    c. Canaanite and Egyptian
    d. Hittite and Syrian

17. Which event caused the Hebrews to be called Jews?
    a. the exodus from Egypt
    b. the Assyrian conquest of Israel
  * c. the rescue of Judah from the Babylonian Captivity (p. 136)
    d. the destruction of the Third Temple in Jerusalem by the Romans

18. All are true of the Jewish Temple in Jerusalem EXCEPT:
    a. The First Temple was built by Solomon.
    b. Three different temples have been built over the centuries.
    c. The Third Temple was destroyed by the Romans in A.D. 70.
  * d. No part of the Temple still stands today. (pp. 136–138)

19. From Zoroastrianism, the ancient Jews borrowed the notion of:
    a. ethical monotheism
  * b. apocalypse (p. 136)
    c. a chosen people
    d. a universal deity

20. Who were the Zealots? The Jewish:
  * a. revolutionaries who committed mass suicide at Masada rather than be conquered by the Romans (p. 137)
    b. exiles taken into captivity in Babylon
    c. leaders who preached the message of social justice
    d. ascetics who retreated into the desert to await the coming of the Messiah

21. A famous episode in Flavius Josephus' *History of the Jewish War* is the:
    a. Exile of the Hebrews in Egypt
    b. Babylonian Captivity
    c. Maccabean Revolt
  * d. Burning of the Temple in Jerusalem (Personal Perspective)

22. Women's role in Hebrew society diminished with the founding of the kingdom of Israel and during and after the Babylonian Captivity because of which of the following reasons:
    a. Male leaders wished to protect the new political system.
    b. Male leaders wanted to ensure the integrity of their religion.
    c. Male leaders desired to promote the Hebrew way of life.
  * d. all of the above (p. 138)

23. All of these apply to the Jewish Bible EXCEPT:
    a. The Law was the first section canonized, in the fifth century B.C.
    b. The Prophets was the second section canonized, in the first century B.C.
    c. The Writings was the third section canonized, in A.D. 90.
  * d. The Apocrypha was the fourth section canonized, in A.D. 150. (p. 140)

24. The biblical books of Genesis, Exodus, Leviticus, Numbers, and Deuteronomy constitute the:
  * a. Torah (pp. 139–140)
    b. Gospels
    c. Prophets
    d. Epistles

25. The oldest copies of Jewish scriptures were discovered in 1947 and are known as the:
    a. Septuagint
    b. Apocrypha
  * c. Dead Sea Scrolls (p. 140)
    d. Pseudepigrapha

26. All are legacies of biblical Judaism EXCEPT the:
    a. notion of social justice for all people, including the poor and the powerless
  * b. idea of original sin (p. 140)
    c. belief in monotheism
    d. expectation of high moral standards for society

27. The word "diaspora" means:
    a. promise
  * b. dispersion (p. 136)
    c. grief
    d. homeland

28. Which Jewish practice or belief was accepted by the early Christians?
    a. circumcision
    b. the Jewish calendar
    c. prohibition against depicting God or any earthly creatures in art
  * d. the Jewish liturgy (prayers, Bible reading, singing of the psalms) (pp. 143–147)

29. Christianity began in:
    a. Egypt
  * b. Judea (p. 143)
    c. Greece
    d. Italy

30. A major source for the life of Jesus is:
  * a. the Gospels (p. 144)
    b. his autobiography called the *Confessions*
    c. the records of the Roman authorities
    d. the records of the Jewish authorities

31. The Gospels of the New Testament CANNOT be described as:
    a. the writings of men who were witnesses to Jesus' message
    b. probably first recorded about 70 A.D.
    c. more or less taking the same point of view of Jesus' life
  * d. secular histories in the style of Thucydides (p. 144)

32. What are the earliest writings in the New Testament?
  * a. the letters of Paul (p. 145)
    b. the Gospels
    c. the Book of Revelation
    d. the Acts of the Apostles

33. The Christian Bible does NOT include the:
    a. Book of Revelation
    b. Torah and the Prophets
  * c. writings of Origen (pp. 146, 148, 152)
    d. Acts of the Apostles

34. The Acts of the Apostles described the following as a turning point in Christian history:
    a. the teaching career of Jesus
  * b. the opening of Christianity to gentiles (p. 145)
    c. the crucifixion of Jesus
    d. the shift from Greek to Latin in the church

35. Paul's Letters constitute:
    a. a factual account of the life and teachings of Jesus
  * b. the first Christian theology (p. 145)
    c. an early attempt to patch up differences between Christians and Jews
    d. an exchange of letters between Jesus and Paul

36. Paul's interpretation of the life of Jesus was based on the Jewish scripture about:
  * a. the Suffering Servant (p. 145)
    b. Job
    c. David
    d. Moses

37. Which was NOT a key teaching of Paul's in his Letters?
  * a. the notion that Jesus was exclusively divine and without human qualities (pp. 145–146)
    b. the idea that all humans are born with original sin
    c. the belief that Jesus' death atoned for the sins of humankind
    d. the concept that Jesus' resurrection guaranteed everlasting life for others

38. The New Testament is written originally in:
    a. Hebrew
    b. Aramaic
  * c. Greek (p. 146)
    d. Latin

39. This Christian belief was adopted from early Judaism:
    a. God is a Trinity with three aspects.
    b. God will reward the faithful and punish the sinners in an afterlife.
  * c. God demands social justice for all people. (p. 146)
    d. God's covenant is with the human race.

40. This Jewish religious practice was NOT adopted by the early Christians:
    a. the rite of baptism
  * b. the observance of dietary laws (p. 146)
    c. the use of hymns, prayers, and Bible reading as part of the liturgy
    d. the idea of the Sabbath

41. Zoroastrianism influenced Christianity in this way:
    a.   the celebration of Easter
    b.   the belief that Jesus was born of a virgin
 * c.   the concept of Satan as the personification of evil (p. 146)
    d.   the idea of the resurrection

42. What Stoic idea was incorporated into early Christianity?
 * a.   the universal kinship of humanity (p. 147)
    b.   the salvation of the human race through the sacrifice of a savior
    c.   the superiority of the spiritual realm to the physical world
    d.   the stress on duty to family and the demands of the state

43. Within a generation of Jesus' death, the Romans treated the Christians as:
    a.   a new religion to be fully tolerated within Roman society
    b.   a traitorous sect to be stamped out
 * c.   a suspect religious group subject to occasional persecutions (p. 147)
    d.   a minor sect of no consequence or threat to law and order

44. The earliest converts to Christianity were:
    a.   aristocratic men and women
    b.   middle-class traders and merchants and their families
 * c.   foreign women and slaves (p. 152)
    d.   people drawn from every social class

45. Why did early Christianity appeal to women?
 * a.   It offered a refuge from the cruelty of Roman society. (p. 148)
    b.   It allowed them to become priests.
    c.   It made divorce legal.
    d.   It promised sexual equality in church government.

46. This early Christian author helped free Christianity from its Jewish roots and wrote books
    that appealed to Roman intellectuals:
 * a.   Origen (p. 148)
    b.   Tertullian
    c.   Celsus
    d.   Galen

47. Tertullian's writings helped to launch this tradition of early Christianity:
 * a.   denunciation of women as sexual temptresses (p. 148)
    b.   blending of Christian ideas with humanistic learning
    c.   use of theater to teach moral lessons
    d.   compromise with Judaism

48. What Greco-Roman philosophical idea did Origen develop in his Christian theology?
 * a.   identifying Jesus with the Stoic notion of the *logos* or reason (p. 148)
    b.   using Epicurean arguments to disprove the resurrection of the body
    c.   showing Jesus' message to be the same as Aristotle's: moderation
    d.   advocating the Platonic notion that Christian saints should become philosopher-kings

49. Vibia Perpetua is remembered in early Christianity as one of the first women:
    a.   writers of philosophical tracts
 * b.   martyrs (Personal Perspective)
    c.   priests
    d.   missionaries

50. Early Christian painting and sculpture were used primarily to decorate:
    a.   churches and meeting places
 * b.   underground burial chambers and tombs (pp. 148–149)
    c.   private dwellings
    d.   isolated caves

51. An early artistic symbol of the Christian faith was:
 * a.   the shepherd with his flock as an image of Jesus and the church (p. 149)
    b.   a mother with a child as a representation of Mary and Jesus
    c.   thirteen male figures around a table as a symbol of the Last Supper
    d.   Jesus hanging on a cross

52. The most popular image of Jesus in early Christian art was as a:
    a.   bearded man
 * b.   beardless youth (p. 149)
    c.   dying man on a cross
    d.   nude athlete

53. In early Christian art, Jesus is often portrayed in the guise of the:
    a.   Homeric hero Achilles
    b.   tragic hero Oedipus
    c.   Greek philosopher Plato
 * d.   Orphic cult leader Orpheus (p. 149)

54. Which Jewish biblical story was used by Christian artists to symbolize Christian refusal to worship the Roman emperor?
    a.   Jonah and the Whale
    b.   Noah and the Flood
    c.   Good Shepherd
 * d.   Three Hebrews in the Fiery Furnace (caption for Fig. 6.15 and p. 150)

55. The early Christians did NOT:
    a.   redirect Jewish monotheism to an international audience, regardless of racial and ethnic backgrounds
 * b.   continue the Jewish practice of prohibiting God's image from being depicted in art (pp. 148–150)
    c.   substitute Jesus' golden rule for Judaism's ethical teachings
    d.   perpetuate the Jewish commandment to give social justice to all

7

LATE ROMAN CIVILIZATION

TEACHING STRATEGIES AND SUGGESTIONS

The instructor can treat this chapter using various strategies, for its themes offer a rich assortment of ways to approach the material. The central theme—the death of one civilization and the birth of another—can be taught using the Pattern of Change or the Spirit of the Age model. Another helpful approach could be that of the Case Study, because the long decline of Rome enables the teacher to introduce many topics that relate to the life of any civilization. Specifically, Diocletian's reforms can be used to raise questions about how other states, including the United States, attempt to solve deep-seated social and economic problems with governmental intervention.

A variation on the teaching strategies can be used by formulating a classroom debate over the causes of the fall of the Roman Empire. Aside from the obvious and often-quoted reasons given, the instructor can argue that there was no "fall"; instead, it could be argued that this period witnessed the beginning of another era as evidenced by the rise of Christianity, the emergence of new social and political systems among non-Roman peoples, and the appearance of new ways of understanding the world and human nature. This classroom tactic is actually a modification of the Diffusion model. In addition, the instructor could adopt the Comparison/Contrast approach to highlight Christianity's beliefs vis-à-vis other ancient religions and to show why the Christian faith survived and the other cults did not.

One of the most challenging objectives for the instructor is to analyze the transition from Classical humanism to Christian civilization. The Spirit of the Age model might be effective here. The teacher, by using St. Augustine as an example, can also show how attitudes toward the most fundamental issues confronting humans, such as the purpose of life and the meaning of history, were being dealt with in new ways. Furthermore, the instructor can use the Slide Lecture to illustrate changing social attitudes and artistic motives in late Roman civilization.

LECTURE OUTLINE

Non-Western Events

I. The Last Days of the
Roman Empire
  A. Historical overview
    1. Survey of imperial problems
    2. Phases of late Roman history
  B. Diocletian's reforms and the
     triumph of Christianity,
     284–395
    1. The Great Persecutions and
       Christian toleration
      a) Techniques and phases of
         persecutions

A.D. 284–500
In Africa, Ethiopia becomes
    Christian in fourth century
    A.D.; Ghana kingdom
    begins; the Nobatian
    kingdom, famous for its
    cavalry in fifth century

       b) Constantine and the spread
            of Christianity
  2. Early Christian controversies
    a) Arianism
        (1) The triumph of Bishop
              Athanasius
        (2) The Nicene Creed
        (3) Ulfilas, an Arian bishop
    b) The rise of ascetic movements
        (1) Pachomius
        (2) Antony
    c) Triumph of Christianity

C. Christian Rome and the end of the
    Western Empire, 395–476
  1. Invasions by the Germans
  2. Collapse of Roman institutions

II. The Transition from Humanism
to Christian Civilization
A. Literature, theology, and history
  1. The decline of secular writing
  2. The Fathers of the Church
    a) Ambrose
        (1) Writings
        (2) Influence
    b) Jerome
        (1) Writings
        (2) Influence
    c) Augustine
        (1) Writings
        (2) Influence

A.D.; introduction of rice into the Niger delta; the palace at Enda Mikael, Ethiopia

In Andean culture, Early Intermediate period, 200 B.C.–A.D. 500; flutes and horns, about 475

In China, period of Disunity, or Six Dynasties, 220–581; Nanking, capital of southern dynasties; poets Tao Qian, 365–427, and Xie Lingyun, 385–433, exploring the theme of retreat in a time of chaos, reflecting both their era and the tension between the Confucian principle of service to society and Daoist mysticism; tea growing now common south of Yangtze River; Buddhism popular in North China, after fourth century; invention of the stirrup, about 350; Buddhist cave temples in North China, about 476

In Himalayan region, in Nepal, the rise of the Licchavi dynasty to 585; Thakuri dynasty, founded by Amsuvarman, 585–650

In India, Gupta dynasty, 320–550; the zenith of Buddhism in India, soon to be eclipsed by Hinduism; *Yoga Aphorisms of Patanjali,* the classic textbook of yoga, fourth or fifth century A.D.; *Eight Anthologies* and *Ten Songs,* the corpus of classical Tamil poetry, first century B.C. to third century A.D.; Kalidasa, *Meghaduta,* monologue on being separated from one's love, in Sanskrit, about 400; Kalidasa's *Shakuntala,* a heroic drama with a romantic theme, in

3. Church history: Eusebius
    a) New literary genre
    b) Influence
B. The visual arts
    1. Late Roman style
    2. Architecture
        a) Palaces
        b) Arches
        c) Basilicas
        d) Domed structures
    3. Sculpture
        a) Secular developments
            (1) Free-standing works
            (2) Colossal statues
            (3) Reliefs
            (4) Stylistic changes
        b) Christian art
            (1) Sarcophagus art
            (2) Stylistic changes
    4. Painting and mosaics
        a) Book illustrations
        b) Mosaics
            (1) Subjects and themes
            (2) Contrast with secular art
            (3) Developments in the Eastern Roman Empire
C. Music
    1. Sacred hymns
    2. The contributions of Ambrose

III. Why Did Rome Fall?
    A. Internal and external pressures
    B. Theories and interpretations

IV. The Legacy of Late Roman Civilization

Sanskrit, about 400; Sudraka's *Little Clay Cart,* a romance, in Sanskrit, about 400; Bhartrihari's cynical love poems, in Sanskrit, fifth century; temple no. 17, at Sanchi, fifth century; invasions of Huns, about 455–528; Huns and other central Asian tribes destroy Gupta empire

In Japan, Tomb period, about A.D. 300–645; great earthen grave mounds and funerary objects; Yamato clan, whose leaders began the imperial dynasty currently ruling Japan; first records of Japanese history, about 400; first Shinto shrines, 478; native kingdoms; earliest haniwa (tomb models), fifth century; founding of the capital, Osaka, fourth to fifth centuries; settlers from central Asia may have given Japan a seminomadic tradition, as seen in houses not built to last and with few furnishings

In Mesoamerica, Classic period, 200 B.C.–A.D. 900; the Huaxtecs, a Mayan people, were cut off from the mainstream and flourished near Tampico, from 700 B.C. to about A.D. 1000; the Huaxtecs are noted for their expressive and dramatic stone sculpture

In Sri Lanka, complex urban center at Anuradhapura with monasteries, Brazen Palace, amusement garden, stone baths, sacred buildings, hospital, third century; monasteries have hygienic facilities with sewers and water pipes for baths nearby

LEARNING OBJECTIVES

To learn:

1. The reasons for the crises in the Late Roman Empire and the various solutions applied by the government

2. The phases in the rise of Christianity

3. The controversies within early Christian thought

4. The ideas and contributions of the church fathers

5. The central role and importance of St. Augustine in early church history

6. The impact of the new Christian faith on the visual arts, especially in sculpture and painting

7. The various interpretations regarding the collapse of the Roman Empire

8. Historic "firsts" achieved by late Roman civilization: the beginnings of the Germanic kingdoms, the rise of the first Christian state, Christianity as the official religion of Rome, the literary genre of church history, the first Latin Bible, and the writings of the church fathers

9. The role of late Roman civilization in transmitting the heritage of earlier times: synthesizing a new civilization from Greco-Roman and Christian elements, fusing Classical values with Christian beliefs in architecture and music, establishing an official church organization, and originating a conception of society in which the Christian church held a pivotal position

SUGGESTIONS FOR FILMS

The Christians: A Peculiar People. McGraw-Hill, 39 min., color.

Decline of the Roman Empire. Coronet, 14 min., color.

In Defence of Rome. McGraw-Hill, 16 min., color.

SUGGESTIONS FOR FURTHER READING

Bandinelli, R. B. *Rome. The Late Empire. Roman Art, A.D. 200–400.* Translated by P. Green. New York: Braziller, 1971. An important resource for the art of Rome's last centuries.

Brown, P. *Augustine of Hippo.* London: Faber, 1967. A careful biography of the life and thought of this early church father.

Chuvin, P. *A Chronicle of the Last Pagans.* Translated by B. A. Archer. Cambridge: Harvard University Press, 1990. A splendid evocation of pagan culture in Rome between Constantine's Edict of Toleration in 313 and the death of Justinian in 565.

Canfora, L. *The Vanished Library. A Wonder of the Ancient World.* Berkeley: University of California Press, 1990. A difficult but rewarding monograph on the famous Library at Alexandria, but which incidentally touches on several other ancient doomed libraries such as the one of Rameses II at Thebes, that of Hadrian at Athens, and the personal books of Aristotle.

Grabar, A. *Early Christian Art.* Translated by S. Gilbert and J. Emmons. New York: Odyssey Press, 1968. An older but still valuable presentation of Christian art in its infancy, by a distinguished French scholar.

Irmgard, Hutter. *Early Christian and Byzantine.* Translated by A. Laing. London: Herbert, 1988. An excellent work that shows how Christians, both in Rome and the Orthodox East, adapted the art of Classical antiquity to new conditions; published first in German in 1971.

MacMullen, R. *Corruption and the Decline of Rome.* New Haven: Yale University Press, 1988. Using the methods of historical sociology, this work explores the reasons for Rome's decline, covering the period from 250, when the state began to disintegrate, until about 420, when outside forces finally broke through the border defenses.

Milburn, R. L. P. *Early Christian Art and Architecture.* Berkeley: University of California Press, 1988. A very useful survey of Christian art and architecture from the beginning to about 550; includes floor plans of early churches.

Murray, C. *Rebirth and Afterlife: A Study of the Transmutation of Some Pagan Imagery in Early Christian Funerary Art.* Oxford: BAR, 1981. A monograph demonstrating the early Christians' appropriation of pagan imagery in funerary art.

Sordi, M. *The Christians and the Roman Empire.* Norman: University of Oklahoma Press, 1986. Revisionist history that presents the conflict between pagan Rome and early Christianity as ethical, religious, ideological, and emotional, but not at its deepest level, political.

Wilken, R. L. *The Christians As the Romans Saw Them.* New Haven: Yale University Press, 1984. Surveys the differing attitudes of Romans toward the Christians, from the birth of the new faith to its eventual triumph as the sole religion of Rome.

IDENTIFICATIONS

symbolic realism	aisles
peristyle	clerestory windows
medallion	atrium
attic	transept
basilica	cruciform
apse	baptistery
nave	impressionistic

PERSONAL PERSPECTIVE BACKGROUND

Paulina, Epitaph for Agorius Praetextatus

Anconia Paulina was wed forty years to Vettius Agorius Praetextatus, the chief pagan intellectual of his time. She shared her husband's beliefs, and the epitaph (Personal Perspective) she wrote for him expresses the hope that they will be united in the afterlife. The epitaph survives today only because St. Jerome, in one of his treatises, reproduced its language in order to expose the falsehood of pagan beliefs. For Jerome, the destination of Praetextatus and Paulina is hell, not "the heavenly palace of her imagination."

St. Jerome, Secular Education; the Fall of Rome

A passionate Christian, St. Jerome had an on-again, off-again love affair with the Latin and Greek classics. During his youthful studies in Germany, he developed such a passion for these works that he feared he had fallen into sin. Taking monastic vows in the Near East, he had visions of being punished on Judgment Day for preferring the classics to Christian works. Thereafter, he "read the books of God with greater zeal than [he] had ever given to the books of men." In his middle years, when he had sworn off the classics, he was in Rome (382–385) as secretary to the pope, and after 385, back in the

Near East, where he completed his translation of the Hebrew Bible into Latin, perhaps the greatest literary achievement of the fourth century. In his last years, he once again read the classic authors. Jerome's life came to symbolize the church's ideal of placing Greco-Roman learning in the service of Christianity. (See *The Western Humanities* for additional information on St. Jerome.)

DISCUSSION/ESSAY QUESTIONS

1. Discuss the major military and social problems facing the emperor Diocletian in 284.
2. Compare and contrast the last years of the Roman Republic with the last centuries of the Roman Empire.
3. Analyze Diocletian's solutions to Rome's imperial and foreign problems and note his successes and failures.
4. Discuss the changing policies of the Roman government toward the Christians. Was the issue dividing Romans and Christians political or religious? Explain. How successful were the Roman authorities in dealing with the Christians?
5. Discuss the emperor Constantine's roles as a preserver of Roman values and as a proponent of Christianity.
6. What were some of the debates that raged inside the early Christian community? How were they resolved?
7. What were the major threats to the Roman Empire by 395, and how did the Romans respond to these threats?
8. Note two fathers of the church, and discuss their contributions to early Christianity.
9. Show how St. Augustine spoke for both the Classical age and the Christian era.
10. In what ways did St. Augustine's *Confessions* and *The City of God* reveal his heart and his mind as a Christian thinker?
11. Compare and contrast Eusebius's Christian view of history with that of the Greek and Roman historians.
12. What values were reflected in the architecture of late Rome?
13. Discuss the architectural features of the basilica and describe how the Christians adapted this building to their own uses.
14. Explain why Neo-Platonism appealed to women.
15. Do you think that the Roman Empire "fell from within" or was "overwhelmed from the outside"? State your case from either point of view.
16. What were the most lasting contributions of the Romans to Western civilization?

MULTIPLE-CHOICE QUESTIONS

1. Life in the Late Roman Empire CANNOT be described as a time when:
   a. The old Roman values were brought into question.
   b. The political and social institutions appeared unable to change or correct society's ills.
   c. A line of weak and warring emperors ruled the empire.
 * d. Roman culture was at its peak. (p. 155)

2. This emperor, in the late third century, reformed the Roman Empire:
   a. Commodus
   b. Constantine
 * c. Diocletian (p. 155)
   d. Augustus Caesar

3. One of the major problems facing Diocletian was:
   a. distributing the surplus foods produced by the farmers
   * b. dealing with an unruly army and its many soldiers (p. 155)
   c. deciding how to treat the newly conquered peoples of Italy
   d. defeating the Carthaginians

4. What issue confronted the Roman army in 284?
   a. a large male populace who wanted to join the army
   * b. a restless set of troops often underpaid and ill-equipped (p. 155)
   c. a peaceful civilian population along the frontiers
   d. a ready pool of recruits from Christians and Germans

5. Diocletian, as the emperor, saw himself as:
   a. simply another human being trying to do a job
   b. a mortal whom Fate had chosen to lead his people
   * c. a divine ruler who isolated himself from the populace (pp. 155–156)
   d. one who mingled with his subjects on a daily basis

6. Diocletian's reforms were NOT successful in which of the following areas?
   a. controlling the Roman army
   * b. solving Rome's harsh tax problems (pp. 156–158)
   c. containing the barbarians
   d. restoring calm to the city of Rome

7. Diocletian tried all of these reforms EXCEPT:
   a. shifting around the capital sometimes
   b. dividing the empire into two parts
   c. setting up a tetrarchy of rulers
   * d. establishing a free-market economy (pp. 156–157)

8. Diocletian's reforms raised the status of Roman women by:
   a. providing educational opportunities for women
   * b. including the wealth of women in the state census (pp. 157–158)
   c. allowing married women to control their own property
   d. permitting women to have equal access to the judicial system

9. Which of the following statements does NOT apply to the Christian church in the early 300s?
   a. The emperor Diocletian began the Great Persecution.
   b. For eight years Roman rulers forbade Christian worship and destroyed churches and books.
   c. The persecutions actually won many converts because of the courage of martyrs.
   * d. The Edict of Milan outlawed the pagan cults and made Christianity the official religion of Rome. (p. 158)

10. The Arian Controversy was settled at the church council of:
    * a. Nicaea (p. 159)
    b. Constantinople
    c. Alexandria
    d. Rome

11. Constantine did NOT:
    a. Help expand the Christian faith across the empire.
    b. Return confiscated property to the church.
    c. Build new churches.
    * d. Eliminate rival faiths to Christianity. (p. 158)

12. The Edict of Milan issued in 313:
    a. pardoned all Christians for their past sins
  * b. permitted Christians to worship openly (p. 158)
    c. demanded that all pagans convert to Christianity
    d. made Christianity the state religion

13. The earliest emperor to convert to Christianity was:
    a. Diocletian
    b. Decius
    c. Julian
  * d. Constantine (p. 158)

14. The founding of Constantinople was NOT a signal that:
  * a. The language of the empire was shifting from Latin to Greek. (p. 158)
    b. The basis of political power was moving from the West to the East.
    c. Christianity was now an official religion of the empire.
    d. The new city was to become a center of culture and art.

15. One of the issues dividing the early Christians was the:
    a. nature of the Virgin Mary
    b. power of congregations instead of the pope to make decisions
  * c. divine nature of Jesus (p. 159)
    d. relationship of the pope to the Roman emperor

16. The early Christians who asserted that Jesus was similar but not identical with God advocated a belief known as:
    a. Athanasium
    b. agnosticism
    c. atheism
  * d. Arianism (p. 159)

17. Christianity appealed to many because it:
  * a. recognized the spiritual worth of the poor (p. 158)
    b. was well organized with control from Rome
    c. solved all of its disputes without controversy
    d. was popular, from its beginning, with the ruling classes

18. Heresy within the Christian church was NOT a sign that:
    a. Dogma and rituals are often areas of disagreement.
    b. Differences of opinion were inevitable given that many converts came to Christianity from other religions.
    c. Classical thought and Christian belief were often incompatible.
  * d. Believers took their faith lightly. (pp. 158–159)

19. The original founders of Western monasticism are:
    a. Jerome and Ambrose
  * b. Pachomius and Antony (p. 159)
    c. Tertullian and Origen
    d. Augustine and Arius

20. Late Roman literature can be described as:
    a. releasing a new and vital spirit
  * b. unable to comprehend the profound changes occurring in society (p. 161)
    c. seeming to care only about the present
    d. having insights into moral behavior

21. Late Roman Christian authors:
  * a. admired Classical writings and adopted Classical literary styles (pp. 161–162)
    b. ignored Classical writings and pioneered new styles appropriate to Christian themes
    c. burned Classical writings because they seemed to contradict Christian beliefs
    d. adopted Aristotle's writings but ignored the rest of Classical literature

22. Three of the most renowned church fathers were:
    a. Ambrose, Augustine, and Plotinus
    b. Jerome, Augustine, and Constantine
  * c. Ambrose, Jerome, and Augustine (p. 161)
    d. Ambrose, Jerome, and Plotinus

23. Ambrose's leadership in the church was NOT based on his:
    a. service as a capable ecclesiastical administrator
    b. fusion of Christian and Greco-Roman ideas in his thinking
  * c. position as pope (p. 161)
    d. contributions as an effective composer of hymns

24. Jerome's most lasting contribution to the church was his:
    a. discovery of the True Cross on which Christ was crucified
  * b. translation of the Bible into Latin (p. 161)
    c. missionary work among the barbarians
    d. support for the official view in disputes over church dogma

25. Jerome's response to the crisis of his age included all of the following EXCEPT:
    a. a description of the shedding of Roman blood defending the empire
    b. his belief that the Roman world was falling
  * c. his advice to abandon secular literature and relay exclusively on the Christian Bible
       (Personal Perspective)
    d. his reaction to the sacking of churches and monasteries

26. Augustine was NOT famous for his:
    a. monumental work on the causes of the fall of Rome
  * b. missionary work among the Germanic invaders (pp. 162–163)
    c. autobiography in which he revealed his innermost thoughts
    d. defense of the church's official point of view in doctrinal disputes

27. Which was NOT part of Augustine's background before becoming a Christian?
  * a. He spent a portion of his life as a convert to Judaism. (pp. 162–163)
    b. He was educated in the Greek and Roman classics.
    c. He was well acquainted with many philosophies, including Neo-Platonism.
    d. He began life as a pagan from North Africa.

28. In *The City of God,* Augustine asked and answered this question:
    a. Why did God create the world?
  * b. Why does the Roman Empire suffer so much? (pp. 162–163)
    c. Will Rome be powerful again?
    d. Where did evil originate?

29. What event compelled Augustine to write *The City of God?*
    * a.   the sack of Rome by the Visigoths (p. 163)
      b.   the conquest of Constantinople by the Ottoman Turks
      c.   the fall of Athens to the Germanic invaders
      d.   the death of Constantine

30. Augustine has been recognized for:
      a.   his contributions to pagan philosophy
      b.   his reconciling Arianism with Christian thought
    * c.   explaining the relationship between God and human beings within the context of history and theology (pp. 162–163)
      d.   his identification of happiness as the goal of human life

31. The early church historians believed that:
      a.   Good would triumph, regardless of the presence of evil in the world.
      b.   Human beings were the primary movers of history.
      c.   History moved in cycles.
    * d.   God played the central role in history. (pp. 163–164)

32. The first historian of the Christian church was:
      a.   Jerome
      b.   Augustine
    * c.   Eusebius (p. 163)
      d.   Constantine

33. The writer Eusebius did NOT:
      a.   draw inspiration from Greco-Roman historians
      b.   seek out historic sources for his facts
    * c.   downplay the role of the divine element in events (pp. 163–164)
      d.   use dramatic emphasis in the style of pagan writers such as Homer

34. *The History of the Christian Church* was:
      a.   a work of divine inspiration
      b.   a realistic and dispassionate account of the early church
    * c.   a work that is important for its information even if it is not always presented in an objective way (p. 163)
      d.   not based on documents and historical records

35. Which was NOT part of the changed circumstances of Late Roman art?
      a.   Patronage shifted from the emperor to the church.
      b.   Classical forms gave way to abstract spiritual qualities.
      c.   Artists abandoned Greco-Roman forms.
    * d.   Religious paintings became part of the decorative scheme in Christian homes. (p. 164)

36. In Late Roman times, which Italian city became a center for the new trends in the visual arts?
    * a.   Ravenna (p. 164)
      b.   Rome
      c.   Florence
      d.   Milan

37. Ravenna, as the new capital of the Late Roman Empire:
    a. was under constant siege by the barbarians
  * b. reflected Eastern influences in its art styles (p. 164)
    c. was the center of a strong centralized government
    d. was the city in which Augustine was bishop for about thirty years

38. The first Roman emperor to support Christian art and architecture was:
    a. Diocletian
    b. Commodus
  * c. Constantine (p. 165)
    d. Marcus Aurelius

39. In the fifth century, as Christianity spread:
  * a. Churches came to be supported by bishops as well as emperors. (p. 165)
    b. More underground centers of worship were built.
    c. The Roman government sometimes prohibited any building.
    d. Rival religions constructed more temples.

40. Diocletian's Palace on the Dalmatian coast did NOT have this aspect:
  * a. It was the Roman Empire's first specifically Christian palace. (p. 165)
    b. It was like a Roman camp in its layout and purpose.
    c. It was a tribute to this powerful ruler.
    d. It was intended to impress visitors with the power of Rome.

41. The Arch of Constantine may NOT be viewed as:
    a. a monument whose scenes have helped historians understand late Roman civilization
    b. a work that inspired later builders of triumphant arches
    c. one of the last great architectural works of the Roman Empire
  * d. the originator of the triumphal arch artistic form (pp. 165–166)

42. Christians adopted which Roman building type for their churches?
    a. cathedral
    b. forum
  * c. basilica (p. 166)
    d. amphitheater

43. A typical basilica includes all of these EXCEPT:
    a. It has an oblong hall that is curved on the eastern end.
    b. It contains windows in the upper walls of the central section.
    c. It is usually divided into three areas by columns.
  * d. Its exterior is decorated with many carvings. (p. 166)

44. The shape of the floor plan of many early Christian churches was the:
  * a. cruciform (p. 167)
    b. square
    c. rectangle
    d. "X" cross form

45. Why was a baptistery built as a separate structure from a church?
    a. It accommodated large crowds at baptisms.
  * b. Christians felt that those who were not yet baptized should not be allowed in the church building. (p. 169)
    c. The baptistery was based on a tradition established by Constantine.
    d. It was the home of the priest.

46. Late Roman secular sculpture can be characterized as:
    a. based on the Classical rules of balance, simplicity, and restraint
    b. little changed from secular sculpture in the pre-Christian era
    * c. dedicated to enhancing the power and image of the emperor (p. 169)
    d. influenced by German ideals and forms

47. One of the generalizations that can be made about surviving sculpture from the Late Roman Empire is that:
    a. Relief work has nearly disappeared.
    b. Sculptured statues were smaller than those made in the early empire.
    * c. The portraits were more like stereotypes than individuals. (p. 169)
    d. Roman sculptures imitated the Greek Archaic style.

48. The leading location of early Christian sculpture is:
    * a. on underground burial vaults or sarcophagi (p. 170)
    b. inside the forums
    c. on the walls of public buildings
    d. within private homes

49. Carvings on Late Roman burial vaults or sarcophagi reveal that:
    a. Rich non-Christian Romans preferred plain, unadorned monuments.
    b. Christians wanted only biblical themes and figures on these tombs.
    * c. The Christian belief in life after death made the sarcophagus a likely object for art. (p. 170)
    d. Christians cremated the dead and thus did not use burial vaults.

50. The early Christian artists used many art forms to express their beliefs, including all of the following EXCEPT:
    a. mosaics
    b. burial vaults
    c. tomb frescoes
    * d. panel paintings (pp. 169–173)

51. Mosaics became very popular in the churches controlled by the:
    a. newly converted barbarian kings who settled in northern Italy
    * b. rulers from the eastern regions of the Late Roman world (p. 173)
    c. newly converted invading tribes from Gaul
    d. rulers in Spain

52. The style of early Christian art can be described as:
    a. abstract and geometric
    * b. symbolic and impressionistic (pp. 169–170)
    c. emotional and expressionistic
    d. traditional and naturalistic

53. An important hymn writer in the early Christian church was:
    a. Jerome
    b. Augustine
    * c. Ambrose (p. 174)
    d. Plotinus

54. According to the French thinker Montesquieu, Rome fell because:
    a. The barbarians were too powerful to be stopped by the Romans.
    b. The population declined.
    c. The climate changed and made the Romans lazy.
    * d. Power ended up in the hands of one person, the emperor. (p. 174)

55. Christianity was a major cause for the fall of Rome according to the writings of:
    * a. Edward Gibbon (p. 175)
    b. Montesquieu
    c. Jerome
    d. Ambrose

COMPARATIVE QUESTIONS, CHAPTERS 1 THROUGH 7

1. All of the following are valid statements about ancient religions EXCEPT:
   a. Judaism and Christianity were monotheistic; the Greek and Roman religions were polytheistic.
   b. Christianity and Greek and Roman mystery cults promised immortality; Judaism and other Greek and Roman cults accepted the finality of death.
   c. Christianity and the Greek and Roman religions represented the deity in their art; Judaism forbade religious images.
   * d. Judaism and Christianity made use of prayers and rituals; the Greek and Roman religions did not.

2. All of the following matchups between a society and its type of government are correct EXCEPT:
   * a. Hellenistic Macedonia—parliamentary government
   b. Ancient Egypt—theocracy
   c. Hellenic Athens—democracy
   d. Rome, 509 to 31 B.C.—republic

3. All of the following matchups between a literary form and its cultural origin are correct EXCEPT:·
   a. epic—Mesopotamia
   * b. sonnet—Egypt
   c. tragedy—Hellenic Athens
   d. satire—imperial Rome

4. All of the following are valid statements about ancient sculpture EXCEPT:
   * a. Greek sculpture borrowed the Egyptian technique of always depicting humans facing either right or left.
   b. The kouros and kore of Archaic Greek sculpture was influenced by the Egyptian practice of placing the left foot forward.
   c. Etruscan sculpture, as in the Apollo Veii, sometimes used the enigmatic smile of Archaic Greek sculpture.
   d. Early Christian sculptured images of Jesus as a beardless youth dressed in classical draperies show the influence of Greek and Roman statues.

5. All of the following are correct statements about the goal of the indicated philosophy EXCEPT:
   a. In Arisoteleanism, the goal is a life of moderation.
   b. In Stoicism, the goal is living in harmony with the *logos.*
   c. In Platonism, the goal is the perfecting of the soul (mind).
   * d. In Neo-Platonism, the goal is satisfaction of the bodily desires.

8

THE SUCCESSORS OF ROME
Byzantium, Islam, and the Early Medieval West

TEACHING STRATEGIES AND SUGGESTIONS

The best way to introduce Rome's successors—Byzantium, Islam, and the Early Medieval West—is through a teaching strategy that combines the Patterns of Change method with Historical Overviews. This combined strategy will allow the instructor, using broad strokes, to lay out the origins, major phases and turning points, and characteristics and cultural highlights of the three civilizations and, simultaneously, to show how the Roman heritage was adapted to new conditions in each society. The instructor can also employ the Comparison/Contrast approach to set forth the similarities and differences among these cultures as well as point out the enduring legacies of Byzantium and Islam to the West.

Having briefly surveyed Rome's successors, the instructor can then concentrate on the Early Medieval West, using the Diffusion method to illustrate how Classical, Germanic, and Christian elements were united into a new civilization. With the Patterns of Change model, the instructor can describe how the West was evolving from a relatively simple stage to a more complex model. Shifting to a strategy that blends a Slide Lecture with a Reflections/Connections approach, the instructor can identify the West's major artistic and literary achievements and show how they mirrored developments in political, social, and economic history. In addition, Charlemagne's reign can be treated as a Case Study in which various questions may be raised, such as the validity of monarchy as a form of government, the usefulness of the "Great Man" theory of history, and the viability of the term *Renaissance* as a label for the cultural awakening of this period.

In a concluding lecture for the entire chapter, the teacher could opt for the Spirit of the Age approach, thus raising questions about the *zeitgeist* of a civilization; that is, in surveying future prospects for all three civilizations from the vantage point of about A.D. 1000, the instructor could speculate on why some civilizations expand and grow, while others stagnate and a few disappear.

LECTURE OUTLINE

Non-Western Events

I.   Successors of Rome: Relative Strengths and Weaknesses

II. The Eastern Roman Empire and
     Byzantine Civilization, 476–1453
     A. Shifting fortunes but stable features
     B. History of the Byzantine Empire
        1. Rulers and ruling dynasties
           a) Justinian

500–1000
In Africa, in Nubia, the first Christian mission established, 543; Nubia remains Christian until the thirteenth century, when Egyptian Muslims invade and introduce Islam; rise of

      b) The Macedonian dynasty and the Golden Age of Byzantium, 867–1081

      c) The Comneni dynasty

      d) The Paleologian dynasty

  2. Civilizing mission in eastern Europe

  3. Patterns of social change

  4. Surrounded by enemies in later years

C. Byzantine culture: Christianity and Classicism

  1. Conflict inherited from Rome

  2. The Orthodox religion

      a) The office of patriarch

      b) Differences between Orthodox and Western Christianity

      c) Religious disputes

         (1) Iconoclastic Controversy

         (2) Other dissension

      d) Monasticism

  3. Law and History

      a) Heir to Roman law

      b) The Justinian Code

         (1) Principles

         (2) Influence

      c) Anna Comnena, the *Alexiad*

  4. Architecture and mosaics

      a) The Byzantine style

         (1) Elements of Byzantine architecture

         (2) The pendentive

         (3) The dome

      b) Outstanding buildings and their characteristics

         (1) The church of Hagia Sophia, Constantinople

         (2) The church of San Vitale, Ravenna

         (3) The church of Sant' Apollinare in Classe

      c) Mosaics

         (1) Contrast with the Roman style

         (2) The portrayals of Justinian and Theodora and their courtiers

      d) Impact of the Iconoclastic Controversy

         (1) Destruction of past art

         (2) Inauguration of a theological art

III. The Islamic World, 600–1517

  A. Overview of Islamic civilization

kingdom of Ghana; permanent settlements in Madagascar by Southeast Asians; merchant colonies established at Kumbi Saleh, Timbuktu, and Jennejeno; in Ife, Nigeria, terra-cotta and bronze sculptures, characterized by two trends, idealized naturalism and extreme stylization, about 500–1000

In Andean culture, Middle Horizon period, 500–900; Late Intermediate period, 900–1438; collapse of Moche culture, about 600; rise of the Wari people in the southern highlands of Peru and the Tiwanaku peoples near Lake Titicaca in Bolivia; Wari tapestries; the capital city of Wari was abandoned in about 800 and remains unexcavated today; the city of Tiwanaku covered 4 square miles and numbered about 60,000 people at its height; Tiwanaku ceramics; the Bennett Monolith is the largest (24 feet) Adean stela; end of Tiwanaku culture in about 1000

In China, Period of Disunity, or Six Dynasties, 220–581; the pagoda at the Song Yue temple in Henan, 523; first Chinese roll painting, 535; the square pagoda of Shen-t'ung'ssu in Shantung, 544; Sui dynasty, 581–618, China is reunified; Tang dynasty, 618–906; an era of cosmopolitanism and cultural flowering; height of Buddhist influence in China, until repressed, about 845; capital of Changan numbers 1 million; silver dishes, decorated silks, ceramic figures, including the Tang

1. Meaning of *islam* and *muslim*
2. Geographic setting
3. The pre-Islamic Arabs
   a) Desert Bedouins
   b) Urban Arabs
4. Jewish and Christian neighbors

B. History of Islam
   1. Life and teachings of Muhammad
      a) The Quraish tribe
      b) The cities of Mecca and Medina
      c) *Jihad* and the expansion of Islam
      d) The purification of the Kaaba
   2. The Islamic Empire and Muhammad's successors
      a) Theocracy and the role of the Caliph
      b) The Abbasid dynasty, the golden age of Islam, 754–1258
      c) Collapse of the caliphate and the rise of mutually hostile Islamic states

C. Islamic religious and cultural developments
   1. Brilliance of Islamic civilization
      a) Brief survey
      b) Central role of religion in Islamic life
   2. Islamic religion
      a) Two central beliefs
      b) Relation to Jewish and Christian prophetic tradition
      c) The Koran
      d) The Hadith, or the Tradition
      e) Five Pillars of the Faith
         (1) The affirmation of faith
         (2) Prayer
         (3) Fasting
         (4) Alms-giving
         (5) Pilgrimage
      f) The Shari'a, or holy law
   3. History
      a) Various types
      b) The pioneering work of Ibn Khaldun
   4. Science
      a) Link between Roman science and medieval Western science
      b) Original contributions
         (1) Medicine
         (2) Mathematics
      c) Adaptations from Hindu science

horse; Tang poetry, the golden age of Chinese poetry with Wang Wei, 699–761, Li Bai, 701–762, Du Fu, 712–770, Bo Juyi, 772–846, and Hanshan, eighth to ninth centuries; renewed trade with the West; Changan connected by canals with Luoyang, a second capital; Tang rulers control the Tarim Basin in central Asia, including the Silk Roads linking China to Persia and the Mediterranean; expansion of China until defeat by Arabs at Talas, 751; period of land reform and good government; use of woodblock printing to mass-produce Buddhist and Daoist texts; the hall of the Nanchan Temple in Shaanxi province, China's oldest surviving wooden structure, 782; earliest evidence of gunpowder in ninth century; adoption of chairs; anti-Buddhist persecutions, 845 and tenth century; the world's first printed book, *The Diamond Sutra*, 868; the Chung-hsing-ssu pagoda at Shantung, about 900, a brick version of a wooden pagoda, which becomes the prototype of later Liao and Sung pagodas; Five Dynasties and Liao dynasty, 907–1125; sixth period of Chinese literature, 900–1900; northern Sung dynasty, 960–1126; first printing of the classic texts of Confucius, 932; money economy; growth in commerce and trade; urban growth and technological innovation;

1,000-volume encyclopedia, 978–984; the Bridge of the Ten Thousand Ages, Foochow, 1000

In Himalayan region, in Kashmir, Gonandiya dynasty, from about 500 B.C. to A.D. 622; Karkota dynasty, 622–about 760; Lalitaditya Muktapida, 724–about 760, the greatest ruler in the Karkota line; conquests in India to the Deccan, in Afghanistan Tibet, and in central Asia; Buddhist complexes at Parihasapura and Pandrenthanm, temples at Loduv, Narastan, Martand, Vantipur, and Patan, between seventh and tenth centuries; development of basic elements of Kashmir architecture: the trilobate arch, the triangular tympanum, and the pyramidal roof; the Utpala dynasty with two strong kings, Avantivarman, 856–883, and Sankaravarman, 883–902, after which decline sets in; in Nepal, end of Licchavi dynasty and founding of Thakuri dynasty by Amsuvarman, 585–650; in Tibet, rise of monarchy and first two kings, K'ri-slon-brtsan, 590–620, and Sron-btsan-sgam-po, 620–645; introduction of Buddhism under latter king; Buddhism made state religion under B'ri-sron-lde-brtsan, 755–797; coming of the magician Padmasambhava and founding of the sect of Red Caps (later opposed by the Yellow Caps); occupation of Changan,

China's Tang dynasty capital; Tibetan religious architecture has two types of monuments, the chorten (a funerary monument that is a modified stupa) and the temple; monastic complex at Samye; period of decline, 850–1000

In India, successive invasions of Huns, about 455 to 528; Huns and other central Asian tribes destroy Gupta empire, 550; temple at Deogarh, sixth century; temple of Durga, the goddess of war, at Aihole, by the Chalukya dynasty, sixth century; dictionary, 650; the *Surangama Sutra,* a Mahayan Buddhist text, written in Sanskrit in the first century A.D. and translated into Chinese in A.D. 705; seventh- and eighth-century mathematicians, Brahmagupta and Lalla, study geometry, trigonometry, and algebra; use of decimals and zero; *The Adventures of the Ten Princes,* by the Sanskrit poet-novelist Dandin, about 700; competing dynasties and clans, from 650 to 1336; Arabs take the city of Sind, 711; the rock-cut temple of Kailasanath at Ellora, built by the Rashtrakuta dynasty, about 650–about 750; Temple of the Sun at Martand, eighth century; raids of Mahmud of Ghazni, 997–1027

In Indochina, in Burma, cultural influence of India, starting in fifth to sixth centuries; introduction of Buddhism from India; conquest of Kyaukse and Pagan regions of north by Tibetan tribes, ninth century; in Cambodia, founding of the Khmer Empire, by Jayavarman II, after 790; stable political and social order and a vigorous art, developed in a series of styles and in imposing architectural monuments; the hydraulic system to bring water to the rice fields, constructed by Indravarman, 877–889, thus ensuring three centuries of prosperity; capital is, first, Angkor, and then, Koh Ker; the basic architectural types of Khmer art are the tower-sanctuary and the temple-mountain; the Bakheng, the royal temple-mausoleum, after 910; return to Angkor during the reign of Rajendravarman, 944–968; the five-level pyramid of Ta Keo, the culmination of the temple-mountain form, about 1000

In Japan, Tomb period, about 300–645; birth of feudal nobility, sixth century; introduction of Buddhism, 552–575; supported by Emperor Shotoky, 593–621; Asuka period, 552–645; Chinese influence, by way of Korea, brings new architectural structures and techniques, new ways of arranging building areas, and principles of urban planning; earliest surviving Buddhist temple, Hōryūji, consisting of a monastery, cloister, pagoda, pavilion, library, "Golden Hall," and temple bell, in Nara, 607–670; Taika reform, 645; reforms made largely on Chinese models; writing system, bureaucratic organization, legal theories; Nara period,

645–784; Nara (near modern Osaka) made the first permanent capital, in 710; Nara laid out in a grid borrowed from China; Nara becomes an important Buddhist center; the Toshodaiji, Nara, a temple synthesizing Chinese and Japanese principles, 755 to 770; the Tōdaiji, the "Great Eastern Temple," the first Buddhist center built wholly at state expense, commissioned by Emperor Shōmu, 701–756; Shōmu decrees that each province establish a monastery for men and a convent for women, in 741; *Kojiki* by Yasumaro Onon, the first history of Japan; *Manyoshu* by Japanese poets, contains 4,516 poems, about 759; Heian period, 794–1185; the Heian goal was to escape from the pervasive influence of Buddhism; Emperor Kwammu, 782–805; Kwammu moves capital to Nagaoka, 784; Nagaoka doesn't work out and a new capital is founded at Miyako, or Kyoto, which remained the imperial residence until 1869; classical Japanese culture in the new capital Kyoto; Kyoto's palaces, temples, and dwellings use the first original Japanese designs; the "phoenix hall" of the Byodoin complex, the only original architecture surviving from about 800; court nobles, especially noblewomen, produce a great body of literature— poetry, diaries, a novel; refined aesthetic sensibility is the hallmark of Heian culture; the first important Japanese painter, Kudawara Kuwanari, d. 853; Kyoto's Diago pagoda, 972; *The Gossamer Years,* an autobiographical narrative of a woman married to a high-ranking aristocrat, tenth century

In Korea, Three Kingdoms period, 57 B.C.–A.D. 668; the pagodas of Miruk-sa at Iksankun and of Chong-nim-sa at Puyo in the Pakche kingdom, the oldest stone structures in Korea, seventh century; the Punhwang-sa pagoda at Kyongju, capital of the Old Silla kingdom, seventh century; Great Silla Kingdom, A.D. 668–935; Korea now unified; the capital Kyongju, built on a square grid with high city walls pierced by twenty gates, containing about 1 million inhabitants; the classic period of Korean architecture, inspired by Chinese Tang style; the Silla type pagoda, with three diminishing stories on a pedestal of two levels and topped by a high finial, such as the twin pagodas of Kam-cun-sa at Wol-ssong Kun, seventh century; the cave temple of Sokkulam, inspired by Indian Buddhist rock construction, eighth century; distinctive glazed pottery; Koryo Kingdom, 918–1392; the medieval phase of Korean culture; imitation of China's Tang period art and architecture

In Mesoamerica, Classic period, 200 B.C.–A.D. 900; burning of Teotihuacán, about 650; Mayan Temple of the Inscriptions, about 700, in Palenque; burial offerings, island of Jaina; Monte Albán abandoned about 750; Mayan murals depicting human sacrifice at Bonampak, in Chiapas, about 800; metalworking introduced, about 800; Mayan cities are deserted by about 900; rise of Mixtec people with the dynasty of the Lords of Tilantoga, 720; Mixtecs conquer Cholula and make it their center; Historic period, 900–1521; trade between Toltecs and Anasazi and Hohokam peoples of the American Southwest

In Muslim World (For founding of Islam, consult Chapter 8 in *The Western Humanities*.),*Golden Odes,* the epic lays of the Bedouin tribes, the only great work of Arab literature predating the dawn of Islam, sixth century; the Koran, 646

In North America, in Arkansas, the Plum Bayou culture, the most complex structure of the American east, about 900

In Sri Lanka, the founding of Anuradhapura, the capital for 1,000 years and home to many Buddhist monasteries, dominated by stupas, such as that of King Mahinda II, eighth century

LEARNING OBJECTIVES

To learn:

1. The successor civilizations to Rome, their major historical periods, their major accomplishments, their adoption of the Roman heritage, and their similarities and differences

2. The strengths of Byzantium that allowed it to survive for more than 1,000 years

3. The characteristics of Orthodox Christianity and how it differed from Western Christianity

4. The significance of the Iconoclastic Controversy

5. To recognize visually the Byzantine artistic style and to identify major examples of Byzantine art and architecture

6. Byzantine contributions to the West: the Orthodox church and religion, the Code of Justinian, and elements of Byzantine art and architecture

7. The leading features of the Islamic religion and the role that it plays in Islamic culture

8. The outstanding achievements in Muslim science and mathematics

9. To recognize visually the Islamic artistic style and to identify major examples of Islamic art and architecture

10. The various cultural influences operating in Islamic civilization

11. Islamic contributions to the West: transmission of the basic philosophical and scientific texts from the ancient world; original contributions in algebra and mathematics; transmission of the concept of zero, Arabic numerals, and the pointed arch

12. The areas in Europe settled by barbarian tribes

13. The stages of the political history of the Frankish kingdom

14. The characteristics and achievements of Charlemagne's reign

15. The structure and organization of the Early Medieval church

16. The accomplishments of the Carolingian Renaissance

17. The characteristics of Early Medieval architecture and painting

18. Historic "firsts" of the Early Medieval West: Benedictine monasticism, earliest successful kingdom in western Europe, the first empire since the fall of Rome, new musical forms, vernacular languages and literature, and the illuminated religious manuscript

19. The role of the Early Medieval West in transmitting the heritage of the Greco-Roman world: revival of learning and scholarship; reshaping the structure of the Christian church; modifying the Latin language; retaining the Classical educational ideal; keeping alive Greco-Roman building and artistic techniques; and, in general, fusing Classical, Christian, and Germanic elements into a new civilization

SUGGESTIONS FOR FILMS

The Byzantine Empire. Coronet, 14 min., color.

Charlemagne and His Empire. Coronet, 14 min., black and white.

The Christians: The Birth of Europe, 410–1084. McGraw-Hill, 39 min., color.

Civilisation: The Frozen World. Time-Life, 52 min., color.

The Fall of Constantinople. Time-Life, 34 min., color.

Islam. McGraw-Hill, 19 min., color.

Islam, the Prophet and the People. Texture Films, 34 min., color.

The Muslim World: Beginnings and Growth. Coronet, 11 min., color.

SUGGESTIONS FOR FURTHER READING

Byzantium

Atroshchenko, V. I., and Collins, J. *The Origins of the Romanesque: Near Eastern Influence on European Art, 4th–12th Centuries.* London: Lund Humphries, 1985. A study that asserts the Romanesque style was heavily influenced by eastern Mediterranean art; some knowledge of Romanesque art will help the student.

Bovini, G. *Ravenna Mosaics.* Greenwich, Conn.: New York Graphic Society Publishers, Ltd., 1956. A splendidly illustrated work about the home of the most beautiful mosaics outside the old Byzantine world.

Browning, R. *The Byzantine Empire.* New York: Scribner, 1980. A general survey whose readable style and numerous illustrations make it a useful introduction for the beginning student.

Grabar, A. *Byzantine Painting.* New York: Rizzoli International, 1979. Full of color plates with clearly written text covering mosaics, frescoes, and mural paintings.

Harvey, A. *Economic Expansion in the Byzantine Empire, 900–1200.* New York: Cambridge University Press, 1989. A case study format that will appeal to the serious student interested in the relationships between economic changes and social consequences.

Mango, C. *Byzantium: The Empire of the New Rome.* New York: Scribner, 1980. An introduction to Byzantium that is topically, not chronologically, organized with chapters on language, economics, religion, literature, science, history, art, and architecture—a different approach for the inquisitive student.

Talbot-Rice, T. *Everyday Life in Byzantium.* London: B. T. Batsford, 1967. A sound overview of daily life among the elite and the other classes.

Vryonis, S. *Byzantium and Europe.* New York: Harcourt, Brace & World, 1967. A standard survey by a well-known scholar, supplemented with numerous color plates; some of the material has been outdated.

Islam

Armstrong, K. *Muhammad: A Western Attempt to Understand Islam.* San Francisco: HarperCollins, 1992. A sympathetic treatment of Muhammad's life and teachings, prefaced by a plea for the West to understand the Prophet and his religion.

Dunlog, D. M. *Arab Civilization to A.D. 1500.* London: Longman, 1971. A valuable work focusing mainly on cultural achievements.

Esposito, J. L. *Islam: The Straight Path.* New York: Oxford University Press, 1991. This introductory text covers Muhammad's life, the formative years of Islam, its beliefs and practices, and modern-day Islam. Very useful for the student who desires an overview.

James, D. L. *Islamic Art: An Introduction.* London: Hamlyn, 1974. A brief survey by a distinguished scholar; good for the beginning student.

Lewis, B. *Islam: From the Prophet Muhammad to the Capture of Constantinople.* New York: Oxford University Press, 1987. In two volumes, one of the outstanding scholars of Islam examines the political, religious, and social history generated by Islam; much more than an overview, and a worthwhile read.

Papadopoulo, A. *Islam and Muslim Art.* Translated by R. E. Wolf. New York: Abrams, 1979. Every example of Muslim art and architecture—from calligraphy to wall decorations—is explained and illustrated. A book for the serious student.

Rodinson, M. *Europe and the Mystique of Islam.* Translated by R. Veinus. Seattle: University of Washington Press, 1987. A study of how Islam is viewed by the West rather than an explanation of Islam.

Watt, W. M. *Muhammad: Prophet and Statesman.* London: Oxford University Press, 1974. Although somewhat outdated, this is a balanced treatment of Muhammad's life and the forces that shaped him, his faith, and his followers.

Early Medieval West

Beckwith, J. *Early Medieval Art.* New York: Praeger, 1973. A standard study for many years, this is still an informative introduction to an important phase of European art—fully illustrated.

Collins. R. *Early Medieval Europe, 300–1000.* New York: St. Martin's Press, 1991. In the History of Europe series, this comprehensive survey, which includes the Byzantine and Islamic worlds, allows the student to pursue many topics and issues.

Conant, K. J. *Carolingian and Romanesque Architecture, 800–1200.* New York: Penguin, 1959. A thorough study that examines the evolution and maturing of the Romanesque style.

Duby, G. *The Early Growth of the European Economy: Warriors and Peasants from the Seventh to the Twelfth Centuries.* Translated by H. B. Clarke. London: Weidenfeld and Nicolson, 1974. An important study by one of the leading scholars in social and cultural history.

Grabar, A., and Nordenfalk, C. *Early Medieval Painting: From the Fourth to the Eleventh Century.* Translated by S. Gilbert. London: Skira, 1957. One of the best treatments of an overlooked area of Western art.

Herrin, J. *The Formation of Christendom.* Princeton: Princeton University Press, 1987. A compact and detailed account of the Christian church from Roman times to the age of Charlemagne that includes discussions of the Byzantine and Muslim worlds.

Hubert, J. *The Carolingian Renaissance.* Translated by J. Emmons, S. Gilbert, and R. Allen. New York: Braziller, 1970. In the Arts of Mankind series, with essays on architecture and its decorations, book painting, sculpture, and applied arts. Profusely illustrated with the series' usual thorough documentation.

Lyon, H. R. *The Middle Ages: A Concise Encyclopedia.* London: Thames and Hudson, 1989. An indispensable handbook for medieval civilization with 250 illustrations. The source book will be quite useful for Chapters 8, 9, and 10 of *The Western Humanities.*

McKitterick, R. *The Frankish Kingdoms under the Carolingians, 751–987.* New York: Longman, 1983. A balance between political and cultural history that presents a sound introduction.

Musset, L. *The Germanic Invasions: The Making of Europe A.D. 400–600.* Translated by E. James and C. James. London: Paul Elek, 1975. Although the work covers a short time period, it is successful in making sense of the many changes that occurred.

Riche, P. *Daily Life in the World of Charlemagne.* Translated by J. McNamara. Philadelphia: University of Pennsylvania Press, 1988. For the more serious student who wants to take a closer look at a specific time; full of fascinating aspects of everyday life.

Stafford, P. *Queens, Concubines, and Dowagers: The King's Wife in the Early Middle Ages*. Athens: University of Georgia Press, 1983. A well-researched study that covers the roles and duties of women in the royal courts.

IDENTIFICATIONS

Byzantine style   mosque
Greek cross   minaret
pendentive   miniature
arcade   Gregorian chant
arabesque   ambulatory
calligraphy   illuminated manuscript

PERSONAL PERSPECTIVE BACKGROUND

Anna Comnena, The Arrival of the First Crusade in Constantinople

Usamah, The Curious Medicine of the Franks

Liudprand of Cremona, A Mission to the Byzantine Court

Throughout the Middle Ages and well into modern times, when people of different cultures interacted, the result was often open warfare or, at best, skepticism about one another's political and cultural views. Such negative attitudes spring from xenophobia (from Greek *xenos* and Latin *xeno*, "stranger")— that is, undue fear or contempt of foreigners. The three Personal Perspectives illustrate the mutual xenophobia of medieval times. What is especially telling is that all three witnesses are representative of the better-educated classes in their respective cultures: Anna Comnena was a princess, the daughter of the Byzantine emperor; the poet, teacher, and writer Usamah was of distinguished Arab ancestry, the son of the lord of a castle on the Orontes River in Syria, who, in his later years, served as an adviser to the great warrior and sultan Saladin; and Liudprand of Cremona held high ecclesiastical and secular posts, including chancellor to the king of Italy, bishop of Cremona, and ambassador for Otto I, the founder of the Holy Roman Empire. Hence, we may conclude that if the educational elite held such views, then fear of foreigners was deeply ingrained in all three cultures. (See *The Western Humanities* and *Readings in the Western Humanities* for additional information on Anna Comnena.)

DISCUSSION/ESSAY QUESTIONS

1. Compare and contrast the strengths and weaknesses of the Byzantine world, the Islamic world, and western Europe in about 900.
2. Discuss the continuities and discontinuities in the Roman legacy as it was adapted to Byzantine civilization.
3. What role did the Orthodox religion play in Byzantine society and culture? Compare and contrast Orthodox religion with the Roman Catholic faith.
4. Select a work of art from the Byzantine period and show how it illustrates the Byzantine artistic style.
5. Summarize the major phases of Byzantine history and note the most important events of each phase.
6. List and discuss the significance of the legacies of Byzantium to the Western world.
7. Which building most clearly embodies the ideals of Byzantine civilization? Explain.
8. Discuss the social, historical, and geographical conditions in the Arab peninsula on the eve of the founding of Islam.
9. Discuss the continuities and discontinuities in the Roman legacy as it was adapted to Islamic civilization.

10. What were the key events in the life of Muhammad, and how did these events affect the rise of Islam?
11. Describe the Islamic religion. What impact did Islam have on society, politics, art, architecture, and literature?
12. Discuss the part played by Muslim science in the chain of events that led to modern science.
13. What are the two types of mosques? Give an example of each type and list its chief features.
14. Which work of art or building most clearly embodies the ideals of Islamic civilization? Explain.
15. Explain how and why the Franks were able to create a relatively stable political system by 750.
16. Analyze the Christian church's leadership and organization in the Early Middle Ages.
17. What were the major characteristics of the Carolingian Renaissance? Was it a real rebirth of learning or a heroic interlude between two dark periods?
18. In what ways were Carolingian architecture and literature reflections of ninth-century life in western Europe?
19. Discuss the development of illuminated manuscripts and illustrate their characteristics, using two examples.
20. "The Early Middle Ages laid the foundations for European civilization." Explain.

MULTIPLE-CHOICE QUESTIONS

1. Byzantine civilization was characterized by all these EXCEPT:
   * a. relatively secure frontiers (pp. 177–178)
     b. Greek as the language of church, state, and culture
     c. exclusive devotion to the Orthodox religious faith
     d. rich and varied urban life, centered in Constantinople

2. Early Byzantine civilization was NOT influenced by:
     a. Diocletian's division of the Roman Empire in the third century
     b. the rapid expansion of its empire in the sixth century
     c. the inroads made by the Islamic world after the eighth century
   * d. the rise of the Frankish state in the seventh and eighth centuries (p. 177)

3. During its thousand-year history, the heartland of Byzantium remained:
     a. Bulgaria and Serbia
   * b. Greece and Asia Minor (p. 178)
     c. Egypt and Syria
     d. Iran and Iraq

4. Byzantium and the Early Medieval West did NOT share which of the following?
     a. an economy whose basic source of wealth was agriculture
     b. a society dominated by a feudal aristocracy
     c. a population composed mainly of peasants
   * d. the Latin language as the language of church and state (pp. 177–178, 196–197, 198–199)

5. Justinian's reign was noteworthy for all of the following EXCEPT:
   * a. the movement to stamp out the human figure in religious art (pp. 178, 181–182)
     b. the reconquest of Italy, southern Spain, and North Africa
     c. a major revision of Roman law
     d. an overextension of Byzantine conquests and the empire that later undermined Byzantine governments

6. When Constantinople was conquered in 1453, the mantle of leadership of Byzantine civilization was claimed by:
   a. the Bulgarian kingdom
   b. the Ottoman empire
   * c. the Russian state (p. 180)
   d. France

7. Which was NOT a legacy of Byzantium to the West?
   a. Orthodox missionaries introduced civilization and religion to the Slavic peoples of eastern Europe.
   b. The Code of Justinian became the standard legal text studied in medieval universities.
   * c. The Byzantine prohibition of human figures in religious art was adopted by the West's Catholic church. (pp. 180–185, 205)
   d. Elements of Byzantine art appeared in Renaissance art in Italy.

8. The Golden Age of Byzantium occurred during the reign of:
   a. Justinian and his dynasty
   * b. the Macedonian dynasty (p. 180)
   c. the Comneni dynasty
   d. the Paleologian dynasty

9. The final conquest of Byzantium was in 1453 by the:
   a. European Crusaders
   b. Seljuk Turks
   * c. Ottoman Turks (p. 181)
   d. Bulgarians

10. Which is NOT a correct distinction between the Western Christian church and the Eastern Orthodox church?
    a. The Western church was ruled by the pope from Rome; the Eastern church was governed by the patriarch of Constantinople.
    * b. The Western church worshiped God in the form of the Trinity; the Eastern church accepted God as being a Unity (One). (pp. 181, 198–200)
    c. Latin was the official language in the West, Greek in the East.
    d. Western priests were celibate; Orthodox priests could marry.

11. Which was NOT a consequence of Byzantium's Iconoclastic Controversy?
    * a. After the controversy ended, Byzantine artists were prohibited from portraying the human figure in religious painting. (pp. 181, 185)
    b. During the controversy, nearly all religious pictures were destroyed.
    c. The controversy contributed to the widening split between the Western Christian church and the Eastern Orthodox church.
    d. The controversy aligned the emperor, the bishops, the army, and the civil service against the monks.

12. All are features of Byzantine law EXCEPT:
    a. Disputes should be settled by court proceedings.
    b. The individual should be shielded against unreasonable demands of society.
    * c. Criminal cases should be adjudicated in trials by a jury of peers. (p. 182)
    d. The limits of a ruler's legitimate power is an issue for courts to determine.

13. The first known work of history by a woman was:
    a. *Muqaddima*
    * b. *The Alexiad* (p. 182)
    c. *History of the Franks*
    d. *History of the English Church and People*

14. Which was NOT an influence on Byzantine architecture?
    * a. The Germanic tradition influenced decorative schemes made of foliage and interwoven lines. (p. 183)
    b. The Oriental tradition contributed rich ornamentation and riotous color.
    c. The Greco-Roman tradition supplied columns, arches, vaults, and domes.
    d. The Christian Bible was the source of subjects for interior decorations.

15. A significant innovation in Byzantine architecture was the:
    a. dome
    * b. pendentive (p. 183)
    c. pointed arch
    d. flying buttress

16. The most magnificent church built in the Byzantine world was:
    a. San Vitale in Ravenna
    * b. Hagia Sophia in Constantinople (p. 183)
    c. Sant' Apollinare in Classe
    d. Dafni near Athens

17. Which was NOT an aspect of the style of Byzantine mosaics and paintings?
    a. Feet point downward.
    b. Figures are rendered in two dimensions.
    * c. Gestures are made expressive. (p. 185)
    d. Figures seem to float in space.

18. Which was NOT an aspect of the church of San Vitale in Ravenna?
    a. It was commissioned by the emperor Justinian.
    b. It is covered with a dome.
    c. It features two impressive mosaics, one of Justinian and his court and the other of the empress Theodora and her retinue.
    * d. It is based on the architectural plan of Rome's Pantheon. (pp. 184–185 and caption for Fig. 8.6)

19. The word *islam* means:
    * a. submission (p. 185)
    b. holy
    c. universal
    d. pure

20. Medieval Islamic civilization did NOT embrace this territory:
    a. southern Spain
    * b. France (p. 188)
    c. Syria
    d. Northern Africa

21. The pre-Islamic Arabs trace their ancestry to:
    * a. Abraham and the Hebrew patriarchs (p. 188)
      b. Homer and the Ionian Greeks
      c. Dido and the Carthaginians
      d. Hector and the Trojans

22. The Arab calendar dates from this historic event:
      a. the first vision that Muhammad received from God
    * b. the flight of Muhammad and followers from Mecca to Yathrib (p. 188)
      c. the conquest of Arabia
      d. the death of Muhammad

23. Muhammad, in his early career, came into conflict with Arab leaders over which of the following locations:
    * a. the Kaaba (pp. 188–189)
      b. the Dome of the Rock
      c. the Alhambra
      d. Hagia Sophia

24. The golden age of Islam occurred:
      a. in the century after the death of Muhammad
    * b. during the Abbasid dynasty of the eighth to thirteenth centuries (p. 189)
      c. after the Abbasid dynasty, in the fourteenth and fifteenth centuries
      d. when the Ottomans came to power in the fifteenth century

25. Between 800 and 1100, Arabic scholarship was more advanced than Western scholarship in all of the following areas EXCEPT:
      a. medicine
      b. mathematics
    * c. history (p. 190)
      d. science

26. All of the following apply to the status of women in Islamic society EXCEPT:
    * a. Muslim women who engaged in manual labor had legal protection. (pp. 189–190)
      b. The Koran gave superior rights to fathers and husbands.
      c. Muhammad's teachings enhanced the general status of women.
      d. The Koran allowed polygamy.

27. What are the two central beliefs of the Islamic religion?
      a. "There are two gods, Ahuramazda and Ahriman, and Zoroaster is their Prophet."
      b. "There is but one god, Yahweh, and Muhammad is his Prophet."
    * c. "There is but one God, Allah, and Muhammad is his Prophet." (p. 190)
      d. "There are two Gods, Yahweh and Satan, and Mani is their Prophet."

28. Which is NOT a required devotional practice by devout Muslims?
    * a. to confess one's sins to the priest (p. 190)
      b. to pray five times a day facing Mecca
      c. to fast during the lunar month of Ramadan
      d. to give alms to the poor

29. Which of these does NOT have authority over devout Muslims?
    a. the Koran
    b. the Hadith
    c. the Shari'a
* d. the Muqaddima (p. 190)

30. Ibn Khaldun argued that history should have this characteristic:
    a. Emphasize the role of divine forces.
* b. Focus on the human desire to bond with certain groups. (p. 190)
    c. Stress the shaping power of economics.
    d. Concentrate on the central role of "great men" in events.

31. In Muslim science, scholars did all of the following EXCEPT:
    a. Translate the Greek scientific texts and preserve them.
    b. Build on the Greek heritage.
* c. Borrow from Chinese medicine. (p. 190)
    d. Transmit their scientific knowledge to medieval Christians.

32. Which was NOT an achievement of Muslim science?
* a. invention of the calculus (p. 190)
    b. development of the algebraic system
    c. first making the clinical distinction between measles and smallpox
    d. transformation of the Hindu numeration system into the Arabic numerals

33. Which was NOT an influence on Islamic architecture?
    a. the Greco-Roman arcade
* b. the Egyptian pyramid (pp. 190–191)
    c. the Persian vaulted hall
    d. the Byzantine pendentive

34. The dominant architectural structure in Islam is the:
    a. temple
    b. fortress-palace
* c. mosque (p. 191)
    d. tomb

35. This type of Islamic art was developed in spite of the Koran's prohibition against figurative art:
    a. arabesque
* b. Persian miniature (p. 195)
    c. calligraphy
    d. decorations of mihrabs in mosques

36. Which is NOT a characteristic feature of an Islamic mosque?
    a. a nearby minaret for prayer calls
    b. an open courtyard
* c. rows of benches to accommodate the faithful (pp. 191–193)
    d. rich decorations of mosaics, Oriental carpets, and calligraphic friezes

37. Which was NOT a feature of life in the West after the collapse of Rome?
    a. It was based on farming.
    b. It exhibited a low standard of living for the bulk of the population.
    c. It had a restricted economy based on barter.
* d. It lacked any central guiding moral authority. (p. 196)

38. Select the INCORRECT matchup of tribe and place of final settlement:
    a. Visigoths in Spain
    b. Vandals in North Africa
    * c. Saxons in Italy (p. 196)
    d. Burgundians in southern France

39. The first important ruler among the Franks was:
    a. Pepin
    b. Charlemagne
    * c. Clovis (p. 196)
    d. Charles Martel

40. Charlemagne's success in holding his vast kingdom together was the result of all of the following EXCEPT:
    a. a relatively efficient bureaucracy
    * b. the backing of the Byzantine emperor (p. 197)
    c. the help of the Roman Catholic Church
    d. a powerful army

41. Early monasteries for women may be described in all of the following ways EXCEPT:
    * a. The female orders adopted the Gregorian rules. (p. 199)
    b. At first, nuns and monks shared the same facilities, but later, separate facilities known as nunneries were established.
    c. Nunneries became havens for women during invasions.
    d. Convents included women forced by their families to take the veil as brides of Christ.

42. Pope Gregory the Great made all of these contributions EXCEPT:
    * a. He crowned the Frankish king as the new emperor. (pp. 198–199)
    b. He sent missionaries to England.
    c. He wrote hymns and music for church ceremonies.
    d. He reformed the clergy.

43. Benedictine monks did NOT:
    a. Follow strict guidelines in their daily lives.
    b. Go through a rigorous education before becoming monks.
    c. Use their days working, praying, and studying.
    * d. Prove their faith by fasting for forty days. (pp. 199–200)

44. The Byzantine historian Anna Comnena, the Muslim writer Usamah, and the German bishop Liudprand shared this attitude:
    a. They respected cultural differences.
    b. They advocated democratic ideas.
    * c. They were critical of foreigners. (Personal Perspective)
    d. They wanted to reduce religious influence in their countries.

45. In the *Consolation of Philosophy*, Boethius:
    a. argued that everything always turns out for the best
    * b. described his search for happiness (p. 200)
    c. denounced Christianity
    d. rejected intellectual inquiry as a way to the truth

46. Which was NOT correct for the Carolingian Renaissance?
   * a. It resulted in innovative literary and artistic works in various genres. (pp. 200–201)
   b. It was the most important intellectual movement between the collapse of Rome and the learning revolution of the twelfth century.
   c. It was essentially an educational movement.
   d. It was led by the best minds at the court of Charlemagne.

47. The leading intellectual who was primarily responsible for the founding of Charlemagne's palace school was:
   a. Einhard
   b. Ethelred
   c. Bede
   * d. Alcuin (p. 201)

48. Which was NOT correct for Einhard's biography of Charlemagne?
   a. It presents a firsthand account of the life of this great man.
   b. It was modeled on the writings of Roman historians such as Suetonius.
   * c. It criticizes the imperialistic ambitions of its subject. (p. 201)
   d. It reflects the author's general admiration for his subject.

49. The new Carolingian minuscule accomplished all of these EXCEPT:
   a. It made documents and other written materials more accessible to the educated.
   b. It created a writing form of capital and small letters.
   * c. It inaugurated a series of literary works that lasted for a century. (p. 201 and caption for Fig. 8.21)
   d. It cut down on the number of errors that monks might make in recopying documents.

50. Which is NOT correct regarding Gregorian chants?
   a. They were named for Pope Gregory the Great, who codified their usage.
   b. They were used in the ceremonies of the church.
   c. They were sung by male voices only.
   * d. They were divided into four parts, to achieve beautiful harmonies. (pp. 201–202)

51. Charlemagne's Palace Chapel can be characterized as:
   * a. a combination of Byzantine, Roman, and Germanic influences (p. 202)
   b. heavily influenced by Islamic architecture
   c. a square building of three stories
   d. an original structure uninfluenced by previous building styles

52. Charlemagne's Palace Chapel:
   a. symbolized the ruler's earthly power
   b. was constructed to impress those who stood within its walls
   c. became a sacred place for later ceremonies, such as coronations
   * d. all of the above (p. 202 and caption for Fig. 8.22)

53. Illuminated manuscripts had this purpose:
   * a. to decorate sacred writings and Bibles (p. 202)
   b. to impress the masses with the power of the emperor
   c. to transmit secret messages among the monkish scribes
   d. to educate the illiterate

54. Which was NOT correct regarding medieval illuminated manuscripts?
    a. Their decorative schemes became more complex over the years.
    b. They were filled with Christian symbols.
  * c. Monastic scriptoria (painting studios) could mass-produce them. (pp. 202–203)
    d. They allowed monk-artists to express both their devotion to God and their artistic talents.

55. By the end of the Early Medieval period, the West could be characterized as:
    a. directly affected by events in Byzantium and Islam
  * b. a fusion of Classical, Germanic, and Christian elements (p. 205)
    c. the dominant power to emerge after the collapse of Rome
    d. in danger of falling back into a dark age

9

THE HIGH MIDDLE AGES
The Christian Centuries

TEACHING STRATEGIES AND SUGGESTIONS

The High Middle Ages can be introduced with a Standard Lecture that gives a Historical Overview, setting forth the key historical and cultural milestones of this period. After this opening, either of two approaches may be used to teach the section on feudalism. One approach is the Patterns of Change model, which will allow the instructor to analyze the origins of feudalism and trace its development from its simple beginning to its later, more complex stages. A second strategy is to focus on the feudal monarchies, using a Comparison/Contrast approach to point out their similarities and differences. Whichever approach is used, the instructor should underscore the idea that the papal monarchy functioned just like a secular monarchy in the High Middle Ages.

Another major theme in the High Middle Ages is Christianity, which may be approached in two ways. A variation on the Reflections/Connection model can be adopted to show the relationships between the church and other medieval institutions (political, social, and economic) as well as the way that Christian values helped to shape standards of public and private morality. Second, the Patterns of Change model can be applied to demonstrate the fluctuating fortunes of the church. As part of this presentation on the church, the instructor can also discuss institutions in general, dealing with such features of institutional development as life cycles, purposes for seeking power, and innate contradictions.

Scholasticism can also be treated with the Patterns of Change model. For almost the first time since teaching the Classical period, the instructor has enough material to delve into the personalities of many key figures being studied, including Peter Abelard, Peter Lombard, and Thomas Aquinas. The teacher can also apply the Diffusion model to show the significant impact of Arab artists and intellectuals on Christian civilization. In light of the contemporary debate about opening the canon of Western culture, it is important to stress the role of the Arabs in the development of medieval Christian science, architecture, and literature.

The teacher can use the Reflections/Connections model to show influences—particularly those of feudalism and the church—on the medieval arts and humanities. With the Diffusion model, the instructor can set forth the shift from the monastic, feudal culture of the first half of this period to the courtly, urban culture of the second half; in literature, this shift is represented by the change from the chansons de geste to romances, from monkish poets to the secular Dante; and, in theology, by the change from Abelard to Thomas Aquinas. In addition, the instructor, employing the Patterns of Change approach, can trace the evolution of architecture from the Romanesque to the Gothic; and a Slide Lecture or films can illustrate the two artistic styles. As a conclusion to the High Middle Ages, the instructor can use the Spirit of the Age approach to demonstrate the medieval synthesis that embraced Dante's *Divine Comedy*, the Gothic cathedrals, Thomist philosophy, and scholastic reasoning.

LECTURE OUTLINE

I. Historical Overview
   A. Major events of the High Middle Ages
   B. The medieval synthesis
   C. The two phases of the era

II. Feudalism
   A. The feudal system and the feudal society
      1. Origins of feudalism
      2. Characteristics of feudalism
      3. Spread of feudalism
      4. Chivalric code
         a) Impact on men
         b) Impact on women
   B. Peasant life
      1. Serfdom
      2. Daily routines
   C. The rise of towns
      1. Rise in population and migrations
      2. Town life
         a) At odds with feudal system
         b) Work and commerce
            (1) Trade routes
            (2) Role of women
   D. The feudal monarchy
      1. The French monarchy
         a) The Capetian kings
         b) Institutional developments
      2. The English monarchy
         a) Norman England
         b) Conflicts between kings and barons
      3. The Holy Roman Empire
         a) Lay investiture
         b) Failure to centralize
      4. The papal monarchy
         a) Reform movements
         b) Powerful popes

III. Medieval Christianity and the Church
   A. Structure and hierarchy
   B. Christian beliefs and practices
      1. Church as way to salvation
      2. Rituals and ceremonies
         a) Inseparable from doctrine
         b) Seven sacraments
   C. Religious orders and lay piety
      1. Monasteries and nunneries
         a) Hildegard of Bingen
         b) *Scivias* or *May You Know* or *Know the Way*
      2. Mendicant orders

1000–1300

In Africa, Bantu, Arab, and Indian cultures blend in Swahili civilization on eastern African coast, 1110–1500; rise of the kingdom of Mali, after 1200; Benin becomes the richest Nigerian forest kingdom, after about 1100; in Nigeria, the terra-cotta art of the Yoruba people In Andean culture, Late Intermediate period, 900–1438; rise of the Chimú peoples; the Chimú capital, Chan Chan, with its palaces, offices, and graves, built largely of adobe In China, Northern Sung dynasty, 960–1126; in eleventh century, women's status declined as result of foot-binding, a practice continued among the upper classes until the twentieth century; the founding of the Imperial Academy of Painting, 1101; Chang Tse-tsuan's (1085–1145) scroll painting of the Northern Sung capital of Kaifen; the "Ying Tsao Ea Shih," a building manual, 1103; Southern Sung dynasty, 1127–1279; landscape painting at its height, 1141–1279; Neo-Confucianism, 1130–1200; explosive powder used in weapons, 1150; Yüan dynasty, 1271–1368; Mongols found Yüan dynasty and make Beijing their capital; Kublai Khan, 1260–1294, extends Mongol empire to southern China and Southeast Asia; high level of religious tolerance as Kublai recruits bureaucrats from all faiths and Buddhist, Taoist, and Confucian temples, Christian churches, and Muslim mosques are tax-exempt; drama flourishes; Wang Shifu's *Story of the Western Wing,* one of China's most popular dramas, thirteenth century; Marco Polo in China, 1275–1292; the Tibetan-style Miao-ying-ssu pagoda in Peking, 1271

In Himalayan region, in Kasmir, the temple of Siva at Pandrenthanm, twelfth century; in Nepal, Malla dynasty, 1200–1768; founding of three great capitals, Katmandu, Patan, and Bhadgaon; in Tibet, revival after 1100 under Indian influence; conquest by Mongols, thirteenth century

In India, gradual Muslim dominance, after 1000; invasions of Muslims from central Asia lead to Muslim dominance in north India and introduction of Persian culture and Islamic religion into south Asia; Jayadeva's *Gitagovinda,* an erotic poem about the god Krishna, in Sanskrit, twelfth century; two large rock-cut *sangharama,* monasteries, at Ellora, eleventh to twelfth centuries; Delhi sultanate, 1192–1526; famous iron- and steelwork, especially swords, eleventh century

In Indochina, in Burma, stable and centralized rule under Anawrahta, 1044–1077, and Kyanzittha, 1084–1112; great building program, including the cave-buildings of Ananda, 1091,

V. The Legacy of the Christian Centuries

and Thatbyinnyu, 1144; the stupa of Mingalazedi, begun 1274; conquest by the Mongols led by Kublai Khan, in 1287 and end of Burmese dynasty; in Siam, freedom from Khmer rule and founding of first independent state at Sukhodaya, under King Ram Kamheng, 1281–1300; this dynasty lasts until 1767; Brah Prang Sam Yot, a Khmer sanctuary in the Lop Buri region; Wat Kukut at Lamphun, a Buddhist monument, 1218

In Japan, Heian period, 794–1185; Hachiman sanctuary at Tsurugaoka, twelfth century; the Jingoji temple, Kyoto, early twelfth century; *The Pillow-Book of Sei Shonagon*, the diary of a lady-in-waiting to an empress, early eleventh century; *The Tale of Genji* by Lady Murasaki, a classic of world literature, 1015; the Great Buddha, Kamakura, Honshu, in about 1250; acme of swordmaking, 1185–1333; the first instance of a ritual suicide (*seppuku*) by a feudal warrior, 1170; Kyoto in 1185 has 500,000 people, larger than any city in the West, except perhaps Córdoba and Constantinople; Shogunate established, 1192; Kamakura period, 1185–1333; start of military rule, as samurai warriors replace nobles as actual rulers; "warrior style" architecture, as seen in use of narrow moats or stockades and grouping buildings to ensure defense and replacing gardens with training grounds; Buddhist religious architecture included the Indian style, as in the reconstructed Tōdaiji, Kyoto, the Chinese style, as in the Kenninji monastery, Kyoto, and the Wayo, the national style of Japan; imperial court remains in Kyoto but shogun's governing organization is based in Kamakura, south of Tokyo; Zen Buddhism in Japan, 1200; Sanjusangendo Temple, Kyoto, 1266; Toshio starts porcelain manufacture, 1227; *The Confessions of Lady Nyō,* a novel of a court lady's love affairs, thirteenth to fourteenth centuries; "An Account of My Hut," by Kamo no Chōmei, a Buddhist poet disenchanted with the world, 1212

In Korea, Koryo Kingdom, 918–1392; successive invasions by the Bitan, the Jurchen, and the Mongols; the nine-story pagoda of Wol-chong-sa at P'yong-ch'ang Kun, eleventh century; the temple of Keuk-nak Chon of the Pong-chong-sa at An-dong Kun, twelfth to thirteenth centuries; the capital of Song-do (Kaesong), with its palaces, gardens, and staircases, is destroyed during these invasions

In Mesoamerica, Historic period, 900–1521; rise of Toltec culture and the founding of Tula in the Valley of Mexico and the revitalization of Tajín in Veracruz and Xochicalco, near Cuernavaca, about 1000; bloodthirsty rituals, demanded by the god of war, practiced at Tajín and depicted in the stone reliefs; great temple at

Tajín; Toltec stone caryatids from the temple at Tula; introduction of the Toltec warrior code; the *Great Chac-Mool,* reclining limestone figure from Maya-Toltec culture, 1100 (an influence on Henry Moore's modern sculpture); Toltec defeated in 1160, though the capital of Tula remained inhabited until 1224, when it was destroyed by the Chichimecs; Toltecs built a new city at Chichén Itzá, in the Yucatán, which was filled with buildings, figures of chac-mool, and a sacred well; decline of Mayan culture in the thirteenth century and continual warfare among the rival cities; Mixtecs dominate the Puebla-Oaxaca regions; the Mixtecs produce several books in pictographic writing, including the Codex Nuttall, the Codex Vindobonensis, the Codex Bodleian, and the Codex Colombino; Mixtec decorative art; Mixtec additions to the Zapotec temple-city of Monte Albán; the architecture of Mitla near Oaxaca

In Muslim world, expansion of Islam, 1000–1500; Firdausi (about 940–about 1020), *The Book of Kings,* the Persian epic, a poetic chronicle of the entire history of Persia, from the creation to the Sasanian Empire, about 1010; Rumi, 1207–1273, Persian poet, founder of the Order of Dancing Dervishes, considered the greatest mystical poet of Persia; Rumi's fame rests on the *Mathnawi,* a collection of poems; Sadi, a didactic poet, about 1213–1292, author of the poem collection called *Rose Garden*, 1258; Avicenna, Arab philosopher, d. 1037; Averroes, Arab philosopher, 1126–1198; Omar Khayyam, d. 1123, Persian poet, author of the *Rubaiyat*

In North America, in American Southwest, trade in cotton yarn; trade in jade with Mexico; in Alaska, ivory figurines in the Punuk culture; Cahokia in Illinois becomes largest town (10,000) in North America, about 1050

In Polynesia, Easter Island, one of the last unsettled areas of the world, is colonized, about 600; the erection of rows of giant statues, after 1000

In Southeast Asia, spread of Buddhism from India, adoption of Sanskrit, the Indian script

LEARNING OBJECTIVES

To learn:

1. The origins, evolution, and spread of feudalism

2. The impact of the chivalric code on feudal society and how it helped shape relationships between men and women

3. The rise, characteristics, and impact of courtly love

4. The nature of peasant life

5. The way of life in medieval towns

6. The similarities and differences among the feudal monarchies

7. The reasons for the successes and failures of feudal monarchies, including the papacy

8. How the church maintained its dominance of society and culture

9. The origins and influence of the new monastic orders for both men and women

10. The development and impact of lay piety

11. The sources of the heresies and the fate of the Albigensians

12. The nature and characteristics of scholasticism

13. The issues involved in the medieval intellectual debates and how they were resolved

14. The medieval synthesis of Thomas Aquinas

15. The characteristics of monastic writing and a representative example of this literary genre

16. Examples of feudal writing and its themes

17. The characteristics of courtly romances and examples of this literary genre

18. The importance of Dante and examples of his writings, in particular the structure and meaning of the *DivineComedy*

19. The development of Romanesque architecture and its main features

20. The transition from the Romanesque to the Gothic style

21. The Gothic cathedral styles, including different phases with examples, chief features, and decorative principles

22. The role, evolution, and impact of music in the High Middle Ages

23. Historic "firsts" achieved in the High Middle Ages that became legacies for later Western developments: the writings of Dante; the theology of Thomas Aquinas, or Thomism; Romanesque and Gothic artistic styles; the epic, the romance, and the chivalric tale; courtly love with its shared social roles for men and women; the legends of King Arthur and the Knights of the Round Table; the basic theoretical system for composing music; and the love song

24. The role of the High Middle Ages in transmitting the heritage from earlier civilizations: redefining the liberal arts curriculum within the context of Catholic faith; rediscovering ancient Classical philosophy and science from Muslim scholars; and reviving Aristotelianism and the rationalist tradition and integrating it with the teachings of the Christian faith

SUGGESTIONS FOR FILMS

Art of the Middle Ages. Encyclopedia Britannica, 30 min., color.

Chartres Cathedral. Encyclopedia Britannica, 30 min., color.

Civilisation: The Great Thaw. Time-Life, 50 min., color.

The Medieval Mind. Encyclopedia Britannica, 26 min., color.

Medieval Times: The Role of the Church. Coronet, 14 min., color.

Middle Ages: Rise of Feudalism. Encyclopedia Britannica, 20 min., color.

SUGGESTIONS FOR MUSIC

German Plainchant & Polyphony. Schola Antiqua. Elektra/Nonesuch H-71312; 71312-4 [cassette].

Gregorian Chant. Deller Consort. Harmonia Mundi 234.

The Memory of Thomas à Becket. (twelfth-century Mass). Schola Hungarica. Hungaroton SLPD-12458 (D); MK-12458 [CD].

The Play of St. Nicholas. (twelfth-century liturgical drama). New York Ensemble for Early Music. Musicmasters 20001X; 20001 W [cassette].

Songs of Chivalry. Martin Best Medieval Ensemble. Nimbus NI-5006 [CD].

Troubadours, Trouveres and Minnesingers (Songs and Dances of the Middle Ages). Augsburg Ensemble for Early Music. Christophorus CD-74519 [CD].

SUGGESTIONS FOR FURTHER READING

Agius, D. A., and Hitchcock, R., eds. *The Arab Influence on Medieval Europe.* Reading, England: Ithaca Press, 1994. Seven essays dealing with Arabic influences on medieval European culture.

Aries, P., and Duby, G., eds. *A History of Private Life.* Vol. II, *Revelations of the Medieval World.* Translated by A. Goldhammer. Cambridge: Harvard University Press, 1988. Groundbreaking work that deals with ordinary life, particularly that of often neglected groups, such as women and homosexuals.

Barraclough, G. *The Medieval Papacy.* New York: Harcourt, Brace & World, 1968. Still the standard in the field, with many well-chosen illustrations.

Bloch, M. L. B. *Feudal Society.* Translated by L. A. Manyon. London: Routledge, 1989. Bloch's study, first published in France in 1961, is regarded today as the standard treatise on European feudalism.

Cantor, N. F. *The Civilization of the Middle Ages.* New York: HarperCollins, 1993. A completely revised and expanded edition of Cantor's highly respected work, *Medieval History, the Life and Death of a Civilization.*

Duby, G. *The Three Orders: Feudal Society Imagined.* Translated by A. Goldhammer. Chicago: University of Chicago Press, 1980. A learned study by one of France's leading scholars.

Ennen, E. *The Medieval Town.* Translated by N. Fryde. Amsterdam: North-Holland, 1979. First published in Dutch in 1972, this translation is the best general account in English of the flourishing cities of Europe's Middle Ages.

Herlihy, D. *Women, Family, and Society in Medieval Europe: Historical Essays, 1978–1991.* Providence, R.I.: Berghahn Books, 1995. Interpretive essays on medieval society by an acknowledged expert in feminist and family history.

Jackson, W. T. H. *Medieval Literature: A History and a Guide.* New York: Collier Books, 1966. Still the best survey in this field; covers both Latin and vernacular writings.

Kirshner, J., and Wemple, S. *Women of the Medieval World.* Oxford: Basil Blackwell, 1985. A good introduction to the study of women in medieval Europe.

Knowles, D. *The Evolution of Medieval Thought*. London: Longman, 1988. An update by D. E. Luscombe and C. N. L. Brooke of Knowles's popular study, so that it remains a serviceable guide to the main currents of European thought in the Middle Ages.

Labarge, M. W. *Women in Medieval Life: A Small Sound of the Trumpet*. London: Hamish Hamilton, 1986. A survey of the activities of several women from various social groups.

Snyder, J. *Medieval Art. Painting, Sculpture, Architecture. 4th–14th Century*. New York: Abrams, 1989. An authoritative survey of a thousand years of medieval art; especially good discussions of architectural types and symbols; divided into five parts, one of which deals with Byzantium.

Stokstad, M. *Medieval Art*. New York: Harper & Row, 1986. A readable guide based on recent scholarship.

Wilson, C. *The Gothic Cathedral: The Architecture of the Great Church, 1130–1530*. New York: Thames and Hudson, 1990. A handsome survey of Gothic cathedral architecture with the focus on the "Great Churches" built for wealthy corporate patrons, such as monasteries, collegiate foundations, and city parishes.

IDENTIFICATIONS

chivalric code	tympanum
friars	narthex
cathedral	ribbed vault
scholasticism	pier
Realism	flying buttress
Nominalism	choir
via media	rose window
goliard	blind arcade
chanson de geste	gargoyle
vernacular language	gallery
canzone	*Rayonnant*
minstrel	tracery
troubador	trope
romance	liturgical drama
lay	polyphony
terza rima	organum
Romanesque style	motet
Gothic style	lute
bay	

PERSONAL PERSPECTIVE BACKGROUND

Hildegard of Bingen, *Scivias*

Hildegard of Bingen's heavenly visions illustrate the problem the medieval church faced in dealing with those who claimed to speak with inspired authority. The general view held by ecclesiastical authorities was that in the earthly church, only ordained priests could communicate directly with God, and even in those instances the pope had the last word. Hence, when Hildegard reports (in the Personal Perspective) what "a voice said to me from heaven," she is claiming divine authority for her views. Fortunate for her, church leaders such as St. Bernard of Clairvaux and secular rulers such as Emperor Frederick Barbarossa received her letters with equanimity and corresponded with her on equal terms. (What they made, however, of some of her pronouncements is unclear; for example, "[T]he Empire and the Papacy, sunk into impiety, shall crumble away together.") The church's policy of toleration toward mystic utterances changed, however, in the Late Middle Ages, when the messages of visionaries often were directed against what were perceived as church corruption and abuses. (More information on Hildegard of Bingen may be found in *The Western Humanities* and *Readings in the Western Humanities*.)

DISCUSSION/ESSAY QUESTIONS

1. Discuss the origins of feudalism and its impact on society.
2. In what ways did the rise of feudalism indicate that life was becoming more settled and organized in western Europe?
3. What was the chivalric code, and how did it manifest itself in feudal society?
4. Discuss the separate roles that men and women played in the feudal aristocracy, and describe how these roles affected their relationships with each other.
5. Discuss the impact of women on feudal society and feudal values.
6. Compare and contrast the life of a peasant on a manor with that of a town merchant.
7. Discuss the characteristics of medieval secular monarchy (France, England, and the Holy Roman Empire), and note some common problems and issues and how they dealt with them.
8. Discuss the contributions of the three major medieval popes, and assess their impact on the church and medieval society.
9. Compare and contrast the papal monarchy with the medieval secular monarchies.
10. Show how the medieval church was both helped and hindered by its institutional organization.
11. Discuss the impact of new religious orders and the lay piety movements on the medieval church.
12. Discuss the life of Hildegard of Bingen, and assess her impact on medieval literature and religious thought.
13. What is meant by the term *medieval synthesis*? Show how this term applies, or does not apply, to medieval society and culture.
14. What is meant by the term *scholasticism*? What does the style of scholastic reasoning reveal about the nature of the medieval mind?
15. Explain the differences between Realism and Nominalism. Who were the major supporters, and what were their basic arguments for each of these philosophical positions?
16. How did Thomas Aquinas reconcile faith and reason?
17. Summarize the ideas in Aquinas's thought.
18. What was Thomas Aquinas's most important contribution? Explain.
19. What were the main themes in *The Song of Roland*? How did these themes express the ideals of feudalism?
20. Discuss the origins and characteristics of courtly romances.
21. Write an essay comparing *The Song of Roland* with the romances of Chrétien de Troyes, and show how they reflected the changing nature of feudal society.
22. Discuss the main allegorical and theological features of Dante's *Divine Comedy*. Explain how this work summarizes medieval thought.
23. Identify the major characteristics and features of Romanesque architecture, and show how they are evident in the church at Vézelay.
24. How does Notre Dame cathedral, Paris, manifest the Early Gothic style?
25. Describe the High Gothic style, and show how Amiens cathedral is representative of this style.
26. Define *medieval synthesis*. How do Dante's *Divine Comedy* and Notre Dame cathedral, Paris, respectively express the ideal of medieval synthesis?
27. Trace the evolution of music in the High Middle Ages, and describe its use by the church.
28. Name at least three legacies from the High Middle Ages, and show how they are still part of the Western tradition.

MULTIPLE-CHOICE QUESTIONS

1. During the High Middle Ages:
    a. The Christian church suffered many setbacks and lost its followers.
    * b. Feudalism emerged as a stabilizing influence in society. (p. 207)
    c. Town life continued to stagnate with no growth.
    d. The class structure was the same as in Roman times.

2. The feudal system rested primarily on:
    a. economic coercion by the wealthy
    b. the moral foundations of the church
    * c. personal loyalty and kinship (p. 207)
    d. the lingering influence of Charlemagne's kingdom

3. Feudalism evolved into a set of relationships between:
    a. lords and peasants
    b. lords and clerics
    * c. lords and vassals (pp. 207–208)
    d. popes and kings

4. The obligations of vassalage did NOT include:
    a. responsibilities for both lord and vassal
    * b. farmwork from the vassal (p. 208)
    c. military service from the vassal
    d. military protection from the lord

5. The chivalric code can be best described as:
    a. a set of feudal regulations for peasants
    b. the guidelines for new monastic orders
    * c. an unwritten code of conduct for vassals (p. 208)
    d. the business charters for towns

6. Which does NOT apply to the role of women in medieval culture?
    a. In courtly literature, they were made objects of veneration.
    b. In religious literature, they were condemned because of Eve's sin.
    c. In reality, some women exercised power through a father or a husband.
    * d. In reality, they were recognized as equal to men. (p. 208)

7. Which would NOT describe the life of a peasant?
    a. Peasants worked hard but found some relief on Holy Days.
    b. Peasant families found it difficult to move from the manor.
    * c. Peasant life was the same all across Europe. (p. 209)
    d. Life improved for some after more efficient farming methods were introduced.

8. During the High Middle Ages, the population in Europe:
    a. declined
    b. remained stationary
    c. grew at a slow rate
    * d. nearly doubled (p. 209)

9. Medieval townspeople protected themselves from the feudal system by:
    a. forming alliances with the Muslims
    b. appealing to the pope for divine help
  * c. forming guilds to regulate and to improve the local economy (p. 209)
    d. rebelling against the feudal lords

10. One of the outgrowths of the feudal system was the:
    a. creation of Christendom
  * b. feudal monarchy (p. 210)
    c. unification of Europe
    d. further fragmentation of feudalism

11. The major domestic problem facing medieval monarchs was:
    a. how to keep the peasants happy
    b. what to do about the rise of the chartered towns
    c. the need to protect Europe against Muslim invasion
  * d. how to build a centralized rule (pp. 210–211)

12. Which was NOT a defining event in England during the High Middle Ages?
    a. the granting of the Magna Carta
    b. the Norman invasion
    c. the summoning of the first parliament
  * d. the investiture controversy (p. 211)

13. The lay investiture controversy centered on the question of:
    a. who possessed the power to control the fief—the lord or vassal
  * b. whether local lords or the church should appoint certain bishops to their office (p. 213)
    c. when a vassal should become a lay leader
    d. whether or not it was legal to give fiefs to subvassals

14. The major church reform that began in the tenth century started at:
    a. the castle of Louis the Pious
  * b. the Benedictine monastery at Cluny (p. 213)
    c. Rome under Pope Zacharius
    d. the church at Vézelay

15. The most powerful pope in the High Middle Ages was:
    a. Gregory VII
    b. Boniface VIII
    c. Urban II
  * d. Innocent III (p. 214)

16. Christian beliefs and ceremonies were NOT based on:
  * a. the wishes and opinions of believers (p. 215)
    b. the biblical scriptures
    c. the writings of church fathers and later commentaries
    d. past traditions and practices

17. The Christian practices of confession and penance meant that:
    a. A sinner could sin without fear of punishment.
  * b. A sinner could be absolved from sins and penalties could be erased. (p. 215)
    c. A sinner would be allowed into heaven.
    d. A sinner would automatically go to hell.

18. The medieval church taught that purgatory was:
    a. a place where the sinful dead were purged eternally for their sins
  * b. a place where the sinful dead suffered before going to heaven (p. 215)
    c. another name for Hell
    d. another name for Heaven

19. Which is NOT correct for the new religious orders of the High Middle Ages?
    a. They were originally created to work among the urban poor.
    b. They later became involved in higher education.
    c. They often began as mendicant, or begging orders.
  * d. They became hotbeds of heresy. (pp. 215–216)

20. Hildegard of Bingen's *Scivias* may be best described as:
    a. a treatise on political thought
    b. a comprehensive summary of theology
  * c. a visionary tract (p. 216)
    d. an allegorical romance

21. Hildegard of Bingen's achievements included all of the following EXCEPT:
    a. composer of the first morality play to be sung
    b. correspondent with major figures of her time
    c. author of works on the medical arts and science
  * d. philosopher who contributed to the Nominalist-Realist debate (p. 216)

22. The lay piety movement of the late twelfth century involved all of the following EXCEPT:
  * a. leadership of royal figures, such as Marie de France (p. 217)
    b. rise of unorthodox lay orders, such as the beghines and beghards
    c. appearance of freethinkers, such as Mechthild of Magdeburg's *The Flowing Light of the Godhead*
    d. caring for the sick at home and in hospitals

23. Which was NOT an influence on medieval culture?
    a. European peoples across national boundaries
    b. the arts and thought of the Classical world
  * c. Chinese civilization (pp. 218–220)
    d. Muslim civilization

24. Before the medieval universities appeared, most education in Europe was associated with all of the following EXCEPT:
    a. cathedral schools usually run by the bishops
    b. monastic schools operated by monks
    c. surviving schools from the time of Charlemagne
  * d. the schools of Plato and Aristotle in Athens (pp. 218–219)

25. Medieval church schools may NOT be described as:
    a. using Latin in the classroom
    b. being founded to train young men for careers in state and church
    c. having a curriculum based on the seven liberal arts
  * d. appealing mainly to the middle class (pp. 218–219)

26. Scholasticism's primary task was to:
    a. Reconcile the state-versus-church controversy.
    * b. Bring Aristotle's ideas into accord with Christian doctrine. (p. 219)
    c. Reconcile Platonism with Christian beliefs.
    d. Discover new areas of knowledge.

27. Peter Abelard's theological goal was to:
    a. Undermine the morals of his day.
    * b. Use reason to reconcile differences between church doctrine and biblical writings. (p. 219)
    c. Attack church dogma.
    d. Find proofs for the existence of God.

28. The debate between the Realists and Nominalists:
    a. was settled by a church council in 1215
    * b. centered on the issue of universals (p. 219)
    c. arose from attempts to reconcile Arabic thought and Christian beliefs
    d. was fought between the papacy and scholarly monks

29. The Nominalists believed that universals:
    a. were real and actually existed
    * b. existed only in the mind as useful devices to identify and categorize things (p. 219)
    c. were planted in the mind by God
    d. had existence only in an invisible world of truth

30. Which is NOT correct for those thinkers classified as Realists?
    * a. They were strict empiricists. (p. 219)
    b. They were influenced by Plato's theory of ideas.
    c. They believed that abstractions or ideas existed as universals.
    d. They opposed the Nominalists.

31. The Greek philosopher whose works became the heart of Scholasticism was:
    a. Protagoras
    * b. Aristotle (p. 220)
    c. Zeno
    d. Empedocles

32. Which is NOT true of the writings of Aristotle during the Middle Ages?
    a. They came to the West by way of Arabic scholars.
    * b. They were studied in secret as forbidden knowledge. (p. 220)
    c. They eventually became central to Christian thought.
    d. They became the point of disputes among medieval thinkers.

33. Thomas Aquinas in his writings about faith and reason:
    a. adopted the same position as the medieval thinker Bonaventure
    * b. tried to reconcile Aristotelian thought and Christian doctrine (p. 220)
    c. agreed with Averroes's teachings
    d. rejected Abelard and his tradition

34. Thomism might be best described as a:
    a. thought process that reconciled Greek and Arabic philosophy
    * b. synthesis of the faith-versus-reason debate (p. 220)
    c. failure to reconcile the dispute between the popes and the secular monarchs
    d. last effort in philosophy to prove the existence of God

35. Thomas Aquinas, in addition to writing on philosophical and theological topics, also:
    * a. addressed himself to such issues as the best form of government (p. 220)
    b. supported a new system for choosing the popes
    c. attacked the rigorous asceticism of monastic orders
    d. joined the soldiers of the crusade against the Albigensian heresy

36. The *goliards* are best known for their:
    a. lectures in the universities
    * b. songs and poems performed at aristocratic courts (pp. 220–221)
    c. contributions to the faith-versus-reason debate
    d. etiquette books aimed at middle-class readers

37. The *chanson de geste* is a literary genre known as:
    a. a morality play
    b. a mystery drama
    c. a sonnet
    * d. an epic poem (p. 221)

38. Which medieval ideal is NOT found in *The Song of Roland?*
    a. allegiance to the chivalric code
    * b. devotion to a highborn lady (pp. 221–222)
    c. support for Christianity against Islam
    d. loyalty to one's king

39. The *chansons de geste* were replaced after about 1150 by:
    a. secular plays
    * b. courtly romances (p. 222)
    c. religious dramas
    d. romantic novels

40. The most popular subject of medieval romances focused on:
    a. King Henry II and his wife Eleanor
    * b. King Arthur and his knights (p. 222)
    c. the Capetian dynasty
    d. ancient Greek myths

41. Which of the following is NOT correct regarding Chrétien de Troyes's *Lancelot?*
    * a. He blames Lancelot and Guinevere's love for the collapse of King Arthur's court. (p. 222)
    b. He identifies the suffering of Lancelot with that of Christ.
    c. He combines aristocratic, courtly, and religious themes.
    d. He portrays Lancelot as undergoing humiliation in order to earn Guinevere's love.

42. The literary genre *lay* was NOT:
    a. something like a shorter version of a *romance*
    b. usually sung to a court audience
    c. associated with the writings of Marie de France
    * d. written as a disguised religious allegory (p. 222)

43. In the *Divine Comedy*, Dante does NOT recount:
    a. in allegorical terms the experience of all human beings
    b. the claim that both reason and revelation are needed to understand God
    * c. the view that earthly fame is the only way to achieve eternal life (p. 223)
    d. in poetic form many theological arguments of his day

44. Besides Dante himself, the two main figures in the *Divine Comedy* are:
    a. Ganelon and Roland
  * b. Vergil and Beatrice (p. 223)
    c. Thomas Aquinas and the Virgin Mary
    d. Plato and Aristotle

45. The rhyme scheme of the *Divine Comedy* is:
  * a. *terza rima* (p. 223)
    b. *bel canto*
    c. rhymed couplets
    d. fourteen-line sonnet form

46. In its complex structure the *Divine Comedy* is the equivalent of a:
  * a. Gothic cathedral (passim)
    b. Romanesque church
    c. religious crusade
    d. chivalric tale

47. The dominant visual art of the medieval ages was:
  * a. architecture (p. 224)
    b. fresco painting
    c. portrait painting
    d. sculpture

48. The arts in the High Middle Ages were:
    a. treated separately, each being judged by different standards
    b. dominated by painting
  * c. subservient to religion and had no independent status (p. 224)
    d. used to entertain the public

49. In medieval art the four evangelists (Matthew, Mark, Luke, and John) are represented as:
    a. a winged lion, a dog, a fox, and a serpent, respectively
  * b. a man, a lion, a winged bull, and an eagle, respectively (caption for Fig. 9.10)
    c. a book, a fiery sword, a cross, and a banner, respectively
    d. a woman, an angel, a child, and a winged horse, respectively

50. Which of the following does NOT apply to Romanesque architecture?
  * a. Its dominant feature was the choir. (pp. 225–226, 228)
    b. It grew out of the basilica tradition.
    c. It reflected the needs of monastic life.
    d. It appeared to be a spiritual fortress in an unsettled period.

51. Which does NOT apply to Romanesque sculpture?
    a. It was a teaching device to carry the Christian message to the illiterate.
    b. It was primarily a decoration for churches.
    c. It seldom copied Greco-Roman models.
  * d. Its realistic nature was more important than its spiritual values. (pp. 226, 228)

52. The Gothic cathedral was identifiable by its:
  * a. flying buttresses, ribbed vaulting, stained glass windows (pp. 228–229)
    b. ribbed vaulting, rounded arches, thick walls
    c. flying buttresses, domed ceiling, many statues
    d. ribbed vaulting, stained glass windows, and simple decorations

53. Which of the following does NOT apply to Notre Dame cathedral, Paris?
    a. It exhibits the Gothic ideal of harmony.
    b. It contains an enormous choir.
*   c. It is erected with the Classical building method of post-beam-triangle construction.
        (pp. 230–231, 233)
    d. It integrates sculptural details into building units.

54. Early Gothic differed from High Gothic in all the following ways EXCEPT:
*   a. Early Gothic was taller with more elaborate spires than the High Gothic. (p. 234 and
        caption for Fig. 9.30)
    b. Early Gothic used rounded arches; High Gothic employed pointed arches.
    c. Early Gothic had simple apses, while High Gothic used massive choirs.
    d. Early Gothic was practically devoid of sculpture, while High Gothic used rich decorative
        schemes, including sculpture.

55. Developments in Gothic music included the:
*   a. appearance of the motet (p. 238)
    b. decline of secular music
    c. creation of the first symphony orchestra
    d. spread of opera

10

THE LATE MIDDLE AGES
1300–1500

TEACHING STRATEGIES AND SUGGESTIONS

The instructor can introduce the Late Middle Ages with a Standard Lecture that is organized as a Historical Overview, presenting the major milestones in the cultural sphere as well as the key political, economic, and social developments. With a Pattern of Change approach, the instructor can show the changes that occurred as High Gothic gave way to Late Gothic civilization; and a Slide Lecture can illustrate the accompanying stylistic shifts in the arts and architecture. In addition, the instructor can use the Reflections/Connections strategy to demonstrate that the change from High Gothic to Late Gothic was rooted in the period's multiple calamities.

Besides constituting the final phase of medieval civilization, the Late Medieval period also marks the first stirrings of the modern world. The best way to deal with this topic is to use a blend of the Spirit of the Age approach with the Comparison/Contrast technique, setting forth the death of the Middle Ages as the modern world struggles to be born. In this combined approach the instructor should concentrate on three major aspects of the emerging modern world: first, the shift from the medieval ideal of a unified Christian Europe to the modern reality of a system of rival states; second, a decline in the power of the church coupled with the rise of secular consciousness; and, third, the appearance of the painter Giotto, who set art on its modern path. A Slide Lecture is essential for understanding the radical nature of Giotto's artistic achievements. If circumstances allow, the instructor can organize a Discussion on the Late Middle Ages as a transition period, encouraging students to consider what has been gained and what has been lost by the shift from medieval to modern times.

LECTURE OUTLINE

Non-Western Events

I. Historical Overview
   A. The "calamitous" fourteenth century
   B. Breakup of the unique culture of the
      High Middle Ages

II. Hard Times Come to Europe
   A. Ordeal by plague, famine, and war
      1. The plague
         a) Its pattern and the death toll
         b) Types of plague
         c) Impact on culture
      2. Famine
         a) Patterns
         b) Impact on society

1300–1500
In Africa, Swahili civilization
   on eastern African cost,
   1100–1500; Egypt ruled by
   Mameluke sultans, former
   Turkish slaves, 1250–1517;
   Mali defeated by Sonni Ali
   of Songhay; at Benin,
   capital of the Edo
   kingdom, famous bronze
   sculpture; in West Africa,
   a Portuguese squadron
   returns from West Africa
   with a cargo of slaves,

3. War
   a) Patterns
   b) Impact on society and economics
B. Depopulation, rebellion, and industrialization
   1. Depopulation
      a) Reasons
      b) Impact on society and economics
   2. Rebellion
      a) Patterns
      b) Impact on society
   3. Industrialization
      a) Textiles
      b) New industries
C. The secular monarchies
   1. France
      a) Wars with England and Burgundy
      b) Rise of modern France
   2. England
      a) Wars with France
      b) The emergence of a strong Parliament
      c) The Tudor dynasty
   3. The spread of the French-English ruling style
D. The papal monarchy
   1. An age of decline
      a) Dislocation
         (1) The Avignon papacy
         (2) Impact on the church
      b) Schism
         (1) The Great Schism
         (2) Impact on the church
         (3) How settled
      c) The conciliar movement
   2. Restoration of papal power in about 1450

III. The Cultural Flowering of the Late Middle Ages
A. Breakdown of the medieval synthesis
B. Religion
   1. Absence of monastic reform
   2. Lay piety
      a) The *devotio moderna*
      b) The flagellants
   3. Heresies
      a) John Wycliffe
      b) Jan Hus
   4. The Inquisition
   5. Witchcraft
C. Theology, philosophy, and science
   1. The *via antiqua* versus the *via moderna*

1460—the beginning of the slave trade with Europe; Portuguese explorers reach Africa's Gold Coast, 1470; the Portuguese explorer Diego Cao discovers the mouth of the Congo River, 1484

In Andean culture, Late Intermediate period, 900–1438; Late Horizon, 1438–1534; the meteoric rise of the Inca people, starting in about 1438 with their first conquest; by the late 1400s, the Incas controlled the central Andes, from Quito in Ecuador to below Santiago in Chile, about 3,400 miles; great state builders; sculpting nature, terracing mountains, modifying stone outcrops, nestling cities into mountain peaks, and piling stone on stone; agricultural terraces at Pisac, the Sacred Rock at Machu Picchu, the Inca "throne" at Sacsahuaman; the capital of Cuzco was a city of fine buildings, noted for superb megalithic construction and fine masonry; the city of Machu Picchu, the most famous monument in ancient South America; the Observatory at Torreon; Inca tapestries and ceramics; Pizarro's conquest of the Incas, 1534

In Asia, Tamerlaine begins conquest

In China, Yüan dynasty, 1271–1368; Ni Tsan, poet and painter, 1301–1374; Ming dynasty, 1368–1644; Ming rule was authoritarian; despite early expansion and imperial-sponsored sea voyages, 1421–1433, Ming period is inward-looking with an emphasis on farming; growth of commerce and important changes in the economy and society; vibrant culture; silk brocade, a mixture of tapestry and silkweaving; encyclopedia in 22,937 volumes, begun 1403; restoration of the Great Wall, 1368; Great Temple of the Dragon, Beijing, 1420; the Temple and Altar of Heaven, 1420–1430, in Beijing

In Himalayan region, in Kashmir, conquest by Muslims, 1339; in Tibet, founding of Lamaistic state by the Dalai Lama, about 1450 to 1950s; Potala, the residence of the Dalai Lama, begun after 1450

In India, Delhi Sultanate, 1192–1526; Muberak, 1316–1320, last of the Khilji rulers of Delhi; Gharzi Khan, Sultan of Delhi, in 1320 became first of the Tughlak dynasty; famine, 1335–1342; Bubonic plague begins in 1332; rise of Vijayanagar, a Hindu kingdom in South India, 1336–1646; remains independent of Muslim rulers until 1565; the Tomb of Khan-i-Jahan Tilangani, at Tuqhluqabad, built in 1368–1369, an example of Indo-Muslim style of architecture; Jamma Musjid Mosque of Husain, Juanpur, 1438; Portuguese traders arrive, 1498

In Indochina, in Burma, the city of Pagan, 5,000 stupas (dome-shaped Buddhist monument containing relics), tenth to fourteenth centuries; Mongol rule from 1287 to about 1500; in Siam, Thai dynasty from the Lop Buri region centralize the

b) Burgundy
  (1) The Burgundian setting
  (2) Claus Sluter
4. Late Gothic painting and the rise of new trends
  a) Radical changes
  b) Illuminated manuscripts
    (1) Secular influences
    (2) The Limbourg brothers
  c) New trends in Italy
    (1) Giotto
    (2) The new style
  d) Flemish painting
    (1) The Burgundian setting
    (2) Characteristics
    (3) Jan van Eyck
    (4) Hieronymus Bosch

IV. The Legacy of the Late Middle Ages

state, about 1350–1767; conquest of Angkor, 1353; capital city of Ayuthia with 500 pagodas and the royal chapel, or Wat P'ra Si Sanpet, fifteenth to eighteenth centuries; in Cambodia, the Angkor Wat complex, the temple mountain of Suryavarman II, the most famous monument of Khmer art, 1113–1150; Angkor Thom, the temple-mountain of the Bayon, the last great work of Khmer art, built by Jayavarman VII, 1181–1220; decay of the central power and collapse of the economy begins, after 1220
In Japan, Kamakura period, 1185–1333; Kemmu Restoration, 1333–1336; dual rule between the civil (ornamental) power of the emperor and the military (actual) power of the shogun, 1192–1867; Muromachi period (Ashikaga Shogunate), 1333–1572; warrior power base is Kyoto's Muromachi District; influence of Zen Buddhism and samurai and court society; influence from China's Yüan and Ming dynasties along with a trend toward decoration and a taste for luxury; introduction of the tea ceremony and the Zen garden; rise of daimyo ("Great Names"), 1300–1500; civil war against Hojo regents; *Jinno-shotaki*, by Kitabatake Chikafusa, a history of Japan, 1339; the "No" (more than 240) plays of Motokiyo Zeami, d. 1443; the Golden Pavilion in Kyoto, 1397; Kyoto's

Ryōanji (rock garden)
designed by a Zen priest,
1473; the "No" play
Ataka by Nobumitsy,
1435–1516; the Kinkakuji,
Kyoto, a three-story
building, late fourteenth
century; the Ginkakuji,
Kyoto, a pavilion, early
fifteenth century

In Korea, Koryo Kingdom,
918–1392; the ten-story
pagoda of Kyong-ch'on-sa,
Seoul, 1348; Li dynasty,
1392–1910; rigid application
of Confucian principles,
and gradual diminution of
Buddhism; art and
architecture imitate older
styles; the ten-story pagoda
of Won-gak-sa, Koryo-
revival style, Seoul, 1468;
the pagoda of Nak-san-sa
at Yang-yang-kun, late
fifteenth century; the
zenith of celadon porcelain

In Mesoamerica, Historic
period, 900–1521; the
culture of Mixteca-Puebla
with the ceremonial site
of Mitla and the rich
treasures found in a tomb
at Monte Albán; the
settling down of the
Chichimec nomads and
establishing rule over parts
of the Valley of Mexico,
with Texcoco the capital,
after 1327; Totonac pottery
on the Gulf Cost; rise of the
Aztec people, a warrior
culture with ritual human
sacrifice; the crowning of
the first Aztec king in 1376;
the Aztecs founded an
empire, based in the
highlands of Mexico; the
founding of Tenochtitlán,
an island city of temples,
pyramids, palaces,

aqueducts, music, dance, sculpture, and murals, in 1325; the Aztec rock temple at Malinalco, west of Mexico City; Aztec books include Codex Borbonicus and the Codex Florentino

In Muslim world, Hafiz, about 1320–about 1390, Persia's greatest lyric poet, the master of the *ghazal*, or ode, literary genre

In New Zealand, endemic warfare among Maori tribes

In North America, rise of Middle and Upper Mississippi phases of Mound Builders, after 1400; the Iroquois build communal longhouses at Howlett Hill, New York, fourteenth century

In Southeast Asia, introduction of terraced rice paddies

LEARNING OBJECTIVES

To learn:

1. The calamities that occurred in the fourteenth century and the impact they had on society and culture

2. To recognize visually Late Gothic art and architecture and to identify their leading characteristics

3. To understand the foundations of the modern world that were laid in this period

4. To trace the decline of the papacy from its pinnacle of power and prestige in 1200 to its nadir during the Great Schism, ended in 1417

5. The lay movements and heresies that arose at the same time as the decline in the prestige and power of the papacy

6. The theological struggle between the *via antiqua* and the *via moderna* and its outcome

7. The significant developments in Late Medieval science

8. The highlights of Late Medieval literature, especially the writings of Petrarch, Boccaccio, Chaucer, and Christine de Pizan

9. Giotto's achievements and their significance for later painters

10. The contributions of the Flemish painters

11. Historic "firsts" of the Late Middle Ages that became part of the Western tradition: the growth of the middle class as a dominant force in society, the emergence of secular rulers ready to curb church power, the birth of the tradition of common people challenging aristocratic control of culture and society, the release of a powerful secular spirit, and the invention of the technique of oil painting

12. The role of the Late Middle Ages in transmitting the heritage of earlier civilizations: continuing development of vernacular literature, separating Greco-Roman philosophy from Christian theology, freeing the practice of painting from its bondage to architecture, making painting the leading artistic medium, and reviving the realistic tradition in painting that stretched back to ancient Greece

SUGGESTIONS FOR FILMS

Art Portrays a Changing World: Gothic to Early Renaissance. Alemann Films, 17 min., color.

Chaucer's England. Encyclopedia Britannica, 30 min., color.

Faith and Fear. CRM/McGraw-Hill, 40 min., color (Reaction to the Black Death).

Giotto and the Pre-Renaissance. Universal Educational and Visual Arts, 47 min., color.

Joan of Arc. Learning Corporation of America, 26 min., color.

Medieval England: The Peasants' Revolt. Learning Corporation of America, 31 min., color.

SUGGESTIONS FOR FURTHER READING

Duby, G. *The Age of the Cathedrals: Art and Society, 980–1420.* Translated by E. Levieux and B. Thompson. Chicago: University of Chicago Press, 1981. Cultural history at its best, this book analyzes Europe's rebirth after about 1000; it focuses on three successive periods, with each symbolized by a building: the monastery, the cathedral, and the palace; the French original was published in three volumes, between 1970 and 1975.

Ennen, E. *The Medieval Woman.* Translated by E. Jephcott. Oxford: Basil Blackwell, 1984. A historical overview from 500 to 1500 that weaves together the changing roles of women from various classes and social groups.

Gottfried, R. *The Black Death: Natural and Human Disaster in Medieval Europe.* New York: Free Press, 1983. Examines the Black Death in a broad context of epidemiology while explaining its origins, spread, and consequences in Late Medieval Europe.

Harbison, C. *The Mirror of the Artist. Northern Renaissance Art in Its Historical Context.* New York: Abrams, 1905. A concise guidebook, arranged topically in six chapters.

Hofstatter, H. H. *Art of the Late Middle Ages.* Translated by R. E. Wolf. New York: Abrams, 1968. An excellent guide to Late Medieval painting, sculpture, and architecture with abundant illustrations, more than half in color.

Holmes, G. A. *Europe, Hierarchy and Revolt, 1320–1450.* New York: Harper & Row, 1975. Still useful for the student who wants a more detailed understanding of the last phases of medieval Europe and the beginning of Renaissance Europe.

————, ed. *The Oxford Illustrated History of Medieval Europe*. Oxford: Oxford University Press, 1988. In separate essays, several scholars trace the evolution of Europe from the fall of Rome to the emergence of monarchies; richly illustrated.

Huizinga, J. *The Autumn of the Middle Ages*. Translated by R. J. Payton and U. Mammitzsch. Chicago: University of Chicago Press, 1996. A classic of Late Medieval studies, this brilliant work helped to reclaim the Late Middle Ages as a subject of study from Renaissance scholars who were making this their own. First published in the Netherlands in 1919 and later translated into English, this new translation captures much that the first translation failed to convey.

Lambert, C. *Medieval Heresy: Popular Movements from Bogomil to Hus*. 2nd ed. Cambridge, Mass.: Blackwell, 1992. For the serious student who wants to learn more about heretical movements and how they affected the Catholic church organization and faith.

Mâle, E. *Religious Art in France: The Late Middle Ages: A Study in Medieval Iconography and Its Sources*. Translated by M. Mathews. Princeton: Princeton University Press, 1986. A handsome reprint of the 1908 classic that has become indispensable for understanding the symbolism in medieval religious art.

Meiss, M. *Painting in Florence and Siena after the Black Death*. Princeton: Princeton University Press, 1964. A study of painting, in its meaning and form, within the context of a specific event—the Black Death. Touches upon religious thought and literature, too. This is a pioneering work in art history research and interpretation.

Oakley, F. P. *The Western Church in the Late Middle Ages*. Ithaca, N.Y.: 1980. A survey of the fourteenth- and fifteenth-century church when it faced many crises and assaults.

Shahar, S. *The Fourth Estate: A History of Women in the Middle Ages*. Translated by C. Galai. London: Metheun, 1983. A study of women who lived in the High and Late Middle Ages. Topics include women's public and legal rights, witches, and heretical movements, and focuses on women who were nuns, wives, and from various strata of society.

Swann, W. *The Late Middle Ages: Art and Architecture from 1350 to the Advent of the Renaissance*. London: Paul Elek. 1977. A useful introduction to the art and architecture of the Late Gothic period in northern Europe and the Iberian peninsula—fully illustrated.

Ziegler, P. *The Black Death*. New York: John Day Company, 1969. A detailed and long study; perhaps somewhat outdated, but still a "classic" work.

IDENTIFICATIONS

devotio moderna   fan vault
via antiqua   campanile
via moderna   Italo-Byzantine style
Late Gothic style   perspective
Flamboyant style   triptych
Perpendicular style

PERSONAL PERSPECTIVE BACKGROUND

Franco Sacchetti, On the Changeableness of Fashion

Sacchetti's chief claim to fame rests on a literary work entitled *Three Hundred Tales*, a collection of stories inspired by Bocaccio's *Decameron*. Some of Sacchetti's tales have perished; only 215 complete ones survive along with fragments of others. Writing in the gloomy aftermath of the Black Death,

Sacchetti soberly claimed that his purpose was "to mingle a little gaiety with the sadness and weariness of life." His stories are filled with satirical commentary on the people and customs of his time.

Sacchetti's point of view may have reflected a downturn in his own fortunes. Born into a wealthy merchant family, he abandoned commerce to practice politics in his native Florence. After serving as ambassador and holding other respected posts, he lost everything during the political and social turmoil that beset Florence in the late 1300s.

DISCUSSION/ESSAY QUESTIONS

1. Discuss the political, social, and religious changes from 1300 to 1500, which brought an end to Europe's Middle Ages. How did these changes affect the culture of the period? Be specific.
2. What natural and human calamities occurred during the fourteenth century? Discuss the impact of these misfortunes on society and culture.
3. In what way were the foundations of the modern world laid in the Late Middle Ages?
4. Discuss the short-term and long-term consequences of the demographic crisis in Europe during the fourteenth century. Did this crisis influence the period's arts and humanities? Explain.
5. Why were the English and French rulers able to unify their countries in the fifteenth century? Why did other rulers want to imitate them? How was this development reflected in the period's culture?
6. Describe the decline of the church and especially its ruling hierarchy, the papacy, during the Late Middle Ages. How did this religious decline affect the age's culture and society?
7. How did developments in Late Medieval science and philosophy-theology foreshadow the end of the medieval world?
8. Discuss the issues and personalities involved in the theological struggle between the *via antiqua* and the *via moderna*. What was the outcome of this theological controversy? What was the significance of this controversy for the future?
9. Discuss medieval contributions to science.
10. How was literature being changed by new forces in the Late Middle Ages? Show specifically how those forces affected the works of the Italian writers Petrarch and Boccaccio, the English writers Langland and Chaucer, and the French writer Christine de Pizan.
11. Identify the characteristics of Late Gothic architecture. Choose a building from this period and show how it embodies this style.
12. Identify the characteristics of Late Gothic sculpture. Choose a work by Pisano or Sluter and show how it expresses this style.
13. In what way did Giotto "rescue and restore" painting in the fourteenth century? Compare and contrast a painting by Giotto with one by his contemporary Cimabue in order to demonstrate the nature of Giotto's achievement.
14. Discuss the contributions of Burgundian artists in the fifteenth century, concentrating on the works of the Limbourg brothers, Jan van Eyck, Claus Sluter, and Hieronymous Bosch.
15. Using an example of literature and architecture from the Late Middle Ages, show how these works reflected the changing values of this period.
16. What is the most significant legacy of the Late Middle Ages to the modern world? Explain.

MULTIPLE-CHOICE QUESTIONS

1. Which was NOT a sign that the High Middle Ages' unique blend of the spiritual with the secular was breaking down in the Late Middle Ages?
   a. warfare among the rival Christian states
 * b. the religious subjects of Late Medieval art (p. 241)
   c. separation of theology and philosophy
   d. decline in the power and prestige of the church

2. Which did NOT disrupt fourteenth-century life in Europe?
   a. the onset of the plague
   b. an extended period of economic depression
 * c. an invasion of Muslim soldiers sweeping up from Greece (pp. 241, 243)
   d. urban riots and peasant unrest

3. The Black Death of the fourteenth century was:
   a. AIDS
   b. tuberculosis
 * c. bubonic plague (p. 241)
   d. smallpox

4. As a result of the devastating plague, the leading image in Late Medieval art and literature became the:
 * a. Dance of Death (p. 243)
   b. Final Judgment
   c. Garden of Eden
   d. Fountain of Youth

5. Which was NOT a natural calamity during Europe's fourteenth century?
   a. periodic bad harvests
   b. general famine and poor distribution of foodstuffs
   c. local wars and conflicts
 * d. cataclysmic earthquakes (p. 243)

6. Who tried to carve out a "middle kingdom" between France and Germany?
   a. the Kings of England
 * b. the Dukes of Burgundy (p. 243)
   c. the Counts of Champagne
   d. the Ottoman Turks

7. Which was NOT a consequence of the demographic crisis of the fourteenth century?
 * a. greater power to the landlords over peasants (pp. 243–244)
   b. a sharp decrease in the density of the rural population
   c. the rise of new economic centers in Bohemia, Poland, Hungary, Scandinavia, and Portugal
   d. the decline of manorialism in western Europe

8. Which was an important technological innovation made in the Late Middle Ages?
   a. the wheel
   b. the steam engine
 * c. movable type (p. 244)
   d. gunpowder

9. The Hundred Years' War was fought between:
 * a. France and England (p. 244)
   b. Italy and Germany
   c. Spain and Portugal
   d. the Netherlands and Scandinavia

10. The court of the Burgundian dukes was located in:
    a. Amsterdam
    b. Paris
    c. Brussels
 * d. Dijon (p. 244)

11. Which is NOT correct for England and France in 1500?
    a. Each had a national assembly that represented various interests.
 * b. Each had a flourishing overseas empire. (p. 245)
    c. Each had a strong centralized government.
    d. Each had an efficient national bureaucracy.

12. During most of the fourteenth century, the popes ruled the church from:
    a. Rome
 * b. Avignon (p. 245)
    c. Milan
    d. Madrid

13. Which was NOT a threat to papal power during the Late Middle Ages?
    a. the Avignonese papacy
 * b. the Albigensian heresy (pp. 245–246)
    c. the Great Schism
    d. the conciliar movement

14. What was the Great Schism?
 * a. the forty-year period when there were two and sometimes three popes, each claiming papal authority (p. 245)
    b. the seventy-year period when the popes ruled from Avignon
    c. the split in the church when the Orthodox separated from the Roman Catholics
    d. the division in the church between Protestants and Catholics, started by Martin Luther

15. The Late Medieval papacy did NOT:
    a. wage wars and, in general, intrude into Italian politics
    b. get caught up in the art and learning of the Early Renaissance
    c. have to fight heresy and schism within the church
 * d. launch a wave of religious reforms (pp. 245–246)

16. Late Medieval religion was characterized by all of these EXCEPT the:
    a. rise of lay piety
 * b. development of new monastic orders (pp. 246–247)
    c. emergence of new heresies
    d. spread of anticlerical feelings

17. Which is NOT an example of lay piety in the Late Medieval church?
 * a. the Abbey of Thelème (pp. 246–247)
    b. the *devotio moderna*, or the "new devotion"
    c. the Brethren and Sisters of the Common Life
    d. the Friends of God

18. The "new devotion" or *devotio moderna* was best expressed in the works of:
    a. John Wycliffe
 * b. Thomas à Kempis (p. 246)
    c. Jan Hus
    d. William of Ockham

19. The Wycliffite heresy advocated the:
    a. opening of the priesthood to women
 * b. abolition of church property (p. 247)
    c. elimination of the sacraments
    d. denial of Jesus' humanity

20. This medieval religious heresy became a vehicle for Czech nationalism:
    a. the Wycliffite
    * b. the Hussite (p. 247)
    c. the Waldensian
    d. the Albigensian

21. All are correct for the Inquisition EXCEPT:
    a. It was a church court.
    * b. It was founded to deal with the Wycliffite heresy. (p. 247)
    c. It flourished mainly in Spain and Italy.
    d. It was used to rid the church of heresy and witchcraft.

22. Which was NOT associated with the *via antiqua* of Late Medieval theology?
    a. It was identified with the beliefs of Thomas Aquinas.
    * b. It aimed to separate Aristotle's ideas from Christian beliefs. (p. 248)
    c. It urged that faith and reason be combined in order to reach divine truth.
    d. It was championed by Duns Scotus.

23. In Late Medieval theology, the *via moderna*:
    a. urged the combination of faith and reason
    b. ignored reason altogether and concentrated on faith
    * c. advocated the complete separation of faith and reason (p. 248)
    d. supported the system of Thomas Aquinas

24. Which was NOT a contribution of William of Ockham to medieval philosophy?
    * a. He denied the power of reason to understand the natural world. (p. 248)
    b. He originated a closely reasoned style of argument.
    c. He helped to separate theology from philosophy.
    d. He contributed to the triumph of Nominalism in the universities.

25. What was Ockham's "razor"?
    a. a technological breakthrough, which allowed for more efficient shaves
    * b. a philosophical method for eliminating superfluous information (p. 248)
    c. a literary device used by critics to dissect poetry
    d. a military formation employed during the Hundred Years' War

26. This medieval thinker pioneered the experimental system in science:
    * a. Roger Bacon (p. 248)
    b. William of Ockham
    c. Duns Scotus
    d. Nicholas Oresme

27. This Late Medieval thinker questioned the then-prevailing view that the earth did not move:
    a. Jan Hus
    b. William of Ockham
    c. Duns Scotus
    * d. Nicholas Oresme (pp. 248–249)

28. Which was NOT a force for change in Late Medieval literature?
    a. The invention of movable type gave birth to printed books.
    * b. The shift of universities to vernacular languages led to the death of Latin in scholarship. (p. 249)
    c. Vernacular literature began to replace literature written in Latin.
    d. The rich middle class started to supplant the nobility as audience and patrons.

29. Petrarch's *My Secret* has all these aspects EXCEPT:
    a. It is written in the form of a dialogue.
    b. It has a religious theme.
    c. It features a conversation between St. Augustine and Petrarch.
  * d. It demonstrates that Petrarch was free of medieval values. (p. 250)

30. Which was NOT an example of the impact of the plague on medieval culture?
    a. It gave rise to the flagellants.
  * b. It provided the setting for Chaucer's *Canterbury Tales*. (pp. 246, 250, 253, and caption for Fig. 10.1)
    c. It provided the setting for Petrarch's *Decameron*.
    d. It led to the image of the Danse Macabre.

31. The author of the *Decameron* was:
    a. Petrarch
  * b. Boccaccio (p. 250)
    c. Langland
    d. Chaucer

32. The *Decameron* helped bring into existence the modern:
    a. novel
  * b. short story (p. 251)
    c. verse-drama
    d. comic play

33. The most original developments in Late Medieval literature occurred in:
    a. France and western Germany
    b. Scandinavia and eastern Europe
  * c. England and northern Italy (p. 249)
    d. Spain and southern Italy

34. This work reflected the social tensions caused by the 1381 Peasants' Revolt:
    a. Petrarch's *My Secret*
    b. Bocaccio's *Decameron*
  * c. Langland's *Vision of Piers Plowman* (p. 251)
    d. Chaucer's *Canterbury Tales*

35. Chaucer's poetry was written for:
  * a. the royal court of the king of England (p. 251)
    b. London's rich middle class
    c. the noble court of the Duke of Norfolk
    d. the ecclesiastical court of the Archbishop of Canterbury

36. The poetry of Chaucer, a commoner, caused him to be honored by being:
    a. elevated to the nobility
    b. made poet laureate
    c. inducted into the Order of the Garter
  * d. buried in Westminster Abbey (p. 251)

37. What is the setting for the *Canterbury Tales?*
    a. a castle outside Canterbury
  * b. a pilgrimage to Canterbury (p. 251)
    c. a harem at Canterbury
    d. a monastery at Canterbury

38. In literary form, Chaucer's *Canterbury Tales* most closely resembles:
    * a. Boccaccio's *Decameron* (p. 251)
      b. Petrarch's *My Secret*
      c. Langland's *Vision of Piers Plowman*
      d. Dante's *Divine Comedy*

39. Chaucer's Canterbury pilgrims:
      a. are drawn exclusively from the upper classes
      b. are drawn exclusively from the lower classes
    * c. represent all walks of medieval society (p. 253)
      d. represent idealized portraits of medieval types

40. Which type of tale was NOT included in Chaucer's *Canterbury Tales?*
      a. *fabliau*
      b. romance
    * c. *chanson de geste* (pp. 251–252)
      d. beast fable

41. The Wife of Bath is a famous character in:
      a. Petrarch's *My Secret*
      b. Boccaccio's *Decameron*
      c. Langland's *Vision of Piers Plowman*
    * d. Chaucer's *Canterbury Tales* (p. 251)

42. Christine de Pizan, in *The Book of the City of Ladies,* argues that:
      a. Women should have financial independence.
    * b. Women should be educated. (p. 252)
      c. Women should be given the right to vote.
      d. Women should give up their traditional role.

43. Which was NOT an achievement of Christine de Pizan?
      a. She was the first known Western woman to earn a living through her writings.
      b. She contributed to the triumph of vernacular language over Latin.
    * c. She was the first woman to lecture at the University of Paris. (p. 252)
      d. She was the first Western writer to raise "the woman question."

44. The hallmark of Late Gothic builders was to:
      a. Return to the basics of the Gothic style.
      b. Treat in a balanced manner the Gothic style's fundamental elements.
    * c. Push the Gothic style to extravagant limits. (p. 252)
      d. Continue the aesthetic goals of the High Gothic style.

45. Which is NOT a characteristic of Late Gothic architecture?
    * a. domes and cupolas on churches (p. 252)
      b. ever greater heights for buildings
      c. elaborate decoration
      d. delicate, lacy details

46. Late Gothic architecture in France culminated in the:
    * a. Flamboyant style (p. 252)
      b. Perpendicular style
      c. Exuberant style
      d. Vertical style

47. Late Gothic architecture in England is called the:
    a. Flamboyant style
  * b. Perpendicular style (p. 252)
    c. Exuberant style
    d. Vertical style

48. A unique feature of England's Late Gothic architecture was:
    a. calligraphic ornamentation
  * b. fan vaulting (p. 252)
    c. circular towers
    d. atriums in the vestibules

49. Late Gothic sculpture and painting was characterized by:
    a. athletic bodies
  * b. willowy, swaying bodies (p. 252)
    c. abstract designs
    d. primitive effects

50. Of the following artworks, which was NOT commissioned by a person or persons associated
    with the Dukes of Burgundy?
    a. Sluter, The Well of Moses
    b. the Limbourg brothers, Très Riches Heures du Duc de Berry
  * c. Pisano, Pulpit in Pisa Cathedral (pp. 257–258, 261, 265)
    d. van Eyck, Arnolfini Wedding Portrait

51. This artist turned painting in a new direction, one that led to the Renaissance:
    a. the Limbourg brothers
    b. Cimabue
  * c. Giotto (p. 261)
    d. Jan van Eyck

52. The painter Giotto achieved all of the following EXCEPT:
    a. a three-dimensional art
    b. full expression of human emotions
    c. naturalistic treatment of figures
  * d. mathematical perspective (pp. 261–265)

53. Fifteenth-century Flemish art was primarily concerned with:
  * a. symbolic realism (p. 265)
    b. psychological truth
    c. abstract purity
    d. idealized perfection

54. All of the Following statements apply to Van Eyck's *Arnolfini Wedding Portrait* EXCEPT:
    a. It expresses the symbolic realism of northern European painting.
    b. It records an actual event.
    c. It includes details that refer to wedding customs or beliefs.
  * d. It indicates that the marriage rite is purely secular, because it omits any references to
       religion. (p. 265 and caption for Fig. 10.22)

55. The paintings of Hieronymus Bosch can be characterized as:
    a. conventional religious art of the Late Gothic period
    b. focused on scenes of domestic life
  * c. often ambiguous in their moral message (pp. 265, 269)
    d. foreshadowing High Renaissance art

11

THE EARLY RENAISSANCE
Return to Classical Roots
1400–1494

TEACHING STRATEGIES AND SUGGESTIONS

The teacher can begin the section on the Early Renaissance with a Standard Lecture using either the Diffusion or the Pattern of Change approach to show the connections and discontinuities between this first modern period and the Middle Ages. At the same time, a general survey can be made between these two cultural periods, contrasting the religious, corporate-minded Middle Ages with the secular, individualistic Renaissance. Because the nature of the Renaissance is such a hotly debated topic, the instructor may want to help students sort through the rival interpretations summarized in the textbook; these interpretations can also be used as the basis for a more general discussion on the nature of historical writing, such as what motivates historians and why they do not always agree.

The teacher will be able to use fifteenth-century Italy as a Case Study to show the interrelationship of politics, diplomacy, economics and war—a recurring theme in history. The Reflections/Connections model will work well in illustrating that in Early Renaissance Florence the brilliant developments in the arts were directly tied to political changes, economic prosperity, and ambitious families.

Various paths may be followed in the lectures on Early Renaissance intellectual and artistic developments. The Pattern of Change model can be applied to the arts and ideas by tracing their evolution over the century. Innovations in education can be contrasted with medieval education, using the Comparison/Contrast approach. The arts can be illustrated with visual aids—slides, films, or both—and should probably be presented as an evolution in techniques, local traditions, and generational differences while underscoring the revival of Greco-Roman Classicism. The instructor might want to use the "Great Individual" argument in discussing the lives and contributions of such key figures as Donatello, Brunelleschi, or Leonardo da Vinci. A final lecture can deal with two topics: first, using a Spirit of the Age approach, the underlying unity of the cultural developments in the Early Renaissance; and, second, using a Diffusion approach, the impact that this age had on subsequent periods, including our own.

LECTURE OUTLINE

Non-Western Events

I. The Renaissance: Schools of Interpretation
   A. Burckhardt and his critics
   B. Phases of the Renaissance

(See Chapter 10 for non-Western events.)

II. Early Renaissance History and Institutions
   A. Italian city-states during the Early Renaissance

171

1. Wars, alliances, treaties
2. Trade and commerce
3. The role of the family
B. Florence, the center of the Renaissance
1. Phases of governments
2. The Medici family
C. The resurgent papacy, 1450–1500
1. Popes caught up in pursuit of power
2. Patrons of Renaissance culture
3. Three powerful popes

III. The Spirit and Style of the Early Renaissance
A. Humanism, scholarship, and schooling
1. Humanistic studies
a) Textual criticism
b) Civic humanism
2. Educational reform and curriculum
B. Thought and philosophy
1. Platonism in Florence
a) Ficino
b) Pico della Mirandola
2. Relation to Classicism
C. Architecture, sculpture, and painting
1. Artistic ideals and innovations
a) Classical influences
b) Late medieval influences
c) Types of perspectives
d) Secular values in art
2. Architecture
a) Brunelleschi
b) Alberti
3. Sculpture
a) Donatello
b) Verrocchio
c) Ghiberti
4. Painting
a) Changes and innovations in painting
b) Masaccio
c) Fra Angelico
d) Piero della Francesca
e) Botticelli
f) Leonardo da Vinci
D. Music
1. Influences on Renaissance music
2. The leading composers
a) John Dunstable
b) Josquin des Prez

IV. The Legacy of the Early Renaissance

LEARNING OBJECTIVES

To learn:

1. The various schools of interpretation of the Renaissance

2. The phases of fifteenth-century Italian politics and diplomacy

3. The phases of Italian economic trends during the fifteenth century

4. The role of Florence as the center of the Early Renaissance

5. The impact of the Medici family in Florentine history

6. The nature of the Renaissance papacy, its leaders, and their contributions

7. The characteristics of the Early Renaissance

8. The characteristics and evolution of Renaissance humanism

9. The development of Renaissance scholarship and learning, including its leaders and their contributions

10. The characteristics of Early Renaissance architecture, including the chief architects, their innovations, examples of their works, and their influence

11. The nature of Early Renaissance sculpture, including its origins, the major sculptors, and their influence

12. The characteristics of Early Renaissance painting and its impact on later styles, with references to specific painters and their innovations

13. To compare and contrast selected works of Early Renaissance architecture or sculpture or painting, noting the artists, what influenced them, and their contributions

14. The changes in music—types of works and new techniques and other innovations

15. The cultural changes in the areas of the arts and how these changes, including the revival of Classicism, affected the arts until modern times

16. Historic "firsts" of Early Renaissance civilization that became part of the Western tradition: textual criticism, realistic painting based on mathematical perspective, the educational ideal, called the "Renaissance Man," and the drive to individual fulfillment

17. The role of Early Renaissance civilization in transmitting the heritage of earlier civilizations: rediscovering Classical art styles and redefining them, reviving Greco-Roman humanism and restoring it to the primary place in the educational curriculum, reinvigorating humanistic studies, freeing painting and sculpture from their tutelage to architecture in imitation of the Classical tradition, and making skepticism a central part of the consciousness of the educated elite as had been characteristic of ancient Greece and Rome

SUGGESTIONS FOR FILMS

Civilisation: Man the Measure of All Things. Time-Life, 52 min., color.

I, Leonardo da Vinci. McGraw-Hill, 52 min., color.

Renaissance: Its Beginnings in Italy. Encyclopedia Britannica, 26 min., black and white.

Renaissance and Resurrection. ABC News, 55 min., color.

The Spirit of the Renaissance. Encyclopedia Britannica, 31 min., color.

SUGGESTIONS FOR MUSIC

The Castle of Fair Welcome (fifteenth-century courtly songs). The Gothic Voices. Hyperion CDA-66194.

Josquin des Prez. *La Deploration sur la mort de Johannes Ockeghem.* New London Chamber Choir. Amon Ra CDSAR-24.

————. *Missa Gaudeamus.* Capella Cordina. Lyr. 7265.

Guillaume Dufay. *Hymns (with Introductory Gregorian Chants from the Cambrai Antiphonal).* Schola Hungarica. Hungaroton HCD-12951.

John Dunstable. *Motets.* Hilliard Ensemble. Angel CDC-49002.

————. *Sacred and Secular Music.* Ambrosian Singers. EA S-36E.

Medieval English Music (from the fourteenth and fifteenth centuries). Hilliard (Vocal Ensemble). Harmonia Mundi HMA-190.1153.

SUGGESTIONS FOR FURTHER READING

Baron, H. *In Search of Florentine Civic Humanism: Essays on the Transition from Medieval to Modern Thought.* Princeton: Princeton University Press, 1988. Readable essays that root the ideal of civic humanism within the reality of Florentine politics.

Burckhardt, J. *The Civilization of the Renaissance in Italy.* New York: Harper Torchbooks, 1958. The mid-nineteenth-century classic that first described the Renaissance for the modern world and that scholars have debated since its publication.

Burke, P. *The Italian Renaissance: Culture and Society in Italy.* Rev. ed. Cambridge: Polity, 1987. An up-to-date study of Renaissance Italy's educated and wealthy urban society that expressed its new attitudes through the arts, literature, and styles of life; findings partly based on computerized data.

Cole, A. *Art of the Italian Renaissance Courts. Virture and Magnificence.* London: Everymans Art Library, 1995. An illustrated study of the art of five of Italy's princely Renaissance courts: Naples, Urbino, Milan, Ferrara, and Mantua.

Cole, B. *The Renaissance Artist at Work.* New York: Harper & Row, 1983. A pioneering work that focuses on the social world in which Renaissance artists worked.

Edgerton, S. *The Renaissance Rediscovery of Linear Perspective.* New York: Basic Books, 1975. In this thought-provoking work Edgerton links the revival of linear perspective with contemporary religious beliefs.

Goldthwaite, R. A. *The Building of Renaissance Florence: An Economic and Social History.* Baltimore: Johns Hopkins University Press, 1980. An enlightening study of the social and economic background to the birth of Renaissance architecture in Florence.

Hartt, F. *A History of Italian Renaissance Art.* 3rd ed. New York: Abrams, 1987. An authoritative work by one of the outstanding art historians of our time.

Henry, D. *The Listener's Guide to Medieval & Renaissance Music.* New York: Facts on File, 1983. A brief, masterly introduction with an annotated guide to some of the best available recordings.

Herlihy, D., and Klapisch-Zuber, C. *Tuscans and Their Families.* New Haven: Yale University Press, 1985. A brilliant work of social and economic history that uses the tax returns of 1427 in Tuscany as the basis for an analysis of the region's families.

Jensen, D. *Renaissance Europe: Age of Recovery and Reconciliation.* 2nd ed. Lexington, Mass.: Heath, 1992. A comprehensive and up-to-date history of Renaissance Europe that takes into account the findings of the new social historians.

Klapisch-Zuber, C. *Women, Family, and Ritual in Renaissance Italy.* Translated by L. Cochrane. A well-respected volume in the new social history being written today.

Murray, P. *The Architecture of the Italian Renaissance.* Rev. ed. New York: Schocken, 1986. A knowledgeable overview of Italian Renaissance architecture with many helpful illustrations and drawings.

IDENTIFICATIONS

Renaissance	chiaroscuro
studia humanitatis	*sfumato*
Early Renaissance style	mass
vanishing point	chanson
pilaster	a cappella
relief	

PERSONAL PERSPECTIVE BACKGROUND

Laura Cereta, Defense of the Liberal Instruction of Women

In this letter, Laura Cereta defends women's rights against a critic whom she addresses as "Bibulus," or "drunkard." "Bibulus" may have been an actual person or simply an epithet to describe those men who denigrated women. In particular, she aligns herself with other women and refuses to cast herself as superior to them simply because of her education.

DISCUSSION/ESSAY QUESTIONS

1. Discuss the various schools of interpretation of the Renaissance. Which is the most valid? Explain.
2. Italian artists and writers in the fifteenth century believed that they were living at a time of the rebirth of civilization. Using the work of one artist and one writer of this period, show how this belief influenced the way that they created. This essay will require you to explain both what these artists and writers were reacting against as well as what was affecting their outlook.
3. Trace military and diplomatic developments in the Italian peninsula from 1400 to 1494. What impact did these events have on society and culture?

4. What changes occurred in the Italian economy during the fifteenth century? Describe the social impact of these changes.

5. In what ways did the changes in the Italian economy influence social and family patterns and habits and the status of women? Is there any evidence that these economic changes affected the arts and humanities? Explain.

6. Summarize the major stages of Florentine political history from 1300 to 1494 and discuss the Medici family's role in events.

7. Identify three Early Renaissance popes and explain their contributions to this cultural movement.

8. What were the intellectual characteristics of the Early Renaissance? How did these ideas manifest themselves in painting, sculpture, architecture, and literature?

9. What is meant by "humanistic studies"? What are its origins? How did this new learning take root in Italy?

10. Define civic humanism and show how it was a part of the Italian Renaissance, noting its goals and its advocates.

11. Was there a radical break between the Early Renaissance and the Middle Ages? Explain your answer.

12. What influence did fifth-century B.C. Athens have on fifteenth-century Florence?

13. Discuss the impact of Neo-Platonism on the Italian Renaissance. Who was the major voice of this movement? What were his contributions?

14. "Pico della Mirandola is the personification of Early Renaissance thought and life." Write a defense of this cultural generalization.

15. How did Brunelleschi change the direction of architecture during the Early Renaissance? Use one of his buildings in your discussion.

16. Explain the role of Classical ideals in Alberti's aesthetic code.

17. Show how Donatello used Classicism to revive sculpture in the Early Renaissance.

18. Discuss the contributions of the painter Masaccio to the Early Renaissance, and use at least one of his works in your essay to illustrate his innovations.

19. What was Botticelli's contribution to Early Renaissance painting? Compare and contrast his style with that of Masaccio.

20. Discuss how painting and sculpture became free of architecture during the Early Renaissance, touching on such matters as the reason for this change, the new ideals for painting, sculpture, and architecture, and the leading advocates for this change.

21. How is Leonardo da Vinci the ideal "Renaissance Man"?

22. Trace the evolution of Early Renaissance painting, from Masaccio to Botticelli and Leonardo, noting specific artists, their achievements, and the guiding themes of their works.

23. What brought about the changes that led to Renaissance music? Was interest in Classicism involved? Who are the leading composers of the Early Renaissance, and what are their contributions?

24. Are you a "child of the Renaissance"? Explain your answer.

MULTIPLE-CHOICE QUESTIONS

1. Historians of the Renaissance:
   a. agree about the general nature of the movement
   b. agree that the movement made a complete break with the Middle Ages
   * c. have recently concluded that it was a very complex cultural movement (p. 273)
   d. accept Burckhardt's interpretation

2. The Peace of Lodi signed in 1454:
   a. ended the Hundred Years' War between England and France
   * b. brought on several decades of peace in the Italian peninsula (p. 275)
   c. resulted in the expulsion of the French from Italy
   d. made the papacy the most powerful state in Italy

3. The most significant consequence of Renaissance warfare was the:
   a. introduction of cannon
   b. use of mercenary soldiers
   c. creation of alliances
 * d. development of diplomacy as an alternative to war (pp. 274–275)

4. The status of women during the Early Renaissance in Italy:
   a. declined significantly as they lost financial power
 * b. probably improved with increased opportunities for education (pp. 275–276)
   c. changed dramatically as they won new political rights
   d. improved socially as they were allowed to marry whomever they chose

5. The center of the Early Renaissance was:
   a. Venice
   b. Rome
 * c. Florence (p. 276)
   d. Siena

6. The Medici family in Florence can be described as a family:
   a. that used its wealth to back the pope
 * b. with a keen political sense and a love of the arts (p. 277)
   c. led by men more interested in war than in peace
   d. dominated by women more interested in peace than in war

7. The late-fifteenth-century popes:
   a. initiated a series of reforms aimed at improving the morals of the clergy
   b. supported the conciliar movement
 * c. were patrons of the Renaissance (p. 277)
   d. held aloof from Italian politics

8. The Early Renaissance pope most attuned to Classical learning was:
 * a. Pius II (pp. 277–278)
   b. Nicholas V
   c. Sixtus IV
   d. Alexander VI

9. Italian humanists expanded their interests by:
 * a. looking beyond official Christian dogma (p. 278)
   b. seeking answers in Chinese philosophy
   c. examining the writings of Indian thinkers
   d. joining in the Scientific Revolution

10. The Early Renaissance drew inspiration from:
 * a. Classical sculpture and architecture (pp. 278–279)
    b. medieval art and architecture
    c. Chinese civilization
    d. Byzantine art

11. The Early Renaissance can best be described as:
    a. a period that made a complete break with the Middle Ages
    b. an age of great scientific advances
 * c. an age when emerging secular values threatened long-accepted religious beliefs (p. 278)
    d. a stagnant period with little cultural innovation

12. Early Renaissance scholars were especially attracted to:
    a. the philosophy of Aristotle
    b. the ideas of the Stoics
  * c. the writings of Cicero (p. 278)
    d. Greek dramas

13. Laura Cereta, in her own defense, claims that she:
    a. is superior intellectually to other women
    b. thinks just as a man does
  * c. is a typical woman in that she is capable of learning (Personal Perspective)
    d. can outthink any man

14. The term *studia humanitatis* does NOT mean:
    a. the comparison of texts to determine which are authentic
  * b. practical guidelines for taking care of the socially disadvantaged (p. 278)
    c. education in Latin literature and language
    d. learned inquiries regarding morals, grammar, history, and rhetoric

15. The earliest humanistic scholars were convinced that:
    a. the scholastic method was the path to truth
  * b. language and writing changed as society changed (pp. 278–279)
    c. the purpose of education was vocational preparation
    d. medieval church Latin was the language of scholarship

16. Which did NOT result from the rise of textual criticism in the Renaissance?
  * a. The Bible was shown to be completely error-free. (pp. 278–279)
    b. A general skepticism developed regarding the authenticity of ancient texts.
    c. Forgeries were now uncovered, such as the Donation of Constantine.
    d. Many medieval documents were now subjected to close scrutiny.

17. The early humanists thought that an educated person ought to:
  * a. spend time in government service (pp. 279–280)
    b. live in isolation from society
    c. live solely for personal pleasure
    d. take orders in the church

18. Lorenzo Valla contributed to the Early Renaissance as a:
    a. painter who first used linear perspective
  * b. literary scholar who studied comparative texts (p. 279)
    c. sculptor who reintroduced contrapposto
    d. founder of a school for humanistic studies

19. The founding patron of the Platonic Academy in Florence was:
    a. Lorenzo ("the Magnificent") de' Medici
  * b. Cosimo de' Medici (p. 280)
    c. Giuliano de' Medici
    d. Piero de' Medici

20. Ficino, the leader of Florence's Platonic Academy:
    a. reconciled Greek and Byzantine thought
    b. harmonized Platonic and Aristotelian thought
    c. wrote a treatise on painting
  * d. developed a spiritualized interpretation of love (p. 280)

21. Early Renaissance Neo-Platonism:
    a. was essentially the same as Late Roman Neo-Platonism
    b. could not be made compatible with Christianity
 * c. taught that Platonic love was superior to erotic love (p. 280)
    d. failed to capture the attention of many thinkers and artists

22. Pico della Mirandola was a:
    a. modest individual who refused to speak out for his views
    b. monk who denounced the Florentine art movement
 * c. scholar trained in philosophy, language, and history (p. 280)
    d. follower of mystical and pietistic learning

23. Underlying much of Pico della Mirandola's writing was the assumption that:
    a. All people share basic truths.
    b. Christianity is only part of a totality of truthful knowledge.
    c. The individual is of primary importance.
 * d. all of the above (pp. 280–281)

24. Central to the thought of Pico della Mirandola was the belief that:
 * a. Individuals can raise or lower themselves. (p. 281)
    b. All human beings are morally imperfect.
    c. All human beings must trust in God's mercy for salvation.
    d. God helps those who help themselves.

25. The visual arts of the Classical era had a strong impact on Early Renaissance Italy because:
 * a. In Italy the ruins of ancient Rome survived. (pp. 281–282)
    b. The Italians often traveled to nearby Greece for study.
    c. The church in Italy kept the Classical tradition alive.
    d. The Italian monasteries were built in a Classical style.

26. The visual arts of the Early Renaissance followed the ideals of:
 * a. balance and harmony (p. 282)
    b. grandiosity and exuberance
    c. abstraction and nonobjectivity
    d. sentimentality and prettiness

27. This fourteenth-century painter inspired Early Renaissance artists:
    a. Cimabue
 * b. Giotto (p. 282)
    c. Masaccio
    d. Pisano

28. Which does NOT apply to the painting technique called linear perspective?
    a. It was pioneered by a series of experiments conducted by Brunelleschi.
    b. It is a mathematically based procedure for giving depth.
 * c. Its results are contrary to the actual way that humans see. (p. 282)
    d. It is a way to create a sense of three dimensions on a two-dimensional surface.

29. Which was NOT a principle of Alberti's theory of art?
 * a. The Classical tradition is outdated and should be discarded. (pp. 282–283)
    b. Paintings should present a noble subject to enlighten the viewer.
    c. A building's ultimate beauty rests on the mathematical harmony of its separate parts.
    d. Painters are creators in much the same way as God.

30. Brunelleschi's most lasting work is the:
    a. dome on the Santa Croce church
    * b. dome on the Florentine cathedral (p. 283)
    c. bell tower next to the Florentine cathedral
    d. city hall of Florence

31. Brunelleschi solved the problem of the dome for the Florentine cathedral by:
    a. constructing a dome of wedged stones as in the Pantheon in Rome
    * b. employing sets of diagonal ribs based on the pointed arch (p. 283)
    c. using reinforced rods and a new type of concrete
    d. borrowing the Classical post-and-lintel model

32. In building the Pazzi chapel, Brunelleschi:
    a. put a Gothic spire on the chapel
    b. turned to Gothic sculpture for decorations
    * c. adhered to Classical design and proportions (p. 283)
    d. copied the basilica floor plan

33. This architect also wrote a treatise on painting:
    * a. Alberti (p. 283)
    b. Masaccio
    c. Lorenzo Valla
    d. Ficino

34. Which does NOT apply to the sculptor Donatello?
    * a. He sculpted figures whose swaying manner suggested Late Gothic art. (pp. 286–287)
    b. He embraced the principles of realism.
    c. He drew inspiration from Classical ideals.
    d. He revived the ancient practice of contrapposto.

35. In his sculpture of *David*, Donatello was able to:
    a. imitate the mysticism of Gothic sculpture
    * b. capture the latent power of the male figure (pp. 286–287and caption for Fig. 11.11)
    c. demonstrate the expressive properties of marble
    d. represent the biblical hero precisely as described in the scriptures

36. Which does NOT apply to Donatello's *Gattamelata*?
    a. It expresses the boldness and power of an actual soldier.
    * b. It idealizes the face of the military leader as a handsome man. (p. 287)
    c. It is the first successful equestrian statue since Roman times.
    d. It was commissioned by the Venetian Senate.

37. Which Renaissance artist did NOT sculpt a statue of David?
    a. Donatello
    * b. Masaccio (pp. 286–290)
    c. Verrocchio
    d. Michelangelo

38. Ghiberti's panels for the east doors of the Florentine Baptistery:
    a. depict scenes from the New Testament
    b. were cast so as to fit inside Gothic quatrefoils
    * c. show his debt to Classicism (pp. 287–288)
    d. are known as the "Gates of Hell"

39. All of the following began with the Early Renaissance EXCEPT the:
   a. rise of textual criticism
   b. drive to individual fulfillment
 * c. beginning of the concept of "the sound mind in the sound body" (p. 297)
   d. origin of the idea of the "Renaissance Man"

40. In comparison to the changes occurring in architecture and sculpture, those that transpired in Early Renaissance painting were:
 * a. more radical and far reaching (p. 289)
   b. less innovative
   c. about the same in terms of styles and techniques
   d. less influential on later artistic developments

41. Masaccio's paintings were influenced by the perspectival experiments of:
   a. Botticelli, the painter
 * b. Brunelleschi, the architect (p. 290)
   c. Pico della Mirandola, the philosopher
   d. Cosimo de' Medici, the patron of arts

42. Which is NOT correct of Masaccio's *The Holy Trinity* painting?
   a. It used a light source to illuminate the figures.
   b. It is one of the first paintings to use linear perspective.
 * c. Its mystical subject is depicted in a supernatural way. (pp. 290–291)
   d. The figures are portrayed within a simulated chapel.

43. Which was NOT an innovation in Masaccio's *The Tribute Money?*
   a. It depicts each figure in precise, mathematical space.
   b. It represents human figures realistically, fully modeled in the round.
 * c. It portrays three episodes at one time. (p. 291)
   d. It uses chiaroscuro.

44. Fra Angelico painted with a sense of the new style Renaissance as evidenced by his:
 * a. treatment of realistic space (pp. 291–292)
   b. use of drab colors
   c. inclusion of gold foil in the painting
   d. depiction of swaying human figures

45. Which is NOT correct for Piero della Francesca's *The Flagellation?*
   a. It was influenced by Fra Angelico's style.
   b. It uses linear perspective.
 * c. It is a scene shrouded in darkness. (pp. 292–293)
   d. It has an odd displacement of the human figures.

46. Botticelli's early paintings were influenced by:
   a. Aristotelianism
 * b. Neo-Platonism (p. 294)
   c. Epicureanism
   d. Stoicism

47. Botticelli's early paintings are famous for their:
   a. Christian themes
 * b. chaste female nudes (p. 294)
   c. realistic landscapes
   d. chiaroscuro effects

48. Which is NOT correct for Botticelli's *The Birth of Venus?*
    a. It appears flattened with little sense of perspective.
    b. Its theme is the birth of love.
  * c. It reflects the influence of Neo-Aristotelianism. (p. 294 and caption for Fig. 11.4)
    d. It unites the images of water, baptism, and rebirth.

49. Leonardo da Vinci is called a Renaissance Man because:
    a. He was a model of courtly behavior.
  * b. He was intellectually curious about nearly every subject. (p. 295)
    c. He was deeply influenced by Neo-Platonism.
    d. He was a strict Classicist.

50. Which is NOT a distinctive aspect of Leonardo's *The Virgin of the Rocks?*
    a. Its four figures are composed into a pyramidal design.
    b. It depicts a religious subject in a very natural setting.
  * c. It is bathed in sunlight, yet there are no shadows. (p. 295)
    d. Expressive hand movements by the figures create internal tensions within the painting.

51. Innovations in Early Renaissance music came from the influence of:
    a. rediscovered Classical compositions
  * b. the seductive harmonics of English music (p. 295)
    c. the tradition of Byzantine music
    d. the use of mathematical proportion in composition

52. Which did NOT distinguish the Franco-Netherlandish school of music?
    a. its blending of the English style with north European and Italian traditions
    b. its Latin Masses
  * c. its reliance on folk melodies (p. 295)
    d. its a cappella singing

53. Which is NOT correct for Josquin de Prez, the composer?
    a. He belonged to the Franco-Netherlandish school of music.
    b. He composed expressive music.
  * c. He composed only in the minor scales. (p. 295)
    d. He matched the sounds with the words of the texts.

54. The Early Renaissance was marked by:
  * a. changes in the arts and architecture, based on Classical ideals (p. 297)
    b. an integration of painting and sculpture into architecture
    c. a decline in the popularity of painting
    d. the emergence of a fully secular art

55. Early Renaissance painting in Italy was characterized by all of the following EXCEPT:
    a. realism
    b. linear perspective
    c. psychological truth
  * d. emotionalism (pp. 289–295)

12

THE HIGH RENAISSANCE AND EARLY MANNERISM 1494–1564

TEACHING STRATEGIES AND SUGGESTIONS

The period 1494–1564 embraces two different but related cultural styles: the High Renaissance and Early Mannerism. To introduce this complex period, the instructor can begin with a Standard Lecture organized as a Historical Overview that stresses, in particular, the critical events of the 1520s as a watershed, including Luther's break with the church and the sack of Rome by the emperor Charles V's troops. The instructor can then shift to a Comparison/Contrast approach to show the similarities and differences between the two cultural styles, the humanistically oriented High Renaissance and the antihumanistically inclined Early Mannerism. A Slide Lecture is indispensable for helping students to distinguish between the two styles in art and architecture. A Music Lecture would also be appropriate to show developments in music, although there was no radical break between Early Renaissance and High Renaissance music, and Mannerism as a term in music is meaningless.

Having established the identifying characteristics of the High Renaissance and Early Mannerism, the instructor can then focus on these contrasting styles. The best approach is to use the Reflections/Connections strategy in order to demonstrate how each cultural style was affected by its historical setting. The Pattern of Change method can also be used to illustrate how the High Renaissance evolved out of the Early Renaissance. In addition, the instructor should highlight the influence of ancient Classicism on the High Renaissance—the most Classical period in Western civilization after fifth-century B.C. Greece. For this purpose the instructor's best approach is the Diffusion model, setting forth how Classical ideals were reborn and revised in High Renaissance Italy.

A good way to conclude this unit is with a Case Study strategy. With this strategy the instructor can challenge the students to ponder the peculiar fate of Classical ages in Western culture; these ages—such as fifth-century B.C. Greece, early-sixteenth-century Italy, and late-eighteenth-century France—were remarkably brief in duration and were followed by periods of upheaval that sharply repudiated Classical ideals. The instructor can also include observations on the current debate regarding the validity of the Western canon and the seemingly contradictory but concurrent revival of Greek and Roman culture, such as the recent translations of Greek dramas and the *Iliad* and the *Odyssey*.

LECTURE OUTLINE

	Non-Western Events
I. Period of Genius	*1494–1564*
A. Key writers and artists	In Africa, West African
B. The High Renaissance	empire of Songhay,
1. Characteristics	1464–1591
2. Centered in Rome	In Caribbean region,
C. Early Mannerism	Columbus discovers the
1. Antihumanistic vision	islands of Jamaica,

2. Characteristics

II. The Rise of the Modern Sovereign State
   A. Emergence of unified, stable kingdoms
      1. The balance-of-power principle
      2. Overview of France's and Spain's involvement in international affairs
         a) Characteristics of a typical sovereign state
         b) The decline of the feudal nobility
         c) French and Spanish wars
   B. The struggle for Italy, 1494–1529
      1. Charles VIII's determining role
      2. Louis XII's and Francis I's continued aggression
      3. Charles V and the first Hapsburg-Valois war
      4. The independence of Venice
   C. Charles V and the Hapsburg Empire
      1. Hapsburg-Valois struggles, 1530–1559
      2. Charles V, a ruler of paradox and irony
      3. The lands of Charles V
      4. The abdication of Charles V and the division of the Hapsburg inheritance
         a) Ferdinand and the German-Austrian Hapsburg territories
         b) Philip and the Spanish-Hapsburg territories

III. Economic Expansion and Social Development
   A. Period of increasing prosperity
      1. Recovery from plague years
      2. Commercial shift from Mediterranean to the Atlantic coast
   B. Population growth
   C. Prosperity and attendant problems
   D. Delayed impact of new raw materials
   E. Introduction of slavery to Europe's colonies in the New World

IV. From High Renaissance to Early Mannerism
   A. Definition of High Renaissance style
      1. Inspired by ancient Classicism
         a) Humanistic
         b) Secular
         c) Idealistic
      2. Relationship to Early Renaissance style
      3. Central role of Rome and the popes

Guadeloupe, Montserrat, Antigua, St. Martin, Puerto Rico, and the Virgin Islands, 1944; Columbus sights St. Vincent and Grenada and discovers Trinidad, 1498; slave trade begins, 1509

In China, Ming dynasty, 1368–1644; Wang Yang-ming, philosopher, 1472–1528; Hsu Wei's *Ching P'Ing Mei*, first classic Chinese novel

In Himalayan region, in Tibet, Lamaistic state, about 1450 to 1950s

In India, Delhi Sultanate, 1192–1526; Mughal Empire, 1526–1858; Mughal Empire unifies north and parts of south India; fusion of Persian and Indian culture in its courts and lands; the Portuguese sailor Vasco da Gama discovers sea route to India, 1498; the poet Furu Nanak establishes the tenets of the Sikh religion, d. 1539

In Japan, Sengoku ("Country at War") period, 1500–1600; "No" dance-dramas at zenith, 1400–1600; Kano Motonobu, court painter, 1476–1559; Zen landscape painting at its height, fifteenth and sixteenth centuries; Antonio da Mota enters Japan as first European, 1542; Japanese pirates besiege Nanking, 1555

In Mesoamerica, Historic period, 900–1521; Cortés destroys the Aztec capital Tenochtitlán and the Spanish conquest of Mexico and Central America follows; slave trade begins, 1509; chocolate brought from Mexico to Spain, 1520;

B. Definition of Mannerism
  1. Inspired by the religious crisis and the sack of Rome, 1527
  2. Reaction against Classical ideals
     a) Antihumanistic
     b) Odd perspectives in painting
     c) Twisted figures placed in bizarre poses in sculpture
     d) Architecture that tries to surprise
     e) Negative view of human nature
C. Literature
  1. High Renaissance
     a) Gaspara Stampa and Venetian culture
        (1) High Renaissance poetry
        (2) Petrarchan style and themes
        (3) The superiority of the suffering lover
     b) Castiglione and the court of Urbino
        (1) Revival of the Platonist dialogue
        (2) *The Book of the Courtier*
           (a) The ideal gentleman
           (b) The ideal lady
  2. Early Mannerism
     a) Machiavelli and the republic of Florence
     b) *The Prince*
        (1) Negative view of human nature
        (2) A treatise on "how to govern"
D. Painting
  1. Primary art form of the age
  2. Leonardo da Vinci
     a) *The Last Supper*
        (1) Description
        (2) Characteristics
     b) *Mona Lisa*
        (1) Description
        (2) Characteristics
  3. Michelangelo
     a) His aesthetic creed
     b) The Sistine Chapel ceiling frescoes: High Renaissance
        (1) Description
        (2) Characteristics
     c) *The Last Judgment* fresco: Early Mannerist
        (1) Description
        (2) Characteristics

silver mines of Zaatear, Mexico, mined by Spanish, 1548; tobacco brought to Spain, 1555; founding of the National University of Mexico, 1551; Aztec dictionary published, 1555
In Muslim world, in Persia, the Safavid dynasty, 1502–1736; religious persecutions, 1502
In North America, John Cabot reaches Labrador, 1497; Ponce de León discovers Florida, 1513
In the Philippines, the Spanish found Manila, 1564
In South America, Columbus reaches perhaps the Orinoco River, 1498; Pedro Alvares Cabral claims Brazil for Portugal, 1500; Portuguese settlement of Brazil, 1530; Buenos Aires founded by Pedro de Mendoza, 1536; Bogotá founded by Jiminez de Quesada, 1538; silver mines of Potosí, Bolivia, discovered, 1544; founding of University of Lima, 1551

4. Raphael
    a) His aesthetic creed
    b) *The School of Athens*
       (1) Description
       (2) Characteristics
    c) *Sistine Madonna*
       (1) Description
       (2) Characteristics
5. The Venetian School: Titian
    a) The Venetian tradition
    b) *Presentation of the Virgin in the Temple*
       (1) Description
       (2) Characteristics
6. The School of Parma: Parmigianino
    a) His aesthetic ideal
    b) *Madonna with the Long Neck*
       (1) Description
       (2) Characteristics

E. Sculpture
  1. Introduction: Michelangelo
  2. *Pietà*, 1498–1499, High Renaissance
    a) Description
    b) Characteristics
  3. *David*, High Renaissance
    a) Description
    b) Characteristics
  4. *Pietà*, before 1555, Early Mannerist
    a) Description
    b) Characteristics

F. Architecture
  1. Bramante
    a) His aesthetic code
    b) The Tempietto, High Renaissance
       (1) Description
       (2) Characteristics
  2. Michelangelo
    a) His aesthetic code
    b) St. Peter's Basilica, High Renaissance
       (1) Description
       (2) Characteristics
  3. Andrea di Pietro, called Palladio
    a) His aesthetic code
    b) The Villa Capra, or the Villa Rotonda—Early Mannerist
       (1) Description
       (2) Characteristics

G. Music
  1. Josquin des Prez and the High Renaissance musical style
  2. Adrian Willaert

3. The invention of families of
   instruments called consorts

V. The Legacy of the High Renaissance and Early Mannerism

LEARNING OBJECTIVES

To learn:

1. The leading characteristics of the High Renaissance and Early Mannerism and to distinguish between the two cultural and artistic styles

2. The prominent role played by Classicism in the High Renaissance and Early Mannerism

3. How the High Renaissance and Early Mannerism reflected their historic settings

4. The determining role played by events of the 1520s in shaping the Mannerist outlook

5. The sources of the Hapsburg-Valois wars

6. The dominant control exercised by France and Spain over international affairs in this period

7. The pivotal part played by the popes in the High Renaissance

8. That Venice, of all Italy's states, remained free of foreign control or influence after 1530

9. That a commercial revolution shifted economic power from the Mediterranean to Europe's North Atlantic coast in this period

10. The achievements of Stampa, Machiavelli, and Castiglione in literature

11. The major contributions in painting of Leonardo, Michelangelo, Raphael, Titian, and Parmigianino

12. The major achievements in architecture of Michelangelo and Palladio

13. The characteristics of the High Renaissance musical style and the achievements of its leading composers, Josquin des Prez and Adrian Willaert

14. The historic "firsts" of the High Renaissance and Early Mannerism that became part of the Western tradition: the golden age of European painting, sculpture, and architecture; the beginning of modern political thought; the origins of the modern secular state; the birth of etiquette for ladies and gentlemen; and the rise of the belief that free expression is both a social and a private good

15. The role of the High Renaissance and Early Mannerism in transmitting the heritage of the past: reviving and updating Classical ideals in the High Renaissance arts and humanities; pushing Classical principles in new and unorthodox directions while continuing to copy Classical forms in Early Mannerism; and persisting in the trend to secularism that had begun in the Late Middle Ages

SUGGESTIONS FOR FILMS

Civilisation: The Hero as Artist. BBC/Time-Life, 52 min., color.

I, Leonardo da Vinci. McGraw-Hill, 52 min., color.

Michelangelo: The Last Giant. McGraw-Hill, 68 min., color.

Michelangelo: The Medici Chapel. West, 22 min., color.

Music and Art; Italy and Music and the Court; The German Court of Maximilian I (Music and the Renaissance Series). Indiana University, 30 min. each, black and white.

SUGGESTIONS FOR MUSIC

Josquin des Prez. *Chansons.* Ensemble Clement Janequin & Ensemble les Eléments. Harmonia Mundi HMC-901279

———. *Mass, "Hercules Dux Ferraiae."* New London Chamber Choir. Amon Ra CDSAR-24.

———. *Motets.* Chapelle Royale Chorus. Harmonia Mundi HM-901243.

———. *Missa, "La sol fa re mi."* The Tallis Scholars. Gimell CDGIM-009.

Music in the Age of Leonardo da Vinci. Ensemble Claude-Gervaise. Musica Viva MVCD-1022.

Adrian Willaert. *Motets.* Boston Camerata Motet Chorus. Elektra/Nonesuch H-71345.

SUGGESTIONS FOR FURTHER READING

Chastel, A. *A Chronicle of Italian Renaissance Painting.* Translated by L. Murray and P. Murray. Ithaca, N.Y.: Cornell University Press, 1983. A superb narrative of the evolution of Renaissance painting, firmly rooted in the everyday documents that affected the lives of the artists; beautifully illustrated.

de Grazia, S. *Machiavelli in Hell.* Princeton: Princeton University Press, 1989. Using political and literary sources, the author examines the Florentine's life and influence in this new study.

Grafton, A., and Jardine, L. *From Humanism to the Humanities: Education and the Liberal Arts in Fifteenth- and Sixteenth-Century Europe.* Cambridge, Mass.: Harvard University Press, 1987. A reinterpretation of how and why scholasticism gave way to the study of the humanities.

Hale, J. R. *War and Society in Renaissance Europe, 1450–1620.* Leicester, England: Leicester University Press, 1985. A recent study that focuses on changes in warfare and the role of the ordinary soldier.

Hauser, A. *Mannerism.* Cambridge, Mass.: Belknap Press, 1986. A brilliant study of one of the most complex periods in cultural history; successfully integrates the arts, architecture, philosophy, and literature.

King, M. L. *Women in the Renaissance.* Chicago: University of Chicago Press, 1991. A highly readable look at Renaissance women: in their families and church, and as "exceptional" women in leadership. This useful introduction to a complex topic also addresses the broader issue of the nature of the Renaissance for women.

Koenigsberger, H. G. *The Hapsburgs and Europe: 1516–1660.* Ithaca, N.Y.: Cornell University Press, 1971. One of the best brief accounts of this powerful family.

————, and Mosse, G. L. *Europe in the Sixteenth Century.* 2nd ed. London: Longman, 1989. Still ranks as one of the best surveys for the student who wants to gain additional insights into this period.

Levy, M. *High Renaissance.* New York: Penguin, 1975. A good, short introductory overview.

Mannix, D. P. *Black Cargoes: A History of the Atlantic Slave Trade.* New York: Viking, 1962. A moving chronicle of the slave trade showing how it corrupted all involved, from Yankee sea captains to African kings.

Miskimin, H. A. *The Economy of Later Renaissance Europe, 1460–1600.* New York: Columbia University Press, 1977. A short but very readable work well supported by tables and charts.

Murray, L. *The High Renaissance and Mannerism: Italy, the North, and Spain, 1500–1600.* London: Thames and Hudson, 1977. A good survey of Italian painting but too brief on the North and Spain.

Parry, J. H. *The Age of Reconnaissance.* Rev. ed. Berkeley: University of California Press, 1981. A wide-ranging survey of Europe's first colonies in the fifteenth through seventeenth centuries.

Partridge, L. *Michelangelo: The Sistine Chapel Ceiling.* New York: Braziller, 1996. A brief but informative study that examines the frescoes regarding design, style, and theological significance; a useful introduction.

Pope-Hennessy, J. W. *Italian High Renaissance and Baroque Sculpture.* 3rd ed. Oxford: Phaidon, 1986. Presupposing that the reader has an understanding of the era, the author takes the student on a detailed journey through a complicated topic.

Reese, G. *The New Grove High Renaissance Masters: Josquin, Palestrina, Lassus, Byrd, Victoria.* New York: Norton, 1984. In the composer biography series, it combines the life and works of each musician. Includes an extensive bibliography.

Smart, A. *The Renaissance and Mannerism in Northern Europe and Spain.* New York: Harcourt Brace Jovanovich, 1972. The author argues that while Northern European art in the Late Middle Ages possessed its unique style and themes, this art would be forever changed in the sixteenth century when the Renaissance made its way across the Alps. The curious student who desires a deeper understanding of cultural changes will learn much from Smart's work.

Stinger, C. *The Renaissance in Rome.* Bloomington: Indiana University Press, 1985. A study of the city of Rome, of the Catholic church in Rome, and the Renaissance of the fifteenth and sixteenth centuries; a work for the ambitious student.

IDENTIFICATIONS

High Renaissance	scenographic
Mannerism	balustrade
machiavellianism	consort
Pietà	

PERSONAL PERSPECTIVE BACKGROUND

Giorgio Vasari, *Lives of the Most Eminent Painters, Sculptors, and Architects*

Vasari's *Lives*, first published in 1550, established the West's conventional way of interpreting Renaissance art until an appreciation for medieval art developed in the twentieth century. In Vasari's survey, following the Renaissance view of history, he depicted the Middle Ages as the Dark Ages, when art was made by incompetent artists. He also showed that the Italian Renaissance revived Classical culture, beginning in the city-state of Florence with the works of Giotto and culminating in those of Michelangelo. The chapter devoted to Michelangelo was the first biography of an artist to appear while the person was alive, and thus initiated a new literary genre. Despite its admiring tone, Michelangelo was offended and arranged for an assistant to write a rival biography (1553), probably based on his own words as he wished to be remembered.

DISCUSSION/ESSAY QUESTIONS

1. Discuss the conditions that led to the flowering of the High Renaissance and the reasons for its abrupt end.
2. Compare and contrast the High Renaissance and Early Mannerism as cultural styles.
3. Discuss the causes of the rise of the new nation-states and describe at least one new nation-state as an example. What impact did the new nation-states have on the arts and humanities?
4. Analyze the strengths and weaknesses of Charles V's empire, and assess how successful he was as a ruler. What was the impact of Charles V's wars on the culture of the times?
5. What were the causes of the Hapsburg-Valois wars, and what was the final outcome of this bloody struggle?
6. How did historic events in the 1520s contribute to the rise of Mannerism?
7. Discuss the role of Gaspara Stampa as both a poet and a woman of the Renaissance era.
8. Show how Machiavelli's *Prince* and Castiglione's *Book of the Courtier* embody the styles of the High Renaissance and Early Mannerism, respectively.
9. Compare and contrast Mannerist artists and Renaissance artists.
10. Discuss the different roles played by Classicism in the High Renaissance and Early Mannerism.
11. What were some of Michelangelo's contributions to painting, sculpture, and architecture? Show how his genius helped to define both the High Renaissance and Early Mannerism.
12. Discuss Michelangelo's artistic creed and show how it was manifested in his Sistine Chapel ceiling.
13. Compare and contrast the architectural ideal of Michelangelo with that of Palladio.
14. Describe the sound of High Renaissance music. Who were the leading composers in this style, and what were some of their principal achievements?
15. Select a painting, a sculpture, and a building from both the High Renaissance and Early Mannerism and compare and contrast them, with the goal of setting forth the distinguishing characteristics of these two artistic styles.
16. What was the single most important development in this period? Explain.

MULTIPLE-CHOICE QUESTIONS

1. The three most famous artists associated with the High Renaissance in Rome are:
   a. Leonardo da Vinci, Michelangelo, and Titian
   b. Leonardo da Vinci, Raphael, and Parmigianino
 * c. Leonardo da Vinci, Michaelangelo, and Raphael (p. 299)
   d. Leonardo da Vinci, Michelangelo, and Parmigianino

2. The cultural center of the High Renaissance was:
 * a. Rome (p. 299)
   b. Florence
   c. Venice
   d. Parma

3. The leading patrons of the High Renaissance were the:
   a. rich middle class
 * b. popes (p. 299)
   c. nobles
   d. monks and nuns

4. Which was NOT an ideal of the High Renaissance?
    a. rational design
    b. beauty
  * c. asymmetry (p. 299)
    d. serenity

5. The three newly unified and stabilized nations in western Europe to emerge in the first half of the sixteenth century were:
    a. Germany, Spain, and France
  * b. Spain, France, and England
    c. Spain, Austria, and England
    d. Ottoman Empire, Spain, and France

6. An important political development between 1494 and 1564 was the:
    a. emergence of Germany as a unified state
    b. triumph of France in Europe
    c. end of the Hundred Years' War
  * d. birth of the concept of the balance of power (p. 299)

7. Between 1494 and 1564, Europe's international political life was dominated by:
    a. England and the Netherlands
  * b. France and Spain (p. 299)
    c. Italy and Greece
    d. Scandinavia and Russia

8. Which was NOT a consequence of the sack of Rome in 1527?
    a. It cast doubt on Rome's ability to control Italy.
  * b. It assured the Italians of a voice in European affairs. (p. 302)
    c. It ended papal patronage of the arts for almost a decade.
    d. It contributed to the rise of Mannerism.

9. Which Italian state maintained its independence from foreigners throughout the 1500s?
  * a. Venice (pp. 302–303)
    b. Florence
    c. Rome
    d. Naples

10. All of the following were causes of the Valois-Hapsburg wars EXCEPT:
    a. The Valois kings felt encircled by Hapsburg power.
  * b. France and Spain both wanted to show England which was the most powerful country in Europe. (p. 303)
    c. The Hapsburgs thought that the French king stood in the way of their dream of a united Christendom of Europe.
    d. Each state struggled to maintain the balance of power.

11. Charles V can be described as a ruler who:
    a. went from one conquest to another
    b. lacked the financial resources to support his ramshackle empire
  * c. represented both the old and new Europe (p. 303)
    d. came to power through a series of military victories

12. Charles V's territories included all of these EXCEPT:
    a. Spain and Austria
    b. Burgundy and the Low Countries
    c. most of South and Central America
    * d. Scandinavia and Finland (p. 303)

13. On Charles V's abdication, his vast holdings were:
    a. inherited by his son Philip
    * b. divided between his brother (the German-Austrian inheritance) and his son (the Spanish territories) (p. 304)
    c. parceled out among a wide number of enemies
    d. taken over by the Valois dynasty

14. Between 1494 and 1564, a revolution occurred that shifted the center of commerce from the Mediterranean to the:
    a. Black Sea
    * b. Atlantic coast (p. 304)
    c. Baltic Sea
    d. German Rhineland

15. Which is a socioeconomic development in this period?
    * a. the establishment of slavery in the European New World colonies (p. 304)
    b. the creation of a tariff-free trade zone in Europe
    c. the beginning of industrial capitalism
    d. the end of peasantry in Europe

16. Studies indicate that all of the following occurred in Europe between 1400 and 1600 EXCEPT:
    * a. The population tended to shift from the west to the east. (p. 304)
    b. The population nearly doubled.
    c. People were beginning to move to urban areas.
    d. The number of cities of over 100,000 increased.

17. One of the distinguishing differences between the Early Renaissance and the High Renaissance was that:
    a. The former was occupied with the Gothic style while the latter was not.
    b. The former concentrated on architecture and the latter on painting.
    c. The former was based solely on scholarship and the latter produced no literature.
    * d. The former experimented with the Classical style whereas the latter created masterpieces of disciplined form and idealized beauty reflecting the Classical past. (pp. 304–305)

18. High Renaissance literature was NOT based on the:
    a. conviction that life has a basic secular purpose
    b. belief that human nature is inherently rational and good
    c. idea that social values are created by people of good sense
    * d. notion that humans require moral guidance by external forces (p. 306)

19. The Mannerist viewpoint was anti-Classical in its:
    a. belief that human nature is basically good
    b. acceptance of the principle that art should imitate nature
    * c. support for an art of odd perspectives and distortions (p. 306)
    d. endorsement of the ideal of balanced design

20. Classical idealism is NOT evident in the:
    a. description of the lady and gentleman in *The Courtier*
    * b. paintings of Parmigianino (pp. 305–322)
    c. treatment of space in the *School of Athens*
    d. body of David in Michelangelo's sculpture of that name

21. Gaspara Stampa may be described in all of the following ways EXCEPT:
    a. She was influenced by Petrarch and his poetry.
    b. She experienced hurt from her love affairs.
    * c. She revealed the joys of life through her novels. (p. 306)
    d. She reflected the age's changing mores through her confessional poetry.

22. The subject of Castiglione's *Book of the Courtier* is:
    a. international diplomacy
    * b. civilized behavior (p. 306)
    c. artistic aesthetics
    d. romantic love

23. Castiglione's model courtier was NOT:
    a. educated in the humanities
    * b. trained to be a priest (pp. 306–307)
    c. skilled in horsemanship and swordplay
    d. knowledgeable about painting and sculpture

24. Castiglione's model lady was described as:
    a. a good mother
    b. an excellent housekeeper
    * c. a charming hostess (p. 307)
    d. an excellent weaver

25. Castiglione argued that in social relations:
    a. Men should dominate women.
    b. Men should be better educated than women.
    c. Women should be superior to men.
    * d. Men and women should be ruled by Platonic love. (p. 307)

26. Castiglione's *Courtier* can be seen as a modern work in that:
    * a. He encouraged the education of women. (p. 307)
    b. He advocated equal rights for men and women.
    c. He called for the abolition of slavery.
    d. He argued that all men are created equal.

27. "Machiavellianism" means:
    a. "Handsome is as handsome does."
    * b. "The end justifies any means." (p. 308)
    c. "Love God and do as you please."
    d. "Still waters run deep."

28. Machiavelli dedicated *The Prince* to this ruler, whom he hoped would become his patron:
    a. Cesare Borgia, the illegitimate son of Pope Alexander VI
    b. Leo X, the Medici pope
    * c. the Medici prince who governed Florence (p. 308)
    d. Charles V, the Holy Roman Emperor

29. Machiavelli's *Prince* reflected the author's:
   * a.   anguish at Italy's domination by foreigners (p. 308)
     b.   experience as a courtier of Charles V, Holy Roman Emperor
     c.   background as a Venetian official
     d.   years as a papal official

30. Machiavelli's political advice to rulers was to:
     a.   Follow the Bible in the conduct of government.
   * b.   Practice conscious duplicity in all matters. (p. 308)
     c.   Be virtuous and upright in all relationships.
     d.   Always be cruel and unforgiving.

31. This writer laid the foundation for modern political theory:
     a.   Castiglione
   * b.   Machiavelli (p. 307)
     c.   Palladio
     d.   Aretino

32. The following Classical value was evident in High Renaissance painting:
   * a.   harmonious colors (p. 308)
     b.   distorted faces
     c.   unbalanced figures
     d.   obscure backgrounds

33. An Early Mannerist painting was:
     a.   Leonardo's *Mona Lisa*
     b.   Michelangelo's *Creation of Adam*
   * c.   Parmigianino's *Madonna with the Long Neck* (p. 319)
     d.   Raphael's *Sistine Madonna*

34. Which was NOT a Classical aspect of Leonardo's *Last Supper*?
     a.   the realistic space and perspective
     b.   the restrained expression of emotions
     c.   the balanced composition with six disciples flanking Jesus
   * d.   the heavenly light that causes the bodies to glow (pp. 308–310)

35. The subjects of Michelangelo's Sistine Chapel ceiling frescoes were NOT based on:
     a.   biblical narrative
     b.   Classical references
     c.   Neo-Platonist philosophy
   * d.   characters from Roman poems (pp. 311, 316)

36. Which was NOT a Neo-Platonic influence on Michelangelo's Sistine chapel ceiling frescoes?
   * a.   the harmonious color scheme (p. 311 and caption for Fig. 12.8)
     b.   the use of geometric shapes
     c.   the portrayal of the pagan sibyls
     d.   the depiction of Adam half-awakened and reaching to God

37. Which was NOT a Mannerist effect in Michelangelo's *Last Judgment* fresco?
     a.   the elongated bodies with heads reduced in size
     b.   the expressive faces
     c.   a chaotic surface appearance with bodies swirling around the central image of Jesus
   * d.   the serene image of Jesus as he sits with downcast eyes (p. 316)

38. Raphael is acknowledged as the supreme painter of:
    a.   psychological truth
 * b.   ordered space (p. 316)
    c.   scientific accuracy
    d.   expressive faces

39. Which High Renaissance master painted a likeness of Castiglione, author of *The Book of the Courtier?*
    a.   Leonardo da Vinci
    b.   Michelangelo
 * c.   Raphael (p. 306 and caption for Fig. 12.5)
    d.   Titian

40. Venetian art was famous for the tradition of:
    a.   subdued lighting
    b.   pale colors
 * c.   sensual surfaces (p. 318)
    d.   simple, uncomplicated scenes of peasant life

41. The outstanding Venetian painter between 1494 and 1564 was:
    a.   Correggio
 * b.   Titian (p. 318)
    c.   Parmigianino
    d.   Caravaggio

42. Parmigianino's *Madonna of the Long Neck* is Mannerist in its:
    a.   well-balanced design
 * b.   distorted figures (p. 319 and caption for Fig. 12.16)
    c.   plain moral message
    d.   idealized proportions

43. What is the subject of a "pietà" scene?
 * a.   the Virgin Mary and the dead Christ (p. 319)
    b.   the crucifixion of Jesus flanked by two other crucified persons
    c.   the birth of Jesus with angels and shepherds
    d.   the journey of Jesus into Jerusalem, riding a donkey

44. Which is NOT a Classical ideal manifested in Michelangelo's *David?*
    a.   graceful contrapposto
 * b.   distorted face (pp. 319, 321)
    c.   heroic nudity
    d.   athletic, muscular body

45. The founder of High Renaissance architecture was:
 * a.   Bramante (p. 323)
    b.   Leonardo da Vinci
    c.   Raphael
    d.   Alberti

46. Which is NOT a Classical ideal visible in Bramante's Tempietto, or Little Temple?
    a.   Ornamentation is restricted to a few architectural details.
    b.   Its proportions are computed using ancient mathematical formulas.
 * c.   It towers over the nearby buildings. (p. 323)
    d.   It functions like a work of sculpture, being placed on a pedestal with steps.

47. Michelangelo's outstanding architectural monument is the:
    a. plan of the Tempietto, Rome
  * b. dome of St. Peter's basilica, Rome (pp. 323–324)
    c. dome of the Florentine cathedral
    d. Villa Capra, or the Villa Rotonda

48. What unifying agent was used by Michelangelo to give a harmonious appearance to the exterior of St. Peter's basilica?
    a. stained glass windows arranged into sets of eight
    b. flying buttresses along the walls of the nave and apse
  * c. double Corinthian columns (p. 324)
    d. statues of saints set into niches on the facade

49. What is the basic plan of the Villa Rotonda?
    a. a Roman rectilinear temple raised on a pedestal
  * b. four identical wings surrounding a domed central area (p. 324)
    c. a meandering shape determined by the eccentric topography of the site
    d. a circular temple covered by a dome

50. Who designed the Villa Capra, or Villa Rotonda?
    a. Alberti
    b. Bramante
    c. Michelangelo
  * d. Palladio (p. 324)

51. Which national school dominated High Renaissance music?
    a. the English
  * b. the Franco-Netherlandish (p. 326)
    c. the Italian
    d. the German

52. What musical innovation occurred in the High Renaissance?
    a. the birth of the orchestra
    b. the development of opera
  * c. the invention of families of instruments, called consorts (p. 326)
    d. the emergence of the piano

53. Which was NOT a feature of High Renaissance music?
    a. a cappella singing
  * b. all voices sing the same line in unison (p. 326)
    c. multiple voices, usually two to six
    d. clearly sung texts

54. The dominant composer in this period was:
  * a. Josquin des Prez (p. 326)
    b. Gabrieli
    c. Willaert
    d. Byrd

55. Which was NOT an enduring legacy of this period to the Western tradition?
  * a. the creation of the concept of Christendom (p. 327)
    b. the belief that free expression is both a private and a social good
    c. the beginning of the modern secular state
    d. a new code of etiquette for gentlemen and ladies

13

THE RELIGIOUS REFORMATIONS, NORTHERN HUMANISM, THE NORTHERN RENAISSANCE, AND LATE MANNERISM 1500–1603

TEACHING STRATEGIES AND SUGGESTIONS

The instructor, again, can choose from several teaching models—the Comparison/Contrast, the Diffusion, or the Spirit of the Age—for the first lecture. The Comparison/Contrast approach is probably the most effective, comparing and contrasting the Italian Renaissance with Northern Humanism and then contrasting the Italian Renaissance with the religious reformations. Other teaching strategies can include using the Patterns of Change model to explain the causes of the Protestant and Catholic reformations and the Case Study approach to draw parallels between the Reformation and later reform movements, such as the Enlightenment or the American Great Awakening.

The teacher can apply the Comparison/Contrast model in analyzing the topics of the Protestant order and the Counter-Reformation. The Diffusion model can then be used to treat Northern Humanism, showing how it grew out of Italian Humanism and took on its own characteristics; the Reflections/Connections approach can establish the historical framework for the presentations on literature, thought, the arts, and music. A Music Lecture can illustrate the music of this period, particularly the music of Palestrina, the central figure of the Catholic Reformation. Late Mannerism in literature and the visual arts can be explained with the Patterns of Change strategy, showing the evolution from Early Mannerism into more and more complex forms. Another option is to teach Late Mannerism using the Reflections/Connections model to demonstrate how the values and beliefs of the Reformation, the Counter-Reformation, and Northern Humanism were expressed in literature and the visual arts.

LECTURE OUTLINE

Non-Western Events

I. Overview of Mannerism, the Northern Renaissance, and the Religious Reformations

II. The Breakup of Christendom: Causes of the Religious Reformations
   A. Conditions in the church
   B. Situation in Germany
   C. The Protestant order
      1. Luther's revolt
         a) The Ninety-Five Theses

1500–1603
In Africa, growth of black slave trade, 1500–1800; Idris Aloma (d. 1603) builds Bornu in the strongest state between the Niger and the Nile; Afro-Portuguese ivory carvings of salt-cellars, hunting horns, spoons, forks, many

       b)   Luther's beliefs
       c)   Social and political implications
              of Luther's revolt
       d)   Luther's Bible
    2. The reforms of John Calvin
       a)   Calvin's beliefs
       b)   Impact of Calvin's beliefs
              on society
       c)   The success of Calvinism
    3. The reform of the English Church
  D. The Counter-Reformation
    1. The reformed papacy
    2. New monastic orders
       a)   For women, the Ursulines:
              Angela Merici
       b)   For men, the Jesuits:
              Ignatius Loyola
    3. The Council of Trent
  E. Warfare as a response to
      religious dissent, 1520–1603
    1. Charles V and the Religious
        Peace of Augsburg
    2. Spain's bid for power

III. Northern Humanism (also known as
     Christian Humanism)
  A. Characteristics of the movement
  B. Northern Humanists: Rabelais,
     Marguerite of Navarre (also called
     Margaret of Angoulême), and
     Erasmus

IV. The Northern Renaissance and
     Late Mannerism
  A. The setting and duration
  B. Northern Renaissance literature
    1. Michel de Montaigne
    2. William Shakespeare, *Hamlet*
  C. Northern Renaissance painting
    1. Albrecht Dürer
    2. Mathias Grünewald
    3. Pieter Bruegel the Elder
  D. Mannerist painting in Spain
    1. El Greco
    2. Sofonisba Anguissola
  E. Italian culture, 1564–1603
    1. Late Mannerist painting
        in Italy: Tintoretto
    2. Late sixteenth-century music
        in Italy and England

V. The Legacy of the Religious Reformations,
    Northern Humanism, the Northern
    Renaissance, and Late Mannerism

by Benin artists, sixteenth century
In China, Ming dynasty, 1368–1644; Ming products, such as blue-and-white porcelain and enamel wares, find overseas markets in Africa, Europe, and Central America, from the 1560s; Beijing, the Ming capital, becomes the largest and most populous city in the world; wall erected around Beijing; Jesuit missionaries active, 1550–1650; worst earthquake in history hits Shanxi province, 1556; churches designed in a Western style by the Jesuit Matteo Ricci, in Macao and Canton, about 1600; the play, *The Peony Pavillion,* by Tang Xiansu, 1598
In Himalaya region, in Tibet, Lamaistic state, about 1450 to 1950s
In India, Delhi Sultanate, 1192–1526; Mughal Empire, 1526–1858; Akbar, the Great Mughal, 1556–1605; the saint-poets Kabir, Ravidas, Nanak, Mirabai, Surdas, and Tulsidas compose devotional poetry in medieval Hindi, about 1400 to about 1600; the *ghazal,* a poetic literary genre, developed in Urdu, from about 1500 to the present
In Indochina, in Burma, rebirth of the arts and architecture, after 1500
In Japan, Muromachi period, 1333–1573; Momoyama period, 1573–1614; "Country at War" period, 1500–1600; first Europeans arrive, 1542; beginning of Western influence; introduction of firearms and fortress architecture; the "White Heron" castle

of Himeji, with its four
towers joined by passages
with turrets; origin of
Kabuki theater; Osaka
Castle, 1583; Nagasaki
begins to emerge as a
major port, 1570;
introduction of printing
press, 1591; Jesuit
missionaries active,
1550–1650

In Korea, Li dynasty, 1392–
1910; Japanese invade and
sack and burn the capital
Kyongju, destroying most
of its buildings and
monuments, 1592–1598

In the Muslim world, in
Persia, Isfahan becomes
capital, 1587, and
beautified with palaces,
mosques, gardens, bridges,
and markets

In North America, formation
of the Mohawk, Oneida,
Onondaga, Cayuga, and
Seneca tribes into a
confederacy called the
Iroquois, 1570

In the Philippines, the
University of San Carlos,
founded 1595

In Siberia, colonization by
Russia begins, 1579

In South America, in
Ecuador, founding of the
Central University of
Quito, 1594; in
Colombia, founding of
Caracas by Spanish
settlers, 1566

LEARNING OBJECTIVES

To learn:

1. The causes of the Protestant Reformation

2. The political conditions in Germany and the Holy Roman Empire in the early sixteenth century

3. The major phases of the life of Martin Luther and the events in Germany during his early years

4. The basic beliefs and tenets of Lutheranism

5. The impact of Luther's revolt on social and political movements

6. The major phases of and influences on John Calvin's life

7. The basic beliefs and ideas of Calvinism

8. The impact of Calvinism on social and political developments

9. The causes of the rise of the Church of England

10. The results and impact of the religious changes in England

11. The causes of the Counter-Reformation

12. The leaders and contributions of the reformed papacy

13. The origins, development, and results of the founding of new Catholic monastic orders and, in particular, the Ursulines and the Jesuits

14. The central issues of the Council of Trent

15. The major phases and results of the Wars of Religion

16. The characteristics of Northern Humanism, its literary leaders, and their contributions

17. The role played by Erasmus in Northern Humanism and the Protestant Reformation

18. The characteristics of Northern Renaissance literature, its leading writers, and their contributions

19. The major phases of the life of William Shakespeare, his types of plays, and the themes and ideas in *Hamlet* that reflect the Mannerist aesthetic

20. The nature of Northern Renaissance painting, its major painters, and representative examples of this style

21. The nature of Italian culture in the late sixteenth century and representative examples as expressed in painting

22. The influence of the Counter-Reformation on Italian church music, and the impact of the madrigal on Italian and English secular music

23. The historic "firsts" of the age of the Reformations, Northern Humanism, the Northern Renaissance, and Late Mannerism that became part of the Western tradition: the end of the dream of a united European Christendom and the division of Europe between Protestantism and Roman Catholicism, the first European explorations and overseas colonies, beginning of the modern sovereign state and the rivalry among these new political entities, formulation of distinct cultural attitudes between Protestants and Roman Catholics, and the establishment of the commercial theater as a legitimate art form

24. The role of this age in transmitting the heritage of earlier ages: continuing the basic ideas and values of Renaissance humanism as modified by Northern Humanism, furthering the concept of the worth of the individual, making religious differences and preferences the basis of intolerance and persecutions, adapting Renaissance styles in literature and the visual arts to northern European tastes, and bringing Mannerist painting to a brilliant sunset in Venetian art

SUGGESTIONS FOR FILMS

Civilisation: Protest and Communication. Time-Life, 52 min., color.

John Calvin. University of Utah, Educational Media Center, 29 min., color.

Martin Luther and the Protestant Reformation. Time-Life, 30 min., black and white.

The Reformation. McGraw-Hill, 52 min., color.

The Reformation: Age of Revolt. Encyclopedia Britannica, 24 min., color.

SUGGESTIONS FOR MUSIC

Palestrina, Giovanni. *Missa de Beata Virgine.* Ugrin, Jeunesses Musicales Chorus. Hungaraton HCD-12921.

————. *Missa Papae Marcelli.* Phillips, The Tallis Scholars. Gimell CDGIM-339.

————. *Stabat Mater.* Brown, Pro Cantione Antiqua. MCA Classics MCAD-25191 [CD]; MCAC-25191 (digital).

Shakespeare Songs and Consort Music. Deller Consort. Harmonia Mundi HMC-202; HMA-190.202 [CD].

SUGGESTIONS FOR FURTHER READING

Augustijn, C. *Erasmus. His Life, Works, and Influence.* Toronto: University of Toronto Press, 1991. A sympathetic treatment of Erasmus and his times.

Bainton, R. *Here I Stand: A Life of Martin Luther.* New York: New American Library, 1950. A still useful biography that treats Luther's life largely from the perspective of his evolving religious beliefs.

Bakhtin, M. *Rabelais and His World.* Translated by H. Iswolsky. Bloomington: Indiana University Press, 1984. Using the methods of literary criticism, this groundbreaking work focuses on "poeticality," and not on historical, cultural, and genetic approaches; first published in Russian in 1968. For advanced students.

Brady, T. A., Jr., Oberman, H. A., and Tracy, J. D. *Handbook of European History, 1400–1600: Late Middle Ages, Renaissance, and Reformation.* Vol. I: *Structures and Assertions.* Vol. II: *Visions, Programs, and Outcomes.* Leiden, The Netherlands: E. J. Brill, 1994. Concise essays by various scholars who survey the state of scholarship in European culture, covering politics, society, religion, and ideas for this 200-year period. Noteworthy essays in Vol. II: "The Humanist Movement" by R. G. Witt; "International Calvinism" by R. M. Kingdon; "Luther's Reformation" by M. Breacht; "The New Religious Orders" by J. P. Donnelly; "The Radical Reformation" by J. M. Stayer.

Chadwick, O. *The Reformation*. Rev. ed New York: Penguin, 1976.. This balanced survey of the Reformation Europe continues to be an outstanding introduction for beginning students; a reprint of the 1964 original with revisions.

Davidson, N. S. *The Counter-Reformation*. Oxford: Blackwell, 1987. An evenhanded approach to the Catholic Counter-Reformation that focuses on four issues: doctrine, clergy, laity, and missions.

Davis, R. *The Rise of the Atlantic Economies*. London: Weidenfeld and Nicolson, 1973. Useful information on the early stage of the growth of commercial capitalism.

Elton, G. R. *Reform and Reformation: England, 1509–1558*. Cambridge: Harvard University Press, 1977. An authoritative work written by one of the century's foremost scholars of Tudor England..

Erickson, E. H. *Young Man Luther: A Study in Psychoanalysis and History*. New York: Norton, 1962. Luther's personality and motives are analyzed by one of the most influential psychoanalysts of our times; one of the landmarks of psychohistory, first published in 1958.

Haile, H. G. *Luther: An Experiment in Biography*. Garden City, N.Y.: Doubleday, 1980. A popular biography that reveals the actual man behind the reformer.

McGrath, A. E. *A Life of John Calvin: A Study of the Shaping of Western Culture*. Cambridge: Blackwell, 1990. An up-to-date biography of Calvin and an assessment of his role in shaping European culture.

Ozment, S. *The Age of Reform, 1250–1550: An Intellectual and Religious History of Late Medieval and Reformation Europe*. New Haven: Yale University Press, 1980. Taking a broader view than most scholars, Ozment argues that the origins of the Reformation are found in the attitudes of the populace and their leaders.

Snyder, J. *Northern Renaissance Art: Painting, Sculpture, the Graphic Arts from 1350 to 1575*. Englewood Cliffs, N. J.: Prentice-Hall, 1985. A broad overview of the Northern Renaissance, tracing its stages beginning with the International Style of the Late Gothic through its collision with the Italian traditions of the Renaissance; excellent illustrations.

Sypher, W. *Four Stages of Renaissance Style*. Garden City, N.Y.: Doubleday, 1955. A controversial and uneven work that remains a brilliant attempt to rethink the Renaissance and its aftermath.

Tawney, R. H. *Religion and the Rise of Capitalism*. New York: Harcourt, Brace, 1952. A forceful response to the thesis of Max Weber; forces the reader to reconsider the relationship between religion and economics; originally issued in 1922.

Weber, M. *The Protestant Ethic and the Spirit of Capitalism*. Translated by T. Parsons. New York: Scribner, 1958. A famous English translation of the early-twentieth-century German book that is probably the most influential modern interpretation of the Protestant Reformation.

Wells, S., ed. *The Cambridge Companion to Shakespeare Studies*. Cambridge: Cambridge University Press, 1986. A useful and authoritative guide for students of Shakespeare.

IDENTIFICATIONS

Reformation	Christian humanism
Counter-Reformation	revenge tragedy
Lutheranism	Northern Renaissance
Calvinism	Late Mannerism
Puritanism	madrigal
Anglicanism	word painting
Jesuits	

PERSONAL PERSPECTIVE BACKGROUND

Albrecht Dürer, On Luther

The Personal Perspective is from Dürer's journal, kept on his travels in Holland and Flanders between July 1520 and July 1521. Along the way, Dürer met and was entertained by Erasmus and the region's leading artists, though the trip's purpose was financial. His imperial pension having expired, Dürer hoped for an audience with Emperor Charles V, who was then touring his Netherlandish possessions. Dürer eventually had his pension renewed, though not before chasing Charles through ten or more cities. While in Antwerp, in May 1521, a rumor (mistaken, as it turned out) reached Dürer that Luther had been abducted by hostile soldiers on leaving the Diet of Worms. In his journal, Dürer expressed his fears for Luther's life and the future of the new faith. He concluded his entry (not included here) with an impassioned appeal to Erasmus: "O Erasmus of Rotterdam, where wilt thou remain? Wilt thou see the injustice and blind tyranny of the power now ruling? . . . [O]ld as thou art . . . thou too mayst win the martyr's crown. . . ." (See *The Western Humanities* for additional information on Dürer.)

DISCUSSION/ESSAY QUESTIONS

1. Discuss the religious and political changes in Europe between 1500 and 1603. How were these changes reflected in the map of Europe?
2. Discuss the causes of the Protestant Reformation, noting the "internal" conditions of the church and the "external" situation in Germany.
3. In what ways did the life of Martin Luther contribute to his break with the Catholic Church?
4. What role did politics play in Luther's successful revolt against the Catholic Church? How did Luther's religious ideas, especially toward the relations between church and state, reflect the political situation in Germany?
5. Show how the quarrel over indulgences triggered the Protestant Reformation.
6. Discuss the major beliefs of Lutheranism and note their impact on nonreligious issues.
7. Explain the basic ideas of Calvinism and show how they affected societies where large numbers of Calvinists were citizens.
8. Compare and contrast Lutheranism and Calvinism, noting especially key doctrines, the definition and role of the sacraments, the place of the Bible in doctrine, and the proper relationship between church and state.
9. What were the causes and major phases of the English Reformation?
10. Trace the Catholic Church's response to the rise of Protestantism. How successful was the church in its early encounters with the new movement?
11. Compare and contrast the effect of the reform movements on Protestant and Catholic women.
12. Discuss the origins and beliefs of the Society of Jesus.
13. How did the sixteenth-century reforms of the Catholic Church lay the foundations for the church until the twentieth century?
14. Outline the major phases of warfare in the sixteenth century and explain their consequences for politics and culture.
15. What were the basic characteristics of Northern Humanism, and how did it differ from Italian Humanism?
16. What was Rabelais's achievement as a writer? Why was he outside of the mainstream of Northern Humanism?
17. Discuss the literary achievement of Marguerite of Navarre and describe the social world within which she wrote.
18. Why is Erasmus called the "prince of humanists"? Discuss his beliefs as they were manifested in his writings.
19. How are Montaigne and Shakespeare representative of Northern Renaissance literature?
20. Discuss the phases of Shakespeare's life. How are his insights into human nature expressed in *Hamlet?* Identify Mannerist features of *Hamlet.*

21. Discuss the impact of the Protestant Reformation on north European painting and note the works of two artists affected by this movement.

22. Relate the impact of the Counter-Reformation on El Greco and discuss this impact as revealed in his paintings.

23. How did the Counter-Reformation affect Italian painting and music in the late sixteenth century?

24. Compare and contrast the religious reformations with the Renaissance.

25. How did the rise of the sovereign state affect politics, warfare, and culture in sixteenth-century Europe?

26. As Europe divided into Protestant and Catholic armed camps, how did these two religious areas respond to the arts and to culture in general? Discuss the ways the two areas were similar as well as how they differed.

27. What were the long-range consequences of the religious reformations for European society and its values?

28. What were the most important legacies of Northern Humanism and Late Mannerism to the Western humanistic tradition?

MULTIPLE-CHOICE QUESTIONS

1. Reformation leaders drew inspiration from the:
    a. flourishing church of the High Middle Ages
    * b. struggling early Christian church (p. 329)
    c. missionary zeal of the Crusades
    d. harsh discipline of Irish Christianity

2. What impact did religious reform have on the sixteenth-century Catholic Church?
    a. It had very little, since the reforms were quickly dismantled.
    b. It made the church very similar to the Protestant churches.
    * c. It set the path the church followed until the 1960s. (p. 329)
    d. It divided the church into rival factions.

3. As the Protestants and Catholics went their separate ways in the sixteenth century, they tended to rally around which of the following sets of leaders?
    a. Protestant King John and Catholic Queen Anne
    * b. Protestant Queen Elizabeth and Catholic Philip II (p. 329)
    c. Protestant King Henry VIII and Catholic Emperor Charles V
    d. Protestant Queen Mary and Catholic Philip II

4. Which did NOT contribute to the disintegration of the Catholic Church?
    a. the growing corruption within the church
    * b. the external threat of Islam from the Middle East (pp. 330–331)
    c. the rise of sovereign states
    d. the impact of humanism and humanistic studies

5. Which was NOT a problem confronting the Catholic Church in 1500?
    * a. Fewer people wanted to serve as priests, monks, and nuns. (pp. 330–331)
    b. Increasing anticlericalism made the church an unpopular institution.
    c. A morally weak papacy refused to grapple with corruption in the church.
    d. The issues raised during the Great Schism remained unresolved.

6. The two European states that were beginning to free themselves from papal control at the beginning of the sixteenth century were:
    a. Spain and France
    * b. England and France (p. 331)
    c. England and Germany
    d. France and Germany

7. Which does NOT apply to the situation in Germany on the eve of the Protestant Reformation?
    * a. The area was politically united but lacked a strong national leader. (p. 331)
    b. German princes resented the power of the church and its economic holdings in the area.
    c. German princes were locked in a power struggle with the Holy Roman Emperor.
    d. German princes saw themselves as protecting Germany's interests against a foreign, that is, Italian, church.

8. Regarding the coming of the Protestant Reformation and the political situation in Europe, it happened when:
    a. The towns and the rural areas were at peace.
    * b. The new nation-states and church clashed. (p. 331)
    c. The feudal lords and the serfs were at odds.
    d. The towns and feudal lords fought one another.

9. The one event that upset Luther and ultimately launched the Protestant Reformation was the:
    a. collection of Peter's Pence in his town
    b. appointing of the Bishop of Mainz by the local prince
    * c. selling of indulgences in Germany (p. 331)
    d. crowning of the Duke of Saxony by the pope

10. An indulgence is defined as:
    a. a grant from the pope for a Christian to indulge in sinful living
    * b. a pardon that reduced the time spent for doing penance (p. 331)
    c. the taking of the Holy Eucharist while in a state of sin
    d. the sale of a church office

11. Luther attacked the sale of indulgences in his:
    * a. Ninety-Five Theses (p. 331)
    b. *Address to the Christian Nobility of the German Nation*
    c. treatise on free will
    d. translation of the Bible

12. In his search for answers to his sense of sin, Luther finally found the solution through the:
    a. preachings of the local bishop
    * b. biblical passages stressing the power of one's faith (p. 332)
    c. forgiving quality of the clergy
    d. use of the seven sacraments

13. Which of the following was NOT a feature of Luther's beliefs?
    a. The Bible is all that is necessary to gain Christian truths.
    b. Relics should not be worshiped.
    * c. Purgatory is central for understanding God's mercy. (p. 332)
    d. Every person is, in effect, a priest.

14. The Lutheran reforms positively affected women by:
    a. calling for equality between husbands and wives
    b. opening state-run schools for young women
    * c. enabling clergy to marry and thus giving respectability to marriage (p. 332)
    d. permitting women to become priests

15. Central to John Calvin's beliefs was the:
    a. concept of free will
    b. importance of relics
    * c. doctrine of predestination (p. 333)
    d. efficacy of the sacraments

16. Calvin's concept of predestination meant that:
    a. Each priest had the power to save his congregation.
    b. Every believer who took the sacraments was saved.
    * c. Only God knew who was saved or not saved. (p. 333)
    d. All Christians were predestined to die and go to purgatory.

17. Closely associated with Calvinism was the belief that:
    a. Everyone who makes money will be damned.
    b. Being lazy or industrious has no effect on one's soul.
    c. One's outward behavior has no effect on salvation.
    * d. God approves of worldly success. (p. 333)

18. In England, the event that set off the Reformation was:
    a. the burning of Lutheran missionaries by Catholic priests
    * b. Henry VIII's desire to divorce Catherine (p. 333)
    c. Parliament's plan to confiscate church property
    d. the rumors of scandalous living among the monks and nuns

19. The chief agent of the Protestant Reformation in England was:
    a. the German Martin Luther, who sent over missionaries to effect radical change
    * b. England's King Henry VIII, working through Parliament (p. 333)
    c. the English people themselves, who worked through a mass protest movement
    d. middle-class Londoners, who were influenced by German pietism

20. Which did NOT contribute to the success of the Catholic Reformation?
    * a. the rise of a feeling among Protestants that they had erred in leaving the church and should return to Catholicism (pp. 334–335)
    b. the development of the Index of forbidden books
    c. the beginning of a line of vigorous and reform-minded popes
    d. the founding of new monastic orders, such as the Jesuits and the Ursulines

21. Which is NOT correct for the Ursulines? This religious order was:
    a. founded by Angela Merici in Italy
    b. originally intended for laywomen only
    * c. planned to be under male control (pp. 334–335)
    d. devoted at first to serving the sick and the poor and educating the young

22. The success of the Society of Jesus was due to all of these reasons EXCEPT the:
    a. zeal and leadership of its founder, Loyola
    b. dedication and discipline of its members
    c. support given the order by the papacy
    * d. sympathy of Protestants who secretly admired them (p. 335)

23. Which was NOT an accomplishment of the Council of Trent?
* a. It made significant compromises with Protestant leaders. (p. 335)
   b. It reaffirmed the seven sacraments.
   c. It rid the church of its worst abuses.
   d. It clarified and reaffirmed dogma and rituals.

24. When the Protestants and Catholics failed to resolve their differences, they:
   a. called on Greek Orthodox church leaders to help settle their disputes
* b. turned to warfare and alliances (p. 336)
   c. declared a twenty-year truce
   d. decided that both sides could settle down and live in peace

25. Both Christian humanism and Renaissance thought:
* a. upheld rationalism and respected Classical literature (p. 337)
   b. concentrated primarily on secular matters
   c. dealt with social issues, especially the plight of women
   d. were influenced by the pietistic movement

26. Which was NOT a belief of the Christian humanists?
   a. The medieval church was the best model for the contemporary church.
   b. Relics and sacred objects were overemphasized in ceremonies.
* c. Monasticism should be expanded. (p. 337)
   d. Christ should be at the center of their faith.

27. As part of their goals, the Christian humanists wanted to:
   a. establish schools for the urban classes
   b. work with the papacy and monks
* c. make sure that the translations of early Christian writings were correct (p. 337)
   d. prove the correctness of papal policies

28. Who of the following was NOT a Northern Humanist:
   a. Rabelais
   b. Erasmus
* c. Ignatius Loyola (pp. 337–338)
   d. Marguerite of Navarre

29. How did Rabelais differ from other Northern Humanists?
   a. He affirmed the goodness of human nature.
   b. He demonstrated a secular outlook on life.
* c. He often made obscene references. (p. 337)
   d. He thought that men and women were able to lead useful lives based on reason and common sense.

30. Marguerite of Navarre's lasting achievement was the:
* a. writing of stories in the style of Boccaccio's *Decameron* (p. 337)
   b. painting of portraits modeled on the style of Michelangelo
   c. founding of the religious order of Ursuline nuns
   d. adapting of the Italian madrigal to French musical tastes

31. Which is NOT a correct statement about Erasmus's life?
* a. He lived the life of a devout and pious monk. (p. 338)
   b. He traveled to many royal and ecclesiastical courts.
   c. He was learned in humanistic studies.
   d. He was thoroughly grounded in biblical studies.

32. What was the theme of Erasmus's *Praise of Folly*?
    a. It was a defense of the Catholic Church against its critics.
    b. It offered a justification for Luther's faith.
  * c. It satirized many individuals and institutions of his day. (p. 338)
    d. It defended the doctrine of predestination.

33. The fate of Erasmus was that:
    a. He founded Protestantism.
  * b. He alienated both the Catholics and the Protestants. (p. 338)
    c. In defending the Catholics, he lost the support of the Protestants.
    d. He became a wandering scholar without credibility.

34. The issue that divided Erasmus and Luther was the:
    a. use and efficacy of the seven sacraments
    b. importance of the role of the clergy
  * c. question of free will and predestination (p. 338)
    d. question of salvation and forgiveness of sin

35. In his *Essays*, Montaigne viewed the world and human nature:
    a. with an optimistic outlook, for he had faith in fellow human beings
    b. without any hope, since all humans were sinners
  * c. with some hope for survival, but his skepticism prevented him from having too much faith
       (pp. 338–339)
    d. through the eyes of conventional Christian beliefs

36. Which is NOT correct regarding Elizabethan England?
  * a. It was a country torn by religious differences. (pp. 333–334, 339)
    b. It was a nation beginning to find its national sense of identity.
    c. It reached new heights in the verbal arts, particularly in the theater.
    d. It became the leader of Europe's Protestant states.

37. Which is NOT correct regarding medieval theater?
    a. It consisted mostly of morality and mystery plays.
    b. It offered Christian messages to audiences.
    c. Its plays were simple in terms of plot and characters.
  * d. It was popular throughout most of the medieval era. (p. 339)

38. Shakespeare wrote all of the following types of plays EXCEPT:
  * a. satires (p. 339)
    b. tragedies
    c. historical
    d. comedies

39. Which was NOT a characteristic of a Renaissance revenge tragedy?
    a. It was filled with suspense and violence.
    b. It concentrated on a murder that must be avenged.
    c. It introduced a ghost who urged revenge.
  * d. It grew out of medieval morality plays. (p. 339)

40. Which is NOT a Mannerist feature in Shakespeare's *Hamlet?*
    a. The main character, Hamlet, is seen from several different perspectives.
    b. The moody Hamlet often seems to change his personality.
  * c. Hamlet always believes in himself and what he can do. (pp. 340–341)
    d. Hamlet has a low opinion of the human race.

41. How did the Protestant Reformation impact on painting and sculpture?
    a. Protestants now began to build elaborately decorated churches.
 * b. Zealous Protestants destroyed some works of art. (p. 341)
    c. The fresco became the dominant expression of Protestant creativity.
    d. Religious art was commissioned for Protestant homes.

42. Late Gothic tendencies in the Northern Renaissance are most evident in the paintings of:
    a. Albrecht Dürer
 * b. Matthias Grünewald (pp. 341–343)
    c. Pieter Bruegel the Elder
    d. Hans Holbein the Younger

43. Dürer, writing about Luther's abduction, expressed the hope that Luther would:
    a. be killed by his captors, the emperor's soldiers
 * b. escape in order that Lutheranism would survive (Personal Perspective)
    c. be taken to Rome and tried for heresy
    d. become more powerful in death as a martyr to the Protestant cause

44. Which was NOT a feature of Albrecht Dürer's self-portraits?
    a. He seemed to be fully aware of his own importance.
    b. His vanity led him to prefer likenesses done in profile.
 * c. He usually portrayed himself seated by a window with light illuminating his face.
        (p. 343 and caption for Fig. 13.9)
    d. He bordered on the sacrilegious with his Christlike self-portraits.

45. Besides paintings, Dürer also is known for his:
 * a. engravings (p. 342)
    b. sculptures
    c. bronze castings
    d. architectural designs

46. A theme of the *Isenheim Altarpiece* was the:
 * a. horror and anguish of the fate of Jesus (pp. 342–343)
    b. belief that humanity is basically good
    c. encoding of religious myth within an allegory using animals
    d. use of Classical myth to express a Christian message

47. Pieter Bruegel's paintings were:
    a. products of the Catholic Reformation
 * b. efforts to capture the ordinary lives of peasants (p. 343)
    c. expressions of the Late Gothic style
    d. judged to be lewd and immoral in his day

48. The most representative Mannerist artist in Spain who captured the spirit of the Catholic Reformation was:
    a. Velázquez
    b. Goya
 * c. El Greco (p. 344)
    d. Dali

49. Which was NOT an influence on El Greco's painting style?
    a.   his own Mannerist sensibility
    b.   the tradition of Venetian art
  * c.   the works of his contemporary Sofonisba Anguissola (pp. 344–346)
    d.   the paintings of Michelangelo

50. El Greco's painting style represents:
  * a.   the essence of Spanish emotionalism and religious zeal (p. 345)
    b.   the spirit of Greek art adapted to Spanish conditions
    c.   the restrained ideal of High Renaissance art
    d.   a throwback to the Byzantine style of his native Crete

51. What was Sofonisba Anguissola's artistic achievement?
    a.   She pioneered the three-quarter-length portrait.
    b.   She introduced Italian art to northern Europe.
  * c.   She helped introduce the Italian school of art to Spain. (p. 346)
    d.   She adapted the style of Leonardo to French tastes.

52. Which is NOT correct for the Council of Trent?
    a.   It affected the visual arts by decreeing that paintings should be simple and direct and thus easily understandable.
    b.   It wanted music and the arts to be part of the church's efforts to win over the uneducated.
    c.   It decreed that indecent paintings should be altered for modesty's sake.
  * d.   It made the art of Michelangelo, Leonardo, and Raphael the standard by which painters would be judged. (p. 348)

53. Which is NOT correct regarding Tintoretto's *Last Supper*?
    a.   It differed dramatically from Leonardo da Vinci's arrangement of the same scene.
    b.   It emphasized the spirituality of the Christian faith.
  * c.   The figures of Jesus and the disciples are depicted naturalistically. (p. 348 and caption for Fig. 13.19)
    d.   It appealed to human feelings, not to reason.

54. Which is NOT true of late-sixteenth-century Catholic Church music?
  * a.   Clarity of words was sacrificed to musical sounds. (pp. 348–349)
    b.   It became more simple in many ways.
    c.   The Council of Trent decreed that music should be easily understood by the illiterate masses.
    d.   Palestrina set the standard for the Catholic ideal for the next few centuries.

55. What type of song was most expressive of late-sixteenth-century music?
    a.   Gregorian chant
    b.   *canzone*
    c.   motet
  * d.   madrigal (pp. 348-349)

14

THE BAROQUE AGE
Glamour and Grandiosity, 1603–1715

TEACHING STRATEGIES AND SUGGESTIONS

The instructor can begin the Baroque Age with a Standard Lecture, using a Historical Overview to summarize the historical and cultural events that determined the shape of this glamorous epoch. The lecture should stress the central role played in continental politics and culture by Roman Catholic rulers and patrons, particularly the Italian popes and the French king Louis XIV, perhaps the most powerful Western monarch ever. The instructor can then adopt a Comparison/Contrast approach to show how political and cultural developments in Protestant Europe, notably in England and the Netherlands, differed from those in the Catholic world, though there were some similarities. It is necessary to describe these contrasting developments in some detail because from this background arose three variations on the international Baroque: the Florid Baroque, the French Baroque, and the Protestant Baroque.

The arts and architecture are the supreme expressions of Baroque taste; hence the best approach to the three separate and distinct manifestations of the Baroque style is through a series of Slide Lectures built around a Comparison/Contrast strategy. A film on the Baroque arts and architecture would also help students understand the nuances of this international style. The Comparison/Contrast strategy can also be employed to deal with Baroque literature, especially the works of Roman Catholic France and Protestant England. In addition, a Music Lecture can be used to introduce students to opera, a major innovation of the Baroque era, and to Bach and Handel, two Baroque composers who rank among the West's musical immortals.

A summary lecture will probably be needed to draw the diverse aspects of this sprawling age together. To this end the instructor can choose a Spirit of the Age approach to demonstrate the unity beneath the period's often tumultuous events. And that unifying idea can be expressed as follows: The Baroque writers and artists, sensing themselves adrift in an ever-changing universe, created a style that mirrored their age's expanding horizons and territorial expansion.

LECTURE OUTLINE

Non-Western Events

I.   Brief Historical Overview
   A. Stylistic meaning
   B. Baroque versus Mannerism
   C. Turbulent events
   D. Scientific discoveries

1603–1715
In Africa, downfall of African
   kingdoms of Kongo and
   Ngola, 1665–1671; British
   Royal Africa Co. chartered,
   1672; Portuguese

dominance of African east coast city-states, 1505–1650; growth of African slave trade, 1500–1800; rise of Asante empire, based on Gold Coast trade, 1700–1750; rise of Segu and Kaarta kingdoms on the Upper Niger, 1660

In China, Ming dynasty, 1368–1644; tea trade begins between China and Europe, 1609; Beijing's Pao Ho Tien (1627), one of the three Great Halls of the Purple Forbidden City; Tartars of Manchu invade, 1616–1620; Manchu dynasty, 1644–1912; the Manchus tried to avoid assimilation and impose their customs on the Chinese; prosperity, followed by complacency, and a sharp rise in population under the Manchus; authoritarian and hierarchical state; people now forced to shave their heads and wear the queue (pigtail); Jesuit missionaries active, 1550–1650; Beijing's Great White Pagoda, 1652; Tibetan influences in Pagoda building; Kao-ts'en, *Autumn Landscape*, famous Chinese india-ink drawing, 1672; Emperor Kang Hsi founds factories for development of art industries in China, 1680; Manchus conquer Formosa, 1683; *A Night's Talk*, a collection of proverbs published under the pseudonym of Mr. Tut-Tut

In Himalaya region, in Tibet, Lamaistic state, about 1450 to 1950s

In India, Mughal Empire, 1526–1858; Europeans establish trading posts,

Dutch, 1609, English, 1612, French, 1674; British East India Co. chartered, 1600; Maratha Confederacy, 1650–1760; Jahangir, 1605–1627; Shah Jahan, 1627–1658; Aurangzeb, 1658–1707; Shah Jahan builds Taj Mahal, 1632–1647; compilation of *The Granth,* the sacred scriptures of the Sikhs, 1604; the construction of the Peacock Throne for Shah Jahan, 1627–1634; Golden Temple of the Sikhs, Amritsar, seventeenth century; Great Mosque at Lahore, late seventeenth century; Tulsi Das, Hindu poet, 1532–1623

In Japan, Yedo, or Tokugawa period, 1615–1867; Japanese isolation, 1637–1854; the castle of Yedo (now part of modern Tokyo), the seat of power for the Tokugawa Shogunate; unified country under a military government with 250 years of secluded peace; rich urban, middle-class culture with innovations in the economy, literature, and the arts; decline of daimyo class; Jesuit missionaries active 1550–1650; revival of Shintoism; Mitsui family's trading and banking house founded, 1673; Pagoda at Nikko, 1636; by 1600, more than 300,000 Christian converts in Japan; a Christian rebellion in 1637 leads to a civil war in which the Christian communities are exterminated; first chrysanthemums arrive in Holland from Japan; Takemoto Gidayu begins puppet theater "Joruri" in Tokyo, 1684; *Shusse Kagekiyo,* famous puppet play by Monzaemon, performed in Tokyo, 1686; under Tokugawa Shogunate, the rice economy gives way to a money economy, with an increase in industry, commerce, and national wealth, but also with economic unrest; the first Japanese-built Western-style ship leaves for New Spain, 1612; removal of women from Kabuki Theater at the order of the shogun, who claims that it is immoral for women to dance in public, 1629; *The Life of an Amorous Man* by Saikaku Ihara, 1682; Moronobu Hishikawa (d. 1694) pioneers *ukiyoe* prints that depict scenes of everyday life; Korin Ogata unites the two imperial schools of painting, the Kano and the Yamato, 1702; poems of Bashō (pseudonym of Matsuo Munefusa), 1644–1694, help popularize haiku poetry; *sukiya*-style domestic architecture emerges, a wooden house erected on raised stone platform, often two stories high, with rooms divided by sliding walls and screens, and with floors covered with mats; limits set for building heights; the Shūgakuin and Katsura villas, Kyoto, the architectural masterpieces of this period, early seventeenth century

In Korea, Li dynasty, 1392–1910; the city walls and gates of Suwon, 1794–1796; a vassal of China and isolated from all except Chinese influence, seventeenth century

In Muslim world, in Persia,
   the Royal Mosque in
   Isfahan, 1617
In North America, founding
   of Santa Fé, New Mexico,
   by Spanish, 1605; founding
   of Jamestown, Virginia, by
   English, 1607; founding of
   Jesuit state of Paraguay,
   1608
In Mesoamerica, Mexico
   cathedral completed

LEARNING OBJECTIVES

To learn:

1. The major historical developments that occurred in the Baroque period and how they helped shape the dominant cultural style

2. The impact of the balance- of-power principle on international affairs in the Baroque period

3. The leading characteristics of secular monarchies in the seventeenth century

4. To trace the development of absolutism in France and the defining role played by Louis XIV in shaping the Classical Baroque

5. To trace the development of limited monarchy in England and the defining role played by England in shaping the Restrained Baroque

6. The characteristics of the variations on the Baroque style and how each reflected its historical setting, such as how the Classical Baroque reflected French court society, how the Florid Baroque reflected papal court circles, and how the Restrained Baroque reflected English and Dutch society

7. The role of the wars of Louis XIV in establishing the primacy of French culture on the continent

8. How the church of St. Peter's, Rome, expressed the Florid Baroque building style

9. The leading artists and architects of the Florid Baroque, the Classical Baroque, and the Restrained Baroque—and their contributions

10. How Versailles Palace expressed the Classical Baroque building style

11. The characteristics, major figures, and chief literary genres of Baroque literature and the differences and similarities between the French and the English Baroque

12. The four chief trends operating in Baroque music

13. The reason that opera is the quintessential symbol of the Baroque

14. The sources and early developments of opera

15. The contributions of the Baroque composers Bach and Handel

16. The historic "firsts" of the Baroque age that became part of the Western tradition: the system of great states governed by a balance of power, France and England's dominance of culture and politics, the concept and practice of "world war," mercantilism, the illusionistic ceiling fresco, opera, and oratorio

17. The role of the Baroque age in transmitting the heritage of the past: redirecting Classical ideals into the grandiose and exuberant Baroque style; giving permanent stamp to the religious division of Westerners into Protestant and Catholic camps; bringing the monarchical tradition to its height in France; launching the trend toward rule by the people in the limited monarchy that developed in England; and carrying Western values to overseas colonies

SUGGESTIONS FOR FILMS

The Age of Absolute Monarchs in Europe. Coronet, 14 min., black and white.

Bernini's Rome. Teaching Films: Indiana University, 30 min., black and white.

Civilisation: Grandeur and Obedience. 52 min., BBC/Time-Life, color.

Civilisation: The Light of Experience. BBC/Time-Life, 52 min., color.

Johann Sebastian Bach. International Film Bureau, 27 min., color.

The Restoration and the Glorious Revolution. Coronet, 11 min., color.

Rubens. International Film Bureau, 27 min., color.

The Sun King. Indiana University, 30 min., black and white.

Unquiet Land: Civil War in England. Universal Studio's Educational and Visual Arts Division, 25 min., black and white.

SUGGESTIONS FOR MUSIC

Bach, Johann Sebastian. *The Art of the Fugue.* Hill, harpsichord. Music & Arts CD-279.

————. *Bach's Greatest Hits.* Leonhardt Ensemble. Pro Arte CDM-801.

————. *Brandenburg Concerti (6).* Orchestra of the Age of Enlightenment. Virgin Classics VCD 7 90747-2.

Handel, George Frederic. *Giulio Cesare in Egitto.* Popp, Ludwig, Wunderlich, Nocker, Berry, Leitner, Bavarian Radio Symphony and Chorus. Melodram 37059.

————. *Messiah.* Te Kanawa, Gjevang, Lewis, Howell, Solti, Chicago Symphony and Chorus. London 414396-2 LH2 (cassette); 414396-2 LH2 [CD]; 414396-1 [digital].

————. *Water Music: Suite.* Van Beinum, Concertgebouw Orchestra. Philips 420857-2 PM.

Monteverdi, Claudio. *Il Combattimento di Tancredi e Clorinda.* Clemencic, Clemencic Consort. Harmonia Mundi HUA-190.986.

———. *L'Incoronazione di Poppea.* Donath, Soderstrom, Berberian, Esswood, Harnoncourt, Vienna Concentus Musicus. Teldec 35247 ZC.

SUGGESTIONS FOR FURTHER READING

Adam, A. *Grandeur and Illusion: French Literature and Society 1606–1715.* Translated by H. Tint. New York: Basic Books, 1972. A brief and solid introduction to how French literature both reflected and transcended French history, politics, and society.

Anthony, J. R. *The New Grove French Baroque Masters: Lully, Charpentier, Lalande, Couperin, Rameau.* London: Macmillan, 1986. In the series of composer studies, this volume has been updated with a new essay on Rameau.

Haley, K. H. D. *The Dutch in the Seventeenth Century.* London: Thames and Hudson, 1972. One of the many excellent surveys in the Thames and Hudson publications that may be somewhat outdated but is still useful for understanding the Dutch at the height of power and influence in European politics and culture.

Kahr, M. M. *Dutch Painting in the Seventeenth Century.* Rev. ed. New York: Harper & Row, 1982. A solid survey that sets the artists and their works within their respective historical, cultural, and social backgrounds and also demonstrates how Dutch tastes and the international Baroque movement affected artists and their styles.

Kamen, H. European Society, 1500–1700. Rev. ed. London: Hutchinson, 1985. Fully revised and updated from the 1971 edition, it contains chapters on demographics, prices and wages, capitalism, popular culture, the family, and social organizations—excellent as a survey of social history.

Lewis, W. H. *The Splendid Century: Life in the France of Louis XIV.* Garden City, N.Y.: Doubleday, 1957. A very readable and reliable account of French society and politics that places Louis's power and personality at the center of seventeenth-century events.

Martin, J. R. *Baroque.* New York: Harper & Row, 1977. A refreshing approach to Baroque art, organized by topics such as space, time, and light.

Munck, T. *Seventeenth Century Europe: State, Conflict, and the Social Order in Europe, 1598–1700.* New York: St. Martin's Press, 1990. A well-written, up-to-date survey that explores all aspects of seventeenth-century Europe—for the curious student.

Orrey, L. *Opera: A Concise History.* Rev. ed. London: Thames and Hudson, 1987. Perhaps the best brief history of opera. In the Thames and Hudson format, it includes photographs of scenes from operas, costumes, opera houses, composers, and performers set within a historical narrative that examines the impact of the major social and cultural trends on opera.

Schama, S. *The Embarrassment of Riches: An Interpretation of Dutch Culture in the Golden Age.* New York: Knopf, 1987. A brilliant analysis of the Dutch way of life that weaves together society and the arts.

Skrine, P. *The Baroque: Literature and Culture in Seventeenth Century Europe.* New York: Holmes and Meier, 1978. This closely argued thesis that looks at the relationships between absolute monarchy and the theatrical stage to explain the Baroque style will attract the serious student.

Treasure, G. R. *Seventeenth Century France.* Rev. ed. London: John Murray, 1981. A standard account, newly revised, that traces the evolution of the modern state—in this study, France.

Wolf, J. B. *Louis XIV.* New York: Norton, 1968. Although published some years ago, Wolf's biography of the Sun King remains the most comprehensive and comprehensible study in English; full of details on life at the court.

IDENTIFICATIONS

Baroque   virtuoso
Florid Baroque style   opera
baldacchino   *bel canto*
illusionism   clavier
Classical Baroque style   fugue
Restrained Baroque style   oratorio

PERSONAL PERSPECTIVE BACKGROUND

Louis XIV, On Justice

Under Louis XIV, legal reforms led to the Code Louis (1667–1673), the system of justice that governed France until the early nineteenth century. As the Personal Perspective suggests, Louis did have a concern for justice and this was reflected in certain changes now made in the laws, such as setting up a system of police to check the crime and filth in Paris, ending trials for witchcraft, and abolishing capital punishment for blasphemy. But the code made legitimate many harsh and cruel practices, such as the use of police informers, arbitrary arrests, imprisonment without trial for years, and torture to obtain confessions. These latter practices were all swept away in the changes wrought by the Code Napoléon (1804–1810). (Additional information on Louis XIV may be found in *The Western Humanities.*)

Madame de Sévigné, On Gambling and Cards at Louis XIV's Court

Marie de Rabutin-Chantal, better known as Madame de Sévigné, was one of the West's great letter-writers; her correspondence numbers ten volumes in print. Wed at eighteen to the Marquis de Sévigné, she was widowed seven years later when her husband was killed in a duel over one of his mistresses. She never remarried. Over the fifty-five remaining years of her life, she reared her son and daughter, played the good grandmother, and all the while, wrote more than 1,500 letters, nearly all to her daughter. Accepted in the best houses in Paris and at the royal court, she observed the upper-class society of her time, as may be seen in the Personal Perspective. In today's democratic world, critics have found her insufficiently sensitive to her period's immorality. For example, one critic (David Cairns) wrote: "Madame de Sévigné found Louis XIV the greatest king in the world after having danced with him." Such a judgment is unfair, for it applies today's standards rather than seeing her views as reflective of her class and times.

DISCUSSION/ESSAY QUESTIONS

1. What was the original meaning of the word *Baroque?* How is this term defined and used today?
2. Identify the three variations on the international Baroque style, discuss their characteristics, and show how each style variation reflected its historical setting.
3. Discuss political developments in Europe during the Baroque age, and show what impact they had on the evolution of the Baroque cultural style.
4. Discuss the reign of Louis XIV of France as a personification of the type of government known as absolutism. Why did Louis determine to become an absolute ruler? Explain Louis's use of propaganda in achieving his political aims.
5. Compare and contrast political developments in England and France in the Baroque age, and explain how they affected the distinctive cultural style of each country.
6. What influence did religion have on the Baroque style? What values in Protestantism and Catholicism made for different developments?
7. Define Florid Baroque. Which building embodies the style of the Florid Baroque? Explain.
8. Explain the relationship of the Baroque style to the Renaissance style.

9. What Classical features and ideals survived in the Baroque style? Where was Classicism the strongest in Baroque culture? Why?
10. How did the Council of Trent affect the ideals of the Baroque arts and architecture?
11. Compare and contrast the Baroque buildings of St. Peter's, Rome, and the Palace of Versailles.
12. What new musical form developed in the Baroque period? Why is this new form so expressive of Baroque cultural values?
13. What were the basic trends in music during the Baroque period?
14. Describe Caravaggio's painting style. Show the influence of his art on the works of both Gentileschi and Velázquez, using examples of their works.
15. Compare and contrast the Florid Baroque painting styles of Rubens and Caravaggio.
16. Discuss the prevalence of Classical ideals within the Classical Baroque. Why is Classicism such a prominent feature of France's cultural life?
17. Show how the Palace of Versailles is a fitting symbol of the Classical Baroque.
18. Discuss Baroque artistic developments in the Netherlands, and show how they were related to conditions in the Calvinist Dutch republic.
19. What are the characteristics of Baroque literature? What literary forms flourished during the Baroque era? Compare and contrast literary developments in England and France during this period.
20. Who are the two best-known Baroque composers, and what are their major contributions to Western music?
21. What are the four chief legacies of the Baroque age to the Western tradition?

MULTIPLE-CHOICE QUESTIONS

1. The term *baroque* probably derives from the Portuguese word *barocco* meaning:
   * a. an irregular pearl (p. 351)
   b. a sinking boat
   c. a labyrinthine palace
   d. a concave mirror

2. During the Baroque period Europe was:
   a. undergoing an era of peace
   b. experiencing the rise of industrial capitalism
   * c. engaged in religious wars (p. 351)
   d. withdrawn from the world

3. European politics in the seventeenth century was characterized by all of these EXCEPT:
   a. a system of sovereign states
   b. a balance of power among England, France, Austria, Prussia, and Russia
   * c. the Italian city-states as the center of political life (pp. 353–357)
   d. absolutist monarchies

4. The most spectacular advocate of absolutism in the Baroque age was:
   a. James I of England
   * b. Louis XIV of France (p. 356)
   c. Charles II of England
   d. Henry IV of France

5. Attitudes toward politics and power in the seventeenth century can be summarized in all of the following ways EXCEPT:
   * a. Political leaders were concerned with welfare programs. (pp. 353–357)
   b. Kings and their advisers did not want to share power with church officials.
   c. The heads of state claimed their power by divine rights arguments.
   d. Machiavelli's influence was evident in the acts and thoughts of many of the rulers.

6. Which was NOT a characteristic of seventeenth-century sovereign states?
   a. bureaucracies staffed by university-trained career officials
   b. a permanent diplomatic corps
   * c. a vast welfare program for the poor (pp. 354–357)
   d. a standing army funded with government revenues

7. During Louis XIV's reign:
   a. Political power was in the hands of the business class.
   b. The state teetered on the edge of revolution.
   c. All religious faiths enjoyed toleration.
   * d. The government emphasized the power and glory of the king. (p. 356)

8. Louis XIV's economic policy was called:
   a. laissez faire
   * b. mercantilism (p. 356)
   c. the guild system
   d. capitalism

9. What caused monarchical power to be limited in early-seventeenth-century England?
   a. There was no legal heir to the throne.
   * b. The parliament considered itself the king's partner in government. (pp. 356–357)
   c. Scotland and England divided control of Britain.
   d. France constantly interfered in English domestic affairs.

10. Over the course of the seventeenth century, England:
    a. enjoyed a hundred years of domestic peace
    b. reconverted to Roman Catholicism
    * c. experienced two revolutions (pp. 356–357)
    d. entered the industrial age

11. By 1715 the principle that government should rest on the consent of the governed was successfully established in:
    a. France
    * b. England (p. 357)
    c. Prussia
    d. Austria

12. The Thirty Years' War was fought largely in:
    a. France
    b. Italy
    * c. Germany (p. 357)
    d. Bohemia

13. The major result of the War of the Spanish Succession was that:
    a. The power of Brandenburg-Prussia was reduced.
  * b. France acquired the national boundaries that still exist today. (pp. 357–358)
    c. It showed the unworkability of the balance-of-power concept.
    d. It prevented England from gaining any colonies.

14. The Baroque ideal was:
    a. repose
  * b. exuberance (p. 358)
    c. a single, static perspective
    d. a design complete in itself

15. Which did NOT help to spread the Baroque style across Europe?
    a. Long-distance trade gave business people opportunities to see the style at firsthand in new settings.
    b. Sons of the wealthy went on the Grand Tour and brought back Baroque art to their homelands.
  * c. Soldiers captured Baroque treasures as booty in wartime and brought them home with them. (p. 358)
    d. Scholars, enamored of the Baroque style, moved from region to region.

16. The Florid Baroque:
  * a. was a product of the Counter-Reformation (p. 358)
    b. was aristocratic and courtly
    c. had a strong Classical dimension
    d. was centered in the Netherlands

17. The Classical Baroque:
    a. was dominated by Roman Catholic religious ideals and themes
  * b. followed strict rules of design (p. 366)
    c. was middle class and respectable
    d. was characterized by extravagance and profusion

18. The Restrained Baroque was:
    a. aristocratic and courtly
  * b. simple and controlled (p. 368)
    c. centered in Italy and Spain
    d. dominated by Christian themes

19. The supreme expression of Florid Baroque architecture is:
    a. St. Paul's Cathedral, London
    b. the Palace at Versailles
  * c. St. Peter's Church, Rome (pp. 358–359)
    d. Villa Rotondo, Vicenza

20. Bernini was either the architect or the sculptor of each of these EXCEPT:
    a. the colonnade for St. Peter's, Rome
    b. the baldacchino in St. Peter's, Rome
  * c. the Palace at Versailles (pp. 358–359, 361)
    d. *The Ecstasy of St. Teresa*

21. Which is NOT correct for the Baroque colonnade attached to St. Peter's, Rome?
    a. There is a line of statues above the arcade.
    b. The arms of the colonnade are curved.
  * c. Painted statues are placed beside each column. (p. 359)
    d. The colonnaded area is shaped like a keyhole.

22. Caravaggio's painting style is characterized by:
    a. antinaturalism
  * b. dramatic use of chiaroscuro (p. 361)
    c. simplicity
    d. serenity

23. Which is NOT correct regarding Gentileschi?
    a. She portrayed female assertiveness in her paintings.
    b. She helped to spread the influence of the Caravaggesque style.
  * c. She painted primarily portraits. (pp. 361–363)
    d. She adopted the "night picture" technique.

24. Which was NOT a new art form developed during the Baroque era?
    a. in art, the illusionistic ceiling fresco
  * b. in sculpture, the free-standing figure (pp. 363, 376–378)
    c. in music, the oratorio
    d. in music, the opera

25. In *The Ecstasy of St. Teresa* Bernini was able to:
    a. create a sculpture that characterized the Restrained Baroque
    b. carve, in marble, a saint administering to the poor
    c. make the saint appear in a state of forgiveness
  * d. capture a moment when the saint senses the Holy Spirit (pp. 359, 361, and caption for Fig. 14.6)

26. Pozzo's *Allegory of the Missionary Work of the Jesuits* illustrates the Baroque love of:
  * a. infinite space (p. 364)
    b. repose
    c. serenity
    d. antinaturalism

27. A Baroque theme in Velázquez's painting *Las Meninas,* or *The Maids of Honor,* is:
  * a. the interplay of space and illusion (pp. 364–365)
    b. the love of infinite space
    c. the intersection of the supernatural and the natural
    d. monumentality

28. Rubens's paintings are known for their:
    a. disciplined order
  * b. ripe sensuality (p. 365)
    c. calm beauty
    d. domestic tranquility

29. Which was NOT one of Rubens's accomplishments?
    a. He was named official court painter to the French king.
  * b. He was appointed head of the French Academy. (pp. 365–366)
    c. He borrowed from Caravaggio and Titian.
    d. He created a cycle of paintings devoted to the life of Queen Marie de' Medici.

30. The dominant influence on the Classical Baroque was:
    a. Gothic civilization
  * b. Greco-Roman tradition (p. 365)
    c. Byzantine culture
    d. Christian doctrine

31. What was the distinguishing quality of the Classical Baroque?
    a. glorification of the common people
    b. simplicity in the service of God
    c. exuberant expression of emotions
  * d. influence of the royal court (p. 366)

32. Versailles's decorations were intended to identify King Louis XIV with:
    a. Jesus Christ
    b. the Roman leader, Julius Caesar
  * c. the Greek god, Apollo (caption for Fig. 14.12)
    d. the French ruler, Charlemagne

33. *The Education of Marie de' Medici* can be characterized as a:
    a. work in the Mannerist style
    b. painting that deals with the subject's psychological state
  * c. work that combines Roman mythology with the queen's life (pp. 379–380)
    d. painting produced at the command of Louis XIV

34. What about the Palace of Versailles is NOT Baroque?
    a. the grandiose decorative plan
  * b. the basic design with rounded arches and Classical columns (p. 366)
    c. the great size of the central structure
    d. the monumentality of the setting with support structures, all placed in a vast park

35. The outstanding representative of Classical Baroque art is:
    a. Rubens
  * b. Poussin (p. 368)
    c. Vermeer
    d. Velázquez

36. Poussin's art is renowned for its:
  * a. detached style (p. 368)
    b. lively manner
    c. urban scenes
    d. middle-class values

37. The Netherlands in the seventeenth century:
    a. was ruled by an absolutist king
    b. lagged behind Europe's other trading states
  * c. was dominated by the sober values of the Calvinist religion (p. 368)
    d. was conquered by Louis XIV of France

38. Which was NOT a feature of seventeenth-century Dutch art?
    a. It reflected the sober values of the Calvinist religion.
    b. It expressed the civic ideals of their society.
  * c. Its themes kept domestic life and public service completely separate. (pp. 368–369)
    d. It was created in response to the demands of one of the first art markets.

39. The outstanding artist of the Restrained Baroque is:
    a. Poussin
    b. Rubens
 * c. Rembrandt (p. 369)
    d. Van Dyck

40. Rembrandt's painting style was typified by all of these EXCEPT:
 * a. portrayal of figures modeled on ancient statuary (p. 369)
    b. use of dramatic chiaroscuro
    c. forceful expressiveness
    d. ability to depict the full range of human moods and emotions

41. The Dutch painter Vermeer specialized in:
    a. still lifes
    b. landscapes and seascapes
 * c. domestic genre scenes (p. 371)
    d. portraits

42. Painting in seventeenth-century England:
    a. reflected the fluctuation of the local art market
 * b. was controlled by the courtly but restrained taste of the aristocracy (p. 372)
    c. responded to the demands of middle-class patrons for a civic-minded art
    d. had religious themes as the dominant subject

43. The outstanding architect of the Restrained Baroque was:
    a. Maderno
    b. Bernini
    c. Hardouin-Mansart
 * d. Wren (p. 372)

44. Judith Leyster's career as a Dutch artist:
    a. brought her fame and fortune equal to any male painter
 * b. was subject to the marketplace (pp. 371–372)
    c. was the result of her knowing powerful people in Dutch society
    d. paralleled that of many other famous Dutch female artists

45. The inspiration for the dome of St. Paul's Cathedral, London, was the dome of:
    a. the Pantheon, Rome
    b. Santa Sophia, Constantinople
 * c. St. Peter's, Rome (p. 374)
    d. San Vitale, Ravenna

46. Baroque writers made major contributions in all of these genres EXCEPT:
 * a. romance (pp. 374–376)
    b. tragedy
    c. comedy
    d. epic

47. The zenith of Baroque drama was reached:
    a. at the papal court in Rome
 * b. at the court of King Louis XIV in Versailles (p. 374)
    c. in the commercial theaters of Amsterdam in the Netherlands
    d. at the court of King Charles II in London

48. Which is NOT correct for seventeenth-century French drama?
    a. It observed the unities of time, place, and action.
    * b. It dealt with the lives of ordinary people. (p. 374)
    c. It was governed by strict rules laid down by the French Academy.
    d. It employed elevated language and focused on universal problems.

49. Racine's tragedies were NOT characterized by:
    a. penetrating psychological insights
    b. a study of sex as a motive for action
    * c. occasional comic scenes to give relief to the dramatic tension (p. 375)
    d. lofty language

50. Comic plays were the specialty of:
    a. Racine
    b. Corneille
    * c. Molière (p. 375)
    d. Milton

51. The Baroque literary work *Paradise Lost* is a:
    * a. Christianized epic (p. 376)
    b. satirical epic based on a trivial episode in middle-class life
    c. continuation of Homer's *Odyssey*, picking up the story where the original work ended
    d. historical epic based on the English Civil War

52. Which was NOT a trend in seventeenth-century music?
    a. Major or minor tonality became a central feature.
    b. Music displayed exaggerated expressiveness.
    c. Music practice was dominated by virtuoso performances.
    * d. There was one single musical ideal. (pp. 376–377)

53. In *Oroonoko*, Aphra Behn:
    a. repeated the themes found in *Paradise Lost*
    b. examined political tensions created by the reign of Louis XIV
    * c. wrote a love novel set in a non-European land (p. 376)
    d. relied on Neoclassical themes to illustrate her beliefs

54. The first great composer of opera was:
    * a. Monteverdi (p. 376)
    b. Bach
    c. Handel
    d. Lully

55. Which was NOT an outstanding development in Baroque music?
    a. the French operas of the Italian composer Lully
    b. the London operas of the German composer Handel
    * c. the Masses of the Italian composer Palestrina (pp. 376–377)
    d. the sacred music of the German composer Bach

COMPARATIVE QUESTIONS, CHAPTERS 8 THROUGH 14

1. Which of the following was NOT a cultural achievement by women during this period, roughly 500 to 1700 A.D.?
   a. Anna Comnena was the first known woman historian.
   * b. Eleanor of Aquitaine pioneered the romance literary genre.
   c. Marie de Pizan was the first known Western woman to earn a living through her writings.
   d. Artemisia Gentileschi helped to spread the style of Caravaggio throughout Italy.

2. All of the following matchups between an architectural style and a Classical influence used in it are correct EXCEPT:
   a. Romanesque style—the basilica form
   b. Renaissance style—Doric, Ionic, and Corinthian orders
   * c. Gothic style—the pointed arch
   d. Baroque style—post-beam-triangle construction

3. All of the following matchups between a book and the historic period in which it was written are correct EXCEPT:
   * a. Early Middle Ages—Hildegard of Bingen's *Scivias*
   b. High Middle Ages—Dante's *The Divine Comedy*
   c. Northern Renaissance—Shakespeare's *Hamlet*
   d. Baroque age—Milton's *Paradise Lost*

4. Which development in Western religion is mismatched with its corresponding historical period?
   * a. the final split between Western Christianity and Orthodox Christianity in the Early Middle Ages
   b. the birth of the friar movement (Franciscans and Dominicans) in the High Middle Ages
   c. the Babylonian Captivity of the Church in the Late Middle Ages
   d. the split of the Western church into Protestant and Roman Catholic branches in the sixteenth century

5. Which musical development is mismatched with its corresponding historical period?
   a. the rise of monophony and polyphony in the Early Middle Ages
   b. the development of musical notation by Guido of Arezzo in the High Middle Ages
   c. the origination of harmonious composition, using major and minor scales and their related harmonies by Josquin des Prez, in the Early Renaissance
   * d. the birth of opera in the High Renaissance

15

THE BAROQUE AGE II
Revolutions in Scientific and Political Thought, 1600–1715

TEACHING STRATEGIES AND SUGGESTIONS

The instructor can introduce this second unit on the Baroque age with a Standard Lecture blended with a Spirit of the Age approach, underscoring the distinguishing characteristics of the period's art styles as previously set forth in Chapter 14. This first lecture on Chapter 15 should emphasize two new revolutionary themes: radical changes in science and political theory. As background to these two revolutions, the teacher can employ one of several teaching models: the Diffusion, the Patterns of Change, the Comparison/Contrast, or, again, the Spirit of the Age. The instructor should then concentrate on the Scientific Revolution, since its changes had the more radical impact of the two intellectual movements. Perhaps the best approach is to do a comparison and contrast, showing the extraordinary differences between seventeenth-century and medieval science. The Patterns of Change model can then be used for the two sections of this chapter that are closely connected: the actual scientific discoveries *and* the remnants of magical thinking that survived even in the minds of the scientists themselves. The Patterns of Change method is also useful for setting forth the stage-by-stage developments in astronomy, physics, medicine, and chemistry. Either the Diffusion or the Reflections/Connections approach will work in assessing the impact of science on philosophy and the ironic aspects of the Scientific Revolution.

To introduce the revolution in political thought, the teacher can use a Standard Lecture with a Reflections/Connections slant, since all of the political thinkers were clearly influenced by the politics of their day. The Diffusion model is the most appropriate for examining the topic of European exploration and expansion. As a conclusion for this unit, the instructor can use a Spirit of the Age approach to explain how the revolutions in science and political thinking forever altered Western values and attitudes.

LECTURE OUTLINE

Non-Western Events

I. The Themes of the Baroque Age

II. Theories of the Universe Before
    the Scientific Revolution
    A. Geocentrism: Aristotle
       and Ptolemy
    B. Empiricism, inductive
       and deductive reasoning

1603–1715
(See Chapter 14 for non-
Western events.)

III. The Scientific Revolution:
Discoveries and Theories

IV. The Magical and the Practical in
the Scientific Revolution
   A. The paradox in the movement
   B. The role of technology
   C. Astronomy and physics: from
      Copernicus to Newton
      1. Nicolas Copernicus: a
         heliocentric universe
      2. Johannes Kepler: the
         three planetary laws
      3. Galileo Galilei: revelations
         about the heavens and
         discoveries about motion
      4. Isaac Newton: gravity and synthesis
   D. Medicine and chemistry
      1. Ancient and medieval opinions
      2. Andreas Vesalius: early
         discoveries about the circulatory
         system
      3. William Harvey: the circulatory
         system explained
      4. Marcello Malpighi: identification of
         capillaries
      5. Robert Boyle: beginnings of chemistry
   E. The impact of science on philosophy
      1. Francis Bacon: explaining the new
         learning
      2. René Descartes: skepticism and the
         dualism of knowledge
      3. Pascal: uncertainty and faith
   F. Ironies and contradictions of the
      Scientific Revolution
      1. Work of a minority
      2. Christian faith, superstition,
         and mysticism

V. The Revolutions in Political Thought
   A. Impact of changing political systems
   B. Natural law and divine right:
      Grotius and Bossuet
      1. Hugo Grotius: natural law and
         international law
      2. Bishop Bossuet: divine right and
         God's plans
      3. Absolutism and liberalism:
         Hobbes and Locke
         a) Thomas Hobbes's *The Leviathan*
         b) John Locke's *Second Treatise
            of Civil Government* and
            *Essay Concerning the Human
            Understanding*

VI. European Exploration and Expansion
   A. Into the Americas, Africa, and the Far East
   B. Roles of various European nations in discoveries and settlements

VII. Responses to the Revolutions in Thought
   A. The spread of ideas
      1. Academies
      2. Fontenelle: popularizing science
      3. Bayle: classifying knowledge
   B. Impact on the arts
      1. Baroque painting
      2. Literature and drama

VIII. The Legacy of the Revolutions in Scientific and Political Thought

LEARNING OBJECTIVES

To learn:

1. The foundations of Western science prior to the seventeenth century, in particular the contributions of Aristotle and Ptolemy in formulating the geocentric system

2. The general nature of the Scientific Revolution

3. The magical and practical elements at work in the Scientific Revolution

4. The discoveries of Copernicus, Kepler, Galileo, and Newton and their contributions to the rise of modern astronomy and physics

5. The discoveries of Vesalius, Harvey, Malpighi, and Boyle and their contributions to the rise of modern medicine and chemistry

6. The impact of seventeenth-century science on philosophy

7. The ideas and contributions of Francis Bacon

8. The ideas and contributions of René Descartes and his impact on Western philosophy

9. Pascal's basic beliefs and their influence on Western thought

10. The ironic aspects of the Scientific Revolution

11. The impact of seventeenth-century political events on political thought

12. The definition, origins, and basic concept of natural law and Hugo Grotius's interpretation of the term

13. The definition, origins, and basic concepts of divine right and Bishop Bossuet's interpretation of the term

14. The meaning of political absolutism and Thomas Hobbes's explanation of the theory

15. The origins and definition of political liberalism and John Locke's interpretation of the theory

16. What is meant by the social contract and the ways it may be used to justify a civil society

17. John Locke's theory of the origin of ideas and its influence on modern psychology

18. The early explorations of Europeans, the expansion of European peoples and culture abroad, and the effect of these developments on western Europe

19. The methods of spreading the ideas of the Scientific Revolution and the implications of those ideas for politics and culture

20. The impact of the Scientific Revolution on the arts

21. Historic "firsts" of the seventeenth-century revolutions in scientific and political thought that became part of the Western tradition: the heliocentric system; Newtonian physics and astronomy; Harvey's explanation for the circulation of the blood; new habits of scientific thought, including empiricism and the inductive method; social contract theory; the beginnings of both modern authoritarian and liberal thought; and the opening phase of European expansion and influence around the world

22. The role of this period in transmitting the heritage of earlier civilizations: reshaping medieval science to conform to the new scientific discoveries and ways of thinking; reviving, for the first time since the fall of Rome, skepticism and intellectual restlessness; and reinterpreting medieval Christian political thought along secular lines

SUGGESTIONS FOR FILMS

Ascent of Man: The Majestic Clockwork. Time-Life, 52 min., color.

Ascent of Man: The Starry Messenger. Time-Life, 52 min., color.

The Light of Experience. Time-Life, 52 min., color.

Galileo, the Challenge of Reason. Learning Corporation of America, 26 min., color.

Newton: The Mind That Found the Future. Learning Corporation of America, 21 min., color.

Science and Society. McGraw-Hill, 18 min., color.

Vesalius: Founder of Modern Anatomy. Yale Medical School, 13 min., color.

William Harvey and the Circulation of the Blood. International Film Bureau, 33 min., color.

SUGGESTIONS FOR FURTHER READING

Alioto, A. M. *A History of Western Science.* Englewood Cliffs, J. J.: Prentice-Hall, 1987. A lucid treatment of the historic events that led to what the author calls our "scientific civilization."

Ashcraft, R. *Revolutionary Politics & Locke's Two Treatises of Government.* Princeton: Princeton University Press, 1986. A brilliant study linking political theory to its historical context; the focus is on the language of political theory and how it arose from a past political situation.

Biagioli, M. *Galileo, Courtier: The Practice of Science in the Culture of Absolutism*. Chicago: University of Chicago Press, 1993. An impassioned work of cultural history that analyzes Galileo and his work within his social milieu, especially as the philosophical astronomer to the duke of Tuscany.

Held, J. S., and Posner, D. *17th and 18th Century Art*. New York: Abrams, 1971. A broad survey of Baroque painting, sculpture, and architecture by two respected art historians.

The History of Science and Technology: A Narrative Chronology. New York: Facts on File, 1988. An invaluable resource for understanding science and technology; translated from an Italian work published in 1975.

Kuhn, T. S. *The Copernican Revolution: Planetary Astronomy in the Development of Western Thought*. New York: Vintage, 1959. The standard history of the Copernican Revolution, embracing cosmology, physics, philosophy, religion, and mathematical astronomy; for the serious student; first published in 1957.

————. *The Structure of Scientific Revolutions*. 2nd ed. Chicago: University of Chicago Press, 1970. A landmark book that explained how revolutions in thought originate; introduced the concept of "paradigm shift" into intellectual discourse.

Marks, J. *Science and the Making of the Modern World*. London: Heinemann, 1983. An excellent overview of the role of science in helping to form modern consciousness; concise and well illustrated.

Olby, R. C., et al. *Companion to the History of Modern Science*. London: Routledge, 1990. This selective survey aims to show the broad diversity of subjects in the history of science and the extensive scholarly literature written about it.

Ronan, C. A. *The Cambridge Illustrated History of the World's Science*. A comprehensive survey, global in perspective, of developments in science; profusely illustrated.

Sommerville, J. P. *Thomas Hobbes: Political Ideas in Historical Context*. Basingstoke: Macmillan, 1992. A concise study of the political ideas of Thomas Hobbes and the historic situation that gave birth to them.

Webster. C. *The Great Instauration: Science, Medicine, and Reform, 1626–1660*. London: Duckworth, 1975. A provocative history of the Scientific Revolution in seventeenth-century England, linking it to the general intellectual ferment associated with the century's Puritan Revolution.

————. *From Paracelsus to Newton: Magic and the Making of Modern Science*. Cambridge: Cambridge University Press, 1982. A revisionist study that tries to show the continuity between the thought of Paracelsus, who is generally considered an obscurantist, and Newton, who is the hero of early modern science.

Westfall, R. S. *The Life of Isaac Newton*. Cambridge: Cambridge University Press, 1993. A shortened version of the 1980 biography of one of the founders of modern science.

Willey, B. *The Seventeenth Century Background*. New York: Columbia University Press, 1982. A classic work in European intellectual history; first printed in 1953.

IDENTIFICATIONS

Scientific Revolution

geocentrism

empiricism

inductive reasoning

deductive reasoning

heliocentrism

social contract

liberalism

tabula rasa

virtuoso

PERSONAL PERSPECTIVE BACKGROUND

Johannes Junius, Secret Letter to His Daughter

Witch trials originated in the High Middle Ages and continued until modern times, the last recorded burning of a witch being in Scotland in 1722. Unlike Johannes Junius, the man whose letter constitutes this chapter's Personal Perspective, most suspected witches were women—perhaps reflecting masculine fears of women with power. What makes Junius's story so compelling is the survival of the secret letter setting forth in his own words the horror of his ordeal.

DISCUSSION/ESSAY QUESTIONS

1. Why is the period between 1685 and 1715 called "the crisis of the European conscience"? What scientific and intellectual changes were occurring during this period? How was the intellectual crisis resolved?
2. Show that the Scientific Revolution was both an outgrowth and a rejection of Aristotelean cosmology.
3. What was the long-term impact of the Scientific Revolution on the study of philosophy and theology?
4. Define the term *geocentrism,* and note how the discoveries and ideas of Aristotle and Ptolemy were illustrative of this concept.
5. What is meant by the term "Scientific Revolution" and what areas of study did it encompass?
6. Discuss the paradoxes and the causes that gave rise to the Scientific Revolution.
7. Discuss the ideas of Copernicus, Kepler, Galileo, and Newton and their contributions to astronomy and physics. How did their discoveries threaten the existing view of the universe? What was the outcome of their work in science?
8. Discuss Galileo's research in light of the seventeenth century's ongoing conflict between religion and science. Why was the church afraid of his findings? Ought it to have been? Explain.
9. Define the Newtonian system and explain how it replaced the medieval worldview.
10. What contributions did Vesalius, Harvey, and Malpighi make to the study of the human body?
11. What role did Francis Bacon play in the rise of modern thought and what has been his impact on modern thought?
12. Discuss René Descartes's most important contributions to Western philosophy and assess their value to modern thought.
13. Who was more important to the Scientific Revolution, Bacon or Descartes? Explain the reasons for your choice.
14. In what ways did Pascal's ideas question the Scientific Revolution?
15. Discuss the ironic aspects of the Scientific Revolution and show how it was both medieval and modern.
16. Define "natural law," and demonstrate how it was manifested in the writings of Grotius.
17. What were the major arguments of Bishop Bossuet in his defense of divine right?
18. How did English politics influence Hobbes's political thinking? What impact has *The Leviathan* had on modern political theory?
19. Define the term "social contract" and illustrate how Hobbes and Locke used this term in their writings on political thought.
20. Show the influence of John Locke's political theories on the founders of the United States.
21. Explain how Locke's theory of knowledge has influenced modern psychology.
22. Identify the overseas areas settled by Europeans during the seventeenth century and discuss the impact of these settlements at home and abroad.
23. How were the discoveries and ideas of the Scientific Revolution disseminated to educated Europeans?
24. In what ways did Bayle's *Dictionary* conflict with accepted approaches to learning, and how did it affect literature?

25. Discuss the impact of the Scientific Revolution on Baroque art.
26. Discuss the general impact of the seventeenth century's scientific and political revolutions on the "European Mind."
27. Do you think that the Scientific Revolution was more important than the Renaissance and the Reformation? Defend your position. Explain the impact of all three movements on Western thought.
28. How did the Scientific Revolution affect the rise of skepticism in Western thought?
29. Discuss some of the short-term and long-range effects of European explorations and settlements on modern times.
30. Explain why witchcraft trials continued during the century in which the Scientific Revolution occurred.

MULTIPLE-CHOICE QUESTIONS

1. Which was NOT a feature of the "crisis of conscience" of the late seventeenth century?
    * a. It was a time when advanced thinkers accepted the idea of evolution. (p. 381)
    b. It was an age when progressive scholars began to think in terms of natural law.
    c. It was a period when mathematics became a tool for solving problems.
    d. It was an era when skepticism about traditional religion began to grow among the educated.

2. Aristotelian physics and astronomy were transmitted to the West through:
    a. Chinese and Indian culture
    * b. Roman and Islamic culture (p. 382)
    c. Viking and Slavic culture
    d. Japanese and Mesoamerican culture

3. Which was NOT a feature of the geocentric universe?
    a. The universe is earth-centered.
    b. The planets, sun, and moon each revolve in a separate sphere.
    * c. The planets are composed of the identical materials the earth is made of. (pp. 381–383)
    d. The universe is divided into supralunar and sublunar worlds.

4. Which was NOT correct for the Egyptian scholar Ptolemy?
    * a. He rejected Aristotle's model of the universe. (p. 382)
    b. He modified Aristotle's model with new mathematical calculations.
    c. He thought that the earth was the center of the universe.
    d. His model of the universe was based on the then latest astronomical data.

5. Which was NOT a feature of medieval science?
    a. It was basically Ptolemy's model with minor modifications.
    b. It identified Aristotle's Unmoved Mover with God.
    * c. It rejected the church's teaching that the earth is made of corrupt materials. (pp. 381–383)
    d. It incorporated Muslim findings into its outlook.

6. Which culture modified and improved the Ptolemaic system before it was transmitted to the West?
    a. the Egyptian
    * b. the Muslim (p. 382)
    c. the Byzantine
    d. the Judaic

7. Aristotle's explanation of motion was challenged in the fourteenth century by scholars at the university of:
   a. Bologna
   b. Alexandria
   * c. Paris (p. 382)
   d. Oxford

8. This artist specialized in engravings of New World insects and animals, based on firsthand knowledge gained in Surinam:
   * a. Maria Sibylla Merian (caption for Fig. 15.2)
   b. Frans Hals
   c. Godfrey Kneller
   d. Rembrandt van Rijn

9. In the Middle Ages, Aristotle's science began to be undermined by the:
   a. spread of the deductive method
   b. use of the Bible as a guide for research
   c. acceptance of the Ptolemaic order of the universe
   * d. application of inductive reasoning (pp. 382–383)

10. Which was NOT a feature of the seventeenth-century Scientific Revolution?
    a. new discoveries in astronomy and biology
    b. a radically changed perspective about the physical world
    * c. the development of tools for looking inside the atom (pp. 382–386)
    d. the beginning of the separation of philosophy and theology

11. Which is a correct statement about the Scientific Revolution?
    a. Late medieval technology had little impact on the new learning.
    * b. Early modern scientists built on the work of medieval thinkers. (pp. 382–386)
    c. Most of the new discoveries were done within the context of the Aristotelian-Ptolemaic system.
    d. Mathematics played a minor role in the discoveries.

12. Neo-Platonism affected the rise of modern science by:
    a. rejecting all of the Christian points of view
    * b. emphasizing the power of mathematics (p. 383)
    c. denying mystical properties to the sun
    d. denying the existence of a power greater than humans

13. When Isaac Newton commented that he stood on the "shoulders of giants," he meant that:
    a. All his predecessors were large men.
    b. Only great minds can accomplish anything.
    * c. He simply built on what others had discovered. (pp. 384–386)
    d. He still stood in the shadow of Aristotle.

14. The central issue between geocentrism and heliocentrism was:
    a. which theory had the greatest quantity of data
    b. which theory was supported by the church
    * c. which theory was simpler (p. 384)
    d. which theory was more complex

15. Copernicus's explanation of the universe can be described as a:
   a. brand-new idea
 * b. revival of an ancient Greek theory (p. 384)
   c. system compatible with medieval Christian theology
   d. revival of an ancient Babylonian theory

16. How did religious leaders react to Copernicus's theory?
   a. It was fully accepted by both Catholics and Protestants.
 * b. The Catholics, after an initial acceptance, later rejected it, while the Protestants, lacking a centralized authority, eventually accommodated themselves to his thinking. (p. 384)
   c. It was accepted by the Catholics but rejected by the Protestants.
   d. It was rejected by the Catholics and the Protestants for more than 200 years.

17. Tycho Brahe contributed to the Scientific Revolution by:
   a. inventing the telescope
   b. discovering the moons around the planet Jupiter
 * c. amassing copious observations of planetary movement (p. 385)
   d. giving final form to the law of inertia

18. Kepler's major contribution to the Scientific Revolution was:
   a. the invention of the telescope
 * b. the discovery of three key planetary laws (p. 385)
   c. a convincing explanation of gravity
   d. a treatise on terrestrial motion

19. A consequence of Kepler's scientific research was that:
   a. His startling discoveries made further investigation unnecessary.
   b. The circular movement of planets was proven correct.
 * c. The sun-centered universe could now be understood in mathematical terms. (p. 385)
   d. The belief that the planets moved in irregular orbits was reinforced.

20. Galileo's important discoveries were influenced by his:
   a. determination to win favor with the church
   b. reliance on the theory of Ptolemy
 * c. use of the new technological invention, the telescope (p. 385)
   d. dependence on the writings of Thomas Aquinas

21. Galileo's celestial observations proved that:
   a. The moon looked the same through a telescope as to the naked eye.
 * b. Jupiter has moons, or satellites. (p. 385)
   c. Aristotle's calculations were essentially correct
   d. The universe was about the size of Ptolemy's figures.

22. Besides astronomical research, Galileo also contributed to the:
   a. science of anatomy
 * b. overturning of Aristotle's theory of motion (p. 385)
   c. modern explanation for the circulation of the blood
   d. modern view that the body is composed of tiny cells

23. Regarding Galileo's astronomical writings, the Catholic Church:
   a. readily accepted them as confirming biblical scripture
   b. agreed with his findings after summoning a church council
 * c. arrested Galileo and threatened to torture him (p. 385)
   d. ignored him, although it declared his ideas to be unacceptable

24. Whose scientific research finally confirmed the truth of the Copernican system?
    a. Galileo
    b. Kepler
*   c. Newton (p. 386)
    d. Leibniz

25. Newton's outstanding contribution to the Scientific Revolution was the mathematical basis
    for the:
*   a. law of gravity (p. 386)
    b. law of inertia
    c. theory of opposites
    d. theory of relativity

26. What did the English poet Alexander Pope mean when he wrote: "God said, 'Let Newton be!' and
    All was *Light*"?
    a. that Newton had discovered how electricity operated
    b. that Newton had discovered the source of light
*   c. that Newton had shed light on the mysteries of nature (p. 386)
    d. that Christians would now be able to follow God's light

27. Newton, the pioneer of modern science, was all of the following EXCEPT:
    a. a religious person who never doubted the existence of God
    b. a scholar not fully liberated from medieval habits of thought
*   c. a man fearful that his discoveries would lead the masses to atheism (p. 386)
    d. a Christian who wanted to be remembered for his religious writings

28. Prior to modern times, knowledge of the human body was limited for all the following reasons
    EXCEPT:
    a. There was general ignorance because the church prohibited the dissection of corpses.
    b. The medical schools relied on animal dissection, and this resulted in misinformation since
        animal bodies differed from human bodies.
*   c. Plato was a leading authority, and he advised scholars to ignore the body and concentrate
        on the mind. (pp. 386–387)
    d. The Roman physician Galen was the supreme authority, and he was often incorrect.

29. The earliest research into the true origins of the circulation of blood began at:
*   a. the University of Padua by Vesalius (p. 387)
    b. the University of Paris by Harvey
    c. the University of Bologna by Malpighi
    d. Oxford University by William of Ockham

30. Both William Harvey and Isaac Newton:
*   a. used mathematics to prove their theories (pp. 386–388)
    b. made important discoveries in celestial physics
    c. borrowed from each other in their research
    d. were greatly influenced by Francis Bacon

31. Robert Boyle made this contribution to modern chemistry:
    a. He united alchemy with chemistry.
    b. He organized the periodic table.
*   c. He separated the study of chemistry from other areas of research. (p. 388)
    d. He arrived at his findings using the deductive method.

32. Which is NOT a source of Francis Bacon's fame?
    a. his clear and precise writing style
    b. his complete reliance on the experimental method
  * c. his scientific discoveries (p. 388)
    d. his belief in progress

33. The scientific work of René Descartes resulted in the development of:
    a. calculus
  * b. analytical geometry (pp. 388–389)
    c. logarithms
    d. irrational numbers

34. Which was NOT part of Descartes's scientific method?
  * a. using inductive reasoning (p. 388)
    b. going step-by-step in an orderly fashion
    c. applying mathematics, especially geometry
    d. searching for clear and distinct ideas

35. Descartes, in his search for the truth:
    a. never doubted the existence of God
    b. maintained that his body was always present
  * c. concluded that he existed because his mind questioned (p. 388)
    d. doubted the truth of his own mental processes

36. What is meant by Descartes's dualism?
    a. Everything comes in pairs.
  * b. The mind and body are separate. (p. 389)
    c. Only by dividing objects into two parts can they be understood.
    d. Human beings have both a human an animal nature.

37. This thinker questioned the benefits of the Scientific Revolution:
  * a. Blaise Pascal (p. 389)
    b. Francis Bacon
    c. René Descartes
    d. Thomas Hobbes

38. Which was NOT a belief of Pascal?
    a. Mathematics is a useful tool for understanding the world.
  * b. Knowledge of self is the first step to knowing the world. (p. 389)
    c. God's existence can be proven by using the laws of probability.
    d. The human passions are helpful in reaching God.

39. Which did NOT occur during the seventeenth century?
    a. the culmination of the Scientific Revolution
    b. the origination of liberal political theory
  * c. the end of witchcraft trials (passim and Personal Perspective)
    d. the establishment of the circulation of blood in humans

40. Which was NOT an ironic aspect of the Scientific Revolution?
    * a. The discoveries were made by a scientific elite, but the populace quickly adopted the new findings. (pp. 390–391)
    b. The discoveries were outgrowths of practical studies and not the result of an attempt to reconstruct the universe.
    c. The scientists produced a model of the universe that was fully secular, but they were all Christians who accepted the existence of God.
    d. The scientists overturned earlier scientific thinking, but they still shared ideas and perceptions rooted in medieval thought.

41. The most powerful influence on seventeenth-century political thought was the:
    a. writings of St. Thomas Aquinas
    b. collapse of manorialism in Western Europe
    c. rise of a large laboring class
    * d. English civil war (p. 391)

42. Which was NOT a major source for seventeenth-century political thought?
    a. the Bible and other religious writings
    * b. the writings of Byzantine scholars (p. 391)
    c. the period's scientific discoveries
    d. the natural rights theory of ancient Rome

43. Which was NOT an influence on Grotius's political ideas?
    a. his personal experiences during the Thirty Years' War
    * b. his years as a courtier at the court of Louis XIV (p. 391)
    c. his travels and observations as an ambassador
    d. his education and reading in ancient philosophy

44. Grotius founded his political theories on his belief in:
    a. original sin
    * b. natural law (p. 391)
    c. divine right
    d. the social contract

45. Which was NOT part of Bishop Bossuet's argument for divine right of kings?
    a. God gave certain men the right to rule.
    b. Kings act as God's agents on earth.
    * c. Subjects can rebel when rulers go against God's plans. (p. 391)
    d. Kings have the right to intervene in the lives of their subjects.

46. Hobbes based *The Leviathan* on the assumption that:
    a. Humans are basically good.
    * b. Individuals predictably act out of fear of death and the quest for power. (p. 391)
    c. God controls human activity.
    d. The world is run by chance.

47. Hobbes reasoned that the best form of government is a(n):
    a. constitutional monarchy limited by the doctrine of natural rights
    * b. absolutist state with the ruler completely controlling the people (pp. 391–392)
    c. enlightened aristocracy in which the best people rule
    d. democracy where there is rule of the people, by the people, and for the people

48. Hobbes's legacy to modern political thought was a theory of:
    a. self-government
    * b. absolutism (p. 392)
    c. liberalism
    d. socialism

49. Which was NOT a belief of John Locke?
    a. All men are created equal.
    b. Humans have reason and are basically decent.
    * c. Humans give up their rights to the state in civil society. (pp. 392–393)
    d. Private property has to be protected.

50. Locke argued that the social contract was:
    a. an ironclad agreement that could not be broken
    b. written to give all the power to the state
    c. a gift from God
    * d. arranged to ensure that the people retain their sovereignty (p. 392)

51. When Locke argued that the mind at birth is *tabula rasa,* he meant that the mind is:
    a. already furnished with the germs of ideas
    * b. empty, devoid of ideas (p. 393)
    c. ready to receive the ideas that God inspires
    d. muddled until internal reasoning can take over

52. Both Hobbes and Locke agreed that the basis of government should be a(n):
    a. constitution
    b. entail
    * c. social contract (pp. 392–393)
    d. gentleman's agreement

53. Which was NOT a result of the migration of Europeans overseas during the seventeenth century?
    a. an increase in rivalries among European states
    b. new trade opportunities for the home societies
    * c. relaxation of control over the overseas colonies (pp. 393–394)
    d. the development of the slave trade out of Africa

54. Bayle's *Historical and Critical Dictionary* can be described as:
    a. a book that supported prevailing institutions and traditions
    b. a work that attacked the findings of the Scientific Revolution
    c. the last book that reflected medieval thought
    * d. an encyclopedic work arranged in systematic form (pp. 396–397)

55. How did the Scientific Revolution affect the arts?
    a. It had no impact at all.
    b. The new science became a prominent theme in Baroque art.
    * c. Baroque artists and writers became highly analytical, an influence from the new science.
       (pp. 397–398)
    d. Baroque artists and writers, reacting against the Scientific Revolution, adopted religious
       themes in their works.

16

THE AGE OF REASON
1700–1789

TEACHING STRATEGIES AND SUGGESTIONS

The instructor can begin the Age of Reason with a Historical Overview that describes the West in 1700, treating such matters as the politics (kingship, absolutist or limited), economics (mercantilism), society (aristocratic and hierarchical), religion (state churches and legalized intolerance), education (piecemeal, random, and elitist), and culture (Baroque and soon to be Rococo). This summary will enable students to better understand the program of the Physiocrats and particularly the *philosophes* who wanted radical changes in Western society and culture. The instructor can next introduce the Enlightenment, using a Spirit of the Age approach that sets forth this cultural movement's goals and guiding ideals, including scientific methodology, mathematical reasoning, and healthy skepticism. The instructor, using the Patterns of Change approach, can briefly describe the influences that helped to shape the Enlightenment mentality, specifically the Scientific Revolution, Greco-Roman Classicism, and the Renaissance. A handout listing key figures by country and the major contribution of each is a good device for demonstrating to students that the Enlightenment was truly an international movement as well as for familiarizing them with the leading *philosophes* and their achievements.

The instructor can use a Standard Lecture to establish the Enlightenment's historical setting, focusing briefly on major historical events affecting the great powers (England, France, Prussia, Austria, and Russia) and to a lesser extent the almost-great powers (the Netherlands, Portugal, and Spain) and showing especially the differences between England with its limited monarchy and growing middle class and France with its absolute monarchy and its resurgent aristocracy. This information is vital for students because these events were determining factors in the rise of the Rococo and Neoclassical styles. With the Reflections/Connections approach, the instructor can then show how the Rococo reflected the French and, to a lesser extent, the Austrian aristocracy and how, in England, it led to a backlash by Hogarth, who ridiculed the excesses of this style in his satiric paintings. Similarly, it can be shown how the Neoclassical style was in part a response to the *philosophes'* criticism of eighteenth-century politics and culture and how, after appearing in about 1770, this style was quickly adopted by progressive spirits across the West. The instructor can employ Slide Lectures blended with a Comparison/Contrast approach to set forth the differences between the Rococo and Neoclassical styles. The Comparison/Contrast approach can also be used to treat literary developments in France and England, and a Music Lecture is essential to illustrate the riches of Rococo and Neoclassical music.

An excellent conclusion can be achieved using a Historical Summary—following the topics laid down in the opening lecture—to describe the agenda of the *philosophes* in 1789, touching on such matters as politics (government by the consent of the governed), economics (laissez faire), society (natural rights, including freedom and equality), religion (Deism, natural religion, and religious tolerance), education (the universal panacea as a problem solver), and culture (Neoclassicism). Time permitting, the instructor can conduct a Discussion, encouraging students to identify those aspects of contemporary life that are direct outgrowths of Enlightenment habits of thought, such as representative government, public school systems, free trade, and religious freedom. The instructor can also show that contemporary rights movements, such as those for African Americans, women, the disabled, and gays, have their roots in the struggle for rights that began as an academic discussion by the *philosophes* in the Enlightenment.

LECTURE OUTLINE

I.   Historical Overview
   A. Four trends of the age
      1. Concentration of political power in the great states
      2. The resurgence of the aristocracy
      3. The political eminence of the middle class
      4. The Enlightenment
   B. Reaction against the Baroque
      1. The Rococo style
      2. The Neoclassical style

II. The Enlightenment
   A. Influences
      1. Greco-Roman world
      2. The Renaissance
      3. The Scientific Revolution
   B. Its geographic boundaries
   C. The *philosophes* and their program
      1. Definition of the *philosophes*
      2. Representative thinkers
      3. Their ideals
      4. Their program
   D. Deism
      1. Metaphor of a clockwork universe
      2. Impact
   E. The *Encyclopédie*
      1. Origins
      2. The project
      3. The editorship of Diderot
   F. The Physiocrats
      1. Definition
      2. Critique of mercantilism
      3. Their doctrines
      4. Adam Smith and his advocacy of a free-market economy

III. The Great Powers During the Age of Reason
   A. Less turbulent than 1600s
   B. Society: continuity and change
      1. Growing urbanization of society
      2. Continuation of a traditional, hierarchical society
      3. Subordinate role for women

Non-Western Events

1700–1789

In Africa, between 1730 and 1800, the states of Lunda, Luba, Oyo, Benin, and Asante prospered and became empires; collapse of Kongo, Ngola, and Mwenemutapa, largely a result of contacts with Europeans; Kumasi, the capital of Asante, called a "garden city" by foreigners; revival of Islam in West Africa, 1725; Asante civilization at zenith, 1721–1750; Dahomey, a state built on the slave trade, the most rigidly controlled state of the eighteenth century; Portuguese driven from their stronghold in Mombassa by a combined African-Arab army, 1728; earrings, anklets, pendants, and armbands fashioned from gold and bronze

In China, Manchu dynasty, 1644–1912; greatest extent of empire, 1760; Emperor Kang Hsi, 1661–1722, institutes competitive civil service examinations; a Chinese version of an Enlightened Despot; Tibet brought into China's orbit, 1720; Emperor Ch'ien Lung, 1736–1796, a patron of Jesuit painters and architects; Jesuits Guiseppe Castiglione and Jean-Denis Attiret design Yüan-ming-yüan, the complex of pavilions and park in

Peking; the Altar of Heaven, a Manchu restoration in 1754 of the 1421 original; height of Manchu civilization but also the beginning of the dynasty's decline; emergence of secret societies, such as the White Lotus, that are hostile to the Manchu dynasty; reduction of slavery, 1730; the visual arts flourish; new method of taking census, in 1741—estimated population of 140 million; 1763, the death of Cao Xueqin, author of the unfinished *The Dream of the Red Chamber*, China's only great novel of manners; Chinese fashions exported to Europe, including Chinese-style gardens, pagodas, pavilions, lacquer, sedan chairs, incense, and porcelain; translations of Chinese thought and literature by Jesuits make their way into the West; in 1715, the Jesuit missionary Castiglione arrives in China, influences Chinese painting; the Summer Palace of Emperor Ch'ien Lung, designed by Jesuits; revival of Neo-Confucianism; study of mathematics, astronomy, and geography increases; dictionaries compiled; compilation of Chinese literature and history made for Emperor Ch'ien Lung, numbering 36,000 volumes

In Himalayan region, in Nepal, end of Malla dynasty and founding of Gurkha dynasty, 1768–present; in Tibet, Lamaistic state, 1450 to

1950s
In India, Mughal Empire, 1526–1858; failure in warfare leads to foreign control, as in the rise of the British East India Company, 1757–1858, and the taking of Madras by France, 1746; weak Mughal authority frees local Muslim rulers; rise of indigenous regional powers, such as the Sikhs (Punjab), Rajputs (Rajasthan), and Marathas (West India)

In Japan, Yedo, or Tokugawa period, 1615–1867; Japanese isolation, 1637–1854; an opening in the bamboo curtain, as the shogun allows Western books to be imported, leading to Japanese knowledge of Western science, especially medicine, 1720; death of Korin Ogata, painter of *Tale of Ise* and other screens painted with iris and red and white plum trees, 1716; performance of *The Love Suicides at Sonezaki* by the puppet theater of Monzaemon Chikamatsu at Osaka, 1720—the first of several domestic dramas based on actual incidents, which reflect the growing power of the middle class; Yokai Yagu, poet, 1702–1783; popular form of entertainment for middle- and lower-class patrons; death in 1724 of Kiyonobu Torii, the *ukiyoe* painter who specialized in portraits of Kabuki actors and beautiful women; *Tales of the Rainy Moon*, by Akinari Ueda, containing stories from China and Japan, 1767; Hokusai, 1760–1849, artist famous for woodblock

c) Voltaire
    (1) *Essay on Customs*
    (2) *Candide*
3. Neoclassicism and English literature
  a) The English setting
  b) Pope
    (1) His style
    (2) *Essay on Man*
  c) Gibbon: *History of the Decline and Fall of the Roman Empire*
4. The rise of the novel
  a) Characteristics
  b) Samuel Richardson
    (1) Theme: love between the sexes
    (2) *Pamela,* or *Virtue Rewarded*
    (3) *Clarissa*
  c) Henry Fielding
    (1) Theme: satiric adventures
    (2) *Tom Jones*
5. Music
  a) Rococo music
    (1) *Style galant*
    (2) The harpsichord and the pianoforte
    (3) Couperin
    (4) Rameau
  b) Classical music
    (1) Characteristics
    (2) The sonata form and its impact
    (3) Haydn
    (4) Mozart

V. The Legacy of the Enlightenment

prints and landscapes; Harunobu, 1724–1770, the earliest master of the multicolored print in Japan; Sharaku, woodblock artist, noted for caricatures of actors, late eighteenth century; Yedo (Tokyo) is destroyed by fire, 1772; in 1800, Yedo has a population of 1 million, making it probably the world's largest city at the time; literary rate in Japan during the Tokugawa Shogunate was highest in Asia, 45 percent for males, 15 percent for females; Utamaro, painter, 1753–1806; Okyo, painter, 1733–1795

In India, French lands ceded to Britain, 1763

In Indochina, in Siam, Emerald Buddha Chapel, Bangkok, 1785

In Mesoamerica, translation of *Popul Vuh,* the sacred book of the Quiché Indians of Guatemala, 1701–1721

In Muslim world, in Afghanistan, the Barkzai dynasty, 1747–1929; in Persia, collapse of the Safavid dynasty under invasion, 1736; war and chaos follow until Zand dynasty established, 1750–1794

In North America, French lands in Canada ceded to Britain, 1763

In Polynesia, Dutch explorer Roggeveen discovers Easter Island, 1722

LEARNING OBJECTIVES

To learn:

1. The goals and the ideals of the Enlightenment as well as the leading *philosophes* and their contributions to this cultural movement

2. The influences on the Enlightenment, especially Greco-Roman Classicism, the Scientific Revolution, and the Renaissance

3. The meaning and significance of Deism and its relationship to the Scientific Revolution

4. The role played by the *Encyclopédie* in the Enlightenment

5. The reasons that both the Physiocrats and Adam Smith encouraged laissez-faire economics instead of mercantilism

6. The condition of Europe in 1700 and the historical changes that occurred between 1700 and 1789, particularly in England, France, Prussia, Austria, and Russia (the great powers) and to a lesser extent in the Netherlands, Spain, and Portugal (the almost-great powers)

7. How the Rococo style reflected its origins in France and Austria, where aloof aristocracies dominated society, and how, in England, Hogarth satirized this style in paintings that appealed to middle-class patrons

8. How the Neoclassical style was, in part, a rebellion against the frivolity of the Rococo style and, in part, a reflection of devotion to Greco-Roman values, especially love of country and virtuous behavior

9. How seventeenth-century England and France, two of the age's leading political powers, represented two contrasting approaches to monarchy and the impact this difference had on artistic and literary developments

10. The characteristics of the Rococo, along with leading exponents of this style and their contributions

11. The characteristics of Neoclassicism, along with leading exponents of this style and their contributions

12. The new ideas that originated in the political philosophy of Montesquieu and Rousseau and their later influence

13. The characteristics and leading composers of Rococo music

14. The defining role played by Haydn and Mozart in originating Classical-style music and their major contributions to this style

15. The historic "firsts" of the Age of Reason that became part of the Western tradition: the emergence of the middle class as a potent force for change; the literary form of the novel; in music, the sonata form and the symphony; a democratizing tendency in culture; a progressive view of history; the principle of government by consent of the governed; and the beliefs that the least amount of state interference in the lives of citizens is best and that all people are created equal

16. The role of the Age of Reason in transmitting the heritage of the past: making the idea of absolutist government an indefensible concept, renewing democratic ideals, reviving and adapting Classical principles and forms to new conditions in the Neoclassical arts and architecture and Classical music, making the civilization of Rome and its fate a comparative model for Western states, continuing the new science and applying its methodology and principles to the Enlightenment, and modifying the Baroque into the Rococo style

SUGGESTIONS FOR FILMS

Catherine the Great: A Profile in Power. BBC/Time-Life, 72 min., black and white.

The Christians: Politeness and Enthusiasm (1689–1791). McGraw-Hill, 45 min., color.

Civilisation; The Light of Experience; The Smile of Reason. BBC/Time-Life, 52 min. each, color.

The Market Society and How It Grew. NET, 2 parts, 29 min. each, black and white.

Voltaire Presents Candide: An Introduction to the Age of Enlightenment. Encyclopedia Britannica, 34 min., color.

SUGGESTIONS FOR MUSIC

Couperin, François. *Concerts Royaux (4).* Claire, See, Moroney, Ter Linder, Harmonia Mundi. 901151 [CD].

Haydn, Franz Joseph. *Quartets (6) for Strings, Op. 50.* Juilliard String Quartet. CBS M2K-42154 [CD].

———. *The Seasons (Oratorio).* Mathis, Jerusalem, Fischer-Dieskau, Marriner, St. Martin's Academy & Chorus. Philips 411428-2 PH2 [CD].

———. *Symphonies (104).* Marriner, St. Martin's Academy. Philips 6768003 PSI.

Mozart, Wolfgang Amadeus. *Don Giovanni.* Arroyo, Te Kanawa, Freni, Burrows, Wixell, Ganzarolli, Davis, Royal Opera. Philips 6707022 2.

———. *Piano Music.* Barenboim. Angel CDC-47384 [CD].

———. *Mozart's Greatest Hits.* Cleveland Orchestra. CBS MLK-39436 [CD].

Rameau, Jean Philippe. *Les Boreades (suite); Dardanus (suite).* Bruggen, Orchestra of the 18th Century. Philips 420240-2 PH.

———. *Les Indes Galantes: Airs et Danses.* Herreweghe, Chapelle Royale Orchestra. Harmonia Mundi 1028.

SUGGESTIONS FOR FURTHER READING

Anderson, M. S. *Europe in the Eighteenth Century.* Rev. ed. London: Longman, 1987. Extensively revised and rewritten to reflect recent research since the 1961 edition. In the Longman General History of Europe series, this is a useful work for the student who wants a solid overview of a complex period.

Black, J. *Eighteenth-Century Europe, 1700–1789.* New York: St. Martin's Press, 1990. In the St. Martin's Press History of Europe series, the author takes a topical, not chronological, approach covering demography, economics, social classes, towns, religion, and the Enlightenment.

Braham, A. *The Architecture of the French Enlightenment.* London: Thames and Hudson, 1980. A scholarly study that will challenge the advanced student—fully illustrated.

Chartier, R. *The Cultural Origins of the French Revolution.* Durham, N.C.: Duke University Press, 1991. An essay on a hotly debated issue regarding the origins of the French Revolution from the "bottom up" on such topics as the public sphere, the publishing industry, and popular culture; not a survey but an interpretative work.

Crow, T. *Painters and Public Life in Eighteenth-Century Paris.* New Haven, Conn.: Yale University Press, 1985. A groundbreaking study on the public sphere and art, which the serious student will find rewarding.

Darnton, R. *The Business of Enlightenment: A Publishing History of the Encyclopédie.* Cambridge: Harvard University Press, Belknap Press, 1979. The biography of a book—a study of how this influential compendium of knowledge was written, organized, and published in spite of much opposition.

Fieldhouse, D. K. *The Colonial Empires: A Comparative Study from the Eighteenth Century.* London: Weidenfeld and Nicolson, 1982. A survey of a complex and controversial topic, this book, while now somewhat outdated, raised the issues still being debated by historians.

Gay, P. *The Enlightenment: An Interpretation.* Vol. 1: *The Rise of Modern Paganism,* Vol. II: *The Science of Freedom.* New York: Knopf, 1966–1969. A brilliant interpretation of the Enlightenment from a liberal point of view.

Hampson, N. *A Cultural History of the Enlightenment.* New York: Pantheon, 1968. Analyzes ideas of the Enlightenment and explains how they spread across Europe and through society.

Honour, H. *Neo-Classicism.* New York: Penguin, 1968. A brief study of Neoclassical art, sculpture, and architecture; a useful work for the beginning student.

Levey, M. *Rococo to Revolution: Major Trends in Eighteenth-Century Painting.* New York: Praeger, 1966. A controversial approach ignoring art history divisions between 1700 and 1830 and focusing on artists as a rather unified group; for the ambitious student.

Mellers, W. *The Sonata Principle.* New York: Schocken, 1969. Insightful discussion of the defining role played by the sonata principle in music composition between 1750 and 1900.

Scott, H. M., ed. *Enlightened Absolutism.* Ann Arbor: University of Michigan, 1990. Prefaced by essays on the general topic of Enlightened Absolutism, this is a country-by-country approach, noting reformers and their programs.

Spencer, S., ed. *French Women and the Age of Enlightenment.* Bloomington: Indiana University Press, 1984. A set of essays that helped pave the way for future studies relating women to the Enlightenment.

Woloch, I. *Eighteenth-Century Europe: Tradition and Progress, 1715–1789.* New York: Norton, 1982. In the Norton History of Modern Europe series, this topical survey covers such issues as the social orders, crime and punishment, population shifts, poverty, and religious thought and organization.

IDENTIFICATIONS

Enlightenment	Classical style (in music)
philosophes	sonata form
Deism	symphony
Physiocrats	concerto
Rococo style	sonata
fête galante	key
rocaille	tempo
Neoclassical style	mood
style galant	scherzo
pianoforte	

PERSONAL PERSPECTIVE BACKGROUND

Lady Mary Wortley Montagu, Letter to Lady ———, 1 April 1717

Lady Mary, as her generation called her, knew that her letters represented her claim to future fame. Having sampled Madame de Sévigné's correspondence, she confided to a friend: "I assert, without the least vanity, that [my letters] will be full[y] as entertaining forty years hence." While sojourning in Turkey, Lady Mary's inborn curiosity led her to experience local culture far in advance of most foreign tourists of the day. She studied Turkish language and poetry, adopted Turkish dress, and admired Turkish medicine whose treatment of smallpox was then superior to that of England. The visit to a Turkish bath, as described in the Personal Perspective, was part of her ongoing exploration of Turkish culture.

DISCUSSION/ESSAY QUESTIONS

1. Identify and explain the four trends that characterize the Age of Reason. How do these trends influence the culture of this period?
2. Discuss the nature of eighteenth-century European society, and indicate how this structure affected the arts.
3. Discuss the Enlightenment, identifying its goals, ideals, leading figures, and enduring contributions to the Western tradition.
4. Show how the Greco-Roman world, the Scientific Revolution, and the Renaissance affected the Enlightenment.
5. Discuss why the Enlightenment was essentially a product of French culture, and give examples of French contributions to the movement.
6. How did the *philosophes* avoid censorship in their public criticisms of eighteenth-century politics and culture?
7. Define Deism. What were its intellectual origins?
8. Compare and contrast the economic theories of the Physiocrats and Adam Smith.
9. Summarize historical developments in England, France, Prussia, Austria, and Russia—the great powers—and discuss how these developments helped to shape arts and architecture, literature, and political theory of the Age of Reason.
10. What is enlightened despotism? Where and why did it develop in the eighteenth century? Discuss the successes and failures of this political system.
11. In what ways were the Rococo and Neoclassical art styles reactions to the Baroque style? Note examples from all three schools.
12. Identify the characteristics and leading figures of the Rococo style of art. Explain Hogarth's negative response to the Rococo style.
13. Using a specific painting from each style, compare and contrast the Rococo with the Neoclassical artistic style.
14. What influences helped to bring about the Neoclassical style? What are its characteristics?
15. Compare and contrast the architecture and interior designs of the Rococo and Neoclassical styles.
16. Why did most of the *philosophes* reject absolutism and support an alternative form of government? Discuss the alternative types of government preferred by Montesquieu and Rousseau.
17. Compare and contrast the literary contributions of Montesquieu, Rousseau, Voltaire, Gibbon, and Alexander Pope to the Enlightenment.
18. Discuss the rise of the novel in eighteenth-century England. What conditions encouraged its development, who were the first novelists, and what were their themes?
19. What innovations occurred in music during the Age of Reason?
20. How does Classical music differ from Rococo music? Explain the role played by the sonata form in the evolution of the Classical style.

21. Discuss the contributions of Haydn and Mozart to Classical music.
22. In what way did the Enlightenment lay the foundations of the modern world?
23. What are the three most significant developments in the Age of Reason? Explain.

MULTIPLE-CHOICE QUESTIONS

1. The Enlightenment style of thinking favored:
   a. traditional Catholic beliefs
   b. pietistic feelings
   * c. scientific methodology (p. 401)
   d. Thomist theology

2. Which was NOT a trend during the Age of Reason?
   a. growing concentration of power in the great dynastic states
   * b. decline in the power of the aristocracy (p. 401)
   c. growing political and cultural eminence of the middle class
   d. unfolding of the cultural movement known as the Enlightenment

3. Which was NOT an expression of Classical values in the Age of Reason?
   a. the piano music of Mozart
   b. the poems of Alexander Pope
   * c. the paintings of Watteau (pp. 401, 410–411, 415, 417, 420–421, 424)
   d. the paintings of David

4. The Enlightenment owed intellectual debts to all of these EXCEPT:
   a. the discoveries of the Scientific Revolution
   b. the secular values of the Greco-Roman world
   c. the humanism of the Renaissance
   * d. the religious doctrines of Christianity (pp. 401–402)

5. The Enlightenment, in its relationship to society:
   a. engulfed the whole of the European population
   b. had a larger impact in eastern than in western Europe
   * c. had an impact on a relatively small percentage of Europeans, mainly in the western middle class (p. 402)
   d. appealed particularly to educated laborers

6. The Enlightenment was most influential in:
   a. Italy and Germany
   b. Scandinavia and Russia
   * c. France and Great Britain (p. 402)
   d. Spain and Portugal

7. The European state with the least censorship in the Enlightenment was:
   a. France
   b. Spain
   * c. the Netherlands (p. 402)
   d. Russia

8. The *philosophes* called for all of these reforms EXCEPT:
    a.   religious toleration
    b.   public education
 * c.   women's suffrage (pp. 402–403)
    d.   abolition of slavery

9. Which was NOT a position advocated by Mary Wollstonecraft?
    a.   She opposed all forms of hierarchy.
    b.   She endorsed natural rights for women.
 * c.   She called for a woman to be named prime minister. (p. 404)
    d.   She urged that women be educated the same as men.

10. Which was NOT an aspect of Deism?
    a.   It was based on the Newtonian model of the universe.
 * b.   It stressed the role of prayer. (p. 404)
    c.   It portrayed God as a great clockmaker.
    d.   It showed that secularization was growing in Europe.

11. A central tenet of Deism is that:
    a.   Jesus Christ is the savior of humanity.
 * b.   God created the universe and set the laws of nature in motion and thereafter never again
         interfered in human and natural affairs. (p. 404)
    c.   God reveals himself in the human heart.
    d.   God expresses himself in the human feelings.

12. The *Encyclopédie* was:
 * a.   a monumental work of seventeen text volumes and eleven books of illustrations (p. 405)
    b.   sponsored by the French authorities
    c.   edited by Voltaire
    d.   dedicated to the high culture of the arts and humanities

13. Another name for laissez-faire economics is:
    a.   the guild system
 * b.   free trade (p. 405)
    c.   mercantilism
    d.   a government-run system

14. Which of the following was NOT one of the ways the *philosophes* spread their ideas?
 * a.   official French publications (p. 402)
    b.   essays and books
    c.   private and public discussions and debates
    d.   salons

15. Who were NOT advocates of laissez-faire economics in the Age of Reason?
 * a.   the French kings (pp. 405, 407)
    b.   the Physiocrats
    c.   Adam Smith
    d.   the entrepreneurs who made the Industrial Revolution

16. During the Age of Reason, which class bore the heaviest tax burden?
    a.   the aristocracy
    b.   the middle class
 * c.   the peasants (p. 406)
    d.   the urban working class

17. Which was NOT a symbol of France's decline during the Age of Reason?
    a. the loss of colonies in North America and India to Britain in 1763
    b. the failure of the tax system to provide adequate state revenues
 * c. the loss of cultural leadership to England and Scotland, which came to dominate the Enlightenment (p. 407)
    d. the inability of the kings to reform the state because of the power of the nobility

18. The relationship between the ideas of the Enlightenment and the French court, nobles, and members of the upper class can be best described as:
    a. of no consequence for those groups
 * b. an interaction whereby some members of these groups read the *Encyclopédie* and discussed its content (pp. 402–404, 407)
    c. one of no contact because the French government forbade those of the ruling and upper classes to read any works by the *philosophes*
    d. a conscious rejection of the Enlightenment's beliefs by all three groups

19. This state, as a limited monarchy, became the ideal model for many *philosophes:*
 * a. Great Britain (p. 407)
    b. France
    c. Sweden
    d. Spain

20. The Empress Maria Theresa of Austria:
    a. was one of the most ardent supporters of the Enlightenment
    b. ruled over an empire that included only Austrian Germans
 * c. attempted to reform her government and army (p. 409)
    d. never had the support of her people, who held her in contempt

21. The outstanding example of enlightened despotism in the Age of Reason was:
 * a. Austria under Joseph II (p. 409)
    b. Russia under Peter the Great
    c. France under Louis XVI
    d. Great Britain under George I

22. In comparing the Rococo and Neoclassical styles, it can be noted that:
    a. Both styles appealed to the new middle classes.
 * b. The Rococo reflected the tastes of the French aristocracy and the Neoclassical the tastes of the progressive middle class. (p. 409)
    c. Both styles were rejected by the progressive middle class, which preferred the Romantic style.
    d. The Rococo attracted the middle class, while the Neoclassical was supported by the upper class.

23. The originator of the Rococo style was:
    a. Hogarth
 * b. Watteau (p. 409)
    c. Fragonard
    d. Boucher

24. The painter Watteau specialized in this subject:
    a. domestic interiors
 * b. aristocratic entertainments (p. 409)
    c. portraits
    d. still lifes

25. A feature of Watteau's *Departure from Cythera* was its:
    a. sense of excitement in a new adventure
    b. moral warning against sexual permissiveness
    c. reference to a historical event
 * d. air of melancholy (p. 411)

26. This painter's works were famous for their unabashed sexuality:
    a. Watteau
    b. Hogarth
 * c. Boucher (p. 411)
    d. David

27. The dominant subject of Vigée-Lebrun in her paintings was:
 * a. society portraits (p. 411)
    b. aristocratic entertainments
    c. mythological scenes
    d. historical events

28. Which was NOT a prominent design element in Rococo interiors?
    a. mirrors
    b. chandeliers
 * c. religious images (p. 413)
    d. *rocaille*

29. A splendid example of a Rococo interior is the:
    a. Library of Kenwood House, London
 * b. "Salon de la Princesse" in the Hôtel de Soubise, Paris (p. 413)
    c. Hall of Mirrors in Palace at Versailles
    d. auditorium of the Pantheon, Paris

30. What innovation is associated with Hogarth's art?
    a. He was the originator of the Neoclassical style.
 * b. He was the first artist to run off multiple engravings of his paintings to reach a large audience. (p. 414)
    c. He established the subject of the *fête galante*.
    d. He originated the Romantic landscape.

31. Which is NOT correct regarding Hogarth's *Marriage à la Mode* series?
    a. It is anti-Rococo in style.
    b. It is a satirical view of a loveless marriage made for money.
    c. It appealed to the values of England's Protestant middle class.
 * d. It was commissioned by King George II. (pp. 414–415)

32. Which did NOT contribute to the birth of the Neoclassical style?
    a. the publication of Stuart and Revett's *The Antiquities of Athens*
 * b. the paintings of Boucher and Fragonard (p. 415)
    c. the archeological excavations at Pompeii
    d. the birth of art history in the writings of Winckelmann

33. The principal exponent of Neoclassical painting was:
    a. Hogarth
    b. Watteau
 * c. David (p. 415)
    d. Fragonard

34. Neoclassicism was characterized by:
    a. frivolous subjects
  * b. disciplined perspective (p. 415)
    c. weightless floating images
    d. an undercurrent of eroticism

35. Neoclassical architecture relied on the ideals of:
    a. grandiosity and monumentality
  * b. proportion and simplicity (pp. 417–418)
    c. abstraction and nonrepresentation
    d. airiness and lightness

36. In politics, Voltaire:
    a. was a democrat
  * b. supported enlightened despotism (p. 418)
    c. advocated limited monarchy
    d. was an exponent of socialism

37. Rousseau's democratic ideas reflected his origins as a citizen of:
    a. the nation-state of England
    b. the world
  * c. the city-state of Geneva (p. 419)
    d. the Holy Roman Empire

38. Montesquieu's most enduring idea in *The Spirit of the Laws* is:
    a. Governments should be based on the consent of the governed.
    b. Governments are created to protect property.
  * c. Separation of powers prevents governments from becoming tyrannical. (pp. 418–419)
    d. Natural rights are inalienable.

39. Which was NOT an idea in Rousseau's *The Social Contract?*
    a. The people collectively personify the state.
    b. Obedience to the laws of the state makes the citizens moral.
  * c. The majority is always right. (p. 419)
    d. The state grants civil rights to the citizens.

40. Which is NOT accurate regarding Montesquieu's *Persian Letters?*
  * a. It was a translation from a Persian original. (p. 419)
    b. It satirized French institutions and customs.
    c. It was cleverly written to avoid censorship.
    d. It launched a new literary genre, the letters of a "foreign" traveler who voices social criticism.

41. Which was NOT an aspect of Voltaire's leadership during the Age of Reason?
    a. He dominated the age's literary life with his poems, plays, novels, and histories.
  * b. He used his moral authority to keep peace among the quarreling *philosophes*. (pp. 419–420)
    c. He was a great controversialist who supported unpopular causes.
    d. Voltaire's *Candide* was the most popular novel of the day.

42. Voltaire's chief aim in *Candide* was to satirize the:
  * a. philosophy of optimism (p. 420)
    b. institution of monarchy
    c. practice of arranged marriages
    d. legal system of France

43. English Neoclassical writers and their readers shared these values:
   a. lightheartedness and love of luxury
   b. formality and courtliness
 * c. good taste and moral and religious values (pp. 420–421)
   d. free-spiritedness and unconventionality

44. Pope's optimism in *Essay on Man* was satirized by:
   a. Montesquieu in the *Persian Letters*
 * b. Voltaire in *Candide* (p. 420)
   c. Gibbon in *History of the Decline and Fall of the Roman Empire*
   d. Rousseau in *The Confessions*

45. Which is NOT correct regarding Gibbon's *History of the Decline and Fall of the Roman Empire?*
   a. It appealed to the Age of Reason's Classical interests.
   b. It echoed the *philosophes'* skepticism about the Christian faith.
 * c. It is still read today because its scholarship has not been surpassed. (p. 421)
   d. It reflected the Enlightenment's belief that history should be philosophy teaching through example.

46. What new literary form was developed in the Age of Reason?
 * a. the novel (p. 421)
   b. the epic
   c. the sonnet
   d. the philosophic dialogue

47. Eighteenth-century novelists generally wrote about:
   a. famous historical events
   b. legends or fables
 * c. true-to-life individuals (p. 422)
   d. glamorous personages

48. Which was NOT a technique used by English novelists to make their works realistic?
   a. They followed their characters over the course of minutely observed time.
   b. They focused on the lives of ordinary men and women.
   c. They used a narrative voice that was appropriate to the setting.
 * d. They concentrated on the feelings of their characters rather than the details of their personal lives. (p. 422)

49. Which did NOT express the new power of the middle class during the Age of Reason?
   a. the paintings of Hogarth
   b. most of the writings of the *philosophes*
   c. the English novel
 * d. the paintings of Watteau (passim)

50. The plot of Fielding's *The History of Tom Jones* is a:
   a. sentimental domestic drama
 * b. robust comedy and adventure tale (p. 422)
   c. tragic situation brought on by fate
   d. legendary tale of a famous highwayman

51. The perfect instrument for Rococo music was the:
    a. violin
    b. trumpet
  * c. harpsichord (p. 422)
    d. organ

52. The music of Couperin is a perfect counterpart to the:
    a. paintings of David
    b. poems of Alexander Pope
  * c. art of Watteau (p. 422)
    d. architecture of Robert Adam

53. Which was NOT characteristic of Classical music?
    a. emphasis on form and structure
    b. widespread reliance on the sonata form
  * c. musical themes that evoked exotic places (pp. 422–423)
    d. use of clear, simple harmonies

54. All of the following describe Mozart's private life EXCEPT:
    a. He was a child prodigy.
  * b. As a court musician, he held a high social position wherever he went. (p. 423–424)
    c. He spent several years in the service of the archbishop of Salzburg.
    d. He died a poor man, unrecognized in his day.

55. In *The Marriage of Figaro*, Mozart presents a:
    a. study of the impact of a mythical hero on history
    b. brief one-act opera on the role of women in Austrian society
  * c. humorous account of how the lower class can outwit the upper class (p. 424)
    d. Romantic opera that plays on the theme of rejected love.

17

REVOLUTION, REACTION, AND CULTURAL RESPONSE
1760–1830

TEACHING STRATEGIES AND SUGGESTIONS

The instructor will be challenged to keep this complicated chapter's central threads together, to focus on the main themes of several complex movements, and to connect the material institutions with the intellectual developments and artistic trends. One or possibly two Standard Lectures may be necessary to set the stage for this period. The Historical Overview can be used to introduce the period in the first lecture; the instructor can then employ the Diffusion model to show what precipitated the three "revolutions"—namely, the American, the French, and the Industrial revolutions, specifically posing the question of how much impact the Enlightenment had on the two political upheavals.

A good approach to the Industrial Revolution is to adopt the Patterns of Change method; and the two political revolutions can be presented with the Case Study or the Comparison/Contrast model. However, the instructor should seriously consider giving a brief Historical Overview in order to lay out in a straightforward manner the origins, phases, and outcome of the French Revolution. To supplement the lecture on the French Revolution, it is recommended that the textbook's Table 17.1, titled Shifts in the French Government, be copied and distributed in class; this table will help to keep this period's complex details from becoming overwhelming for students. The section in the textbook titled "Reaction, 1815–1830" should not be scanted when dealing with the topics in this chapter, since it establishes the groundwork for many of the themes that are taken up in the next chapter.

The Reflections/Connections model should be the most effective in setting the themes, trends, and works identified with Neoclassicism and Romanticism. The paintings and architecture of Neoclassicism and Romanticism should be explained by means of Slide Lectures. The origins and causes of Romanticism can be explored with the Reflections/Connections model or the Spirit of the Age approach—the latter being more appropriate, perhaps, since Hegel, the author of this idea, is treated in this chapter. The instructor, using a Music Lecture, can show how the roots of Romantic music reach back to the Rococo and Classical styles.

Because Chapter 17 is so pivotal to the narrative of Western history and so central to *The Western Humanities*, a concluding lecture on the legacy of this period is necessary both as a summary and as an introduction to the nineteenth century, which will be covered in Chapters 18 and 19.

LECTURE OUTLINE

I. General Characteristics of the 1760–1830 Period

II. The Industrial Revolution
  A. Industrialization in England
    1. Conditions and causes
    2. Changes in cotton manufacturing
    3. Social changes
  B. Classical economics: the rationale for industrialization
    1. Adam Smith: *Wealth of Nations*
    2. Thomas Malthus: *Essay on the Principle of Population*
    3. David Ricardo: *Principles of Political Economy and Taxation*

III. Political Revolutions, 1780–1815
  A. The American Revolution
    1. Causes and phases
    2. Results of the revolution
  B. The French Revolution
    1. Causes and phases
    2. The Napoleonic era

IV. Reaction, 1815–1830
  A. Assessment of the results of the revolutions
  B. Reform and restoration across Europe

V. Revolutions in Art and Ideas: from Neoclassicism to Romanticism
  A. Comparison and contrast of the two movements
  B. Neoclassical painting and architecture after 1789
    1. Jacques-Louis David
    2. Jean-Auguste-Dominique Ingres
    3. Thomas Jefferson
  C. Classicism in Literature after 1789
  D. Romanticism: its spirit and expression
    1. Causes and characteristics of Romanticism
    2. The Romantic movement in literature
      a) *Sturm und Drang:* Goethe as a young writer
      b) English Romanticism
        (1) Wordsworth
        (2) Coleridge

Non-Western Events
1760–1830

In Africa, Osei "The Whale" Bonshu becomes king of the Ashanti empire, 1800; Shaka, king of the Zulu, 1818–1828; society to found Liberia for free U.S. blacks, 1820

In Caribbean, in Santo Domingo, Toussaint L'Ouverture leads a slave revolt, 1802

In India, decline of Mughal dynasty, 1526–1858; British dominance, after 1800 through the British East India company, 1757–1858; introduction of Western culture, language, methods of government, and technology into urban centers; Indian adventurer Hyder Ali conquers parts of India, about 1760

In Himalaya region, in Nepal, Malla dynasty, 1768 to present; in Tibet, Lamaistic state, about 1450 to 1950s

In Japan, Yedo, or Tokugawa period, 1615–1867; extravagance and inefficiency at the Tokugawa court, after 1793; death of Utagawa, a *ukiyoe* painter, noted for his new style based on Western perspective, 1814; Katsushika Hokusai, painter, 1760–1849; Okyo, painter, 1733–1795

In Korea, Li dynasty, 1392–1910; the city walls and gates of Suwon, 1794–1796; the temple complex of Pang-hwa Su-ryu Chong at Suwon, 1796

In Mesoamerica, revolts for independence, 1810–1830

In Muslim world, Sayyid Said, ruler of Zanzibar and

c) Goethe: *Faust*
d) Lord Byron: *Don Juan*
e) Mary Shelley: *Frankenstein*
3. Romantic painting
   a) John Constable
   b) J. M. W. Turner
   c) Casper David Friedrich
   d) Francisco Goya
   e) Théodore Géricault
   f) Eugène Delacroix
4. German Idealism
   a) Immanuel Kant
   b) F. W. J. von Schelling
   c) G. F. W. Hegel
5. The birth of Romantic music
   a) Ludwig van Beethoven
   b) Franz Schubert
   c) Hector Berlioz

VI. The Legacy of the Age of Revolution and Reaction

Muscat, 1804–1856; in Persia, Zand dynasty, 1750–1794; Kajar dynasty, 1794–1925

In South America, revolts for independence, 1810–1830; *Silva a la Agricultura de la Zona Torrica*, by the poet Andres Bello, 1826

World's first accurate census in 1801 shows China with 295 million, India 131 million, Ottoman Empire 21 million, Japan 15 million, Russia 33 million, France 27.4 million, the German states and cities 14.1 million, Britain 10.4 million, Ireland 5.2 million, Egypt 2.5 million, and the United States 5.3 million; the world's largest cities are Guangzhou (Canton) with 1.5 million followed by Nanjin, Hangchow, Kingtechchen, and Yedo Tokyo), each with 1 million

LEARNING OBJECTIVES

To learn:

1. Why the 1760–1830 period was so revolutionary and what it produced

2. The characteristics and causes of the Industrial Revolution

3. Why the Industrial Revolution occurred first in England

4. How the Industrial Revolution changed English society

5. The arguments put forward by the Classical economists regarding the nature of the economy and why these arguments seemed to justify the first phases of the Industrial Revolution

6. The causes, phases, and results of the American Revolution

7. The causes, phases, and results of the French Revolution

8. How and why Napoleon rose to power and what he accomplished

9. The differing impact of the French Revolution and the Napoleonic period on women

10. How Europe reacted to the French Revolution from 1815 to 1830

11. The characteristics of Neoclassicism, its major painters, and their contributions

12. The impact of Neoclassicism on American architecture

13. The characteristics and origins of Romanticism

14. How Romanticism was manifested in literature, who its major writers were, and what their works were

15. The role that Goethe played in Romanticism and his influences on later writers

16. How Romanticism was expressed in the visual arts, who its major artists were, and what key examples of their works are
17. The artistic contributions of Francisco Goya

18. The nature of German idealism and its major voices

19. The origins and nature of Romantic music, its chief composers, and their contributions

20. Historic "firsts" of this period that became part of the Western tradition: the Industrial Revolution, the American Revolution, the French Revolution, Classical economics, states based on natural rights theory, a revolutionary tradition, militant nationalism, and Romanticism

21. The role of this period in transmitting the heritage of earlier civilizations: continuing the Neoclassical style, particularly developing an enduring type of public building style; restoring the idea of democracy, which had been in disrepute since fifth-century B.C. Athens, and giving it a modern interpretation; furthering the Renaissance idea of free expression; and reviving beliefs and ideals of the medieval period

SUGGESTIONS FOR FILMS

The Ascent of Man: The Drive for Power. Time-Life Films, 52 min., color.

Bernstein on Beethoven: Ode to Joy from the Ninth Symphony. BFA Educational Media, 27 min., color.

Civilisation: Heroic Materialism. Fallacies of Hope. Time-Life Films, 52 min., color.

English Literature: Romantic Period. Coronet, 14 min., color.

The French Revolution. Coronet, 17 min., color.

The Industrial Revolution in England. Encyclopedia Britannica, 26 min., black and white.

Napoleon: The Making of a Dictator. Learning Corporation of America, 27 min., color.

Seeds of the Revolution: Colonial America 1763–75. Graphic Curriculum, 24 min., color.

Spirit of Romanticism. Encyclopedia Britannica, 27 min., color.

Thomas Jefferson's Monticello. Comco Productions/Paramount, 24 min., color.

SUGGESTIONS FOR MUSIC

Beethoven, Ludwig van. *Symphony No. 3 in E Flat, Op. 55, "Eroica."* Mehta, New York Philharmonic. CBS IM-35883 [digital]; MK-35883 [CD].

———. *"Leonore" Overture No. 3 and Symphony No. 5.* Boult, London Promenade Orchestra. Vanguard CSRV-190 [Cassette].

———. *Beethoven's Greatest Hits.* Various orchestras and performers. CBS MLK-39434 [CD].

Berlioz, Hector. *Symphonie fantastique, Op. 14.* Muti, Philadelphia Orchestra. Angel DS-38210 [digital]; CDC-47278 [CD]; 4DS-32810 [cassette].

———. *Requiem, Op. 5.* Burrows, Bernstein, French National Radio Orchestra. CBS M2-34202.

———. *Harold in Italy, for viola and orchestra, Op. 16.* Christ, Maazel, Berlin Philharmonic and Chorus. DG 415109-2 GH [CD].

Schubert, Franz. *Songs.* Ameling, w. Baldwin. Etcetera ETC-1009; ARN-268006 [CD].
———. *Symphony No. 8 in B, D. 759, "Unfinished."* Marriner, St. Martin's Academy. Philips 412472-2 PH [CD].

———. *Octet in F for Strings and winds, D. 803, Op. 166.* Scott, Heller, Jolley, Genualdi, Falimir, Tenenbaum, Wiley, and Lloyd. Marlboro Recording Society MRSCD-18 [CD].

SUGGESTIONS FOR FURTHER READING

Broers, M. *Europe Under Napoleon, 1799–1815.* London: Arnold, 1996. Good narrative history of this turbulent period in European history.

Canaday, J. *Mainstreams of Modern Art.* 2nd ed. New York: Holt, Rinehart, and Winston, 1981. An authoritative discussion by one of the leading scholars of modern art; weak on treatment of the trend to abstraction.

Clark, K. *The Romantic Rebellion: Romantic Versus Classic Art.* New York: Harper & Row, 1986. A survey of thirteen artists, ranging from David and Goya to Degas and Rodin, by one of the century's leading art historians; based on the television series, published first in 1973.

Doyle, W. *Origins of the French Revolution.* Oxford: Oxford University Press, 1980. A well-respected survey of the varied interpretations of the causes of the great revolution in France.

Egnal, M. *A Mighty Empire: The Origins of the American Revolution.* Ithaca, N. Y.: Cornell University Press, 1988. A revisionist study that claims that the American revolt in every colony was led by an upper-class faction who had long been committed to the rise of a new world.

Hampson, N. *The First European Revolution, 1776–1815.* New York: Harcourt, Brace & World, 1979. Fully illustrated with many examples of high and popular art and a readable account of the major phases of this turbulent era.

Hitchcock, H. R. *Architecture: Nineteenth and Twentieth Centuries.* New York: Penguin, 1977. Thorough coverage with excellent illustrations and documents from the period.

Honour, H. *Romanticism.* New York: Harper & Row, 1979. A serviceable guide to Romanticism in art.

James, C. L. R. *The Black Jacobins.* 2nd ed. New York: Vintage, 1963. A groundbreaking history of the black uprising in Santo Domingo from a Marxist perspective; a reprint of the 1938 classic.

Klingender, F. D. *Art and the Industrial Revolution.* New York: Schocken Books, 1970. Useful cultural history that relates developments in art to its cultural context.

Landes, D. S. *The Unbound Prometheus: Technological Change and Industrial Development in Western Europe from 1750 to the Present.* London: Cambridge University Press, 1969. An excellent overview that analyzes all the phases of the Industrial Revolution.

LeBris, M. *Romantics and Romanticism.* New York: Skira, Rizzoli, 1981. A brilliant though idiosyncratic interpretation of the Romantic movement; beautifully illustrated.

Lefebvre, G. *The Coming of the French Revolution.* Translated by R. R. Palmer. New York: Vintage, 1961. An insightful summary of the causes of the revolution by one of the midcentury's outstanding scholars; first published in 1939.

Morgan, E. S. *The Birth of the Republic, 1763–1789.* 3rd ed. Chicago: University of Chicago Press, 1992. A classic, first issued in 1956; this interpretation argues that the American rebels found common cause in their support for the principle of equality.

Morris, R. B. *The Forging of the Union, 1781–1789.* New York: Harper & Row, 1987. A fine study by an outstanding scholar that explores how the U.S. Constitution was finally created.

Pilbeam, P. M. *Themes in Modern European History.* London: Routledge, 1995. Eleven essays on central themes spawned by the French Revolution and its aftermath; several essays deal with the huge contrast in scale of the revolution's impact in western versus central and eastern Europe.

Rosenblum, R., and Janson, H. W. *19th Century Art: Painting by Robert Rosenblum, Sculpture by H. W. Janson.* New York: Abrams, 1984. The most up-to-date survey of nineteenth-century painting and sculpture by two highly respected scholars.

Snooks, G. D., ed. *Was the Industrial Revolution Necessary?* London: Routledge, 1994. Five provocative essays by leading scholars, along with a concluding summary, offering new perspectives on the Industrial Revolution.

Sterns, P. N. *The Industrial Revolution in World History.* Boulder: Westview Press, 1993. A broad survey of industrialism, ranging from its birth in Great Britain about 250 years ago to its spread around the globe.

Stromberg, R. *An Intellectual History of Modern Europe.* 3rd ed. Englewood Cliffs, N.J.: Prentice-Hall, 1981. A thorough survey of the leading thinkers and intellectual movements.

Sutherland, D. M. G. *France 1789–1815: Revolution and Counterrevolution.* London: Fontana, 1985. Excellent narrative history of events in France from the onset of the great revolution to the restoration of the Bourbon kings.

Thomas, P. D. G. *Revolution in America: Britain and the Colonies, 1763–1776.* Cardiff: University of Wales Press, 1992. A brief survey focusing on constitutional issues between the American colonies and the British government.

Tucker, R. W., and Henderson, D. C. *The Fall of the First British Empire: Origins of the War of American Independence.* Baltimore: Johns Hopkins Press, 1982. A recent survey of the causes of the American Revolutionary War.

Vaughan, W. *Romanticism and Art.* Rev. ed. London: Thames and Hudson, 1994. A revised edition of Vaughan's masterly volume in the World of Art series; first published in 1978.

Wrigley, E. A. *Continuity, Chance and Change: The Character of the Industrial Revolution in England.* Cambridge: Cambridge University Press, 1988. A provocative work that challenges traditional views of the English Industrial Revolution.

Zaller, R. *Europe in Transition, 1660–1815.* New York: Harper & Row, 1984. A brief, serviceable overview.

IDENTIFICATIONS

Romanticism
Sublime
Sturm und Drang

program music
art song (*lied*)
idée fixe

PERSONAL PERSPECTIVE BACKGROUND

Hector Berlioz, "This Harmonious Revolution"

Berlioz, in the midst of launching his career as a composer, was an ardent supporter of France's 1830 revolution that deposed Charles X, the Bourbon king, and brought to the throne Louis Philippe, the so-called Bourgeois Monarch. The bourgeois Berlioz anticipated that the revolution would lead to "freedom for the arts" and glory for himself: "I shall succeed ten times quicker than I should have done without it" (letter dated September 5, 1830). In those last words can be heard Berlioz's hope for a return to the Napoleonic period's policy of "careers open to talent." Later the dream of a more enlightened society evaporated, but, in the immediate aftermath of the July uprising, radical social reform seemed possible. "This Harmonious Revolution" is taken from Berlioz's *Memoirs*, written in 1848 but still true to the heady optimism of the July days of 1830. (See *The Western Humanities* for additional information on Berlioz.)

DISCUSSION/ESSAY QUESTIONS

1. Discuss the industrial and the political revolutions of the late eighteenth century, focusing on the groups who welcomed these upheavals and their reasons for doing so.
2. Discuss England's Industrial Revolution, identifying the conditions necessary for industrialization to occur and showing how these conditions developed there.
3. Discuss the reasons why the Industrial Revolution occurred first in England and describe its impact on English society.
4. Summarize early developments in the Industrial Revolution, using the situation in cloth manufacturing as your example.
5. Show how the writings of Adam Smith, Thomas Malthus, and David Ricardo could be used to justify the Industrial Revolution.
6. What were the causes of the American Revolution, what were the goals of the revolt, and how successful were the American colonists in achieving their goals?
7. Some historians claim that the French Revolution has been the most important political event in the modern world. Explain why this may or may not be true.
8. Discuss the events leading up to the French Revolution, and describe the events of the first year of the revolution.
9. What were the major phases of the French Revolution from 1789 to 1799? How successful were the French in accomplishing their goals of 1789?
10. Why had events come "full circle" with the rise of Napoleon?
11. Napoleon called himself "a child of the Enlightenment." Did his domestic program reflect Enlightenment values? Explain.
12. Contrast the differing impact made by the French Revolution and Napoleon's reforms on women.
13. Discus the various European responses in the years between 1815 and 1830 to the ideals and goals of the French Revolution and Napoleon.
14. What were the roots of Neoclassicism, how would you define the term, and how did the paintings of David and Ingres express Neoclassicism?
15. Show how David's career as a painter reflected the changing political climate in France.
16. Discuss the impact of Neoclassicism on American building styles.
17. Discuss the origins of Romanticism and identify its chief characteristics.

18. What was the *Sturm und Drang* movement? Discuss its relationship to Romanticism.
19. What contributions did Wordsworth, Coleridge, and Lord Byron make to Romantic literature?
20. Goethe has often been cited as the central figure in the Romantic movement. Why?
21. Compare and contrast Neoclassicism and Romanticism, noting their origins, their sources for inspiration, and their basic characteristics.
22. How were the themes of Romanticism expressed in the paintings of Constable, Turner, and Friedrich?
23. How does Goya fit into Romanticism? Discuss at least two of his works to justify your position.
24. Compare and contrast the art styles of Géricault and Delacroix, using a painting by each artist in your discussion.
25. Compare and contrast Neoclassical painting with Romantic painting, using a representative artist and artwork as the basis of your discussion.
26. What is meant by German idealism and how was it expressed in the philosophy of Kant?
27. Discuss the role of Hegel in the evolution of nineteenth-century European thought.
28. What were the origins of Romantic music? How do Beethoven's musical works express the Romantic style?
29. Discuss Romanticism as a cultural movement, relying on Goethe (a writer), Hegel (a philosopher), and Beethoven (a musician) as the basis of your discussion.
30. Which event of the 1760–1830 period has had the most important effect on your life? Justify your answer.
31. What were the "good" and "bad" results of the French Revolution?
32. In what ways is Romanticism still a part of our lives today?

MULTIPLE-CHOICE QUESTIONS

1. The period between 1760 and 1830 can be described as a time when:
   a. Rural values were paramount.
   b. There were few artistic achievements.
 * c. The middle class began to win power from the aristocracy. (p. 427)
   d. Peace reigned on the continent.

2. Which class benefited the most from the revolutions of the late 1700s?
   a . the peasant class
 * b. the middle class (p. 427)
   c. the aristocracy
   d. the working class

3. The Industrial Revolution began in England because:
   a. Its peasants were clamoring for new jobs.
   b. Its feudal system had collapsed.
   c. Its government was willing to fund industrial growth.
 * d. Its colonial empire was a source for raw materials. (pp. 427–428)

4. Which did NOT occur in the English cloth-making industry at the start of the Industrial Revolution?
   a. One invention followed another in rapid succession.
   b. Laborers had to conform to the way machines operated.
 * c. Unions were created to protect workers. (pp. 427–428)
   d. Factories were built near sources of power, such as a river.

5. Adam Smith in his *Wealth of Nations*:
    a. dealt with manufacturing, not with agriculture and commerce
  * b. emphasized the concept of enlightened self-interest (p. 428)
    c. called for the intervention of governments to control their economies
    d. praised mercantilism as the best economic policy

6. The classic expression of laissez-faire economics is:
    a. Hegel's *Reason in History*
    b. Malthus's *On Population*
  * c. Smith's *Wealth of Nations* (p. 428)
    d. d'Holbach's *System of Nature*

7. Malthus's "law" of population meant that:
    a. The future is inevitably brighter than the past.
    b. Wages inevitably fall behind prices.
  * c. Population growth will inevitably outstrip food production, leading to natural calamities, such as famines, plagues, and wars. (p. 428)
    d. Populations remain fairly stable in industrial states because of the widespread use of birth control measures.

8. Ricardo's "iron law of wages" meant that wages for workers:
    a. are at the mercy of supply and demand
  * b. always hover around the subsistence level (pp. 428–429)
    c. reflect the economy's natural justice
    d. are tied to the cost of living

9. The economic conclusions reached by Malthus and Ricardo:
    a. indicated that farmers were prospering under industrialism
    b. forecast a rise in the working-class standard of living
    c. asserted that the economy operated by chance
  * d. led many to believe that the workers deserved what they got (p. 428)

10. By 1830 Europe can be described as a continent that:
    a. was controlled by one power, France
    b. had enjoyed almost fifty years of peace and prosperity
  * c. was divided into two political camps (p. 429)
    d. was about to enter into a period of long decline

11. What was the major issue dividing England and her American colonies in 1776?
    a. cultural differences
    b. class conflicts
  * c. taxes and the cost of upkeep of the colonies (p. 429)
    d. the slave trade

12. One immediate outcome of the American Revolution was that:
    a. All inhabitants were granted the right to vote.
    b. The new country closed its borders to immigrants.
  * c. It became the most democratic government since ancient Athens. (p. 429)
    d. It abolished slavery within its borders.

13. France, under Louis XVI, can be described as a:
    a. country with a uniform high standard of living
    * b. nation with a large national debt (p. 430)
    c. people united under a well-beloved king
    d. country with an equitable tax system

14. The major accomplishment of the French Revolution's first phase was the:
    a. end of the class system in France
    b. triumph of the workers
    * c. creation of a limited constitutional monarchy (p. 430)
    d. right to vote being given to women citizens

15. Which was NOT a feature of the second phase of the French Revolution?
    * a. compromise with the Catholic Church (pp. 430–431)
    b. the Reign of Terror
    c. control by the radicals
    d. foreign wars

16. One of Napoleon's major domestic reforms was a:
    * a. new legal code (p. 431)
    b. state religion based on Deism
    c. state-run farm system
    d. free press

17. In foreign affairs Napoleon:
    a. succeeded in setting up client kingdoms across Europe
    b. convinced other European states that he wanted peace
    * c. failed to liberate oppressed people (pp. 431–432)
    d. proved to be an inept military leader

18. One major change in Europe between 1789 and 1815 was the:
    a. spread of French-style revolutions to many countries
    * b. influence of Napoleon's reforms in much of western and central Europe (pp. 431–432)
    c. creation of government-sponsored industrial centers in western Europe
    d. rise of working-class rebellion across the continent

19. Neoclassicism in literature lingered on in England after 1800 in the works of:
    a. John Constable
    b. William Wordsworth
    c. Lord Byron
    * d. Jane Austen (p. 433)

20. France's revolutionary leaders favored Neoclassicism because:
    a. They liked its elaborately decorated house styles.
    b. They admired its association with the Middle Ages.
    * c. They thought the style morally uplifting. (p. 433)
    d. It reminded them of France's past glory under Louis XIV.

21. Which does NOT apply to David's *The Death of Marat?*
    a. It was an example of classicizing the modern.
    b. It captured a specific moment in history.
    c. It portrayed the ideals of the French Revolution by glamorizing one of its martyrs.
    * d. It foreshadowed the Romantic movement in painting. (p. 434 and caption for Fig. 17.4)

22. David's painting called *The Coronation* can be described as:
    * a. a work of political propaganda (pp. 434–435)
      b. a sentimental interpretation of an event
      c. an exact portrayal of what happened at the coronation
      d. the best group portrait of the era

23. Who introduced the Neoclassical style in architecture to the United States?
      a. George Washington
      b. Benjamin Franklin
    * c. Thomas Jefferson (p. 435)
      d. James Madison

24. The style of Thomas Jefferson's Monticello is:
      a. Neo-Gothic
      b. Baroque
      c. Rococo
    * d. Palladian (p. 435)

25. Which is NOT associated with Romanticism?
      a. It grew out of a rejection of the Enlightenment's ideas.
    * b. It was opposed to sentimentalism in art and literature. (p. 437)
      c. It looked to nature and the Middle Ages for inspiration.
      d. It reflected, in part, the revolutionary values of the French Revolution.

26. Romanticism viewed nature as:
      a. a resource to be exploited
      b. the fount of all evil
      c. a well-ordered system run by mathematical laws
    * d. a power that overawed the individual (p. 437)

27. Which was NOT a response of the Romantics to the French Revolution?
      a. They envisioned it as the wave of the future.
      b. They were appalled by its extreme violence.
      c. They thought its ideals to be too abstract.
    * d. They saw it as a return to the glories of the Middle Ages. (p. 437)

28. Romantic writers and artists expressed:
    * a. an admiration for nonconformity (p. 438)
      b. a deep respect for the middle class
      c. a yearning to be part of the aristocracy
      d. a preference for the Classical world

29. The country that could best claim to be the home of Romanticism was:
      a. England
      b. France
    * c. Germany (p. 438)
      d. Italy

30. Who helped popularize German culture and writers during this period?
      a. William Wordsworth
      b. Mary Shelley
    * c. Madame de Staël (p. 438)
      d. Jane Austen

31. The relationship of Romanticism and nationalism was that they were:
    a. two completely different movements
    b. constantly in conflict with each other
  * c. intertwined in their early years (pp. 437–438)
    d. rebellions against the Rococo movement

32. The *Sturm und Drang* movement:
    a. started in Russia
    b. supported the values of Classicism
  * c. glorified the life of the peasants (p. 438)
    d. was opposed to nationalism

33. Goethe's novel entitled *The Sorrows of Young Werther* was:
  * a. one of the opening works of the Romantic movement (p. 438)
    b. a realistic work about the working class
    c. a defense of society's rules and values
    d. an example of the human mind overcoming the heart

34. English Romanticism was launched by the writings of:
  * a. Wordsworth and Coleridge (p. 438)
    b. Keats and Shelley
    c. Goethe and Lessing
    d. Lord Byron and Dickens

35. The poems of Wordsworth's *Lyrical Ballads:*
    a. were written in a Neoclassical style
  * b. celebrate the joys and pleasures of ordinary events (p. 438)
    c. illustrate the alienation between humans and nature
    d. praise the benefits of the Industrial Revolution

36. Which is NOT correct regarding Goethe's hero Faust?
    a. He symbolized the universal rebel, willing to try anything.
    b. He was a restless intellectual.
  * c. He spent all of his life in his study. (pp. 438–439)
    d. He underwent a series of sordid adventures, including murder and seduction.

37. Lord Byron personified the Romantic ideal because:
    a. He upheld middle-class ideals.
    b. He was a private person with high morals.
  * c. He died as a hero in a noble cause. (p. 439)
    d. He spent his life helping others.

38. The major themes in English Romantic painting were the:
    a. real and the natural
    b. impression and the study
    c. exotic and the Classical
  * d. pastoral and Sublime (p. 439)

39. Which was NOT a theme in Romantic painting?
  * a. kings and aristocrats at play (pp. 439–440)
    b. quiet pastoral scenes
    c. scenes depicting nature's awesome aspects
    d. scenes of country folk and peasants

40. In his paintings Constable:
    a. tended to emphasize the human form
    b. painted "night scenes" in the manner of Caravaggio
    c. relied on Greek and Roman myths for subjects
  * d. emphasized the play of sunlight (p. 441)

41. Which painter's treatment of color later influenced the Impressionists?
  * a. Turner (p. 441)
    b. Ingres
    c. Goya
    d. Friedrich

42. The painter who established the Romantic style in Germany was:
    a. Millet
    b. Delacroix
  * c. Friedrich (p. 441)
    d. Biedermeier

43. Which Romantic artist was noted for portraying figures from the back, thus neglecting the faces?
  * a. Friedrich (p. 441)
    b. Constable
    c. Turner
    d. Goya

44. In his paintings Goya did NOT express:
  * a. a love of nature that he identified with God (pp. 442–443, 445)
    b. a nightmarish vision of the world
    c. a growing despair over the fate of his beloved Spanish homeland
    d. the psychological truth of his subjects, in his portraits

45. Goya's etchings entitled *Caprichos:*
  * a. express his most personal feelings (p. 445)
    b. have optimistic themes
    c. portray idealized subjects
    d. present gentle satires on contemporary topics

46. Géricault's painting of *The Raft of the Medusa* portrayed the theme of the:
  * a. breakdown of civilization (pp. 445–446 and caption for Fig. 17.19)
    b. calmness of nature
    c. strength of sailing ships
    d. forgiveness of God

47. Which is NOT correct for Delacroix's *Liberty Leading the People?*
    a. It made France's tricolor flag the focal point of the painting.
  * b. It became a rallying cry for France's bourgeois monarchy. (pp. 446–447 and caption for Fig. 17.21)
    c. It combines realism and allegory.
    d. It was based on a historical event.

48. Delacroix's *Liberty Leading the People* was inspired by the:
    a. Revolution of 1789
    b. defeat of Napoleon in 1815
  * c. July Revolution of 1830 (p. 447)
    d. restoration of the Bourbons in 1815

49. German idealism is a:
    a. revival of ancient Platonism
  * b. philosophic alternative to religion (p. 448)
    c. philosophy based on atheism
    d. system of thought based on materialism and determinism

50. All of the following are ideas of Hegel EXCEPT:
    a. History evolves through a dialectical process.
    b. The goal of the World Spirit is freedom.
  * c. Individuals have significant roles in the struggle for freedom. (pp. 448–449)
    d. Conflict and strife are essential for historical growth.

51. Which group was NOT influenced by Hegel's ideas?
  * a. democrats, who shared his views on the role of the people in history (p. 449)
    b. historians, who appropriated his idea that history moves through stages
    c. conservatives, who adopted his theory of a strong centralized state
    d. Marxists, who borrowed his concept of the dialectic

52. Which was NOT a change in late-eighteenth-century music, brought about by the impact of the middle class?
    a. the rise of public concerts and performances with admission fees and paid performers
    b. more accessible music to serve the tastes of new audiences
  * c. the hiring of performers, wearing household livery, to perform as family musicians (p. 449)
    d. music written to be performed in homes on the inexpensive musical instruments that were now available

53. Which is NOT correct regarding Beethoven and his music?
    a. His life passed through several stages that were mirrored in his search for new forms of music.
  * b. He pioneered the sonata form in music. (pp. 449, 451)
    c. He personified the new breed of musician, supporting himself with concerts, lessons, and sales of his music.
    d. He represented both the culmination of Classical music and the introduction of Romantic music.

54. Berlioz's *Symphonie fantastique (Fantastic Symphony)* is original in its use of a:
    a. symphonic musical form
  * b. recurring musical theme (p. 452)
    c. sonata form
    d. ballet suite within the symphonic form

55. All of these are innovations of Romantic music EXCEPT:
    a. program music
    b. the art song
    c. the use of choral music within the symphonic form
  * d. the sonata (pp. 449–452)

18

THE TRIUMPH
OF THE BOURGEOISIE
1830–1871

TEACHING STRATEGIES AND SUGGESTIONS

The instructor can introduce the Age of the Bourgeoisie, 1830–1871, with a Historical Overview that summarizes this epoch's key historical developments and, with a Patterns of Change approach, can set forth the accompanying stylistic evolution from the dominant Romantic and Neoclassical styles to the new style of Realism. Turning to a Reflections/Connections approach, the instructor can show how Neoclassicism and Romanticism mirrored historical events prior to 1848, the year of European-wide revolutions and a watershed year, and how Realism expressed the changed situation thereafter. A Slide Lecture combined with a Comparison/Contrast approach can show the changes in the arts and architecture. Special emphasis should be given to the painter Manet, because his "art for art's sake" dictum opened the door to the radical changes that produced modern art. A Music Lecture can illustrate the transformation in music, although Romantic music remained dominant throughout the era. A Standard Lecture organized on the Comparison/Contrast model can demonstrate the literary changes taking place, as Romantic writing gave way to Realism. And a Standard Lecture can be used to explain the contributions in philosophy, religion, and science. The instructor can conclude this series of presentations with a Spirit of the Age approach, emphasizing the role played by the ruling middle class, liberalism, and science in shaping mid–nineteenth-century culture.

LECTURE OUTLINE

Non-Western Events

I. Historical Overview
    A. The legacy of the American and
       French revolutions
    B. The plight of the proletariat
    C. Summary of stylistic developments

II. The Political and Economic Scene:
    Liberalism and Nationalism
    A. Liberalism
       1. Definition
       2. Ideals and influence
    B. Nationalism
       1. Definition

1830–1871
In Africa, Moshesh, king of
  Basutoland, 1824–1868;
  British consulates in coastal
  states, 1830–1860;
  exploration of interior
  continent, 1830–1875;
  decline of slave trade,
  1840–1863; Boer farmers
  found Natal, Transvaal,
  Orange Free State, 1836;
  East Africa is most
  important source of

world's ivory and illicit slaves, by 1850

In China, Manchu dynasty, 1644–1912; end of Opium War in 1842 opens China to wholesale exploitation by the Western powers; Taiping reform program ("Heavenly Peace") advocates examinations based on the Bible instead of Chinese classics, equal distribution of land, property rights for women, common granary, 1853–1864; the Summer Palace, a typical "pleasure palace" of the Manchu dynasty, nineteenth century

In Himalaya region, Malla dynasty, 1768–present; Gurkhali-style architecture, mixing archaic with French and Italian influence; in Tibet, Lamaistic state, about 1450 to 1950s

In India, Mughal dynasty in name only to 1858; actual rule is by British East India Company, 1757 to 1858 when power passes to the British crown (raj), 1858–1947; first telegraph, 1853; the first railroad link, between Bombay and Thana, a 20-mile length, 1853; Rabindranath Tagore, philosopher and poet, 1861–1941

In Indochina, in Siam, King Phra Chom Klao Mongkut, 1851–1868, the inspiration for the book by an English governess about her experiences at this Western-influenced court

In Japan, Yedo, or Tokugawa period, 1615–1867; opening of Japan, 1854; Meiji period, 1868–1912; emergence, through Western stimulus, into international world; marked changes in society, government, and culture;

b) John Stuart Mill
2. Socialism
   a) The utopian socialists
      (1) Owen, Saint-Simon, Fourier
      (2) Failed experiments
   b) The Marxists
      (1) Marx and Engels
      (2) Dialectical materialism
      (3) Formation of international socialist organization
      (4) Little influence before 1871

B. Religion and the challenge of science
  1. The higher criticism
  2. Science
   a) Geology discredits the biblical view of creation
   b) Biology questions the divine image of human beings
   c) Pasteur: the germ theory of disease
   d) Chemistry: advances in atomic theory, anesthetics, and surgery

IV. Cultural Trends: From Romanticism to Realism
  A. Order and Escape
   1. Neoclassicism and Romanticism adopted by the middle class
    a) Art becomes routinized
    b) The development of "official art"
   2. The challenge of Realism
    a) Rejection of Neoclassicism and Romanticism
    b) Art with a moral point of view, focused on ordinary people
    c) Influences on Realism
  B. Literature
   1. Overview
    a) Romanticism: free will
    b) Realism: deterministic
   2. The height of French Romanticism
    a) Hugo
      (1) *Hernani*
      (2) *Les Misérables*
    b) Sand
      (1) Her life and values
      (2) *Indiana*
   3. Romanicism in the English novel: the Brontë sisters
    a) Emily Brontë, *Wuthering Heights*
    b) Charlotte Brontë, *Jane Eyre*
   4. Realism in French and English novels
    a) Balzac and *The Human Comedy*

stone replaces wood in building construction; end of feudalism, 1871; Prince Matsukata, statesman, 1835–1924; Andiro Hiroshige, 1797–1858, painter of series of color prints "Fifty-Three Stages of the Tokaido," 1832; Japanese literature influenced by the Realist literary style of the West, after 1868; Mori Ogai, poet, translator of *Faust*, 1860–1921; the origin of Takashimaya retail store giant, 1831; *Ten Thousand Sketches, ukiyoe* prints by Katsushika Hokusai, 1836; *Nanso Satomi Hakken*, a novel by Bakin Takizawa, 1842; Yedo (Tokyo) in 1843 has 1.8 million, second only to London; infanticide keeps Japan's populatoin low; arrival of first Japanese-built ship in the United States (San Francisco), in 1860; the Paris world's fair of 1867 introduces *ukiyoe* prints to the West; beginning of Mitsubishi industrial empire, 1868; Japan's first public elementary school, in Kyoto, 1869; the Kirin Brewery is founded in Yokohama by an American businessman, William Copeland, 1869; the architects Tadahiro Hayashi and Kisuke Shimizu II, learning from the construction works at the foreign settlement in Yokohama, introduce Western building into Japan; Shimizu's Tsukiji Hotel, Tokyo, 1867–1868

In Korea, Li dynasty, 1392–1910; eastern gateway of Seoul, 1869

In Muslim world, Sayyid Said, ruler of Zanzibar and

b) Flaubert and *Madame Bovary*
c) The English Realists
   (1) Characteristics
   (2) Dickens
   (3) Gaskell
   (4) Evans (George Eliot)
5. The Russian Realists
   a) Characteristics
   b) Tolstoy
   c) Dostoyevsky

C. Art and architecture
1. Neoclassicism and Romanticism after 1830
   a) Ingres
      (1) A power in official art
      (2) *The Turkish Bath*
   b) Delacroix
      (1) Color theories
      (2) *The Abduction of Rebecca*
   c) Romantic architecture
      (1) Characteristics
      (2) Barry and Pugin's Houses of Parliament, London
2. The rise of Realism in art
   a) Background
   b) Courbet
      (1) *A Burial at Ornans*
      (2) *Interior of My Studio*
   c) Daumier
      (1) Satirical subjects
      (2) *The Freedom of the Press*
      (3) *Third Class Carriage*
   d) Millet
      (1) The Barbizon school
      (2) *The Sower*
      (3) *The Gleaners*
   e) Bonheur
      (1) Ideas and subjects
      (2) *The Horse Fair*
   f) Manet
      (1) *Salon des Réfuses (Salon of the Rejects)*
      (2) *Le Déjeuner sur l'Herbe (Luncheon on the Grass)*
      (3) His radical aesthetic

D. Photography
1. Historical background
   a) Daguerre
   b) Fox Talbot
   c) Photography as art
2. Matthew Brady's achievement

E. Music
1. Changes in Romantic music; adherence to Classical forms

Muscat, 1804–1856; France seizes Algeria, 1830; Mehemet Ali founds dynasty in 1833 that rules Egypt until 1952, though British influence dominates after 1882; in Afghanistan, the Barakszi dynasty, 1835–1929

In Mexico, Porfirio Diaz, statesman, 1830–1915; Texas wins independence from Mexico in 1836 and joins the United States, 1845

In North America, Cherokee chief Sequoya, creates Cherokee alphabet, 1770–1843

In South America, Ecuador breaks away from Colombia and becomes a republic, 1830

2. Romantic music: opera
   a) Middle-class audiences and their impact
   b) Verdi
      (1) His style
      (2) *Rigoletto* and other operas
   c) Wagner
      (1) Aesthetic goals
      (2) *The Ring of the Nibelung*
3. Romantic music: orchestral and chamber works and *lieder*
   a) Changes under Romanticism
   b) Brahms
   c) Schumann

V. The Legacy of the Bourgeois Age

LEARNING OBJECTIVES

To learn:

1. The defining events of the Age of the Bourgeoisie

2. The characteristics of the reigning styles of Neoclassicism and Romanticism and how they reflected events to 1848, along with the characteristics of Realism and how it was a product of the post-1848 period

3. The roles played by the middle class and the ideologies of liberalism and nationalism in shaping politics and culture during this era

4. The significance of the revolutions of 1830 and their aftermath

5. How the revolutions of 1848 were a watershed in politics and culture

6. The cultural importance of the Civil War in the United States

7. The impact of industrialism on history and civilization

8. The challenge to religion by the conclusions of higher criticism and the advances in science

9. The major contributions of science to an understanding of the universe

10. The dialectic between liberalism and socialism, with special attention to Marxism and its origins

11. The changed nature of Neoclassicism and Romanticism in the Age of the Bourgeoisie

12. The characteristics of the Romantic novel, along with the leading writers and examples of their novels

13. The characteristics of the Realist novel, along with the leading writers and examples of their novels

14. To compare and contrast the Neoclassical style of Ingres with the Romantic style of Delacroix

15. The significance of the official Salon in helping to shape Romantic and Neoclassical art prior to 1871

16. The characteristics of Realism in art along with the leading advocates and examples of significant works

17. That Manet laid the groundwork for modern painting

18. That photography was developed and became a new art form during this period

19. The characteristics of Romantic music in this era

20. The impact of the bourgeoisie as patrons of opera

21. That Verdi and Wagner dominated opera although with contrasting musical styles

22. That Brahms was the leader of the conservative school against the followers of Wagner

23. Historic "firsts" of the Age of the Bourgeoisie that became part of the Western tradition: the Realist style of the arts, architecture, and literature; the germ theory of disease; anesthesias; advances in surgery; the pasteurization process; Marx's analysis of history; Darwin's theory of evolution; Pasteur's work in immunology and microbiology; the camera; the art of photography; the high-tech tradition; "art for art's sake" credo; higher criticism; and socialism

24. The role of the Age of the Bourgeoisie in transmitting the heritage of earlier civilizations: reviving Gothic architecture as the Neo-Gothic; continuing Neoclassicism in art and Romanticism in the arts and music; meeting the challenges to religious beliefs posed by scientific discoveries; perpetuating Romantic music, especially in the operas of Wagner that pushed this style to the limit; updating liberalism and moving toward democracy; turning nationalism toward greater militancy; maintaining the revolutionary tradition begun in the American and French revolutions; bringing the ancient institution of slavery to an end; and intensifying industrialism

SUGGESTIONS FOR FILMS

Balzac. Radim, 23 min., black and white.

Bismarck: Germany from Blood and Iron. Learning Corporation of America, 30 min., color.

Civilisation: The Fallacies of Hope. BBC/Time-Life, 52 min., color.

Early Victorian England and Charles Dickens. Encyclopedia Britannica, 30 min., color.

Karl Marx: The Massive Dissent. Films, Inc., 57 min., color.

Les Misérables. Indiana University Audio-Visual Center, 54 min., black and white.

Nationalism. Encyclopedia Britannica, 20 min., black and white.

The Victorian Period. Coronet, 14 min., color.

SUGGESTIONS FOR MUSIC

Brahms, Johannes. *Symphonies (4)*. Vienna Philharmonic. DG 423053-1 GH4 [digital].

———. *Quartets (3) for Strings*. Juilliard String Quartet. CBS M2K-45154 [CD].

———. *Brahms's Greatest Hits*. Vienna Symphony et al. Pro Arte CDM-823 [CD].

Verdi, Giuseppi. *Otello*. Freni, Malagu, Vickers, Bottion, Senechal, Glossop, van Dam, Karajan, Berlin Philharmonic. Angel CDMB-69308 [CD].

———. *Requiem Mass*. Amara, Forrester, Tucker, London, Ormandy, Philadelphia Orchestra. Odyssey Y2-35230.

———. *Rigoletto*. Cotrubas, Obraztsova, Domingo, Cappuccilli, Giulini, Vienna Philharmonic and State Opera. DG415288-1 GH3 [Digital]; 415288-2GH2 [CD].

Wagner, Richard. *Der Ring des Nibelungen (orchestral excerpts)*. New York Philharmonic. CBS MK-37795 [CD].

———. *Tristan: Prelude and Liebestod*. Bernstein, New York Philharmonic. CBS MS-7141.

———. *Wagner's Greatest Hits*. Philadelphia Orchestra et al. CBS MLK-39438 [CD].

SUGGESTIONS FOR FURTHER READING

Baumer, F. L. *Modern European Thought: Continuity and Change in Ideas, 1600–1950*. New York: Macmillan, 1977. Covers the major schools of thought over four centuries and shows how thinkers address the perennial questions of philosophy.

Bridenthal, R., and Koonz, C., eds. *Becoming Visible: Women in European History*. Boston: Houghton Mifflin, 1977. A collection of twenty essays by scholars with the common aim of uncovering the hitherto neglected role of women in European history, ranging from ancient Crete and Sumer to Nazi Germany.

Brion, M. *Romantic Art*. New York: McGraw-Hill, 1960. Somewhat outdated in research, the book is still worthwhile for its splendid color plates and excellent black-and-white reproductions.

Chadwick, O. *The Secularization of the European Mind*. New York: Cambridge University Press, 1975. Addresses one of the major fundamental issues of modernity in a perceptive and thoughtful way.

Clark, T. J. *The Absolute Bourgeois: Artists and Politics in France, 1848–1851*. London: Thames and Hudson, 1973. An indispensable analysis of artistic developments in this crucial and revolutionary period, Clark broke new ground in art history by stressing the intersection of economics, politics, and art.

Greenfield, L. *Nationalism: Five Roads to Modernity*. Cambridge: Harvard University Press, 1992. England, France, Russia, Germany, and the United States are the "five roads" to modernity via nationalism. A challenge to the ambitious student, this is a closely reasoned and fully documented historical examination of the dominating force and "idea" of the modern world, of which there are many studies.

Hamerow, T. S. *The Birth of a New Europe: State and Society in the Nineteenth Century*. Chapel Hill: University of North Carolina Press, 1983. Examines the broader impact of industrialization as it affected all of Europe relative to the structure of society, the nature of European state political systems, and continental politics.

Heilbronner, R. L. *The Worldly Philosophers*. New York: Touchstone, 1980. This informative and entertaining collection of short biographies of economists is, today, nearly a classic for undergraduates who want to learn more about the personalities, private lives, and ideas of some of the seminal minds of economic thought.

Hobsbawm, E. J. *The Age of Capital, 1848–1875*. Rev. ed. London: Weidenfeld and Nicolson, 1988. Thoroughly researched and composed in the author's acerbic style with a Marxian interpretation—for the student who wants to experience a particular point of view by a gifted writer.

Lichtheim, G. *A Short History of Socialism*. New York: Praeger, 1969. Continues to be a very helpful introduction to the ways certain persons and groups responded to industrialization. The author attempts to bridge the gap between the historical and sociological perspectives.

Lindeman, A. *A History of European Socialism*. New Haven: Yale University Press, 1983. Somewhat different in approach than Lichtheim, Lindeman combines the theories and shapers of socialism with the workers' movements and attitudes and traces the movement from its origins in the late eighteenth century to the 1980s.

Needham, G. *19th Century Realist Art*. New York: Harper & Row, 1988. An examination of the forms of Realism, their origins and evolution within the context of the broader trends of nineteenth-century culture and history; this work is for the serious student.

Novotny, F. *Painting and Sculpture in Europe, 1780–1880*. London: Penguin, 1973. In the Pelican History of Art series, this covers all aspects of painting and sculpture and is a challenging work for the advanced student.

Rich, N. *The Age of Nationalism and Reform, 1850–1890*. New York: Norton, 1976. In the Norton History of Modern Europe series, it surveys the unification movements, the Second Industrial Revolution, and social reforms in an orderly and clear format and style.

Schumpeter, J. A. *Capitalism, Socialism, and Democracy*. 6th ed. London: Unwin, 1987. A standard in its field, this study sets a series of complex issues into a broad political and cultural framework.

Sperber, J. *The European Revolutions, 1848–1851*. Cambridge: Cambridge University Press, 1994. Combines traditional themes and topics with cultural and social issues and the wider international implications in analyzing those pivotal years. This is a "student textbook" in the New Approaches to European History series.

Sterns, P. *European Society in Upheaval: Social History Since 1800*. New York: Macmillan, 1967. A history of the consequences of industrialization by a leading scholar sympathetic to industrialized life.

Stonyk, M. *Nineteenth-Century English Literature*. New York: Schocken Books, 1984. In the History of Literature series; numerous writers and their major works are offered in thumbnail sketches; useful as a guide for the serious student.

Vaughan, W. *Romanticism and Art*. London: Thames and Hudson, 1994. An updated edition of the author's *Romantic Art* in which he defines Romanticism, sets the movement in its historical and cultural context, and traces its phases throughout the nineteenth century.

Whittall, A. *Romantic Music: A Concise History from Schubert to Sibelius*. London: Thames and Hudson, 1987. A useful companion to the surveys in Romanticism and in Romantic art.

IDENTIFICATIONS

Utilitarianism

socialism

higher criticism

evolution

Realism

aria

recitative

libretto

music drama

leitmotif

PERSONAL PERSPECTIVE BACKGROUND

Gustave Flaubert, Letter to Jules Cloquet, January 15, 1850

As a youth, Flaubert was a Romantic anti-bourgeois bourgeois, afflicted with a detestation of Europe, its cold climate, and its stifling ways. In 1840, after his first trip outside France to Corsica in the Mediterranean, he confided to a friend: "I hate Europe, France—my own country, my succulent motherland that I'd gladly send to hell now that I've had a glimpse of what lies beyond." In other words, he was in the grips of Orientalism, the Romantic passion for the Middle East. He was finally able to satisfy his obsession when he and a friend, Maxime Du Camp, along with a servant, visited several countries in the Middle East (October 1849–June 1851). Ostensibly on government-related business, Flaubert was supposed to gather information for the Ministry of Agriculture and Commerce, though he never filed a report. The Personal Perspective shows his first impression of Egypt. (For more information on Flaubert, consult *The Western Humanities* and *Readings in the Western Humanities.*)

Feodor Dostoevsky, Winter Notes on Summer Impressions

Winter Notes on Summer Impressions is Dostoevsky's journal of his first travel outside his homeland to Europe, what he termed the "land of holy wonders." A hurried trip, covering about two and a half months, he visited (by his own reckoning) "Berlin, Dresden, Wiesbaden, Baden-Baden, Cologne, Paris, London, Lucerne, Geneva, Genoa, Florence, Milan, Venice, [and] Vienna," and some places twice. The Personal Perspective recounts Dostoevsky's disgust at the teeming streets of London, and this disgust is typical of his overall response to other cities. Instead of a "land of holy wonders," he found Europe to be a dying culture—a reflection of his Slavophilism, the belief that the Russian ideal represents the best hope for the future of humanity. (More information on Dostoevsky may be found in *The Western Humanities* and *Readings in the Western Humanities.*)

DISCUSSION/ESSAY QUESTIONS

1. Discuss the triumph of the bourgeoisie after 1830, focusing on the part played by the political revolutions of the period.
2. Define the terms "liberalism" and "nationalism" as understood in Europe before 1848, and note examples of their impact on European affairs.
3. Discuss the major historical and cultural events between 1830 and 1871 and show how they influenced the arts and humanities, particularly the Neoclassical and Romantic styles before 1848 and the Realist style thereafter.
4. Explain the significance of the 1848 revolutions and how they represented a turning point in nineteenth-century culture and politics.
5. How did the coming to power by Europe's middle classes affect the arts, literature, and music during this period?
6. What impact did the middle class and its ideology of liberalism have on nineteenth-century politics and culture? Explain the changed nature of liberalism in the mid-nineteenth century.
7. Define nationalism. Show how this ideology influenced culture and politics in this epoch.
8. Define *Realpolitik*. How did *Realpolitik* influence politics after 1848? What caused *Realpolitik* to develop?

9. What were the causes and the outcome of the American Civil War? Explain this war within the context of general trends in the West during the nineteenth century.
10. Discuss industrial developments in this era. What impact did these changes have on culture, particularly on political philosophy?
11. "The 1851 Exhibition in the Crystal Palace, London, was a fitting symbol of the Age of the Bourgeoisie." Explain.
12. Summarize the key ideas in Marxism. Explain the sources of Marx's philosophy of history.
13. What scientific advances were made between 1830 and 1871? What impact did these advances have on the development of cultural styles?
14. Explain the rise of Realism, in relation to the prevailing styles of Neoclassicism and Romanticism.
15. Discuss Romantic literature, focusing on the major characteristics and the leading authors and their contributions.
16. Compare and contrast Realist literature with Romantic fiction.
17. Discuss the impact of the Royal Academy of Painting and Sculpture on art during the Age of the Bourgeoisie. Define "official art."
18. Who founded Realist art? Why? What are the characteristics of Realism? Who are the leading Realist painters?
19. What was Manet's innovation that laid the foundations of modern art? Explain.
20. What new art form was invented during this era? Explain its significance.
21. Discuss Realism as a cultural style, using an example from both literature and art as the basis of your essay.
22. How did Romantic music change during this Age of the Bourgeoisie? What forces were operating on music and causing it to change?
23. Compare and contrast the contributions of Verdi and Wagner to Romantic opera.
24. Discuss the role of Brahms in the history of Romantic music.

MULTIPLE-CHOICE QUESTIONS

1. The middle class, from 1830 to 1871, found justification for its existence in all of the following EXCEPT:
   a. the hope for political power coming out of the French Revolution
   b. a rising standard of living as a result of the Industrial Revolution
 * c. the goals of socialism (p. 455)
   d. liberalism's political and social ideals

2. The early-nineteenth-century bourgeoisie embraced these styles:
   a. Impressionism and Post-Impressionism
   b. Realism and Naturalism
 * c. Romanticism and Neoclassicism (pp. 455, 469)
   d. Baroque and Rococo

3. A basic principle of nineteenth-century liberalism was that:
 * a. The individual should be free from external control. (p. 455)
   b. Wealth and power should be distributed fairly in society.
   c. The state is a divine institution.
   d. all of the above

4. In nineteenth-century Europe, liberalism was most successful in:
   a. Italy
   b. Russia
 * c. France (pp. 457–458)
   d. Germany

5. Which was NOT a basic idea of nineteenth-century nationalism?
   a. Feelings for one's nation are more important than class interests.
   b. All members of a nation are like brothers and sisters.
 * c. The nations of the world should work together for world peace. (pp. 455, 457)
   d. National identity is bound up with the language and heritage of a specific ethnic group.

6. The 1848 revolutions can be characterized as:
   a. moving from one triumph to another across Europe
   b. failure as soon as they began, since they were immediately crushed
   c. achieving very little at the beginning but finally winning their goals
 * d. starting off with great promise but ending in defeat (pp. 457–458)

7. *Realpolitik,* between 1850 and 1871, had a powerful impact on the:
 * a. unification campaign in Germany (pp. 458–460)
   b. electoral changes in Great Britain
   c. economic policies of Napoleon III in France
   d. economic unification movement in Germany, 1830–1870

8. Who engineered the unification of Germany?
   a. Cavour
   b. Disraeli
 * c. Bismarck (p. 459)
   d. Metternich

9. Italy in 1871 was unified around this small Italian state:
   a. Venetian republic
   b. duchy of Tuscany
 * c. kingdom of Piedmont Sardinia (pp. 459-460)
   d. kingdom of the Two Sicilies

10. The American Civil War had the immediate consequence of:
    a. ending regional tensions
  * b. abolishing slavery (p. 460)
    c. industrializing the national economy
    d. resolving racial problems

11. By 1871 the right to vote was guaranteed to:
    a. women in England
  * b. working-class men in England and America (p. 462)
    c. lower-middle-class men in Austria and Germany
    d. peasants in Russia

12. By 1866 the West was linked together by:
  * a. transatlantic telegraph cables between Europe and America (pp. 460–461)
    b. state memberships in international peacekeeping organizations
    c. a worldwide telephone system
    d. concrete-paved highways across the continent and across Britain

13. All were aspects of the Great Exhibition of 1851 staged in the Crystal Palace, London, EXCEPT:
    a. It was the first world's fair.
  * b. The building was constructed in the reigning Neo-Gothic style. (p. 461)
    c. The exhibition confirmed Britain's status as the world's dominant industrial power.
    d. The exhibition displayed the newest inventions and the latest machine-made goods.

14. Which was NOT an industrial development between 1830 and 1870?
   * a. State programs guaranteeing social security developed across the West. (p. 469)
   b. There was a rapid growth of cities in Britain, France, and Belgium.
   c. Vast slums for poor and ill-trained workers sprang up in all industrialized cities.
   d. Slums became breeding grounds for class hatred and socialist ideas.

15. The seeds of World War I were sown by:
   a. the opening of the Suez Canal in 1869
   b. Britain's introduction of free trade in 1846
   * c. Prussia's humiliating defeat of France in 1870–1871 (p. 459)
   d. the unification of Italy in 1871

16. At the heart of nineteenth-century liberalism was a belief in:
   a. government control
   * b. free expression for the individual (p. 462)
   c. state-funded welfare
   d. government-operated schools

17. The founder of Utilitarianism was:
   * a. Jeremy Bentham (p. 469)
   b. John Stuart Mill
   c. Robert Owen
   d. Charles Fourier

18. Bentham believed that society should be based on "utility," meaning:
   a. natural rights
   * b. "the greatest happiness for the greatest number" (p. 469)
   c. God's law
   d. tradition

19. A leading nineteenth-century Utilitarian was:
   a. Robert Owen
   b. Friedrich Engels
   * c. John Stuart Mill (p. 463)
   d. Napoleon III

20. John Stuart Mill advocated:
   a. voting rights for eighteen-year-olds
   b. gay rights
   * c. voting rights for women (p. 463)
   d. a state-supported church

21. Utopian socialists, in general:
   a. supported the bourgeois values of thrift and hard work as ways for workers to improve their condition
   * b. urged reform of the ills of industrial society based on the experience of model communities (p. 463)
   c. advocated violent overthrow of existing governments
   d. agreed with liberal principles

22. A leading utopian socialist was:
    a. Friedrich Engels
  * b. Comte de Saint-Simon (p. 463)
    c. Jeremy Bentham
    d. August Comte

23. Marx's dialectical reasoning was based on the philosophy of:
  * a. Hegel (p. 463)
    b. Burke
    c. Kant
    d. Fichte

24. Marx theorized that history is propelled by:
    a. individual greed
  * b. class conflict (p. 463)
    c. God
    d. chance events

25. Which was NOT a key idea in Marxism?
    a. The middle class will bring forth its own gravediggers, the proletariat.
    b. Government, law, the arts, and the humanities reflect the values of a particular ruling class.
  * c. The future belongs to the strongest power. (p. 463)
    d. The proletariat will eventually install a classless society.

26. "Higher criticism" refers to the nineteenth-century intellectual movement in which scholars:
    a. focused exclusively on literary texts while ignoring their historical settings
  * b. studied the Bible not as a divinely inspired book incapable of error but simply as a set of writings susceptible to varied interpretations (p. 464)
    c. analyzed all writings, secular and sacred, in accordance with Marxist theory
    d. applied linguistic theory to literature to show that all texts are the same

27. Whose researches in geology cast doubt on the biblical story of creation?
  * a. Charles Lyell (p. 464)
    b. Charles Darwin
    c. Louis Pasteur
    d. John Dalton

28. Between 1830 and 1871 all of these scientific advances were made EXCEPT:
    a. Data were collected showing that modern plants and animals had evolved from simpler forms through a process of natural selection.
    b. The germ theory of disease was established.
  * c. The interior structure of the atom was mapped out. (pp. 464–465)
    d. Chloroform and other anesthesias were introduced.

29. In science Charles Darwin:
    a. established the germ theory of disease
  * b. marshalled data to support the theory of evolution (p. 464)
    c. introduced the anesthetic called chloroform
    d. formulated the periodic table of the elements

30. In science Pasteur:
    * a. established the germ theory of disease (p. 464)
    b. marshalled data to support the theory of evolution
    c. introduced the anesthetic called chloroform
    d. formulated the periodic table of the elements

31. Between 1830 and 1871 Romantic art became:
    * a. respectable and inoffensive (p. 465)
    b. immoral and shocking
    c. popular among the working classes
    d. innovative and experimental

32. Manet's *A Bar at the Folies-Bergère*:
    a. expressed the point of view of the aristocracy
    b. glamorized the life of a barmaid
    * c. caught the gaudy atmosphere of a popular entertainment center (caption for Fig. 18.7)
    d. represented a disappearing style of life

33. Which did NOT contribute to the rise of Realism?
    a. Bismarck's political policies
    b. Darwinian science
    c. the invention of the camera
    * d. the increasing power of Protestantism (pp. 465–466)

34. Art in the Age of the Bourgeoisie was:
    a. dominated by an avant garde
    * b. subject to pressures from official government agencies (p. 465)
    c. under the influence of the Roman Catholic Church
    d. a product of what the aristocrats dictated at the royal courts

35. A leading French Romantic writer was:
    a. Honoré de Balzac
    * b. Victor Hugo (p. 466)
    c. Gustave Flaubert
    d. George Eliot

36. Romantic novelists concentrated on:
    a. scientific accuracy
    b. ordinary people without idealizing them
    * c. the feelings of their characters (p. 466)
    d. the social and economic forces that determined the lives of their characters

37. George Sand has been called "the first modern, liberated woman" because she:
    a. conducted her love affairs in secrecy
    * b. played an active role in the Paris 1848 revolution (p. 466)
    c. submitted to the restrictions of a class-conscious society
    d. led the fight for equal pay for equal work

38. Realistic novelists did NOT:
    a. depict the lives of ordinary men and women
    * b. let their imagination dictate the mood of the work (p. 466)
    c. describe the human world with scientific accuracy
    d. write without romanticizing their characters

39. Which was NOT a Romantic feature in Emily Brontë's *Wuthering Heights?*
    a. the ghostly apparitions and graveyard scenes
  * b. the conventional moral feelings expressed by the characters (p. 467)
    c. the unconventional hero Heathcliff
    d. the tale of mismatched soulmates

40. The English Realist with the largest audience was:
    a. Charlotte Brontë
  * b. Charles Dickens (p. 467)
    c. George Eliot
    d. Elizabeth Gaskell

41. An innovation of Dostoevsky, the Russian Realist, was:
    a. a first-person narrative style
    b. stream-of-consciousness writing
  * c. the anti-hero type (p. 469)
    d. the socialist novel

42. Flaubert, in his *Madame Bovary,* made his heroine a(n):
    a. ideal wife for other women to emulate
  * b. creature caught up in her unrealistic dreams (p. 467)
    c. symbol of the corruption of French politics
    d. innocent victim of a cruel class-conscious society

43. The leading Neoclassical painter between 1830 and 1871 was:
    a. Delacroix
  * b. Ingres (p. 469)
    c. Courbet
    d. Manet

44. All of these are products of the Romantic style EXCEPT:
  * a. Ingres's *The Turkish Bath* (pp. 469, 471, 478)
    b. Delacroix's *The Abduction of Rebecca*
    c. Barry and Pugin's Houses of Parliament, London
    d. Verdi's *Rigoletto*

45. The founder of Realism in painting was:
    a. Delacroix
    b. Ingres
  * c. Courbet (p. 471)
    d. Manet

46. Courbet's painting called *Interior of My Studio:*
    a. uses images taken from Greek mythology
    b. romanticizes the figures in the painting
  * c. summarizes the painter's approach to art until this time (pp. 471, 473)
    d. shows the influence of Neoclassicism

47. The key element in Daumier's approach to painting was:
    a. a love of exotic scenes
    b. a fascination with fiery action
  * c. a satirical eye (p. 473)
    d. a feeling for the geometry underlying nature

48. The French painter Millet was:
    a. a disciple of David
    b. a leading Neoclassicist
 * c. an artist who admired Constable and the English Romantics (p. 474)
    d. noted for his paintings with Oriental themes

49. Which is NOT correct regarding the painter Millet?
    a. He was a member of the Barbizon school.
    b. He painted pastoral scenes without idealizing or romanticizing them.
 * c. He was influenced by David's classical paintings. (pp. 474–475)
    d. He made the rural folk and their labor the center of his work.

50. In what sense was Manet the first modern painter?
    a. He opened the door to abstraction.
 * b. He originated the tradition of "art for art's sake." (p. 477)
    c. He paved the way for Expressionism.
    d. He pioneered the Cubist style.

51. Rosa Bonheur can be considered as:
    a. a Romantic landscape artist who offered escapism for the French middle class
    b. an artist whose Neoclassical style was favored by Napoleon III
    c. the daughter of a famous French painter who capitalized on her father's name
 * d. a member of the Realist school who was influenced by science (p. 475)

52. Romantic music was characterized by the:
    a. movement toward abstract composition
    b. abandonment of Classical forms of music
 * c. use of folk songs and ethnic dance rhythms (p. 478)
    d. trend toward atonality

53. The composer of the opera *Rigoletto* is:
 * a. Verdi (p. 479)
    b. Puccini
    c. Wagner
    d. Brahms

54. Wagner's contribution to opera did NOT include:
    a. a new style of opera that fused all of the arts together
    b. the use of *leitmotifs* as identifying musical phrases for characters, things, or ideas
 * c. a performance style that alternated arias with recitatives (p. 479)
    d. the composing of a type of music with a continuously flowing melodic line

55. Which composer was the leader of the traditionalists who opposed the music of Wagner?
    a. Verdi
    b. Schubert
 * c. Brahms (p. 479)
    d. Chopin

19

THE AGE OF EARLY MODERNISM
1871–1914

TEACHING STRATEGIES AND SUGGESTIONS

Because Chapter 19 covers a shorter time period relative to most chapters in *The Western Humanities*, the instructor can omit the usual introduction (the Standard Lecture with a Historical Overview) and begin lecturing on the topics and themes of the period of Early Modernism. The Spirit of the Age teaching strategy can be used for the opening lecture to describe the characteristics of Modernism, with the emphasis on Early Modernism. It is extremely important to point out the distinction between the Modernist cultural style and the phenomenon known as "modern life," since both were emerging during this period. There are three major topics in this chapter, the Second Industrial Revolution, the emergence of militant nationalism, and the rise of imperialism; and the Comparison/Contrast approach can be used to discuss them, showing how they evolved from earlier versions in the late eighteenth century. Another teaching strategy is to adopt the Case Study method to draw connections between the nationalism and militarism that occurred during Early Modernism and contemporary manifestations of these same phenomena.

After having established the historical background and the chief traits of Early Modernism, the teacher can then use the Reflections/Connections teaching strategy, blended with a Slide Lecture and a Music Lecture, to set forth the leading developments in philosophy, literature, science, and the arts and explain their interrelationship with the wider culture. The instructor should explain carefully the various movements during this time, such as Expressionism, abstraction, and Cubism, since they set the stage for twentieth-century civilization and many of them continue today, even if in a diluted or barely recognizable form.

As a concluding lecture, the instructor can set the stage for the next chapter, which deals with the twentieth century's two world wars, by focusing on the West's long slide into war despite its efforts to maintain the peace.

LECTURE OUTLINE

Non-Western Events

I. Characteristics of Early Modernism

II. Europe's Rise to World Leadership
   A. The Second Industrial Revolution
      and the making of the
      phenomenon of "modern life"
      1. Differences between the First
         and Second Industrial Revolutions

1871–1914
In Africa, Olive Schreiner,
*The Story of an African
Farm*, 1883; end of
involuntary servitude in
sub-Saharan Africa, 1901–
1910; interest in African art
burgeoning among the

a)   Urbanism
b)   The middle class
c)   The working class
d)   The changing role of women

B. Responses to industrialism: politics and crises
1. Domestic policies in the heavily industrialized West: Germany, France, Great Britain, and the United States
2. Domestic policies in central and eastern Europe: Italy, Austria Hungary, and Russia

C. Imperialism and international relations
1. The scramble for colonies: Africa and the Far East
2. World War I: causes

III. Early Modernism
A. Philosophy and psychology
1. Nietzsche
2. Freud
3. Jung

B. Literature
1. Naturalistic literature
a)   Zola
b)   Ibsen
c)   Chekhov
d)   Chopin
2. Decadence in literature
a)   Huysmans
b)   Wilde
c)   Proust
3. Expressionist literature
a)   Strindberg
b)   Kafka

C. The advance of science
1. Mendel
2. The Curies
3. Roentgen
4. Planck
5. Bohr
6. Einstein

D. The Modernist revolution in art
1. Impressionism
a)   Monet
b)   Renoir
c)   Cassat
d)   Morisot
2. Post-Impressionism
a)   Seurat
b)   Cézanne

Parisian avant garde, 1904–1905

In China, Manchu dynasty, 1644–1912; the first railroad, the 80-mile line between Tangshan and Tianjin (Tientsin), 1887; the abortive Boxer Rebellion, an uprising of patriots called the Boxers because they relied solely on their fists and swords against foreigners and their guns, 1900; fall of Beijing to eight affected powers, including Great Britain, Germany, Russia, Japan, and the United States, 1900; Lui E's (1857–1909) *The Travels of Lao Can,* a popular novel written in the wake of the Boxer Rebellion, 1903–1904; revolution, 1911; republic, 1912–1949; Yuan Shih-k'ai, first president, 1912–1916; weak government; Western influence seen in promotion of science and democracy; Sun Yat-sen, revolutionary leader, 1866–1925

In India, British crown (raj) rules, 1858–1947; first Indian National Congress, 1886; R. Tagore, Nobel laureate in literature, 1913; *Handful of Songs,* a collection of poems in Bengali by Tagore, 1909

In Indochina, in Siam, King Chulalongkorn, 1873–1910, abolishes feudalism and slavery, reforms the legal system and education, introduces the telegraph, and opens Siam's first railroad

In Japan, Meiji period, 1868–1912; the Constitution of 1885 sets up a constitutional monarchy; Bank of Japan founded, 1882; samurai revolt, 1877; first general election, 1890; Russo-Japanese War, 1904–1905, won by Japan; Bank of Japan building, by Kingo Tatsuno, 1890–1896; the National Museum, by Toyu Katayama, in 1909; the Imperial Theater, by Tamisuke Tokogawa, 1911; introduction of reinforced concrete; *Journal of the Enlightenment,* a journal dedicated to progressive reform, established in 1874 but suppressed in 1876; literature flourishes, often influenced by Western writers; newspapers of high quality appear; Kiyoshi Shiga, scientist, isolates the dysentery bacillus, 1898; Japan gets its first railroad, 18 miles between Tokyo and Yokohama, 1872; Tokyo Electric Light Co. brings electricity to Japan, 1887; Baron Takaki reports that beriberi can be prevented by a proper diet, 1887; founding of Japanese Musical Instrument Manufacturing Co., by Torakasu Yamaha, 1889; Kokichi Mikimoto pioneers cultured pearls, 1893; Shibasaburo Kitazato of Japan and A. E. J. Yersin at Berlin discover the bacillus for the Black Plague, 1894; *The Tower of London* and *I Am a Cat,* two novels by Soseki Natsume, 1905; *Broken Commandment,* a semiautobiographical work by Shimazaki Toson, which breaks his promise to his father not to reveal that he and his family are members of Japan's outcast group, 1906; *Spring,* a novel by Shimazaki Toson, in 1907; *The River Sumida,* a novel by Kafu Nagai, in 1909; *A Handful of Sand,* nontraditional tanka-style poems by Takuboku Ishikawa, 1910; Taisho period, 1912–1926; *Kokoro,* a novel by Sōseki Natsume, on the theme of the crisis caused by Modernism, 1914; *Seven Japanese Tales,* 1910–1959, by Tanizaki Jun'ichiro, one of Japan's great modern writers

In Korea, Li dynasty, 1392–1910; Japan forces Korea to open certain ports to foreign trade, 1876; Japanese rule, 1910–1945

In Muslim world, in Persia, founding of the Babism religion by Ali Mohammed, whose followers call him the Bab, after 1845; Ali Mohammed is executed for heresy in 1850, and his follower Husayn Ali takes the title Baha'u'llah (Splendor of God) and preaches the Baha'i faith

In Polynesia, Gauguin settles in Tahiti, 1891

In South America, in Brazil, *Epitaph for a Small Winner,* a novel by Joaquim Machado de Assis, 1881; Manaus Opera House, 700 miles up the Amazon, 1896; *Rebellion in the Backlands,* an account of an 1896 uprising by a religious fanatic in Brazil's outback, 1902; A. Carlos Gomez, composer, 1839–1896

In Sri Lanka, the birth of Coomaraswamy, 1877–1947, the art historian who portrayed Indian art as spiritual in contrast to post-Renaissance art of the West

World's cities in 1901: London 6.6 million, New York 3.4 million, Paris 2.7 million, Berlin 1.9 million, Chicago 1.7 million, Vienna 1.7 million, Wuhan 1.5 million, Tokyo 1.45 million, St. Petersburg 1.3 million, Philadelphia 1.3 million, Constantinople 1.2 million, Moscow 1.1 million, Sian (Siam) 1 million

LEARNING OBJECTIVES

To learn:

1. The major characteristics of "modern life" and Early Modernism, 1871–1914

2. The causes and nature of the Second Industrial Revolution and its effect on society—in particular, women

3. How the heavily industrialized nations reacted to the Second Industrial Revolution

4. The social and economic policies of central and eastern Europe, 1871–1914

5. The characteristics, origins, and results of late-nineteenth-century imperialism

6. The long-range and immediate causes of World War I

7. The directions of late-nineteenth-century philosophy and specifically the philosophy of Nietzsche

8. The ideas and achievements of Sigmund Freud

9. The ideas and contributions of Carl Jung

10. In Early Modernist literature, the meaning of Naturalism, Decadence, and Expressionism, the major voices, and representative writings

11. Innovations in science, the discoverers, and their long-range significance

12. The ideas of Albert Einstein and their implications

13. The origins and characteristics of Impressionism, its most important artists, representative paintings, and its influence on later schools of art

14. The Post-Impressionists, representative paintings, and their impact

15. The nature of Fauvism, Cubism, and Expressionism; the leading artists and representative works in each of these styles; and the three movements' influence on later styles

16. Late-nineteenth- and early-twentieth-century trends in sculpture and architecture, the major sculptors and architects, and representative works

17. Developments in music, including innovations, new schools, leading composers, and representative works

18. Historic "firsts" during the period of Early Modernism that became part of the Western tradition: imperialism and colonial empires; Western dominance of the non-Western world through goods, ideas, and values; anti-imperialistic attitudes outside of the West; a new stage of industrialism in the West and the beginning of industrialism outside of the West; Early Modernism (1) in art, Impressionism, Post-Impressionism, Cubism, Fauvism, and Expressionism along with the Post-Impressionist trends of Expressionism, abstraction, and primitivism and fantasy, (2) in literature, Naturalism, Decadence, and Expressionism, (3) in sculpture, the eclectic style of Rodin, (4) in architecture, functionalism and the Organic style, and (5) in music, Impressionism, Expressionism, and jazz; Nietzsche's philosophy; Freudian psychology; Jungian psychology; and psychoanalysis

19. The role of Early Modernism in transmitting the heritage of earlier civilizations: intensifying militant nationalism, absorbing and adjusting to new developments in industrialism, continuing advances in science; increasing the spread of public education, continuing the trend to a secularized culture, reinterpreting Romanticism

SUGGESTIONS FOR FILMS

Europe, the Mighty Continent. Time-Life, thirteen films on Europe from 1900 to the present, 52 min. each, color.

Imperialism and European Expansion. Coronet, 13 min., black and white.

Impressionists. Universal Educational and Visual Arts, 42 min., color.

Nationalism. Encyclopedia Britannica, 20 min., black and white.

Paris, 1900. Brandon, MacMillan, 81 min., black and white.

Pioneers of Modern Painting. International Film Bureau, 40 min., color.

The Post-Impressionists. International Film Bureau, 25 min., color.

What Is Impressionism? Columbia Broadcasting System. 52 min., black and white. (On music).

SUGGESTIONS FOR MUSIC

Debussy, Claude. *Danses sacrée et profane, for Harp and Orchestra (1904).* Tietov, Slatkin, St. Louis Symphony. Telarc DG-10071 [digital]; CD-80071 [CD].

———. *La mer (1903–1905).* Ashkenazy, Cleveland Orchestra. London 417488-1 LH [digital]; 417488-2 LH [CD]

———. *Prélude à l'après-midi d'un faune (1892–1894).* Rubinstein. RCA 5670-2-RC [CD].

Schoenberg, Arnold. *Verklärte Nacht, Op. 4 (1899).* Boulez, Ensemble Intercontemporain, CBS IM-39566 [digital]; MK-39566 [CD]; IMT-39566 [cassette].

————. *Pierrot Lunaire, Op. 21 (1912)*. DeGaetani, Weisberg, Contemporary Chamber Ensemble. Elektra/Nonesuch H-71309; 71251-4 [cassette].

————. *Quartet No. 2 in F sharp for Soprano and Strings, Op. 10 (1907–1908)*. Beardslee, Sequoia Quartet. Elektra Nonesuch D-79005; D1-79005 [cassette].

Stravinsky, Igor. *Petrushka (1911)*. Mehta, New York Philharmonic. CBS MK-35823 [CD]; IMT 35823 [digital].

————. *Le Sacre du Printemps (1913)*. Karajan, Berlin Philharmonic. DG 423214-2 GMW [CD].

————. *Fireworks, Op. 4 (1908)*. Dutoit, Montreal Symphony. London 414409-1 LH [digital]; 414409-2 LH [CD].

SUGGESTIONS FOR FURTHER READING

Biddiss, M. D. *The Age of the Masses: Ideas and Society in Europe Since 1870*. New York: Penguin, 1977. A balanced account examining the influence of the masses both on society and on leading thinkers and writers.

Bullock, A. *The Twentieth Century: A Promethean Age*. London: Thames and Hudson, 1971. Excellent integration of cultural and political history; handsomely illustrated but weak on dates.

Callen, A. *Techniques of the Impressionists*. London: Orbis, 1982. An innovative work that studies the limitations imposed by material and social conditions on the Impressionists; includes detailed analyses of painting techniques used in selected paintings.

Clark, T. J. *The Painting of Modern Life: Paris in the Art of Manet and His Followers*. Princeton: Princeton University Press, 1986. A superb analysis of key artists and their work that is rooted in economic developments; a central text in the movement to return the discussion of art to a consideration of its historical context.

Denvir, B. *Post-Impressionism*. London: Thames and Hudson, 1992. Another fine volume in the World of Art series; includes 148 illustrations and many quotations from the artists.

Evans, R. J. W., and Strandmann, H. P. von, eds. *The Coming of the First World War*. Oxford: Oxford University Press, 1988. A recent work that stresses the actual decisions made by politicians and their impact on public opinion and the popular mood of the times.

Ferriss, T. *Coming of Age in the Milky Way*. New York: William Morrow, 1988. A brilliant and accessible discussion of the discoveries and developments that have created modern science.

Golding, J. *Cubism: A History and an Analysis, 1907–1914*. 3rd rev. ed. London: Faber, 1968. A well-regarded history of Cubism; first published in 1959.

Headrick, D. *Tools of Empire*. New York: Oxford University Press, 1981. A study of the interconnection of imperialism and technology, especially guns, medicine, and steam engines.

Hobsbawm, E. J. *The Age of Empire, 1875–1914*. London: Weidenfeld and Nicolson, 1987. An excellent survey of politics and culture during this period.

Hobson, J. A. *Imperialism: A Study*. London: Unwin Hyman, 1988. First published in 1905, this modern classic identified most of the issues that are still debated about imperialism; a powerful stimulus to Lenin's views.

Hughes, H. S. *Consciousness and Society: The Reorientation of European Social Thought*. Rev. ed. New York: Vintage, 1977. An illuminating study of the ideas and thinkers that helped shape the attitudes of early-twentieth-century governing elites; first issued in 1958.

Joll, J. *The Origins of the First World War*. London: Longman, 1984. A brief look at the diplomatic, military, and economic causes of World War I.

Lafore, L. D. *The Long Fuse: An Interpretation of the Origins of World War I*. Philadelphia: Lippincott, 1965. The standard survey of the various interpretations of the causes of World War I.

Martel, G. *The Origins of the First World War*. 2nd ed. London: Longman, 1996. A useful survey, with documents.

Pascal, R. *From Naturalism to Expressionism: German Literature and Society, 1880–1918*. London: Weidenfeld and Nicolson, 1973. Excellent literary history, which links German writing with the social values of the time.

Pollard, S. *European Economic Integration, 1815–1970*. London: Thames and Hudson, 1974. A masterly survey of Europe's evolving economy in the nineteenth and twentieth centuries.

Rewald, J. *The History of Impressionism*. 4th rev. ed. New York: Museum of Modern Art, 1973. The standard history of the first wave of modern art.

Schorske, C. *Fin-de-Siècle Vienna: Politics and Culture*. New York: Knopf, 1980. An interesting study claiming that Vienna produced political and cultural styles that have dominated the twentieth century.

Stone, N. *Europe Transformed, 1878–1919*. London: Fontana, 1984. A sound country-by-country survey of the five major European powers and how world war changed them.

Wohl, R. *The Generation of 1914*. Cambridge: Harvard University Press, 1979. Using "generation theory," Wohl explores what Europe's 1914 generation had in common and what impact its many untimely deaths had on later events.

IDENTIFICATIONS

Modernism	Post-Impressionism
avant-garde	Pointillism
Naturalism	primitivism
Decadence	Fauvism
Expressionism	Cubism
problem play	collage
local color	*pavane*
Creole	atonality
Cajun	syncopation
aesthete	jazz
abstraction	ragtime
Impressionism	blues

PERSONAL PERSPECTIVE BACKGROUND

Vera Brittain, from *Testament of Youth*

Testament of Youth is the autobiography of the early years (to about 1930) of Vera Brittain (1893–1970), writer, wartime nurse, feminist, socialist, and political activist. Born and reared in a comfortable upper–middle-class home in England's industrial north in the city of Bradford, she describes with humor and insight her coming of age in the early twentieth century. Against the backdrop of the coming of World War I and the rise of the women's movement, she presents her story as she moves from provincial debutante to become a committed feminist, dedicated to keeping her maiden name in marriage and making her own way in the world. Covering also the lives of family and friends, this book is, as its title suggests, a collective portrait of the youthful generation who experienced World War I. Brittain's legacy lives on through her daughter, the politician Shirley Williams.

DISCUSSION/ESSAY QUESTIONS

1. Discuss the uneasy peace between 1871 and 1914, citing the forces that were leading to war. Show how the period's prevailing attitudes as well as its culture reflected this ambiguous time.
2. Define Early Modernism, and using two examples of Early Modernism found in literature and the arts, show how each represents this style.
3. What is meant by the Second Industrial Revolution? What were its phases, and how did it affect European society?
4. In what ways did the Second Industrial Revolution affect the role of women in the European social system?
5. Compare and contrast the ways the heavily industrialized nations responded to the Second Industrial Revolution.
6. What were the patterns of industrial growth in central and eastern Europe, and how did the countries in those regions deal with the economic changes between 1871 and 1914?
7. Describe the nature of late-nineteenth-century imperialism, and briefly identify which European nations claimed what territories around the world.
8. Discuss the fundamental causes of World War I and also the more immediate events that led up to the outbreak of the war. Do you think that the war could have been avoided? Explain.
9. What beliefs of Western thought were questioned by the Early Modernists? How were these doubts manifested in literature and the arts?
10. Identify the ideologies that were challenging liberalism after 1871, and explain the reasons they now appeared on the scene.
11. Define avant-garde and discuss what role the avant-garde played in late-nineteenth-century Western literature and art.
12. Discuss the ideas of Friedrich Nietzsche and assess the influence of his ideas in the modern world.
13. Discuss Sigmund Freud's explanation of human behavior, especially focusing on his conclusions regarding human happiness.
14. What is meant by "psychoanalysis"? Describe Freud's role in the development of this technique.
15. Discuss the influence of Nietzsche and Freud on the Modernist movement, giving specific examples of their impact on arts and ideas.
16. Discuss Early Modernist literature, focusing on the styles of Naturalism, Decadence, and Expressionism. Identify at least two representative works from each style in your essay.
17. Assess the advancements made in biology, chemistry, and physics between 1871 and 1914, identifying the major participants and their contributions.
18. Show how advances in science influenced European writers between 1871 and 1914.
19. Show that Impressionism was both an outgrowth of *and* a reaction to earlier Western styles of art.
20. Demonstrate the characteristics of Impressionism, using the paintings of Monet, Renoir, Cassatt, and Morisot as the basis of your discussion.
21. What is meant by Post-Impressionism? Who were its leading painters? Show how their works expressed this style.
22. Compare and contrast Fauvism, Cubism, and Expressionism, noting the leading artists in each style and their representative works.
23. Discuss Impressionism and Expressionism as the opening phases of Modernism, showing how they broke with the past and established new forms of art. Be specific in your use of examples.
24. Define Cubism in painting and assess its impact on modern art.
25. Briefly discuss the major trends in sculpture and architecture during Early Modernism.

26. Describe Impressionist music. Who were its chief innovators? What are the names of representative Impressionist works?
27. Discuss the origins of jazz and the work of Scott Joplin.
28. Write an essay in which you explain how militant nationalism, imperialism, and militarism affected historical and cultural events during Early Modernism.
29. How has the late-nineteenth-century avant-garde affected Western values?

MULTIPLE-CHOICE QUESTIONS

1. What was the prevailing mood in Europe between 1871 and 1900?
   a. Europe had begun a long decline as a world force.
 * b. Europe had entered an era of peace and tranquility. (p. 483)
   c. Europe was becoming a haven for the world's immigrants.
   d. Europe was in the midst of a religious revival.

2. Modernism was a cultural movement that:
   a. marked the end of the Middle Ages
 * b. rejected both Greco-Roman Classicism and the Judeo-Christian tradition (p. 483)
   c. began with the Renaissance
   d. shared the revolutionary ideas of Marxism

3. Three major forces that helped shape events between 1871 and 1914 were:
   a. Christianity, feudalism, manorialism
   b. war, famine, plague
 * c. imperialism, militarism, nationalism (p. 483)
   d. overpopulation, pollution, class violence

4. Europe between 1871 and 1914:
   a. moved closer to political unity
 * b. was increasingly involved in internal disputes (p. 483)
   c. came increasingly under the influence of American culture
   d. launched a moral crusade against Modernism

5. Which invention was NOT introduced between 1871 and 1914?
 * a. television (pp. 483–484)
   b. telephone
   c. automobile
   d. airplane

6. Which is NOT correct regarding Europe's Second Industrial Revolution, in comparison to the First Industrial Revolution?
   a. Great Britain was no longer the leader of the industrial world.
   b. Scientific research now played a larger role in industry.
 * c. The pace of urbanization had now slowed down. (pp. 483–486)
   d. New forms of energy—electricity and oil—were now introduced.

7. Under Early Modernism, many Europeans moved to the cities because:
 * a. Urban jobs paid better than those in the country. (p. 485)
   b. The cities promised free social benefits to their citizens.
   c. City life was more spiritual than isolated rural areas.
   d. Urban school systems were better than those in the countryside.

8. Life in the growing cities of the late nineteenth century:
   a. was much better for the working class than the middle class
   b. moved at a slower pace than life in the country
   * c. provided women new opportunities for jobs (pp. 485–486)
   d. blurred the lines between the wealthy and the poor

9. Which was NOT a change experienced by women during the Second Industrial Revolution?
   a. It led to more education, since some new jobs required special skills.
   b. It encouraged women to unite in campaigns around common concerns, such as property rights and divorce laws.
   c. It opened up new career paths in teaching, nursing, business offices, and retailing.
   * d. It put them on an equal footing with male employees. (pp. 485–486)

10. Which social change did NOT occur between 1871 and 1914?
    a. the establishment of public school systems
    * b. the passing of laws giving women voting rights (pp. 485–486)
    c. the creation of labor unions and the use of the strike
    d. the opening of work opportunities for women in teaching, nursing, office work, and sales

11. Which did NOT weaken the appeal of liberalism during the Early Modern period?
    * a. Liberalism's emphasis on Christian morals fell on deaf ears in this secular age. (p. 486)
    b. Liberalism's opposition to social welfare programs made the movement's ideas unattractive to workers who wanted more state services.
    c. Liberalism's promise that free trade would lead to a harmoniously working economy was proved untrue.
    d. Socialism offered more benefits to the workers than did liberalism with its emphasis on laissez-faire and individualism.

12. Unlike Germany and France, Great Britain during the 1871–1914 period:
    a. was beset with violence at home
    b. saw the rise of militant socialist parties
    * c. reformed the living conditions of the poor (pp. 486–487, 489)
    d. witnessed the decline of its middle class

13. The United States between 1871 and 1914:
    a. was dominated by the southern farmers
    b. overcame the racial problems stemming from the Civil War
    * c. became a haven for millions of immigrants (p. 487)
    d. became isolationist and got rid of its colonies

14. The quintessential city symbolic of Modernism during this period was:
    * a. Vienna (p. 487)
    b. Budapest
    c. Rome
    d. Prague

15. As the Industrial Revolution came to Russia:
    a. The standard of living improved for all classes.
    b. Agriculture expanded and became a vital source of wealth.
    * c. The government became more oppressive and dictatorial. (p. 489)
    d. The leaders kept the country out of war so the economy could grow.

16. Which was NOT a cause of late-nineteenth-century imperialism?
    a. The industrialized nations needed new markets.
    b. Surplus capital, generated by profits, needed to be reinvested.
  * c. The balance of power in Europe needed to be redressed. (p. 489)
    d. New, cheap sources of raw materials were required.

17. Before World War I, how significant was imperialism as a cause of war?
    a. It had no impact.
  * b. It heightened tensions but did not lead directly to war. (p. 489)
    c. It led directly to warfare in Europe among the great powers.
    d. It lessened tensions among the great powers as all were united by the bond of imperialism.

18. The immediate cause of World War I was a quarrel between:
    a. Germany and Russia
    b. France and Germany
  * c. Austria and Serbia (p. 489)
    d. Austria and Russia

19. Early Modernism's optimism about the future was reinforced by:
    a. a renewal of Christianity
  * b. advances in science and technology (p. 489)
    c. the spread of Marxism
    d. an upsurge in the arts

20. Which was NOT a key idea of Nietzsche?
  * a. All Eastern philosophies are true. (p. 492)
    b. All Western philosophies are false.
    c. There are no moral certainties.
    d. Christianity is a slave morality.

21. Nietzsche's life and thought are ironical in what way?
    a. Despite his anti-Christian views, many Christians admired him.
  * b. Although he was an opponent of a strong German state, his writings were later taken up by the Nazis, who advocated a unified Germany. (p. 492)
    c. A popular thinker during his lifetime, he ceased to have any influence after World War II.
    d. While he glorified socialism, the West's individualistic artists made him one of their heroes.

22. Nietzsche and Freud:
    a. supported the traditional values of Western thought
    b. praised middle-class morality
  * c. explored beneath the surface of human motives to find the underlying truth (p. 492)
    d. accepted the basic decency and common sense of human beings

23. Freud thought that human personality was:
    a. shaped by the environment and was therefore able to be altered by changing the situation
    b. determined by what God had implanted in each person and was thus unchangeable
  * c. the product of an inescapable struggle between inborn instincts and a culturally based conscience (p. 492)
    d. free and spontaneous and could change at will

24. Freud's research led him to emphasize the patient's:
    a. chemical balance in the brain
    b. birth rank within his or her family
  * c. innermost thoughts (p. 492)
    d. response to peer pressure

25. The three styles of Early Modern literature are:
    a. Realism, Impressionism, Romanticism
  * b. Naturalism, Decadence, Expressionism (p. 492)
    c. Functionalism, Organicism, Constructivism
    d. Fauvism, Cubism, Surrealism

26. Which is NOT correct regarding the writers who belonged to the school of Naturalism?
    a. They were spurred on by the methods of science.
    b. They borrowed from sociology to give them insights into social issues.
  * c. They were inspired by the conclusions of higher criticism. (pp. 493–494)
    d. They judged the modern world, especially industrialism, in a realistic way.

27. Zola's novels express Naturalism by:
    a. being set in the countryside
    b. ignoring details and focusing on impressions
  * c. exploring serious social issues (p. 493)
    d. dealing with the power of nature

28. Ibsen's *A Doll's House* is written in which style?
  * a. Naturalism (pp. 493–494)
    b. Decadence
    c. Expressionism
    d. Realism

29. The hero in Huysmans's *Against Nature* expresses what Decadence means by:
  * a. cultivating unfashionable and exotic pleasures (pp. 494–495)
    b. embracing materialism
    c. escaping to a tropical island
    d. becoming a devotee of mass culture

30. An example of Decadence in literature is:
    a. Kafka's *The Trial*
  * b. Wilde's *The Picture of Dorian Gray* (p. 495)
    c. Ibsen's *A Doll's House*
    d. Zola's *Germinal*

31. An example of Expressionism in literature is:
    a. Chekhov's *The Three Sisters*
    b. Wilde's *The Picture of Dorian Gray*
    c. Proust's *Remembrance of Things Past*
  * d. Strindberg's *The Dream Play* (p. 495)

32. The most famous Expressionist in Early Modernist literature was:
  * a. Kafka (p. 495)
    b. Strindberg
    c. Zola
    d. Wilde

33. Kafka's novel *The Trial* has this Modernist theme:
    a. a person brought to a tragic end for having broken the universe's moral code
    b. a person overwhelmed by the spiritual forces of nature
 * c. a person victimized by forces beyond human control (p. 495)
    d. a person forced to choose between conscience and the laws of the state

34. The first scientist to win two Nobel Prizes for science was:
    a. Albert Einstein
 * b. Madame Curie (p. 495)
    c. Max Planck
    d. Gregor Mendel

35. Max Planck is credited with:
    a. discovering X rays
 * b. establishing the quantum theory of radiation (p. 496)
    c. formulating the theory of dominant and recessive genes
    d. explaining the behavior of electrons at the subatomic level

36. Niels Bohr:
    a. established the quantum theory of radiation
    b. proved that the Newtonian system was still valid
 * c. explained the behavior of electrons at the subatomic level (p. 496)
    d. discovered X rays

37. Einstein's theoretical work in physics did all EXCEPT:
    a. eventually lead to the overthrow of Newtonian concepts of space and time
    b. assert that the only absolute in the universe is the speed of light
    c. prove that there are no absolutes in space and time
 * d. overturn what Bohr had proposed (p. 496)

38. Which was NOT an innovation of the Impressionist painters?
    a. They painted spontaneously, not working deliberately from careful study.
    b. They concentrated on the play of light, not caring about precise forms.
    c. They painted out of doors, not in their studios.
 * d. They created the first abstract paintings. (p. 497)

39. The Impressionists were influenced by the:
    a. Neoclassical school
    b. Baroque school
    c. Pre-Raphaelites
 * d. Romantic school (p. 497)

40. The first critics of Impressionist painting:
    a. praised the new style as representing a turning point in art
 * b. ridiculed the new style as being messy and slapdash (p. 497)
    c. ignored the new style, hoping it would go away
    d. greeted it with faint praise, seeing little difference between it and Romantic painting

41. Monet's painting style can be described as depicting his:
    a. obedience to the rules of good taste
    b. ability to find beauty in the industrialized world
 * c. carefree view of the world (p. 497)
    d. restless nature as he experimented with new styles

42. Renoir's painting style can be described as:
    a. pioneering the tradition that led to Cubism
    * b. moving beyond Impressionism to a greater concentration on form (p. 497)
    c. experimenting constantly with various styles
    d. restoring Classical principles to art

43. One of the results of the Impressionist movement was that:
    a. A single international style now emerged.
    b. Content now became more important than form in art.
    c. Myth, literature, and history became the subjects of art.
    * d. Art was freed to move in many directions. (pp. 497–501)

44. All of these are significant Impressionist painters EXCEPT:
    a. Mary Cassatt
    b. Berthe Morisot
    c. Auguste Renoir
    * d. Vincent van Gogh (p. 501)

45. The leading painters of Post-Impressionism were:
    a. Monet, Renoir, Morisot
    * b. Cézanne, Gauguin, van Gogh (pp. 501–504)
    c. Picasso, Matisse, Braque
    d. Courbet, Manet, Millet

46. Cézanne's painting pointed the way to the twentieth century's:
    a. primitivelike art
    * b. abstract art (p. 502)
    c. Expressionist art
    d. Surrealist art

47. Van Gogh launched the Post-Impressionist trend in painting called:
    a. abstraction
    b. fantasy
    * c. Expressionism (p. 503)
    d. primitivism

48. In painting, the term "expressionism" means:
    * a. representing the emotions (p. 503)
    b. finding a painterly vocabulary to symbolize music
    c. capturing the fleeting play of light on humans and objects
    d. working with geometric shapes

49. The leading painters in Paris on the eve of World War I were:
    a. Malevich and Kandinsky
    * b. Matisse and Picasso (p. 505)
    c. Mondrian and van Dongen
    d. Giacometti and Boccioni

50. Picasso's *Les Demoiselles d'Avignon* was significant for all the following reasons EXCEPT:
    a. It foreshadowed later developments, especially nonobjective art.
    b. It opened the door to influences from non-Western art.
    * c. It established Surrealism as the reigning style. (p. 505)
    d. It was the prelude to Cubism.

51. The artist and school identified with the breakthrough to pure abstract art were:
   a. Matisse and Fauvism
 * b. Kandinsky and *Der Blaue Reiter* (p. 507)
   c. Picasso and Cubism
   d. Monet and Impressionism

52. Which architect coined the phrase "form follows function"?
 * a. Louis Sullivan (p. 508)
   b. Frank Lloyd Wright
   c. Auguste Rodin
   d. Georges Seurat

53. A characteristic of Expressionist music is:
   a. music that is harmonious and soothing
 * b. a text that is reflected expressively in the musical sounds (p. 511)
   c. music that incorporates elements of chance into its composition
   d. a text unrelated to the musical sounds

54. What was the most striking feature of Expressionist music?
   a. lyricism
 * b. atonality (p. 511)
   c. word painting
   d. pounding rhythms

55. Which did NOT contribute to the birth of jazz?
   a. ragtime and blues
   b. European harmony
 * c. Gregorian chants (p. 511)
   d. West African and African-Caribbean rhythms

20

THE AGE OF THE MASSES
AND THE ZENITH OF MODERNISM
1914–1945

TEACHING STRATEGIES AND SUGGESTIONS

The instructor can introduce the Age of the Masses and the Zenith of Modernism with a Historical Overview that focuses on the two world wars, the Great Depression, and totalitarianism; and then, using a Reflections/Connections approach, can show how these developments were reflected in the reigning Modernist style. For example, unbridled warfare and its threat contributed to the prevailing mood of pessimism; economic depression encouraged assaults on capitalism and led to the introduction of socialist and protest themes in literature and art; and the growth of Nazism in Germany caused the flight of avant-garde intellectuals and artists to freer countries and, in Germany, to the replacement of innovative, difficult art with a sentimental, easily accessible style. The Historical Overview should also focus on the rise of the masses and their impact on culture and politics, both positively and negatively. With a Standard Lecture, the instructor can set forth the intellectual and scientific advances made in this era. A Slide Lecture, blended with a Patterns of Change approach, can illustrate artistic developments and, at the same time, demonstrate how Modern art shifted from its Early to its High phase. A Music Lecture can show similar changes in Modernist music. A Patterns of Change approach can also illuminate the literary changes taking place in High Modernism.

A good conclusion to this section is to summarize the West's and the world's situation in 1945, making the point that many of the dilemmas then are the same as those being resolved in the 1990s, such as the Soviet Union versus the United States; totalitarianism versus liberal, democratic governments; communism versus capitalism; anti-Semitism versus Jewish assimilation; and art for art's sake versus art with a social conscience. With a Discussion, the instructor can ask students to consider whether and how these issues are being resolved.

LECTURE OUTLINE

Non-Western Events

I. Wars, Depression, and the
    Rise of the Masses

II. The Collapse of Old Certainties and the
    Search for New Values
    A. Historical overview
        1. Liberalism under fire
        2. The world in 1945
        3. The view from the United States

1914–1945
In Africa, South African Max
    Theiler develops a yellow
    fever vaccine, 1930; the
    longest bridge in the world
    opened over the Lower
    Zambesi, 1935; *The Forest
    of a Thousand Demons,* a
    novel by Daniel O.

B. World War I and its aftermath
    1. The Central Powers
    2. The Allied Powers
    3. The events of spring 1917
        a) The United States joins the Allies
        b) Revolution in Russia, which becomes the Soviet Union
    4. The Versailles Treaty
    5. Postwar developments to 1930
        a) Prosperity in Britain, France, and the United States
        b) Contrasting events in Germany and Austria
        c) Stock market crash, 1929
C. The Great Depression of the 1930s
    1. Attempts to restore the economy
        a) France, Great Britain, and the United States
        b) Germany
    2. Prosperity in Japan
D. The rise of totalitarianism
    1. Background
        a) The defeat of democratic hopes after Versailles
        b) Definition of totalitarianism
    2. Russian communism
        a) Lenin's revision of Marxism
        b) Conditions in the Soviet Union
        c) Bolshevik revolution
        d) The struggle for power after Lenin's death
        e) The Stalin era
    3. European fascism
        a) Definition and characteristics
        b) Mussolini and Italy, the first fascist state
        c) Hitler and the Nazis in Germany
        d) Franco and Spain
E. World War II: origins and outcome
    1. Origins
        a) The Versailles Treaty
        b) The Great Depression
        c) Nationalistic feelings
    2. The course of the war
    3. The Holocaust
        a) Jews
        b) Gypsies, homosexuals, and others

III. The Zenith of Modernism
    A. Background
        1. Avant-garde developments
        2. Mass culture

Fagunwa, a Yoruba chief, 1938; in South Africa, *Monologue,* by Afrikaans poet N. P. van Wyk Louw, 1935

In Caribbean, in Jamaica, Rastafarians claim Ethiopia's emperor, Haile Selassie, as the living god, withdrawing from Jamaican society and insisting that blacks must return to Africa, but they contribute to Jamaican culture with reggae music, 1930; in Martinique, *Return to My Native Land,* poetry by Aimé Cesaire, 1939

In Central America, in Nicaragua, *Prosas profanas,* by poet Ruben Dario, 1896

In China, republic, 1912–1949; the era of warlords, 1916–1928; Nationalist regime under Chiang Kai-shek, 1928–1949; government faced with domestic revolt by the Communists and Japanese occupation, 1937–1945; the "May Fourth Movement" launched in 1919, protesting corruption of Chinese society and culture; in the 1930s, rise of Communist revolutionary group, led by Mao Zedong, 1893–1973; between 1934 and 1935, the Communists make the "Long March" to avoid extinction by the Nationalists; capital moved to Chungking, 1937; *Cat Country,* a novel, 1932; *Call to Arms,* a collection of short stories, 1923, by Lu Xun, 1881–1936, considered the founder of modern Chinese literature; exhibition of Chinese art at Burlington House, London, 1935; *The Eclipse,* a novel by Shen Yen-ping,

a) Definition
b) Features
c) The defining role of the United States
d) Relation to Modernism
B. Experimentation in literature
   1. The novel
      a) Stream-of-consciousness writing
      b) Joyce's *Ulysses*
      c) Woolf's *To the Lighthouse* and other works
      d) Hemingway's *The Sun Also Rises*
      e) Faulkner's Yoknapatawpha novels
      f) Lawrence's *Lady Chatterley's Lover*
      g) Orwell: a writer for all seasons
   2. Poetry
      a) Yeats
      b) Eliot
      c) The Harlem Renaissance: Hughes and Hurston
   3. Drama
      a) Brecht and "epic theater"
      b) Cocteau
      c) O'Neill
C. Philosophy and science: the end of certainty
   1. Idealist philosophy replaced
   2. The logical positivist school: Wittgenstein
   3. The existentialist school
      a) Heidegger
      b) Sartre
   4. Physics
      a) Einstein and the general relativity theory
      b) Heisenberg's uncertainty principle
      c) Opening of the nuclear age
D. Art, architecture, and film
   1. Painting
      a) Abstraction
         (1) Malevich and Suprematism
         (2) Mondrian and *De Stijl*
         (3) Picasso's *Guernica*
         (4) O'Keeffe
      b) Primitivism and fantasy
         (1) Duchamps and Dada
         (2) Surrealism: Dali, Klee, and Kahlo

1928; *Thunderstorm*, a drama in the style of Greek tragedy, by Tsao Yu, 1934; *My Country and My People*, a nonfiction work by Lin Yutang, 1935; *Sunrise*, a play by Wan Chia-pao, 1936; *Rickshaw* by Lao She, 1937; the Chung Shan Hospital, Shanghai, 1937, an example of Chinese Revival architecture, 1920–1939

In India, the British raj, 1858–1947; intensification of Indian nationalism, 1919–1947; Amritsar massacre, 1919; Tagore's *The Home and the World*, 1919; the physician C. V. Raman receives Nobel Prize, 1930; Tagore's novel *Gharer baire* (1916) breaks new ground by being in the Bengali dialect rather than in Bengali classical language; opening of city of New Delhi, planned by English architects and inspired by Christopher Wren and Pierre L'Enfant, 1931; the short stories and novels of Premchand (1880–1936) that create a panorama of North Indian society

In Japan, Taisho period, 1912–1926; Showa period, 1926–1989; Japan emerges as a world power; a liberal-leaning regime, 1914–1936; devastating earthquake in Tokyo in 1923 leads to use of new construction methods; Manchuria invaded and becomes Japanese puppet state of Manchukuo, 1932; triumph of militarism, 1936; invasion of China, 1937; Mori Ogai, 1860–1922, a founder of modern Japanese literature; Tsukiji little theatre opens in Tokyo, beginning of Japanese modern theater, 1924; Shintoism abolished in Japan, 1945; the bacteriologist Hideyo Noguchi, 1876–1928; in 1930, Japan has 50,000 automobiles as compared with 23 million in the United States, 18,000 in China, 125,000 in India, 4,822 in Syria; founding of the Hayakawa Electric Co., whose merchandise is sold under the name of Sharp, funded by proceeds from the first mechanical pencil, invented by Tokuji Hayakawa, in 1915; discovery of cancer-causing properties of coal tar, in experiment with animals, by Katsusaburo Yamagiwa, in 1915; *Grass on the Wayside*, a novel by Satsume Sōseki, 1916; Tokyo's Imperial Hotel, completed by Frank Lloyd Wright with Mayan architectural features, 1916; the Kabuki Theater building, 1922, by Shinichiro Okada; founding of Matsushita Electric Co., 1918; *A New Life*, a novel by Shimazaki Toson, 1919; founding of Yoto Kogyo Co., the firm that produces Mazda trucks and automobiles, 1920; founding of Suzuki Motor Co., 1920; Japan's first radio station, Tokyo Shibaura, 1925; *The Izu Dancer*, a novel by Yasunari Kawabata, 1926; Japan's first subway, Tokyo's Chikatetsu, 1927; *Some Prefer Nettles,* a novel by Junichiro Tanizaki, 1928; "Machine," a famous short story by Riichi Yokomitsu, 1930; founding of Fuji Film,

1934; *Gyakko (Dokenohana)*
a novel by Osamu Dazai,
1935; *Sanshiro Sugata*, a
film by Akiro Kurosawa,
1943
In Korea, Japanese rule,
1910–1945
In Mexico, land distribution
under President Cardenas,
1934–1940; 2 million people
killed in revolution, 1910–
1917; the Constitution of
1917 becomes basis of a
reformist, democratic
state; oil fields nationalized,
1930s; founding of *El
Universal*, a newspaper,
1916; mural paintings of
Fall of Cuernevaca and
Cortez and His Mercenaries,
by Diego Rivera for
Mexico City's Palacio de
Cortez, 1930
In Muslim world, in Egypt,
Taha Hussein (1888–1973),
literary critic and author of
The Stream of Days, the
second volume of his
autobiography, 1939; in
Persia, the dictatorship of
Reza Khan Pahlevi, 1925–
1941; *The Blind Owl*, a novel
by Sadiq Hidayat, 1941; in
Saudi Arabia, Abdul-Aziz
ibn Saud proclaims himself
king of Jejaz and renames
it Saudi Arabia, 1925;
Standard Oil of California
receives monopoly of oil
leases, the first step in what
eventually becomes
ARAMCO (Arabian
American Oil Company),
later a fully owned
government (Saudi)
agency, 1933
In Palestine, founding of
Hebrew University in
Jerusalem, 1924
In South America, in
Argentina, 1930 coup leads
to a military-based regime;
growth of local fascist
movement during World

War II; in Brazil, the first dictatorship of President Vargas, 1930–1945; in Chile, the Nobel Prize for literature to the poet Gabriela Mistral, 1945; in Uruguay, the poet Jan Zorila, 1857–1931; on the Chilean-Argentine border, the *Christ of the Andes* statue, commemorating the peaceful settlement of a border dispute, 1904; in Peru, *The Dark Messengers*, poems by Cesar Vallejo, 1918; completion of Lima's Gran Hotel Bolívar, Peru's central meeting place, 1924; in Chile, *Altazor*, poems by Vicente Huidoboro, 1919; in Uruguay, the first World Cup football (soccer) competition, 1930

LEARNING OBJECTIVES

To learn:

1. The characteristics of Modernism and how this style reflected the era's historical events

2. The key historical happenings between 1914 and 1945

3. How liberalism altered during this period and the causes of these changes

4. The history of World War I, including its causes, major events, turning point, and peace settlement, along with its consequences for politics and culture

5. The nature of the Great Depression and its impact on culture and politics

6. About totalitarianism, its definition; its two major types, communism and fascism; and how this authoritarian form of government affected politics and culture during this period

7. The history of World War II, including its causes, major events, turning point, and outcome

8. The historical and cultural situation in 1945

9. About mass culture, its defining characteristics, origins, and relationship to technology and how it affected the course of Modernism

10. The dominant role of the United States in the emerging worldwide mass culture

11. The innovations in the novel, particularly the introduction of stream-of-consciousness technique

12. The leading Modernist novelists, representative works, and literary characteristics

13. The chief Modernist poets, representative works, and style characteristics

14. The principal Modernist dramatists, their innovations, representative works, and literary style

15. The advance in philosophy, notably the founding of logical positivism and existentialism and the influences of these schools of thought on the wider culture

16. The leading scientific developments and how they both influenced and reflected events in politics and culture

17. The major trends in Modernist painting, the leading artists in each trend, and representative works

18. How the Bauhaus was the most significant development in architecture during this period

19. About International-style architecture, its chief exponents, and a representative building

20. How film became an art form in this period and how film differs from movies

21. The impact of artistic and literary refugees from Europe's totalitarian regimes on the free societies in which they sought sanctuary

22. The dominant schools of music in this era, the leaders of the two schools, and representative compositions

23. About the rise of American music with a distinctive style, the leading American composers, and representative works

24. Historic "firsts" of the Age of the Masses that became part of the Western tradition: nuclear power and nuclear weapons, a first modern instance of genocide, the highest standard of living in history for the most people, democracy for millions of citizens, polarization between mass and high culture, film as an art form, American dominance of worldwide mass culture, two superpowers instead of a multipolar arrangement, America as the world's industrial leader, Einstein's general theory of relativity, heisenberg's uncertainty principle, and stream-of-consciousness writing

25. The role of the Age of the Masses and High Modernism in transmitting the heritage of earlier civilizations: keeping Classical influences alive in Neoclassical music, continuing the tradition of world wars begun in the Baroque era, reviving absolutist forms of government in totalitarianism, updating artistic trends that began in Post-Impressionism, and perpetuating Modernism in general and giving it a pessimistic focus

SUGGESTIONS FOR FILMS

The A-Bomb Dropped on Japan. Fleetwood, 4 min., black and white.

And the World Listened: Winston Churchill. University of Wisconsin, 28 min., black and white.

Bolshevik Victory. Films, Inc., 20 min., black and white.

Europe, the Mighty Continent: This Generation Has No Future. Time-Life, 52 min., color.

Expressionism. International Film Bureau, 26 min., color.

Germany—Dada. University Educational and Visual Arts, 55 min., color.

The Great War—Fifty Years After. NBC, 25 min., color.

Igor Stravinsky. Carousel, 42 min., black and white.

Lenin and Trotsky. CBS, 27 min., black and white.

Nazi Concentration Camps. National Audio-Visual Center, 59 min., black and white.

The Spanish Turmoil. Time-Life, 64 min., black and white.

Surrealism. International Film Bureau, 24 min., color.

Twisted Cross (The rise of Nazism). McGraw-Hill, 55 min., black and white.

The World at War Series (1933 to a reunion of WWII veterans). Heritage Visual Sales, 26 parts, 51 min. each, color.

SUGGESTIONS FOR MUSIC

Schoenberg, Arnold. *Concerto for Piano & Orchestra, Op. 42 (1943).* Fellegi, Ferencsik, Budapest Symphony. Hungaroton SLPX-12021.

————. *Moses und Aron (1930–1932).* Bonney, Zakai, Langridge, Mazura, Haugland, Solti, Chicago Symphony and Chorus and Glen Ellyn Children's Chorus. London 414264-1 LH2 [digital]; 414264-2 LH2 [CD].

————. *Concerto for Cello (1932–1933).* Yo-Yo Ma, Ozawa, Boston Symphony. CBS IM-39863 [digital]; MK-39863 [CD].

Stravinsky, Igor. *Oedipus Rex (1927).* Norman, Moser, Nimsgern, Bracht, Davis, Bavarian Radio Symphony & Chorus. Orfeo S-071831 A [digital]; C-071831 [CD].

————. *Pulcinella. (1920; rev. 1949).* Murray, Rolfe Johnson, Estes, Boulez, Ensemble Intercontemporain. Erato ECD-88107 [CD].

————. *Symphony in C (1940); Symphony in Three Movements (1945); Symphony of Psalms (1930).* Stravinsky, CBC Symphony. CBS MK-42434 [CD].

Ellington, Duke. *Sophisticated Ellington.* (Rec. 1927–1966). RCA CPL2-4098E; CPK2-4098 [cassette].

————. *This Is Duke Ellington.* (1927–1945). RCA VPM-6042 [mono].

————. *The Symphonic Ellington.* (Rec. ca. 1950). Trend 529 [mono].

SUGGESTIONS FOR FURTHER READING

Arendt, H. *The Origins of Totalitarianism*. New York: Meridian Books, 1964. Although written three decades ago, this study, which traces the roots of totalitarianism to late-nineteenth-century anti-Semitism, imperialism, and racism, is still relevant to the student of today.

Arnason, H. H. *History of Modern Art*. Englewood Cliffs, N.J.: Prentice-Hall, 1977. A standard survey of modern art that has been outdated in some areas, but remains a useful introduction.

Bell, P. M. H. *The Origins of the Second World War in Europe*. London: Longman, 1986. A challenging study that covers both the events leading up to 1941 and the schools of interpretation over the causes of World War II; in the Origins of Modern Wars series.

Bendersky, J. *A History of Nazi German*. Englewood Cliffs, N.J.: Prentice-Hall, 1992. Examines the origins and development of Nazism, its seizure of power, the nazification of Germany, and World War II in a short but clearly written book.

Cantor, N. F. *Twentieth Century Culture: Modernism to Deconstruction*. New York: Peter Lang, 1988. An engaging account with an invaluable section on Post-Modernism, despite the author's hostility to many of its features.

Carsten, F. L. *The Rise of Fascism*. 2nd ed. London: Batsford, 1980. This brief survey, although superseded by later works, remains a useful introduction to the emergence and triumph of one of the most important "isms" of the twentieth century.

Eksteins, M. *Rites of Spring, the Great War, and the Birth of the Modern Age*. Toronto: Lester and Orpen Dennys, 1989. Offers a perspective on the coming of the modern age within the context and experience of World War I.

Fussell, P. *The Great War and Modern Memory*. New York: Oxford University Press, 1975. Fussell shows how the war in the trenches and those who wrote about these events created the myths that grew out of the horrors of World War I—closely reasoned, thoroughly researched, and passionately presented.

Gilbert, M. *The Second World War: A Complete History*. New York: Henry Holt, 1989. Complete in the sense of coverage of nearly every battle, and full of details and facts.

Goldwater, R. J. *Primitivism in Modern Art*. Cambridge: Harvard University Press, Belknap Press, 1986. An updated and revised "classic" in art history that links the works of primitive artists to Western artists since the late nineteenth century.

Hamilton, G. H. *Painting and Sculpture in Europe, 1880–1940*. New York: Penguin, 1967. A well-organized history of the rise of Modern painting and sculpture; illustrated in black and white.

Hunter, S., and Jacobus, J. *Modern Art: Painting, Sculpture, Architecture*. Rev. ed. Englewood Cliffs, N.J.: Prentice-Hall, 1992. Revised and enlarged, this is a selective rather than encyclopedic work that traces the origins of Modern art from the nineteenth century through its decline and the advent of Post-Modernism.

Johnson, P. *Modern Times: The World from the Twenties to the Nineties*. Rev. ed. New York: HarperCollins, 1991. A lively and argumentative review of twentieth-century politics and culture by a leading conservative analyst.

Keegan, J. *The Second World War*. New York: Viking Penguin, 1990. A survey of the entire war that focuses on five major battles to illustrate the technological and human dimensions of combat.

Kitchen, M. *Europe Between the Wars: A Political History*. London: Longman, 1988. A standard approach covering the 1919 peace treaties, the European economy, events leading up to the war in 1939, plus a chapter on each major country.

Lee, S. J. *The European Dictatorships, 1918–1945.* New York: Methuen, 1987. A geographical and historical survey of "sixteen dictatorships" based on recent scholarship and interpretations.

Marrus, M. *The Holocaust in History.* Hanover, N.H.: University Press of New England, 1987. A first-rate interpretative survey on the many aspects of the Holocaust, not a detailed account. Very useful for looking at the many implications of this event.

Marwick, A. *War and Social Change in the Twentieth Century: A Comparative Study of Britain, France, Germany, Russia and the United States.* London: Macmillan, 1975. One of the first studies of this type of social and cultural history that explores the impact of the two world wars on each country.

Neret, G. *The Art of the Twenties.* Translated by T. Higgins. New York: Rizzoli, 1986. An exciting work that covers all of the arts—painting, architecture, sculpture, film, fashions, photography, posters. Fully illustrated with some of the more famous and some of the seldom exhibited examples of these creative activities.

Newhall, B. *The History of Photography from 1839 to the Present Day.* Rev. ed. New York: New York Graphic Society, 1978. This completely revised and enlarged edition may be somewhat outdated, but it is still a useful survey containing many famous photographs by the world's leading photographers.

Schmitt, B. E., and Vedeler, H. C. *The World in the Crucible, 1914–1919.* New York: Harper & Row, 1984. The last book in the Rise of Modern Europe volumes, this solid treatment of "war and revolution" uses the latest research and, at the same time, maintains the high standards of scholarship and writing identified in this excellent series—even though some of the books are now outdated.

Shirer, W. L. *The Rise and Fall of the Third Reich.* New York: Simon & Schuster, 1960. Written by an American correspondent who witnessed the rise of Hitler and his party in Germany, this is a monumental yet very readable account.

IDENTIFICATIONS

mass culture	Suprematism	Surrealism
stream-of-consciousness	Constructivism	International style
epic theater	Socialist Realism	serial music
logical positivism	*De Stijl*	twelve-tone scale
existentialism	Dada	Neoclassism

PERSONAL PERSPECTIVE BACKGROUND

Elie Wiesel, from *Night*

Wiesel was born in a village in the region known as Transylvania, where he lived until this area was conquered by the German Nazis in 1944. After the conquest, the Germans followed a policy of sending Jews and other "undesirables" to concentration camps. The Wiesel family was first interned in Auschwitz, Poland, where his mother and his youngest sister were killed in gas chambers. Two older sisters were taken elsewhere. Wiesel and his father were then moved to Buchenwald, Germany, where his father died from hunger and disease. When the U.S. Army liberated Buchenwald in 1945, Wiesel was among the survivors. He was liberated to France and placed in an orphanage there. In his adult years, particularly starting with the publication of his first novel, *Night*, in 1958, he has devoted himself to remembering the Holocaust and, in general, fighting bigotry, hatred, and violence. In 1986 Wiesel was awarded the Nobel Peace Prize for his lifelong efforts. (More information on Wiesel may be found in *Readings in the Western Humanities.*)

DISCUSSION/ESSAY QUESTIONS

1. In what ways was the period between 1914 and 1945 an "era of illusions"? What are some examples of these "illusions"?

2. Explain how the impact of events between 1914 and 1945, including the world wars, the Great Depression, the rise of totalitarianism, and the growth of the masses, influenced developments in High Modernism.

3. How did historical events affect the political and economic principles of liberalism between 1914 and 1945? Show how and why different patterns emerged in various regions of the West.

4. Discuss World War I, its causes, major events, turning point, and peace settlement. What impact did the war and its aftermath have on politics and culture?

5. Some historians claim that the Great Depression was the turning point in the first half of the twentieth century. Argue, pro or con, that this event was "the turning point" in contemporary history, noting key events before and after this economic crisis.

6. Describe conditions in the Great Depression, focusing on the countries that suffered most and least. What impact did economic failure have on the era's politics and culture?

7. Define totalitarianism. Compare and contrast the two types of totalitarian governments that arose after 1917. What were the origins of these governments, their accomplishments, and their failures? What part, if any, did these totalitarian regimes have on the outbreak of World War II?

8. Discuss the impact of totalitarianism on politics and culture between 1917 and 1945.

9. Discuss World War II, its causes, major events, turning point, and peace settlement. Summarize the situation in the West and the world in 1945.

10. Define mass culture. What were its contributions between 1914 and 1945? Discuss the complex relationship between mass and high culture during this epoch.

11. Discuss literature in the High Modernist era, setting forth the major writers (novelists, poets, and dramatists) and representative works of each. Compare and contrast their characteristics within the context of the Modernist style. What part did stream-of-consciousness writing have on developments in the novel?

12. Discuss the ways that black American intellectuals, writers, and musicians redefined their place in American life during this period, dealing in particular with the Harlem Renaissance and the writers Hughes and Hurston.

13. What two schools dominated philosophy during this era? What was the goal of each school, and who were its leaders? How did these developments in philosophy mirror events in the wider culture?

14. Discuss the scientific advances made between 1914 and 1945. Show what relationship, if any, these advances had to the era's politics and culture.

15. "The period between 1914 and 1945 represents the 'End of Certainty' in the West." Evaluate this statement in light of the literature written during this period.

16. What Post-Impressionist trends dominated painting during this period? In each trend, identify the leading artists, a representative work of each, and characteristics of each painter's individual style.

17. Discuss the influence of Picasso on the direction of modern art, noting his innovations, evolving styles, and themes. Be specific in your use of examples of his art.

18. Discuss developments in film during the Age of the Masses.

19. What impact did intellectual and artistic refugees from totalitarian regimes have on the states in which they sought sanctuary?

20. Discuss High Modernist music, concentrating on the two dominant schools, their leaders, and their differing styles.

21. What were the unifying characteristics of High Modernism, as seen in the arts, literature, philosophy, and music of the Age of the Masses?

22. Select the artistic or literary work that best symbolizes the Age of the Masses and justify your selection.
23. "American music found its distinctive voice in the Age of the Masses." Explain.

MULTIPLE-CHOICE QUESTIONS

1. The "masses" refers to:
   a. the aristocracy
   b. the wealthy middle class
   * c. the lower-middle and working class (p. 515)
   d. the peasants

2. Many of today's historians believe that the period between 1914 and 1945 can be best understood as:
   a. a time of tremendous economic growth
   b. a period of two wars that were totally unrelated
   * c. an era when the masses became a powerful historical force (p. 515)
   d. an epoch when Europe embraced Eastern culture

3. Which was NOT a contribution resulting from the rise of the masses?
   a. fresh forms of popular entertainment
   b. the birth of mass culture
   * c. a blending of mass and high culture (p. 515)
   d. a negative backlash among "serious" writers and artists

4. Which was NOT a significant outcome of the Treaty of Versailles?
   a. It established the League of Nations.
   b. It helped sow the seeds of World War II by its treatment of Germany.
   * c. It allowed the United States to dominate world affairs thereafter. (p. 517)
   d. It stripped Austria of its empire, so that it never fully recovered from its defeat.

5. The spring 1917 events that helped determine the outcome of World War I were:
   * a. the Russian revolution and the entry of the United States into the war on the side of the Allies (p. 516)
   b. the Germans' unrestricted submarine warfare and the entry of Italy into the war on the side of the Allies
   c. the harsh armistice terms offered by the Allies and the entry of Turkey into the war on the side of the Central Powers
   d. the German revolution and the collapse of the currency in Italy

6. Germany between the Versailles Treaty and the rise of Hitler was known as the:
   a. Berlin Republic
   b. Bonn Republic
   * c. Weimar Republic (p. 517)
   d. Potsdam Republic

7. The first totalitarian state in Europe was:
   a. Spain
   b. Italy
   * c. Russia (p. 519)
   d. Germany

8. The European country that suffered most from the Great Depression was:
   * a. Germany (p. 519)
     b. France
     c. Italy
     d. Spain

9. Lenin and Marx agreed about all of these ideas EXCEPT:
     a. Economic conditions determine the course of history.
     b. History leads inevitably to a communist society.
   * c. A dedicated elite is necessary to initiate revolutionary change. (p. 519)
     d. The goal of history is a society run by and for the workers.

10. Fascism supported:
     a. the supremacy of individual expression
   * b. the fusion of the people into a whole (p. 519)
     c. representative democracy
     d. free enterprise

11. A European fascist leader in the 1930s was:
   * a. Mussolini in Italy (p. 519)
     b. Blum in France
     c. King Alfonso of Spain
     d. Tito of Yugoslavia

12. Which country experienced a civil war in the 1930s and became a testing ground for military weapons and tactics later used in World War II?
     a. Hungary
     b. Portugal
     c. Italy
   * d. Spain (p. 519)

13. The causes of World War II did NOT include:
   * a. France's dissatisfaction with its treatment at the Versailles Peace Conference in 1919 (p. 520)
     b. Germany's aggressive policies in central Europe in the 1930s
     c. Japan's invasions of Manchuria and China in the 1930s
     d. German nationalistic feelings about recovering "lost" German lands and peoples

14. Which was NOT a feature of the Holocaust?
     a. It reflected Germany's anti-Semitic attitudes.
   * b. It was accomplished over the protests of the world's Christian leaders. (p. 520)
     c. It expressed Germany's nationalistic feelings.
     d. It resulted in the death of 6 million Jews and millions of other people who were members of groups considered undesirable.

15. Which is NOT a characteristic of mass culture?
     a. It is inexpensive.
     b. It is mass-produced.
     c. It is easily accessible.
   * d. It is serious. (p. 522)

16. Mass culture, between 1914 and 1945, did NOT reflect the:
    a. tastes of the lower-middle and working class
  * b. spirit of skepticism and experimentation (pp. 522–523)
    c. growth of industrialized society
    d. development of new technologies

17. The leading symbol of America's dominance of worldwide mass culture was:
    a. Igor Stravinsky
    b. Babe Ruth
  * c. Walt Disney (p. 523)
    d. Louis Armstrong

18. A literary innovation of the Modernist novel was:
  * a. stream-of-consciousness writing (p. 523)
    b. fixed realism
    c. an omniscient narrator
    d. focus on precise details

19. Two American novelists who experimented with fiction during the Modernist period were:
    a. Langston Hughes and W. E. B. DuBois
  * b. Ernest Hemingway and William Faulkner (pp. 523–524)
    c. T. S. Eliot and William Butler Yeats
    d. George Orwell and D. H. Lawrence

20. Which novel reflected the author's debt to popular hardboiled detective fiction of the 1930s?
    a. Joyce's *Ulysses*
    b. Woolf's *To the Lighthouse*
  * c. Hemingway's *The Sun Also Rises* (p. 524)
    d. Faulkner's *The Sound and the Fury*

21. This novel was a satire on Stalinist Russia:
    a. Woolf's *Mrs. Dalloway*
  * b. Orwell's *Animal Farm* (p. 524)
    c. Lawrence's *Lady Chatterley's Lover*
    d. Hemingway's *The Sun Also Rises*

22. What Modernist symbol was intended to reflect the hollowness of contemporary life?
    a. Yeats's Byzantium
  * b. Eliot's waste land (p. 525)
    c. Hughes's river
    d. Faulkner's Yoknapatawpha County

23. Langston Hughes's poetry reflected:
    a. the values of the late Roman poets
  * b. his anguish as a black man in a white world (p. 525)
    c. his hatred of totalitarian governments
    d. his black separatist politics

24. Which did NOT contribute to the Harlem Renaissance?
  * a. the American government's grants for the arts (p. 525)
    b. the growing popularity of jazz
    c. the avant-garde cult of primitivism
    d. the population shift of American blacks from the rural south to northern cities

25. Zora Neale Hurston faced a number of difficulties because:
    a. Her background, from an upper-class family, made it difficult for her to relate to the masses.
    b. She could never decide if she wanted to write novels or poetry.
    c. She tended to fall into stereotypes in depicting her characters.
*   d. She was a black female dealing with both race and gender. (525–526)

26. What type of theater was developed by Bertolt Brecht?
*   a. epic theater (p. 526)
    b. modernized Greek classics
    c. tense family dramas
    d. absurdist plays

27. Cocteau's drama *The Infernal Machine* is a Modernist version of the story of:
    a. Orestes
*   b. Oedipus (p. 527)
    c. Orpheus
    d. Odysseus

28. This author's philosophy helped to lay the groundwork for logical positivism:
*   a. Wittgenstein (p. 527)
    b. Heidegger
    c. Sartre
    d. Heisenberg

29. Existentialism is concerned primarily with:
    a. defining terms
    b. clarifying statements
*   c. authenticity (p. 527)
    d. spiritual values

30. A key value in Sartre's existentialism is:
    a. the limits to human choice
    b. submitting to forces beyond one's control
    c. faith in God
*   d. individual responsibility (p. 527)

31. Which is NOT correct regarding Heisenberg's uncertainty principle?
    a. It states that absolute certainty is impossible in subatomic physics.
*   b. It reflects the Freudian belief that truth is relative. (pp. 528–529)
    c. It means that scientists, with their instruments, inescapably interfere with the accuracy of t heir studies of atomic structure.
    d. It is based on the inability of physicists to identify both an electron's exact location and its path at the same time.

32. The scientist who headed the team that built the first atomic bomb was:
    a. Einstein
    b. Heisenberg
    c. Planck
*   d. Oppenheimer (p. 529)

33. The prevailing style of art encouraged by Lenin between 1917 and 1922 was:
    a. Cubism
    b. Futurism
  * c. Constructivism (p. 530)
    d. Surrealism

34. Which was NOT correct regarding Malevich's style of painting?
    a. He believed that Christian mysticism is superior to Marxist materialism.
    b. He thought that art should be nonobjective.
  * c. He asserted that feelings are supreme over every element of life. (p. 530)
    d. He advocated a representational style of painting.

35. The *De Stijl* movement was led by:
    a. Picasso
  * b. Mondrian (pp. 530–531)
    c. Matisse
    d. Malevich

36. All of these are correct statements about Picasso's *Guernica* EXCEPT:
    a. It is a protest against Franco's unbridled warfare.
    b. It is executed in a modified Cubist style.
  * c. Its vivid colors express the artist's rage. (p. 532)
    d. It is a visual symbol of the era's conflict between totalitarianism and human freedom.

37. Which does NOT apply to Georgia O'Keeffe?
    a. She avoided pure abstraction in her paintings.
  * b. Her work reflected the mysticism of the northwest. (pp. 532–533)
    c. Often her works dealt with the theme of death.
    d. She painted objects unique to the American setting.

38. Dada artists were famous for their:
  * a. outrageous acts (p. 533)
    b. spiritual values
    c. humanistic beliefs
    d. pure abstraction

39. Surrealist art was inspired by the theory of:
    a. Marx
  * b. Freud (p. 533)
    c. Einstein
    d. Heisenberg

40. The most influential exponent of Dada was:
    a. Picasso
  * b. Duchamp (p. 533)
    c. Malevich
    d. Mondrian

41. A leading Surrealist was:
    a. Beckmann
    b. Matisse
  * c. Dali (p. 533)
    d. O'Keeffe

42. Paul Klee can be described in all of the following ways EXCEPT:
   * a. Klee reflected the despair of the Dada style. (pp. 534–535)
   b. Klee related his art to children and their scribbling.
   c. Klee was an opponent to the rise of fascism.
   d. Klee was both an academic and a practicing artist.

43. Frida Kahlo expressed her creative talents best as:
   a. an artist of the Neoclassical school
   b. a poet of the Harlem Renaissance
   * c. a painter of many revealing self-portraits (pp. 535–536)
   d. a playwright of existential dramas

44. Which was NOT correct regarding the Bauhaus?
   a. It was the leading art institute in Germany between 1919 and 1933.
   * b. It reflected the values of the Nazi political movement. (p. 538)
   c. It brought together artists, craftspeople, and architects.
   d. It developed a spartan (all-white) type of interior decoration.

45. Matisse's art in the 1930s is noted for its:
   a. social protest themes
   * b. expressiveness (pp. 536–537)
   c. religious values
   d. pure abstraction

46. This artist's paintings reflected his hatred of Nazism:
   a. Mondrian
   b. Malevich
   c. Matisse
   * d. Beckmann (p. 537)

47. International-style architecture was characterized by:
   * a. sleek exteriors (p. 538)
   b. the Classical orders
   c. Gothic towers
   d. ornamented facades

48. The Russian director Eisenstein pioneered this film technique:
   a. the close-up
   * b. the montage (p. 539)
   c. cross-cutting
   d. the handheld camera

49. Which did NOT change moviemaking between 1914 and 1945?
   * a. the handheld camera (pp. 539–540)
   b. the addition of sound
   c. the three-color cinematography process
   d. the flight of talented German filmmakers to Hollywood

50. Which was NOT one of the composer Schoenberg's achievements between 1914 and 1945?
   a. He was the leader of the atonal school of music.
   * b. He revived the Classical operatic forms inspired by Pergolesi and Mozart. (p. 540)
   c. He pioneered serial music.
   d. He composed with a twelve-tone scale.

51. Between 1919 and 1945 the Neoclassical school of music was led by:
    a. Ives
    * b. Stravinsky (p. 540)
    c. Copland
    d. Harris

52. Who was NOT the pioneer of a distinctively American style of music, between 1914 and 1945?
    * a. Igor Stravinsky (p. 540)
    b. Aaron Copland
    c. Ella Fitzgerald
    d. Duke Ellington

53. Stravinsky's music between 1919 and 1945 was characterized by all of these EXCEPT:
    * a. serial composition (p. 540)
    b. complex rhythmic patterns
    c. Classical operatic forms inspired by Pergolesi and Mozart
    d. small orchestras and musical structures based on Baroque models

54. Which of the following does NOT describe the American composer George Antheil?
    * a. He was interested in using American folk tunes to develop a unique American sound.
       (pp. 540–541)
    b. He lived much of life abroad in Europe.
    c. He was fascinated with the modern machine age.
    d. He experimented with a number of musical forms and sounds.

55. Which is NOT an example of the influence of mass culture on Modernism?
    a. Copland's incorporation of jazz elements into his serious music
    * b. Faulkner's use of advertising copy in the Yoknapatawpha novels (pp. 524, 527, 540)
    c. Cocteau's use of film in his play *The Infernal Machine*
    d. Hemingway's adoption of a popular detective fiction style in *The Sun Also Rises*

21

THE AGE OF ANXIETY AND BEYOND
1945–

TEACHING STRATEGIES AND SUGGESTIONS

Because of the press of time, the instructor often must either omit or condense material at the end of the term. The tendency, therefore, is to rush through the last class lectures without much thought to the teaching model. Yet, these last lectures sometimes demand the most care in determining teaching strategies. The instructor should not fall into the trap of simply giving an encyclopedic listing of events and names just to "cover" the material in the final chapter. A minimum of three lectures should be scheduled for the last chapter.

Since the time frame in Chapter 21 is approximately fifty years, the instructor need not begin with the standard Historical Overview but can open the final set of lectures regarding Late Modernism and Post-Modernism with either the Spirit of the Age or the Comparison/Contrast approach. The Patterns of Change model and/or the Diffusion model can then be used effectively with two major topics: first, the distinctions between Late Modernism and Post-Modernism, and second, the globalization of bad culture, particularly under Post-Modernism. In the closing lecture, the instructor can use the Reflections/Connections approach to make some educated guesses about the future of the emerging global culture. Such remarks must, of necessity, be guarded and can touch on such matters as impending directions of political, social, and economic trends; the projected influence of such trends on intellectual, literary, and artistic developments; and finally, the continuing relationship between the world today and the civilizations of Mesopotamia and Egypt where Western civilization arose almost 5,000 years ago.

LECTURE OUTLINE

Non-Western Events

I. Characteristics of the Age of Anxiety
    and Beyond: Late Modernism and
    Post-Modernism

II. From a European to a World Civilization
    A. The era of the superpowers, 1945–1970
        1. Postwar recovery and the new world
            order
            a) Divisions and alliances in
                Western Europe and around the
                globe
            b) The Soviet Union
            c) The United States

1945–
In Africa, the transformation
of Europe's African
colonies into independent
states, ruled by Africans,
1950–1970; riots in
Johannesburg against
apartheid, 1950;
Organization of African
Unity (OAS), 1963; in
Ghana, Africa's best-known
woman writer, Ama Ata
Aidoo, *Our Sister Killjoy*,

2. The cold war
  a) Division of East and West
       in Europe
  b) Spreads to other parts
       of world
  c) Military conflicts and
       international tensions
3. Emergence of the Third World
  a) The end of colonialism
  b) New states and new economic
       systems
B. Toward a new global order, 1970–1994
  1. National issues and international
     realignment
    a) Economic trends and crises
    b) Domestic challenges and changes
         in the United States and in
         the Soviet Union
  2. Problems with a global dimension
    a) Exploding populations
    b) Growing environmental issues

III. The End of Modernism and the Birth of
Post-Modernism
  A. Philosophical, political, and
     social thought
    1. Existentialism
    2. Structuralism
    3. Feminism
    4. Black consciousness movement
  B. Science and technology
    1. Communications and computers
    2. Medical discoveries
  C. The literature of Late Modernism:
     fiction, poetry, and drama
    1. Existentialist writings
      a) Sartre
      b) Camus
    2. Black literature
      a) Richard Wright
      b) James Baldwin
    3. The novel and other literary forms
      a) Norman Mailer
      b) Alexander Solzhenitsyn
      c) Dylan Thomas
      d) Alan Ginsberg
      e) Samuel Beckett
  D. The literature of Post-Modernism
    1. Latin American writers
      a) Borges
      b) Marquez
    2. Eastern European writers—Milan
       Kundera

a novel, 1977; in Ivory Coast, the opening of Our Lady of Peace, the tallest church in Christendom, designed by Pierre Fakhoury and modeled after St. Peter's in Rome, 1989; in Kenya, *A Grain of Wheat,* a novel by Ngugi wa Thiong, 1967; in Lagos, Antonio Olinto, *The Water House,* 1981; the woman writer Buchi Emecheta, *The Rape of Shavi,* a novel, 1986; in Nigeria, *People of the City,* a novel by Cyprian Ekwenski, 1954; *Things Fall Apart,* a novel by Chinua Achebe, 1958; Tutuola, b. 1920, storyteller, *Palm Wine Drinkard,* 1952; the woman writer, Zaynab Alkali, *The Stillborn,* a novel, 1984; Wole Soyinka, Nobel Prize for literature, 1986; in Senegal, "Chaka," a poem by Leopold Sedar Senghor, 1956; *O Pays, Mon Beau Peuple,* and *Xala,* novels by Sembene Ousmane, 1957 and 1976, respectively; in South Africa, *Sarafina,* a stage musical by Mbongeni Ngema, 1987; *The Wanderers,* a novel by Es'kia Mphahelele, 1971; Fugard, Kani, Ntshona write plays on treatment of blacks; Nadine Gordimer, Nobel Prize for literature, 1991; Albert John Luthuli, Nobel Peace Prize, 1960; Bishop Desmond Tutu, Nobel Peace Prize, 1984; F. W. de Klerk and Nelson Mandela, Nobel Peace Prize, 1993
In Caribbean, in Cuba, *Paradise,* a novel by Jose Lezama Lima, 1966; in

Jamaica, "I Shot the Sheriff," a popular song by reggae composer-performer, Robert Nesta "Bob" Marley, 1973; in St. Lucia, *Omeros,* an epic poem modeled on Homer, by Derek Walcatt, 1990; Derek Walcott, Nobel Prize for literature, 1992; in Trinidad, the novelist V. S. Naipaul, b. 1932, author of the novel *A House for Mr. Biswas,* 1961

In Central America, in Costs Rica, *The President,* a novel by Miguel Asturias, 1946; Oscar Arias Sanchez, Nobel Peace Prize, 1987; in Guatemala, Rigoberta Menchu, Nobel Peace Prize, 1992

In China, republic, 1912–1949; civil war with Communists victorious; Nationalists flee to Taiwan after defeat; Communist government led by Mao Zedong, 1949–1976; Great Leap Forward virtually eliminates houseflies, mosquitoes, rats, and bedbugs over wide areas, 1957; culturalrevolution of the 1960s has disastrous impact on traditional Chinese culture; "Quotations of Chairman Mao," 1966; China explodes a hydrogen bomb, 1967; rapprochement with United States, 1971; ascendancy of Deng Xiaoping, a pragmatic leader, 1976–1989; economic reform and political retrenchment since about 1978; Beijing's Fragrant Hills Hotel, designed by Chinese-American I. M. Pei opens, 1982; "Massacre of Tiananmen Square,"

Beijing, 1989; resurgence
of hard-liners, 1989–

In Himalaya region, Malla
dynasty, 1768–present;
Gurkhali-style architecture,
mixing archaic with French
and Italian influence; in
Tibet, Lamaistic state, about
1450 to 1950s, when
Chinese rule began; the
Dalai Lama, Nobel Peace
Prize, 1989

In Hong Kong, the Bank of
China Building, designed
by the Chinese American
I. M. Pei, 1989; transfer of
Hong Kong to China,
July 1, 1997

In India, end of British raj,
1947; partition of India
into modern countries of
India and Pakistan (East
and West); war between
the two Pakistans leads
to a separation into two
states, Pakistan and
Bangladesh, 1971; the age-
old "untouchability" caste
(15 percent of the
population) is outlawed,
though vestiges remain
for years, 1946; *Aparajito*,
a film by Satyajit Ray,
1956; *The Middleman and
Other Stories* by Bharati
Mukherjee, 1988; Anita
Desai's *Fire on the
Mountain*, a novel dealing
with the plight of women
in India, 1977; Salman
Rushdie's *Midnight's
Children*, a novel about
Hindu-Muslim identity,
1980; U. R. Anantha
Murthy's *Samskara*, a
novel in the Kannada
language that explores the
passing of the Brahman
tradition, 1965; Zubin
Mehta, Indian-born
conductor, chosen to lead
the New York
Philharmonic, 1978; Ravi
Shankar, b. 1920, sitar

player; Mother Teresa of Calcutta, Nobel Peace Prize, 1979

In Indochina, in Myanmar (Burma), Daw Aung San Suu Kyi, Nobel Peace Prize, 1991

In Japan, Showa period, 1926–1989; Western-style constitution, 1946; women gain the right to vote, 1946; land reform, tenant farmers decline from nearly one-half to one-tenth the population, 1946; Prime Minister Yasukiro Nakasone, the "Japanese Reagan," two terms in the 1980s; "the Idiot," a short story by Ango Sakaguchi, 1946; *The Setting Sun,* a novel by Osamu Dazai about the decline of aristocratic life, 1947; *Confessions of a Mask,* a semi-autobiographical novel by Yukio Mishima, 1948; "No Consultation Today," a short story by Masuji Ibuse, 1949; Junji Kinoshita, b. 1914, author of the drama *Twilight Crane,* 1949; NHK, Japanese television, begins broadcasting, 1953; *The Sound of the Mountain,* a novel by Yasunari Kawabata, 1954; Yasunari Kawabata, Nobel Prize for literature, 1968; *The Crucified Lovers,* a film by Kenji Mizoguchi, 1954; *Gate of Hell,* a film by Teinosuke Kinugasa, 1954; *Throne of Blood,* a film by Akira Kurosawa, 1957; Yuichi Inoue: *Fish,* a painting, 1959; Josaku Maeda, *Mystagogie d'espace,* a painting, 1965; Tsugouharu Foujita, painter, 1899–1968; Kenzo Tange, b. 1913, architect and town planner, designer

of Peace Center,
Hiroshima, 1955; *The
Waiting Years*, by Enchi
Fumiko (1905–1986) who
continues Japan's tradition
of outstanding women
writers; *Chushingura*, a film
by Hiroshi Imagaki, 1962;
Woman in the Dunes, a film
by Hiroshi Teshigahara,
1964, based on the novel of
the same name by Abe
Kobo, 1962; Japan becomes
the free world's second
strongest economic power,
in 1968; Yusunari Kawabata,
1899–1972, author of the
novel *Snow Country*, 1948
and recipient of Nobel Prize
for literature,
1968; Minoru Takeyama,
architect designer of
Tokyo department store;
Kenzo Tange, designer
of the Ehime Convention
Hall and the building
complex at Hiroshima;
Double Suicide,
a film by Masahiro
Shinoda, 1969; *Shogun
Assassin*, a film by Kenji
Misumi, 1981; Metropolitan
Teien Art Museum opens,
1983; *A Taxing Woman*, a
film by Juzo Itami, 1988;
Heisei period, 1989–
present; Socialist party
headed by a woman,
Takako Doi, 1989; *The
Japan That Can Say No*, a
political analysis by
Shinaro Ishihara and Sony
founder Akio Morita, 1990;
Tokyo's City Hall,
designed by Kenzo Tange,
1990; Eisaku Sata, co-
winner, Nobel Peace Prize,
1974; Kenzaburo Oe, Nobel
Prize for literature, 1994
In Korea, division into two
states, North and South
Korea, 1948; Korean War,
1950–1953; Sun Myung
Moon founds the

Unification Church, 1954

In Mexico, David Siqueiros, muralist, 1897–1974; Carlos Chávez, composer, 1899–1978; Alfonso Garcia Robles, co-winner Nobel Peace Prize, 1982; Octavio Paz, Nobel Prize for literature, 1990

In Muslim world, Arab League founded, 1945; in Egypt, *The Beginning and the End*, a novel by Naquib Mahfouz, 1949; in Morocco, *The Sacred Night*, a novel by Tahar Ben Jelloun, 1987; OPEC "oil crisis," 1974; Anwar el-Sadat, co-winner, Nobel Peace Prize, 1978; Naquib Mahfouz, Nobel Prize for literature, 1988

In New Zealand, *Sweetie*, a film by Jane Campion, 1990, and *The Piano*, 1993

In North Vietnam, Le Duc Tho, co-winner, Nobel Peace Prize, 1973

In South America, in Argentina, the semiabstract painter, Aquiles Badi, 1893–1976; *Hopscotch*, a novel by Julio Cortazar, 1963; *The Kiss of the Spider Woman*, a novel by Manuel Puig 1976; Adolfo Perez Esquivel, Nobel Peace Prize, 1980; in Brazil, Oscar Niemeyer, the architect, designer of the city of Brasilia, 1956–1963; Brasilia becomes new capital, 1960; Pelé's soccer career, 1956–1974; in Chile, the poet Pablo Neruda (1904–1973) wins Nobel Prize for literature, 1971; in Columbia, Gabriel Garcia Márquez, Nobel Prize for literature, 1982; in Peru, *The War at the End of the World*, a novel by Mario Vargas Llosa, 1984; in Uruguay, *The Short Life*, a

novel by Juan Carlos
Onetti, 1950

World's population in mid-1996 is 5.78 billion; China 1.2 billion, India 952 million, the USA 266 million, Indonesia 206 million, Brazil 162 million, Russia 148 million, Pakistan 129 million, Japan 125 million, and Bangladesh 123 million; the largest cities are Tokyo-Yokahoma 28.4 million, Mexico City 23.9 million, São Paulo 21.5 million, Seoul 19.0 million, New York City 14.6 million, Osaka-Kobe-Kyoto 14.0 million, Bombay 13.5 million, Calcutta 12.8 million, Rio de Janeiro 12.7 million, and Buenos Aires 12.2 million

LEARNING OBJECTIVES

To learn:

1. The differences between Late Modernism and Post-Modernism

2. The causes and characteristics of the two postwar economic and political systems of the superpowers and their allies

3. The major economic and political trends among the nations of Western Europe

4. Domestic developments within the Soviet Union from 1945 to 1970

5. Domestic developments within the United States from 1945 to 1970

6. The origins and course of the cold war

7. The causes and results of the emergence of the Third World states

8. The causes of the changes in international relations since 1970

9. The course and results of Soviet-American relations from 1970 to 1994

10. The major global problems confronting the world in 1994

11. The major intellectual and cultural movements and their leaders since 1945.

12. The renewal of feminism, its chief advocates and their messages.

13. The discoveries and inventions in science and technology and their impact on Western culture from 1945 to 1991

14. The characteristics of existentialism, its major voices, and representative literature

15. The development of the novel and poetry after World War II

16. The rise of black consciousness, its chief advocates and their messages

17. The trends and changes in the theater after World War II

18. The Post-Modern novel and novelists

19. The characteristics, innovations, and themes of Late Modernist painting, examples of these changes, and the leading artists

20. The major developments, trends, and sculptors of Late Modernism

21. Late Modernist architecture and architects

22. The general characteristics of Post-Modernism and its most important features

23. The Post-Modernist painters, sculptors, and architects and representative works

24. The key developments, important innovations, and leading composers in Late Modernist and Post-Modern music

25. The rise and meaning of mass culture

26. The world in 1997, reflecting its heritage from earlier civilizations: making militant nationalism once again a force for disruptive change around the world, specifically in the former Soviet Union and the former Yugoslavia; moving away from an international scene dominated by the superpowers to one governed by a multipolar arrangement; continuing Classical influences in the Post-Modernist arts and architecture; updating nineteenth-century Expressionism and Realism as trends in Post-Modernism; reviving and drastically refurbishing Hellenistic attitudes in Post-Modernist literature and philosophy and in the multiethnic, multiracial, multicultural states that seem to be emerging, particularly in the United States and Great Britain; returning to the roots of Western civilization in Mesopotamia and Egypt in the works of Anselm Kiefer, perhaps the most influential artist working today; restoring harmonious sounds and simple techniques to the music of Post-Modernism; and making American mass culture the world's common denominator

SUGGESTIONS FOR FILMS

American Art in the Sixties. Blackwood Productions, 58 min., color.

American Sculpture of the Sixties. Visual Resources, 19 min., color.

Cold War. McGraw-Hill, 20 min., black and white.

Europe, the Mighty Continent. (The concluding films in this thirteen-part series examine the decline of Europe and European unification.) Time-Life, 52 min., color.

Music: Electronic Edge. Documents Associates, 22 min., color.

Today and Tomorrow. Films for the Humanities, 60 min., color.

A Woman's Place. Xerox Films, 52 min., color.

SUGGESTIONS FOR MUSIC

Cage, John. *The Seasons (ballet) (1947)*. Davies, American Composers Orchestra, CRI S-410.

—————. *Sonatas and Interludes for Prepared Piano (1946–1948)*. Fremy. Etcetera ETC-2001; KTC-2001 [CD].

—————. *Song Books I–II (1970); Empty Words III (1975)*. For Speaker and Chorus. Cage, Schola Cantorum. Wergo 60074.

Glass, Philip. *Einstein on the Beach*. Glass Ensemble. CBS M4-38875; M4K-38875 [CD]; MXT-38875 [cassette].

—————. *Glassworks*. Glass Ensemble. CBS FM-37265; MK-37265 [CD]; FMT-37265.

—————. *The Photographer, for Violin, Chorus & Instruments (1982)*. Kukovsky, Glass Ensemble. CBS FM-37849; MK-37849 [CD].

—————. *Koyanisqaatsi*. Antilles/New Direction 90626-1; 906260-2 [CD]; 90626-4 [cassette].

Stravinsky, Igor. *Agon (ballet) (1957)*. Irving, New York City Ballet Orchestra. Elektra/Nonesuch 79135-1; 79135-2 [CD] 79135-4 [cassette].

—————. *Elegy for J.F.K. (1964)*. Fischer-Dieskau, Gruber, Adler, Berger. Orfeo S-015821 A.

SUGGESTIONS FOR FURTHER READING

Ashton, D. *The New York School: A Cultural Reckoning*. New York: Viking, 1973. Outstanding discussion of the generation that founded Abstract Expressionism; superbly illustrated.

Banks, O. *Faces of Feminism: A Study of Feminism as a Social Movement*. New York: St. Martin's Press, 1982. One of the first histories of feminism as a popular movement, extending from 1840 to 1980.

Crouzet, M. *The European Renaissance Since 1945*. Translated by S. Baron. London: Thames and Hudson, 1970. Full of relevant paintings, photographs, and examples of popular culture to illustrate Europe's recovery and rebirth.

Gardner, H. *The Quest for Mind*. New York: Vintage, 1974. A succinct treatment of structuralism and its varieties by a well-respected Harvard psychologist.

Guilbaut, S. *How New York Stole the Idea of Modern Art: Abstract Expressionism, Freedom and the Cold War*. Translated by A. Goldhammer. Chicago: University of Chicago Press, 1983. A brilliant interpretation of the linkage between cold war politics and Late Modernist culture.

Hughes, R. *Shock of the New*. 2nd ed. New York: Knopf, 1991. An authoritative overview of the rise of Modernist art.

Jencks, C. *Post-Modernism: The New Classicism in Art and Architecture*. New York: Rizzoli, 1987. Despite the narrowly focused title, this authoritative synthesis surveys all the varieties of Post-Modernism.

————. *The Post-Modern Reader*. New York: St. Martin's Press, 1992. A collection of essays that together define Post-Modernism; Jenck's introductory essay is a classic of lucidity about this difficult movement.

Johnson, P. *The Birth of the Modern: World Society, 1815–1830*. New York: HarperCollins, 1991. Johnson's thesis is that the Modern world was born between 1815 and 1830; overly ambitious (it runs to 1095 pages), but there are many useful sections.

Kennedy, P. *The Rise and Fall of the Great Powers*. New York: Random House, 1987. A provocative analysis that interprets changes in the fortunes of the great powers in terms of the competing demands of economic growth and military needs.

Keylor, W. R. *The Twentieth-Century World: An International History*. 3rd ed. New York: Oxford University Press, 1996. An excellent overview of developments in world history during this century.

Laquer, W. A *Europe Since Hitler: The Rebirth of Europe*. Rev. ed. New York: Penguin, 1982. A first-rate study of Europe to 1970.

Lucie-Smith, E. *Movements in Art Since 1945: Issues and Concepts*. Revised and expanded 3rd ed. London: Thames and Hudson, 1995. The best survey available of developments in art since 1945.

Rosecrance, R. N. *The Rise of the Trading State: Commerce and Conquest in the Modern World*. New York: Basic Books, 1986. Presents the provocative thesis that a new international order is emerging based on cooperation among trading states.

Schell, J. *The Fate of the Earth*. New York: Knopf, 1982. An influential study on what civilization is doing to the natural environment.

Smith, J. *The Cold War, 1945–1965*. Oxford: Blackwell, 1989. A brief overview of the cold war, covering its origins and the changing climate that led to an end of the Age of Superpowers and the inauguration of a bipolar world after 1965.

Von Laue, T. H. *The World Revolution of Westernization: The Twentieth Century in Global Perspective*. New York: Oxford University Press, 1987. A useful survey of world history in the twentieth century; uses an impressionistic approach.

IDENTIFICATIONS

Late Modernism	Neorealism
Post-Modernism	Neoexpressionism
structuralism	Neoclassicism
theater of the absurd	high tech
magic realism	glissando
Abstract Expressionism	synthesizer
assemblage art	Performance Art
Pop Art	

PERSONAL PERSPECTIVE BACKGROUND

Ann Douglas, "High Is Low"

Ann Douglas, professor at Manhattan's Columbia University, is an able interpreter of contemporary culture. In this excerpt from her article in the *New York Times Magazine* she offers a concise summary of the Post-Modern situation: willingness to trespass against the historic boundaries separating high and low culture, openness to hitherto unheard voices, such as members of minorities at home and representatives of the Third World abroad, acceptance of the world as a global village, and, most important, claiming American mass culture as a microcosm of that global culture.

DISCUSSION/ESSAY QUESTIONS

1. Discuss the impact of military armaments and modern technology on the culture of the world between 1945 and 1970.
2. Define the terms "Late Modernism" and "Post-Modernism" and explain the differences between the two terms.
3. How have international issues changed between Late Modernism (1945–1970) and Post-Modernism (after 1970)? Discuss how these changes are reflected in the arts and humanities.
4. What is meant by the term "cold war?" Which nations were involved in this conflict, and what were the causes of this "war"?
5. Discuss the ways that both the defeated and victorious nations confronted the postwar years and describe their successes and failures.
6. Discuss the Soviet Union's domestic and foreign policies from 1945 to 1970.
7. What were the major internal problems confronting the United States from 1945 to 1970, and how successful was it in solving these problems?
8. What were the reasons for the end of European colonialism after 1945, and how did colonialism end in Asia and Africa?
9. Discuss the forces and issues that have led to a new global order since 1970.
10. Analyze the reasons for the end of the cold war, and note how the internal policies of the United States and the Soviet Union influenced the course of events.
11. Briefly describe the major global problems confronting the world today.
12. "Late Modernism was an 'Age of Anxiety.' " Defend or refute this statement in a short essay, drawing on literature and art from the period.
13. Define structuralism and discuss some of its major supporters and their works.
14. Analyze the role of Simone de Beauvoir in the feminist movement, and trace the history of this movement to today.
15. Discuss how the rise of modern feminism has helped shape the culture (literature, thought, and art) since 1945.
16. Discuss black consciousness, its definition, and the reasons for its birth, using the writings and actions of its chief supporters as background for your discussion.
17. Show how Existentialism was expressed in the works of Sartre and Camus.
18. Describe the major developments in Late Modern literature, and give representative examples of writers working in this field.
19. Define the "theater of the absurd," using the dramas of Beckett as the basis for your discussion.
20. Compare and contrast Post-Modernist with Late Modernist literature. Discuss at least two Late Modernist and Post-Modernist writers and their works in the essay.
21. Define Abstract Expressionism; how was it manifested in painting, and who were its most important painters?
22. What is meant by Pop Art? Which artists were associated with this movement?
23. Write a brief essay setting forth the differences between Late Modern and Post-Modern painting, focusing on at least two painters working in each style.
24. How have painters made social issues a central concern in their art since 1945? What causes have attracted them? How are these issues manifested in their works? How has this development influenced the nature of Late Modern and Post-Modern painting?
25. What distinguishes Late Modern from Post-Modern architecture, and who are the leading representatives of each style?
26. Discuss the contributions of Cage, Glass, Wilson, and Anderson to music after 1945. How is Post-Modernism reflected in today's music?

27. Define Performance Art and discuss the contributions of Anderson and Sherman to this type of art.
28. What is meant by mass culture, and how is it a reflection of the influence of the United States in the expanding world culture?

MULTIPLE-CHOICE QUESTIONS

1. The greatest threat to the West in the immediate postwar years was the fear of:
   a. the Germans and the Japanese rearming
 * b. nuclear war (p. 545)
   c. uprisings in the Third World
   d. an international economic depression

2. A cause of increased international tensions between 1945 and 1970 was:
   a. rising nationalism in Central and Eastern Europe
   b. the resurgence of Japan and Germany as military threats
   c. the collapse of international financial markets
 * d. developments in Third World countries (p. 545)

3. Which is NOT an issue facing the world after 1970?
   a. an international population explosion
   b. a growing shortage of food and the onset of famine
 * c. a decline in technology and inventions (p. 545)
   d. environmental crises of historic proportions

4. Which was NOT a characteristic of the postwar world?
   a. democracies in the American bloc, collectivist regimes in the Soviet bloc
 * b. rampant materialism in the American bloc, spiritual revival in the Soviet bloc (p. 547)
   c. piecemeal social welfare in the American bloc, comprehensive social welfare programs in the Soviet bloc
   d. booming economies in the American bloc, stagnating or slow-growth economies in the Soviet bloc

5. All of the following characterize what was happening in Great Britain and France after World War II EXCEPT:
   a. Both nations experienced moderate economic growth.
   b. They nationalized some of their basic industries.
   c. The two nations founded or extended their public health programs.
 * d. Laborers in both nations were satisfied with their situation. (p. 548)

6. In the 1950s the United States:
 * a. emerged as the leader of the democracies around the world (p. 548)
   b. continued to struggle with its low standard of living
   c. was unable to return to a peacetime economy
   d. found itself torn by racial riots and social problems

7. Which was NOT a cause of the civil rights movement in the United States?
 * a. the full backing of the federal government (pp. 548–549)
   b. the 1954 Supreme Court decision that declared "separate but equal" schools were unconstitutional
   c. the leadership of Martin Luther King, Jr.
   d. the refusal of Rosa Parks to sit in the back of a bus in Alabama

8. Which was NOT a sign of the cold war?
   a. the race to stockpile weapons by the two superpowers
   b. the forming of NATO and the Warsaw Pact alliance
   c. the outbreak of the Korean War and the Cuban missile crisis
 * d. the cultural exchanges of artists and intellectuals between the superpowers (pp. 549–550)

9. Which was NOT a consequence of the United States' failure in Vietnam?
   a. The United States emerged as a divided nation over the war and its goals.
   b. The United States' leaders were now reluctant to exercise military power abroad except in the Western Hemisphere.
   c. The United States was perceived to be weakened as a superpower.
 * d. The lessons of Vietnam brought the citizens together. (p. 551)

10. The first Third World country to win independent status after 1945 was:
    a. Algeria
 * b. the Philippines (p. 551)
    c. India
    d. Union of South Africa

11. The shift in Soviet-American relations that eased international tensions starting about 1970 is known as:
    a. laissez-faire
    b. bilateral agreements
 * c. détente (p. 551)
    d. glasnost

12. The reforms of Gorbachev in the Soviet Union had this result:
    a. a raised standard of living
 * b. progress in opening up political debates (p. 552)
    c. tighter control over the member states of the Soviet Union
    d. an era of prosperity in Eastern Europe

13. Today the two most pressing international issues are:
    a. nuclear war and the arms race
    b. the cold war and regional tensions
 * c. population explosion and a deteriorating environment (p. 553)
    d. growing famine and population migration

14. A characteristic of Late Modernism was:
    a. an undaunting optimism
    b. a commitment to a fixed set of standards in art
 * c. a sense of saving Western civilization from itself (pp. 554–555)
    d. appropriation of images of mass culture

15. The Late Modernists:
    a. advocated a return to religion
    b. welcomed the age of the masses
 * c. wanted to save what they considered worthwhile in Western culture (pp. 554–555)
    d. were hopeful, thinking that with World War II the world had turned a corner

16. Which does NOT apply to Post-Modernism?
    * a. It is existential in outlook. (p. 555)
    b. It is global in scope.
    c. It is multivoiced, since it embraces the works of women, members of minority groups, and representatives of the Third World.
    d. It is willing to trespass the boundaries between high and low culture.

17. Which is NOT a key feature of Post-Modernism?
    a. It draws inspiration from Classical and Pre-Classical cultures.
    * b. It turns away from the roots of Western tradition. (p. 555)
    c. It calls for a global civilization.
    d. It endorses multiculturalism.

18. The intellectual movement identified with Post-Modernism is:
    a. existentialism
    * b. structuralism (pp. 555–556)
    c. Realism
    d. idealism

19. Structuralists maintain that:
    a. Human freedom is unlimited.
    b. Humans act and operate in random, unpatterned ways.
    * c. Civilizations arise from deep-seated modes of thought. (p. 556)
    d. The basic nature of the human mind is unfathomable.

20. Which is NOT an influence of Noam Chomsky and Claude Lévi-Strauss on structuralism?
    a. Their theories imply that a common substructure exists in all human minds.
    b. Their theories have led other researchers to focus on the subconscious mind.
    c. Their theories hint that societies share some common subsurface features.
    * d. Their theories have led to a unified and coherent set of laws about the mind. (pp. 555–556)

21. The revival of the feminist movement after 1945 was first sparked by:
    * a. Simone de Beauvoir (p. 557)
    b. Betty Friedan
    c. Alice Walker
    d. Germaine Greer

22. The earliest significant theorist of black identity was:
    a. Martin Luther King, Jr.
    * b. Franz Fanon (p. 558)
    c. Malcolm X
    d. Whitney Young

23. Martin Luther King, Jr., was influenced by all of these EXCEPT:
    a. the New Testament and the teachings of Jesus
    * b. the philosophy of Nietzsche (p. 558)
    c. the writings of Thoreau
    d. the example of Gandhi

24. Which was NOT an important advance in technology after 1945?
    a. the birth control pill
    * b. the radio (p. 558)
    c. the computer
    d. the communication satellite

25. The chief influences on Jean-Paul Sartre's literary works were:
    a. his Roman Catholic heritage
    * b. existentialism and Marxism (p. 558)
    c. structuralism and logical positivism
    d. Realism and Naturalism

26. In his novel, *The Fall*, Camus dealt with the:
    a. problem of the tragedy of death at an early age
    * b. sense of guilt brought on by moral fraud (p. 559)
    c. consequences of sin to a devout believer
    d. never-ending quest for happiness

27. Black writers in the United States after 1945 discovered all of the following EXCEPT that:
    a. Their works were often not well received at home by white critics and audiences.
    * b. Christian values went hand in hand with their vision of a racially integrated society. (p. 559)
    c. Exile in France was sometimes preferable to living with racial discrimination at home.
    d. Existentialism was one way for them to deal with their sense of isolation.

28. The assassination of Martin Luther King, Jr., affected James Baldwin in this way:
    a. It revived his faith in the American way of life.
    b. It persuaded him that an integrated society was the only solution to America's racism.
    * c. It convinced him that violence was the most effective way to change America's racial attitudes. (p. 559)
    d. It led him to dedicate his life to working among the urban poor.

29. The writer Doris Lessing is noted for the:
    a. bleak vision of her "absurdist" plays
    b. obscurity of her enigmatic poetry
    * c. feminist message in her Realist novels (p. 559)
    d. humor of her romantic short stories

30. Alexander Solzhenitsyn's novels express his:
    a. deep devotion to the religious beliefs of Roman Catholicism
    * b. profound faith and trust in the Russian people (p. 559)
    c. strong endorsement of Marxism
    d. support for a centralized Soviet Union

31. The hero in Solzhenitsyn's *One Day in the Life of Ivan Denisovich*:
    a. is killed during a rebellion against the prison system
    * b. endures the hardships of the labor camp (p. 559)
    c. decides that life is not worth living and commits suicide
    d. renounces Marxism and is executed for his thought crime

32. Which is NOT characteristic of Dylan Thomas's poetry?
    a. It focused on themes accessible to most of his readers.
    b. It was filled with forceful and colorful language.
    c. It often featured local-color details from his native Wales.
    * d. It expressed social and political themes. (p. 560)

33. The poet who led the Beat Generation of the 1950s was:
  * a. Allen Ginsberg (p. 560)
    b. Richard Wright
    c. James Baldwin
    d. Robert Frost

34. The theater of the absurd:
  * a. shared existentialism's bleak vision (p. 561)
    b. obeyed the rules of the Classical tradition
    c. concentrated on the psychology of the characters
    d. romanticized the lives of ordinary people

35. Which is NOT correct regarding Beckett's play *Waiting for Godot?*
    a. It contains little or no action.
    b. It borrows British music hall comedy routines.
    c. It expresses the sense of the futility of life.
  * d. It follows French tragedy in its use of lofty language. (p. 561)

36. This writer's dramatic works belong to theater of the absurd:
    a. Eugene O'Neill
    b. Jean-Paul Sartre
    c. Albert Camus
  * d. Samuel Beckett (p. 561)

37. Post-Modern literature in Latin America is written in this style:
    a. social realism
  * b. magic realism (p. 561)
    c. absurd naturalism
    d. Marxist naturalism

38. Which is NOT correct regarding the novels of Gabriel García Márquez?
    a. They reflect the influence of American writers like Faulkner.
    b. They blend the real and the incredible into the narrative.
    c. They express the author's sense of place and of national traits.
  * d. They reveal an author obsessed with political ideology. (p. 561)

39. The Post-Modern novels of Milan Kundera stress the:
  * a. identity of sexual freedom with political freedom (p. 561)
    b. themes of fantasy and linguistic experimentation
    c. principles of Christian fundamentalism and Slavophilism
    d. ideals of revolutionary politics and social justice

40. The writings of Maxine Hong Kingston:
    a. are concerned exclusively with her matriarchal heritage
    b. argue that Western culture is superior to Eastern culture
  * c. point out the evils of racism and exploitation in America (p. 562)
    d. romanticize life both in China and the United States

41. The center of Western culture shifted after 1945 from Paris to:
    a. Tokyo
    b. London
  * c. New York (p. 562)
    d. Rome

42. Abstract Expressionism can be described as a style of painting that:
* a. tries to liberate the painter from conventional painting methods (p. 563)
  b. borrows themes from popular culture
  c. is based on Classical values
  d. is based on photographic clarity of detail

43. Which Abstract Expressionist is famous for "drip paintings"?
* a. Jackson Pollock (p. 563)
  b. Robert Rauschenberg
  c. Jasper Johns
  d. Mark Rothko

44. An "assemblage" is:
  a. an eclectic style that joins several styles of art into a single work
* b. a put-together structure that mixes junk, odds and ends, and some paint (p. 563, 566)
  c. a performance piece that blends art, music, dance, speech, and theater
  d. a collection of artists who work together simultaneously to create a work of art

45. These two Abstract Expressionists showed the way to Pop Art:
  a. Jackson Pollock and Willem deKooning
* b. Jasper Johns and Robert Rauschenberg (p. 566)
  c. Mark Rothko and Helen Frankenthaler
  d. Kenneth Noland and Morris Louis

46. The sculptor Louise Nevelson worked in a:
  a. Pop Art style
* b. style reminiscent of Abstract Expressionism (p. 567)
  c. Neorealist style
  d. style inspired by Rodin

47. Pop Art focused on:
* a. mass-produced products, such as soup cans (p. 566)
  b. religious themes
  c. color, texture, and line
  d. Third World culture

48. The most famous Pop artist was:
  a. Picasso
  b. David Smith
* c. Andy Warhol (p. 566)
  d. Jasper Johns

49. The Late Modernist architecture of Mies van der Rohe is characterized by:
  a. buildings treated as unified sculptures
  b. a reworking of the Classical orders
  c. many ornate decorations
* d. the "glass box" style (p. 569)

50. The works of the artist Sue Coe:
  a. reflect spiritual values
  b. are concerned primarily with beautiful images
  c. romanticize humankind's relationship with nature
* d. express her social and political ideas (p. 571)

51. Which of the following art styles are identified with Post-Modernism?
    a. Neoimpressionism, Neoabstractionism, and Neonaturalism
  * b. Neorealism, Neoexpressionism, and Neoclassicism (p. 571)
    c. Neocubism, Neoromanticism, and Neogothicism
    d. Neorenaissance, Neobaroque, Neorococo

52. The Neoexpressionist aspect of Post-Modernism is identified with the works of:
    a. Peter Blake
  * b. Sue Coe (p. 571)
    c. Philip Pearlstein
    d. John DeAndrea

53. The Classical aspect of Post-Modernism is apparent in:
    a. Anselm Kiefer's Osiris and Isis
  * b. Philip C. Johnson's AT&T Building (pp. 576–577)
    c. Rogers and Piano's Pompidou Center
    d. Coe's *Modern Man Followed by the Ghosts of His Meat*

54. The Post-Modernist music of Philip Glass:
    a. continues the atonality of Late Modern music
  * b. is emotionally appealing (p. 578)
    c. is composed using the Classical sonata form
    d. returns to the serial music style of Schoenberg

55. Which does NOT apply to Performance Art?
  * a. It always involves music. (p. 579)
    b. It is a mixed media art.
    c. It mixes high and popular art.
    d. It aims at a unique, nonreproducible experience.

COMPARATIVE QUESTIONS, CHAPTERS 15–21

1. The Age of Science had an impact on the Age of Reason in all of the following ways EXCEPT:
    a. The discoveries in astronomy led to the image that God was a clockmaker.
    b. The political writers Hobbes and Locke helped the *philosophes* formulate their
        understanding of how governments work.
  * c. The underlying pessimism of scientific discoveries reinforced the Age of Reason thinkers'
        beliefs that society could not be changed.
    d. Seventeenth-century European explorations and expansions convinced the *philosophes* that
        the world was larger than Europe.

2. Which of the following is correct regarding art and styles?
    a. The Rococo style was a reaction against the Neoclassical style.
  * b. The Neoclassical style was a reaction against Rococo art.
    c. Romanticism and the Neoclassical style shared common artistic goals.
    d. Rococo and Romantic paintings were patronized by the new industrial middle class.

3. Much of the first half of nineteenth-century European history can be described as:
    a. a time when the Rococo style dominated European art
  * b. an era when the impact of the eighteenth-century revolts was felt in many countries
    c. a quiet era of settled governments and stable societies
    d. a period of violent reaction to and successful repression of the liberal ideas generated by the
        French Revolution

4. Both Romanticism and Realism can be described as:
   a. intellectual reactions to the Age of Science
   b. the outgrowth of a sense of optimism in Europe
   c. ways to deal with the rise of Modernism
 * d. literary and artistic forms to confront the Industrial Revolution

5. Modernism has which of the following characteristics?
   a. It has had only one phase.
   b. Modernism has been full of optimism and has embraced the political and economic trends of the modern world.
 * c. The movement has prided itself in being separate from mass society and culture.
   d. It was satisfied with the Judeo-Christian set of values and advocated its continuation as moral standards for society.

LISTENING GUIDES

The following pages contain a selection of listening guides developed by Jack Boyd for *Encore: A Guide to Enjoying Music* (Mayfield Publishing Company, 1991). These guides cover quite a variety of music, all of which is available on tape or cassette from Mayfield, without including so much detail that the music neophyte founders. The guides have been designed to keep the listener moving through the compositions, section by section, item by item. The nontechnical descriptions are coupled with notation to enhance the enjoyment of music readers. Permission is granted for photocopied reproduction of handouts given to students without charge.

The following selections are discussed in greater detail in *Music in the Western Tradition* by Claire Detels, a supplement that can be shrinkwrapped with *The Western Humanities, Third Edition,* at a minimal cost to students.

Anton Webern: *Five Pieces for Orchestra, Op. 10, Piece No.4*

Igor Stravinsky: *The Firebird,* Final Variations

Peter Tchaikovsky: "Dance of the Reed Flutes," from *The Nutcracker*

Trouvère Song, "Or La Truix"

Guillaume de Machaut: "Kyrie," from *Notre Dame Mass*

Thomas Weelkes: "As Vesta Was from Latmos Hill Descending," from *The Triumphs of Oriana*

Giovanni Gabrieli: Motet, *Plaudite, Psallite,* from Sacrae Symphoniae

Henry Purcell: "When I Am Laid in Earth," from *Dido and Aeneas*

Antonio Vivaldi: "Spring," from *Il Quattro Stagione (The Four Seasons)*

J. S. Bach: Fugue in G minor, "Little"

W. A. Mozart: Symphony No. 40 in G minor, Mvt. 4

F. J. Haydn: Symphony No. 94 in G major, Mvt. 2

Ludwig van Beethoven: String Quartet in C minor, Op. 18, No. 4, Mvt. 4, "Rondo"

Franz Liszt: Hungarian Rhapsody No. 2

Modest Mussorgsky: "The Great Gate at Kiev," from *Pictures at an Exhibition*

Guiseppe Verdi: "Libiamo," from *La Traviata*

Richard Wagner: "Ride of the Valkyries," from *Die Walküre*

Claude Debussy: "La Cathédrale Engloutie," No. 10 from *Préludes,* Book I

Arnold Schoenberg: "Mondestruken" (Moondrunk), from *Pierrot Lunaire*

Kzysztof Penderecki: *Threnody for the Victims of Hiroshima*

Traditional: *Bopong*

Traditional: *Beggin' the Blues*

Ludwig van Beethoven: Symphony No. 5 in C minor, Mvt. 3

Aaron Copland: *Fanfare for the Common Man*

Frédéric Chopin: Scherzo in E Major, Op. 54

Charles Ives: "At the River"

WOLFGANG AMADEUS MOZART · "LAUDATE DOMINUM," FROM *SOLEMN VESPERS OF THE CONFESSOR* (1780)

- The violins state the lyrical theme over a spare, elegant accompaniment.
- The solo soprano uses the same long, placid melody to present the Latin text of Psalm 113, *Laudate Dominum* (Praise the Lord).
- The chorus sings the same music, but now with the *Gloria Patri* (Glory to the Father) text.
- The soloist and chorus sing the concluding *Amen*.

LISTENING GUIDE

▣ & CD

ANTON WEBERN · *FIVE PIECES FOR ORCHESTRA, OP. 10, PIECE NO. 4* (1911–1913) (Flowing, extremely tender)

:00	Mandolin	6 notes, *dolce* (sweetly), *Zeit lassen* (strict time)
:01	Harp	3 notes at the same time, *pp*, slowing, then faster
:05	Viola	2 notes at the same time, *pp*
:06	Clarinet	a single note repeated 6 times, *ppp*
:07	Trumpet	4 disjointed notes, *dolce*
:11	Trombone	2 notes, *dolcissimo* (very sweetly), *sehr gebunden* (very controlled)
:14	Drum	3 strokes, *ppp*
:15	Harp	5 notes, gradually faster
	Clarinet	single note trilled
	Celeste	2 notes very close together, twice
	Harp	
	Mandolin	single note, 7 repetitions, *pp*
	Celeste/Harp	
:20	Violin	5 notes, *ppp*, "like a breath"
:25		silence

LISTENING GUIDE

IGOR STRAVINSKY · *THE FIREBIRD*, FINAL VARIATIONS (1910)

Theme (A)	First heard in the horns above a muttered string accompaniment, then repeated exactly.
Variation 1 (A′)	Melody higher in violins, joined by flutes the second time through.
Variation 2 (A″)	Strings and woodwinds play the melody loudly, then other instruments join on the second playing.
Variation 3 (A‴)	Introduced by sudden quiet muttering, followed by very loud, brassy, fast, shortened, and fragmented versions of the theme.
Variation 4 (A⁗)	Melody slows as the full orchestra plays various sized pieces of the theme.
Conclusion	Very loud brassy chords, with a crescendo to the accented final note.

PETER TCHAIKOVSKY · "DANCE OF THE REED FLUTES," FROM
THE NUTCRACKER (1892)

Although he had a full orchestra at his disposal, Tchaikovsky wisely limited himself to virtually a chamber music sound.

Introduction	plucked low strings
A	• Three flutes state the main melody, with the low strings accompanying.
	• The English horn (alto oboe) gives a smooth transitional melody.
	• Three flutes play the main melody again, with more instruments accompanying.

B	The trumpet, very low and in minor, presents a nervous, staccato melody, other brasses accompanying.
A'	Three flutes play the original melody again, with strings accompanying.

LUDWIG VAN BEETHOVEN · "FÜR ELISE," BAGATELLE IN A MINOR (1808)

A   Slow, oscillating, trill-like opening figure, with simple upward accompanying notes in the left hand; the microform is **aababa**.

B   Soaring, songlike melody, ending with an echo of the opening slow oscillating notes.

A   As at the opening, except shorter, might now be thought of as **A'**; the microform is now **aba**.

C   *Ostinato* accompaniment (repeated notes) in the left hand, slow, interrupted melody in the right hand.

A   Same as the second **A** section (**A'**).

TROUVÈRE SONG · "OR LA TRUIX" (14th century)

"Or la truix" is in medieval Provençal French and compares wooing a girl with writing verse.

A *Or la truix trop dure te, voir, voir!*
(It is truly difficult to woo her, truly, truly!
A ceu k'elle est simple te.
Even if she looks simple.

b *Trop por outrecuidiés me taius,*
It may appear simple to the listeners,

b *cant je cudoie estre certains*
but in fact it is very difficult to put together,

a *de ceu ke n'a ve-rai des mois,*
oix, oix!
Ah, me, Ah, me!

A *Or la truix trop dure te, voir, voir!*
It is truly difficult to woo her, truly, truly!
A ceu k'elle est simple te.
Even if she looks simple.)

 **ISTENING GUIDE** **& CD**

GUILLAUME DE MACHAUT · "KYRIE" FROM *NOTRE DAME MASS*

Machaut's mass, written ca. 1350, is in six movements using a four-voice texture throughout.

Kyrie eleison
(Lord have mercy)

Upper two voices "busier" than lower voices. Top voice uses a syncopated rhythm four times.

Christe eleison
(Christ have mercy)

Syncopated, active top voice. Lower three voices almost like an accompaniment. Occasional long-held, chordlike notes.

Kyrie eleison
(Lord have mercy)

Exact repeat of the first *Kyrie*.

LISTENING GUIDE

⚏ & CD

THOMAS WEELKES · MADRIGAL, "AS VESTA WAS FROM LATMOS HILL DESCENDING,"
FROM *THE TRIUMPHS OF ORIANA* (1601)

As Vesta was from Latmos hill *descending*	Four high voices, then descending melodies.
She spied a maiden Queen the same *ascending*	Ascending melodies.
Attended on by *all* the shepherds swain,	All voices sing.
To whom Diana's darlings came *running down* amain.	Downward running notes.
First *two by two,*	Two voices echoed by two voices.
Then *three by three*	Three voices echoed by three voices.
Together,	All voices together.
Leaving their *Goddess*	Music in 3/4 time, the old Trinity concept.
All alone,	Single voice alone.
Hasted thither, and *mingling* with the shepherds of her train	Voices intertwining.
With *mirthful tunes* her presence entertain.	Pleasant tunes in all voices.
Then *sang* the shepherds and nymphs of Diana,	Stately, hymnlike introduction to this section
Long live fair Oriana!	Long notes in the bass voice, in the longest section of the work.

LISTENING GUIDE

GIOVANNI GABRIELI · MOTET, *PLAUDITE, PSALLITE,* FROM *SACRAE SYMPHONIAE* (1597)

The organization is primarily in four sections, each section using a different brief psalm passage. Each section ends with an *Alleluia* setting. Although a single choir begins the individual sections and the *Alleluia* settings, all sections end with everyone singing (playing).

INTRODUCTION

Plaudite, psallite
(Clap hands, sing psalms

Three tenor voices in succession.

SECTION 1

Jubilate Deo omnis terra,
Give praise to God, all the earth

Choir 1 begins, then all voices enter at *omnis* (all).

Alleluia,
praise the Lord,

Choir 3 (low voices), then Choirs 1, 2, and 3 in succession.

SECTION 2

benedicant Dominum, omnes gentes,
bless the Lord, all peoples,

Again, Choir 1 begins and all voices enter at *omnes.*

collaudantes eum,
praising Him all together,

Alleluia,

Exactly as the first *Alleluia.*

SECTION 3

quia fecit nobiscum Dominus misericordiam suam,
because the mercy of the Lord has shown upon us

Choir 2 begins, Choirs 1 and 3 together, then all voices.

Alleluia,

Exactly as the first *Alleluia,*

SECTION 4

Et captivam duxit captivitatem, admirabilis et gloriosus in saecula.
He led captivity captive, this admirable and glorious one)

Choir 3 begins, then Choirs 2, 1, 2, and 3 with short phrases on *captivitatem. Gloriosus* sung in fanfarelike bursts.

Alleluia.

As at the first, but with a short extention to add finality.

ARCANGELO CORELLI · *CONCERTO GROSSO* IN G MINOR, OP. 6, NO. 8., MVT. 4, "PASTORALE" (pub. 1714)

This concerto grosso is in three sections, ABA', and uses two violins and a *basso continuo* for the *concertino*, with strings for the main body of the orchestra.

A

Concertino	Simple, lilting tune in 12/8 by the solo violins, accompanied by long notes in the string orchestra (imitating bagpipes?).
Ripieno	The orchestra concludes the opening section, then repeats the soloists' material.
Concertino	High but downward-pointing melodic sequence (series of similar phrases).
Ripieno	The orchestra finishes the *Concertino* section, then continues with its own statement of the music.
Concertino	High, slow, drooping violin notes, again with the phrase finished by the orchestra.
Ripieno	Orchestra continues in minor, ending the section with dramatic pauses.

B

Ripieno and *Concertino*	The full orchestra alternates loud and soft passages, interrupted by *concertino* passages.

A'

	A shortened version of the **A'** theme using only the first four divisions (**CRCR**).

ISTENING GUIDE  & CD

HENRY PURCELL · "THY HAND, BELINDA" AND "WHEN I AM LAID
IN EARTH" (DIDO'S LAMENT), FROM *DIDO
AND AENEAS* (1689)

RECITATIVE

Thy hand, Belinda! darkness shades me,	Dido sings to her handmaid, with only a *basso continuo* accompaniment.
On thy bosom let me rest.	Free rhythm, very emotional.
More I would, but death invades me.	
Death is now a welcome guest!	

When I am laid, am laid in earth, may my wrongs create no trouble in thy breast.	The ten-note ground (bass melody) is stated alone, then starts again as Dido sings. This vocal section repeats in most editions of this work.
Remember me, remember me, but ah! forget my fate.	This section is also repeated, then the aria concludes with a fully orchestrated playing of the ground.

The opera concludes with the polyphonic chorus of angels singing "With drooping wings, ye cupids come and scatter roses on her tomb."

LISTENING GUIDE

                                                        ▣ & CD

ANTONIO VIVALDI · "SPRING," FROM *IL QUATRO STAGIONE* (*THE FOUR SEASONS*), "ALLEGRO"

Tutti   Strongly rhythmic passage by the full orchestra with echoing loud and soft phrases.

Solo   Actually a violin trio picturing the songs of birds.

Tutti   A shortened version of the first *tutti*, leading directly into pictures of gentle zephyrs, another brief version of the first *tutti*, then a thunderstorm begins.

Solo   The solo violin enters with lightninglike flashes during the "thunderstorm."

Tutti   Very short modified version of the opening material, in minor.

Solo   The bird songs return.

Tutti   The "Zephyr" material of the second *tutti* returns.

Solo   Akin to the "Zephyr" music of the second *tutti*.

Tutti   Shortened version of the opening section, first loud, then soft.

LISTENING GUIDE

& CD

**J. S. BACH · CANTATA NO. 140, *WACHET AUF, RUFT UNS DIE STIMME*
(WAKE UP, A VOICE CALLS US), MVT 1 (1731)**

While listening to Movement 1, "Wachet auf," notice three musical components:

Wachet auf, ruft uns die Stimme
(Wake, awake, cries out the voice

der Wächter sehr hoch auf der Zinne,
the watchman high in the tower,

wach auf, du Stadt Jerusalem!
Wake up, you city of Jerusalem!

Mitternacht heisst diese Stunde;
This is the midnight hour;

sie rufen uns mit hellem Munde:
they cry to us with bright voices:

wo seid ihr klugen Jungfrauen? (etc.)
where are your wise virgins?)

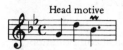ISTENING GUIDE  & CD

J. S. BACH · FUGUE IN G MINOR ("LITTLE")

Three-note head motive (quarter notes)

Downward melody

Downward melody of eight notes (eighth notes)

Oscillating figure

Upward oscillating figure (sixteenth notes)

Complete fugue subject, voice 1

As voice 1 finishes with the subject, a few rapid notes lead into . . .

Following voice 2's presentation of the subject, there is an extended passage — the *codetta* — with free counterpoint. Soon voice 3 enters in the bass clef in the original key, voice 2 continues with the countersubject, and voice 1 presents new material.

In a passage exactly like the original entrance of voice 2, the deep, solid answer is presented in the pedal keyboard.

Pedals

LISTENING GUIDE   ■■ & CD

W. A. MOZART · SYMPHONY NO. 40 IN G MINOR, K. 550, MVT. 4,
ALLEGRO ASSAI (VERY FAST) (1788)

EXPOSITION

A   A fast, frantic upward melody (a typical "rocket theme") in G minor;
no introduction.

Bridge   A long passage stringing out the A theme.

B   A gentler melody, in B-flat major, played softly first by the violins, next
by the clarinet, then varied.

DEVELOPMENT

The first seven notes of the A theme are altered and revised in a jagged, almost
frenetic passage, interrupted by fragments of the B theme. This reworking of the
A theme continues throughout the Development.

RECAPITULATION

A   Returns much like the first statement.

Bridge   Again, stringing out material from the A theme.

B   Also returns, but in the original minor key.

CODETTA

Abrupt, loud, very fast passage for the full orchestra leading to the final chords.

ISTENING GUIDE  & CD

F. J. HAYDN · *SYMPHONY NO. 94 IN G MAJOR ("SURPRISE"),*
MVT. 2, ANDANTE (moving, going) (1791)

Theme   The little tune, consisting of two almost identical halves, has a certain folk song quality, a desirable trait in theme and variation because the listener has only one chance to learn the tune before being plunged into its variation.

Variation 1   The melody remains almost unchanged, but now violin I traces a filigree countermelody above the main melody.

Variation 2   The tonality changes from C major to C minor, and in the second half of the melody it temporarily jumps to the key of A-flat major.

Variation 3   The violins double the number of notes in the melody while the flute and oboe weave a new countermelody.

Variation 4   The woodwinds and brasses state the theme, then the violins play a more sharply rhythmic version.

Codetta   The basic melody returns in the oboe, the flute joins in, and the work concludes gently.

 **LISTENING GUIDE**

 & CD

LUDWIG VAN BEETHOVEN · STRING QUARTET IN C MINOR,
OP. 18, NO. 4, MVT. 4, "RONDO"
(*ALLEGRO*) (fast) (1798)

A	Very rapid running notes, in C minor, reminiscent of a gypsy violinist.
B	A slower, songlike melody in A-flat major.
A	A virtual repeat of the opening **A** section.
C	Upward bursts of notes in (in order) cello, viola, violin II and I.
A	The gypsy song returns (**A**).
B	An almost identical repeat of the first **B** section.
A	The gypsy song returns, but much faster.
Codetta	A downward rush, some high repeated notes, then the upward bursts (borrowed from **C**) finish the movement.

LISTENING GUIDE

LUDWIG VAN BEETHOVEN · *VIOLIN SONATA NO. 9 IN A MAJOR,*
OP. 47 ("KREUTZER"), MVT. 1
(1802–1803) [first 3:30]

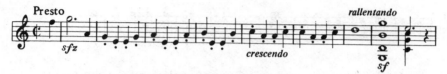

Introduction	Solo violin, often using double stops, followed by a somber piano section, then both together.
A	Fast, short, agitated upward melodies by both instruments.
B	Slower, almost folklike theme, dominated at first by the violin.
(Continuation)	Both themes are taken apart and reworked during the development and recapitulation.

ISTENING GUIDE & CD

ROBERT SCHUMANN · "DIE ROSE, DIE LILIE, DIE TAUBE, DIE SONNE" (1840)

Munter (Lively)

Die Ro - se, die Li - lie, die Tau - be, die Son - ne, die liebt' ich einst al - le in Lie - bes - won - ne.

a *Die Rose, die Lilie, die Taube, die Sonne,*
(The rose, the lily, the dove, the sun,
Die liebt' ich einst alle in Liebeswonne.
I loved them all once with an ecstatic love.

Headlong rush, starting before the piano.

a *Ich lieb' sie nicht mehr, ich liebe alleine*
I love them no more, I only love
Die Kleine, die Feine, die Reine, die Eine;
The Little One, the Dainty One, The Pure One, the One;

b *Sie selber, aller Liebe Wonne,*
She alone, of all love's delight,
Ist Rose und Lilie und Taube und Sonne.
Is rose and lily and dove and sun.
Ich liebe alleine Die Kleine, die Feine, die Reine, die Eine . . . die Eine.
I only love the Little One, the Dainty One, the Pure One, the One . . . the One.)

Upward melody.

For emphasis, repeats some earlier text. Finishes completely out of breath, as the piano continues its accompanying figure, ending with two loud chords.

LISTENING GUIDE

ROBERT SCHUMANN · "IM WUNDERSCHÖNEN MONAT MAI"
(1840)

Im wun - der-schö-ne Mo-nat Mai,   als al - le Knos - pen spring-en,   da

ist in mei - nem Herz-en   die Lie - be auf - ge -gang-en.

A		Piano introduction.
B		
a	*Im wunderschönen Monat Mai,* (In the beautiful month of May, *Als alle Knospen sprangen,* When all the leafbuds were opening,	Simple, expressive. Similar to first line.
b	*Da ist in meinem Herzen* Then in my heart *Die Liebe aufgegangen.* The Love broke forth.	Upward melody, building tension, ending as if "breaking forth."
A		Piano interlude same as the Introduction.
B		
a	*Im wunderschönen Monat Mai,* In the beautiful month of May, *Als alle Vögel sangen,* As all the birds were singing,	Exactly the same melodic structure as the first vocal section.
b	*Da hab' ich ihr gestanden* Then to her I confessed *Mein Sehnen und Verlangen.* My yearning and desire.)	
A		Postlude same as the Introduction and Interlude, trailing off into nothing.

LISTENING GUIDE 📼 & CD

ROBERT SCHUMANN · "BLINDMAN'S BLUFF," FROM
KINDERSCENEN, OP. 15 (1838)

.15 Upward rushing melody, first section repeated. Then, downward melody in the same spirit. Much like a *moto perpetuo* (perpetual motion) or a fast round.

.26 Same melody again, but without the repeated first section.

.32 Shortened version of the melody.

HECTOR BERLIOZ · "DIES IRAE," FROM *REQUIEM (GRANDE MESSE DES MORTS)* (1837, revised twice later)

Introduction

Low strings, slow and soft, like a plainchant.

Dies irae, dies illa,
(Day of wrath, day of judgment,
solvet saeclum in favilla,
when this age shall melt to ashes,
teste David cum Sibylla.
testified of David by the Sibyl.

Sopranos sing softly, gently accompanied by orchestra. Basses, then tenors in two parts, followed by all three voices on the full text.

Interlude

Full orchestra, animated.

Quantus tremor est futurus,
How great the trembling in the future,
quando Judex est venturus,
when that Judge shall come like the wind,
cuncta stricte discussurus!
on whose sentence everyone depends!

Tempo doubled, basses sing the *Dies Irae* melody, Sopranos on a single note, Tenors repeated accented statements of *Dies irae, dies illa.*

Interlude

Full orchestra as before.

Quantus tremor est futurus, (etc.)
How great the trembling.)

Full chorus, very loud, with agitated sounds from the orchestra.

Interlude

Three measures similar to the first Interlude, then the four brass bands enter from four corners of the hall.

FRANZ LISZT · HUNGARIAN RHAPSODY NO. 2 (1847)

Lassan

Introduction   Slow, deliberate, like a fanfare or roll on a drum.

Lassan   A leisurely, seductive, almost arrogant *molto espressivo* dance, with three interruptions for brilliant, free *glissandos* much like a gypsy instrumentalist. The accompaniment is marked *l'accompagnamento pesante* (peasantlike accompaniment). The *Lassan* melody comes back twice more before ending with material similar to the Introduction.

Friska

Friska   Several sections, strongly rhythmic, beginning *pp* (very soft) and *vivace* (very fast), with a hopping, dotted rhythm. Several Liszt trademarks are used, including repeated trumpetlike notes, brilliant octaves, and fast chromatic passages. The work ends *prestissimo* (extremely fast) with the hands alternating octaves, followed by a pause, three slow, strong chords, then three fast, accented concluding chords.

LISTENING GUIDE

📼 & CD

MODEST MUSSORGSKY · "THE GREAT GATE AT KIEV," FROM *PICTURES AT AN EXHIBITION*
(1874; orchestral version, 1923)

Great Gate processional theme

A	A stately, dignified procession through the Great Gate, for full orchestra, loudly, with the brass stating the theme, which is then extended.
A	Repeat of the main theme, even louder.
B	Suddenly soft. Ancient Russian hymn played by the woodwinds imitating an organ.
A	Return of the procession played by the brass, while the strings play faster scale passages.
B	Slavonic chant, again played softly by the woodwinds.
Interlude	Bells (from the chapel of the Great Gate) sound, then the brasses play the melody of the Promenade (from earlier in the set) as the strings again play scales.
A	A triumphal ending for full orchestra using the orginal processional theme.

LISTENING GUIDE

 & CD

GIUSEPPE VERDI · "LIBIAMO," FROM *LA TRAVIATA* (1853)

Li - bia - mo, li-bia-mo ne' lie - ti ca - li-ci, che la__ bel-lez-za__ in - fio - ra;

Introduction

Orchestra, *allegretto* (moderately quick), with a bright waltz rhythm.

VIOLETTA

a   *Libiamo, libiamo ne' lieti calici,*
We find abandonment in this cup,
che la bellezza infiora;
which is the most beautiful flower;

The same melody as presented by the orchestra, ornamented and flowing.

a   *e la fuggevol, fuggevol ora*
it is a fleeting, fleeting hour
s'innebrii a voluttà.
it is an intoxicating delight.

b   *Libiam ne' dolci fremiti*
With sweet ecstasy of abandonment
che suscita l'amore,
let us drink to love,

b'   *poichè quell'occhio al core*
since such glances of the heart
onnipotente va.
overwhelm us.

a   *Libiamo, amor fra' calici*
Love and abandonment in the cup
più caldi baci avrà.
with many warm kisses.

SOLOISTS AND CHORUS

Ah! libiam, amor fra calici
Ah! love and abandonment in the cup
più caldi baci avrà.
with many warm kisses.

A rousing echo of Violetta's last phrase.

VIOLETTA	Violetta repeats her solo with more emphasis on friendship and happiness but with snide references to the fleeting quality of love.
SOLOISTS AND CHORUS	Everyone sings in unison, urging a night of revelry and wine.
VIOLETTA AND ALFREDO	The two lovers alternate phrases, then sing together of the joys of the evening. The chorus joins quietly, then all get gradually louder as they sing, "Let us enjoy every moment until the dawn."

LISTENING GUIDE

☐☐ & CD

RICHARD WAGNER · "RIDE OF THE VALKYRIES," FROM *DIE WALKÜRE* (1870)

Ride of the Valkyries

Valkyries' war cry

Introduction		Agitated high string sounds, then low brass accents.
A	**a**	High brass present the Valkyries motive, which is then repeated to end in a new key. Fragments of the motive are developed into a fanfare.
	a'	Full brass on the motive, shorter section.
	b	Low brass, with downward rushes by the strings playing the Valkyries' war cry.
	a'	Brass repeat the Valkyries theme, ending with held sounds.
B		Sudden explosions, with trembling woodwinds, lightning flashes, and thunder.
A'	**a**	Return of the Valkyries theme in brass, with the sound of quavering woodwinds. Lightning flashes in the high instruments.
	a'	Final presentation of the Valkyries theme, very loud.

LISTENING GUIDE

& CD

GABRIEL FAURÉ · "IN PARADISUM," FROM *MESSE DE REQUIEM*
(1887)

In pa - ra - di - sum   De - du - cant an - ge - li,

FIRST SECTION

In paradisum deducant angeli;
(In paradise may the angels receive you;
in tuo adventu suscipiant te martyres,
at your coming may the martyrs receive you,
te perducant te in civitatem sanctam Jerusalem.
And lead you into the Holy City of Jerusalem.

Serene, high oscillating piping and chiming accompaniment, as the sopranos sing the slow, seraphic, translucent melody. The rest of the voices enter on the word *Jerusalem.*

SECOND SECTION

Chorus angelorum te suscipiat,
There may the choir of angels receive you,
et cum Lazaro quondam paupere,
And with Lazarus, once a beggar,
aeternam habeas requiem.
may you have eternal rest.)

The silver chiming of angelic bells continues as the sopranos sing the melody. Again, the full chorus enters only on *requiem,* and then repeats the final phrase as the angelic chiming fades away.

ISTENING GUIDE   & CD

CLAUDE DEBUSSY · "LA CATHÉDRALE ENGLOUTIE," NO. 10
FROM *PRÉLUDES*, BOOK 1 (1910)

0:00   Gentle, almost random chiming, a wide range that narrows to four single notes, then expands. Two chords lead to . . .

0:50   Muttered low drone builds tension under harmonic chiming, building to . . .

1:29   Sounds similar to the opening, but fuller, louder, and more accented.

1:50   Chiming develops into a more melodic polyphonic section, first loud, then softer.

2:36   Single melody, developing to two-part, then fully harmonic.

3:47   Low rumbling drone section, with opening chimelike sounds, ending with a melody beginning in mid-range and moving upward. The misty chords gradually drift away.

ISTENING GUIDE   📼 & CD

ANTONÍN DVOŘÁK · *SLAVONIC DANCE NO.* 8, OP. 46 (1878)

A   Sections of strongly accented *hemiola* rhythms alternating with bouncy, peasantlike dance music, the first half of the melody in minor, the second half almost identical but in major.

B   Lyrical song by the oboe over muttering strings.

A   Sudden repeat of the opening material.

Coda   A very short version of the **B** material, ending with a single explosion of the **A** motive.

LISTENING GUIDE

& CD

MAURICE RAVEL · *PAVANE FOR A DEAD PRINCESS*
(orchestral version) (1899)

A   Horn over *pizzicato* (plucked) strings. Two phrases divided by a harp glissando.

B   Two phrases, the first featuring the woodwinds, the second muted strings.

A   Similar to the first **A** section, with woodwinds playing the melody.

C   In minor, with various instruments on an upward-reaching melody.

A   Similar to the second **A** section, with added harp accents.

LISTENING GUIDE

📼 & CD

ARNOLD SCHOENBERG · "MONDESTRUNKEN" (MOONDRUNK),
FROM *PIERROT LUNAIRE*, OP. 21, for flute,
violin, cello, piano, and reciter (1912)

Den Wein, den man mit Augen trinkt
(The wine that only eyes can drink
Giesst Nachts der Mond in Wogen nieder,
Pours nightly in waves from the
moon,
Und eine Springflut überschwemmt
And a Springtide flood inundates
Den stillen Horizont.
The quiet horizon.

Light, dancelike piano and flute, then
other instruments, all in their upper
register.

A sudden accent on "Springtide
flood."

Gelüste schauerlich und süss,
Desires, dreadful and sweet,
Durchschwimmen ohne Zahl die Fluten!
Swim through flutes without measure!
Den Wein, den man mit Augen trinkt,
The wine that only eyes can drink,
Giesst Nachts der Mond in Wogen nieder.
Pours nightly in waves from the
moon.

Flute and violin introduce the second
stanza. All instruments still in the upper register.

Der Dichter, den die Andacht triebt,
The poet, under the impulse of piety,
Berauscht sich an dem heilgen Tranke,
Gets befuddled on the holy drink;
Den Himmel wendet er verzückt
He tilts backward toward heaven
*Das Haupt und taumelnd saugt und
schlüret er*
His head, and sucks and sips
Den Wein, den man mit Augen trinkt.
The wine that only eyes can drink.)

Suddenly louder and more agitated
with the piano pounded.

Lighter on "heaven," ending with
light, ethereal mistlike sounds.

 ISTENING GUIDE

& CD

GEORGE ANTHEIL · *BALLET MÉCHANIQUE* (1924, revised 1954)

0:00 Strict rhythm in tympani, followed immediately by the piano introducing the main "melodic" and rhythmic material.

0:25 Tympani and xylophone develop the main musical material.

0:55 Tympani roll into strong piano accents, xylophone dies away.

1:25 Piano alone, strong rhythms, nonmelodic.

2:35 Xylophone added to mostly piano material.

2:50 Xylophone, tympani dominate, then other instruments added.

3:35 Over a tympani roll, nonpredictable rhythms by other instruments.

4:05 The work continues with similar sounds.

 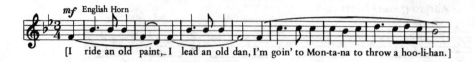

VIRGIL THOMSON · "CATTLE," FROM THE ORCHESTRAL SUITE
THE PLOW THAT BROKE THE PLAINS (1936)

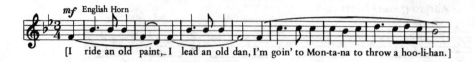

[I ride an old paint, I lead an old dan, I'm goin' to Mon-ta-na to throw a hoo-li-han.]

A English horn (alto oboe) on "I Ride an Old Paint."

B Clarinet, different key, "Laredo."

A English horn, clarinet, English horn, with guitar.

B Flute and guitar with faster notes. Then banjo, clarinet, oboe, flute, with *um-pa-pa* accompaniment, *crescendo.*

A Full orchestra, loud-soft-loud.

B Orchestra, strings predominate.

A Trumpets loud, then soft, then strings and percussion.

B English horn, flute, full orchestra, English horn that dies away.

AARON COPLAND · "HOE-DOWN," MVT. 4 FROM *RODEO* (1942)

- The band tunes up, followed by a quieter section but still with strong rhythms.
- Sudden repetition of the opening music with a fiddle tune added.
- Trumpet, oboe, and fiddle alternate with the fiddle tune, then the full orchestra enters with the same tune.
- After a sudden stop, the percussion and other instruments play an accompanying figure as they gradually slow and stop.
- Sudden repetition of the opening music.

HENRY COWELL · *THE BANSHEE* (1925)

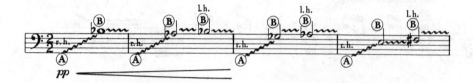

The Banshee is played on the open strings of the piano, the player standing at the crook. Another person must sit at the keyboard and operate the damper pedal throughout the composition. The whole work should be played an octave lower than written. R.H. stands for "right hand"; L.H. stands for "left hand." Different ways of playing the strings are indicated by a letter over each tone, as follows:

- Ⓐ indicates a sweep with the flesh of the finger from the lowest string up to the note given
- Ⓑ sweep lengthwise along the string of the note given with the flesh of finger

LISTENING GUIDE

&CD

KRZYSZTOF PENDERECKI · *THRENODY FOR THE VICTIMS OF HIROSHIMA,* opening 3:10 (1960)

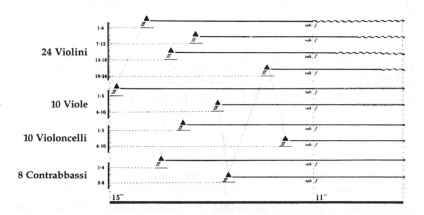

0:00 Extremely high screeches on the stringed instruments bowed right next to the fingers to form tone clusters. Diminishes.

0:47 *Pizzicato* (plucked) lower strings enter, high screaming pitches continue, solo instruments play brief two-, three-, and four-note "melodies." Gradually dies away.

1:45 Mid-range single tone forms, *pizzicato* notes gradually stop.

2:10 Low notes drift into a single tone, then drop a half-step.

2:20 Single tones blossom into discordant bursts of sound.

2:30 Repeated, very high.

3:00 High whine appears. The work continues.

LEONARD BERNSTEIN · *CHICHESTER PSALMS*, MVT. 1 (1965)

Awake, harp and lyre! I will arouse the dawn!	Stately opening chorale-like passage using a text from Psalm 108:2.
Make a joyful noise to the Lord, all the earth. Serve the Lord with gladness; come before his presence with joyful songs. (etc.)	Loud, joyful, dancelike setting of Psalm 100 in highly accented 7/4 meter.
For the Lord is good, his mercy endures forever And his truth continues for all generations.	Bellike instrumental section introducing three vocal soloists.
Awake, harp and lyre! I will arouse the dawn!	The chorus enters briefly just before a loud, abrupt ending.

LISTENING GUIDE

📼 & CD

HEITER VILLA-LOBOS · *BACHIANAS BRASILEIRAS, NO. 5* for eight
cellos and soprano solo (1938–1945)

Introduction	Brief passage for *pizzicato* (plucked) cellos.
A	Soaring, wordless vocalise for soprano, with a solo cello paralleling the voice, but lower. Remaining cellos *pizzicato*.
A	Solo cello repeats the melody over *pizzicato* cellos.
B	Chantlike passage by soprano over rich harmonic cello foundation.
A	Repeat of the first A section.

LISTENING GUIDE

●● & CD

THE JAVANESE (SUNDANESE) GAMELAN · *BOPONG*

Bopong uses three musical components:
1. Continuous high, flute-like, highly ornamented chirpings.
2. Low to mid-range soft gongs, usually slow to medium speed.
3. High, brassy, chiming xylophones, generally fast and interrupting.

The gongs and flutes use a heterophonous texture with the gongs slower, the flutes faster and much more ornamented.

The brassy xylophones are mostly limited to swift, jangling, unpredictable interjections of very rapid notes, almost as if trying to interrupt the musical flow. They are actually marking the musical phrases. Under it all, the sauntering, majestic gongs keep up a placid, constantly evolving melody consisting of three slow notes followed by faster, higher tones.

Midway through, the gongs settle into a repeated 8- or 9-note melody. Twenty seconds before the end, all instruments change to a new, faster melody in unison.

BESSIE JONES · "BEGGIN' THE BLUES" (c. 1920)

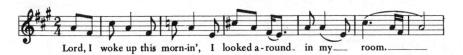

Lord, I woke up this mornin', I looked a-round in my room.

I woke up this mornin', I looked around in my room,
Well, I woke up this mornin' an' I looked around in my room,
I said, "Hello, blues, what you doin' in here so soon."

I knowed it was the blues, 'cause I heard him walkin' in my room,
I knowed it was the blues, 'cause I heard him walkin' in my room,
Lord, I wonder what's the matter, 'cause the blues won't leave me alone.

O the blues jumped a rabbit, run him a solid mile,
O the blues jumped a rabbit, run him a solid mile,
And the rabbit turned over and cried like a nachul chile.

He cried, "Blues, blues, you follow me everywhere,"
He cried, "Blues, blues, you follow me everywhere,
I don't know what's the matter, the blues jus' won't let me be."

LISTENING GUIDE

BOB NOLAN AND THE SONS OF THE PIONEERS ·
"CHANT OF THE WANDERER" (1946)

Introduction

Take a look at the sky where the
whippoorwill trills;
At the mountain so high where the
cataract spills.
Take a look at the falls and the rippling rills;
Hear the wanderer's call from the
whispering hills,

Fast, slow, fast.
Bob Nolan solo.

Other voices enter.

CHORUS

The rippling rills,
The cataract spills,
The whippoorwill trills

Solo high tenor on a single yodel note,
as others sing twice.

Let me live on the range where the
tumbleweeds grow;
Let the silver sands change where the
prairie winds blow;
Let the wanderers sing where the
wanderers go.
Let the melody ring, for it's happy I
know.

CHORUS

The wanderers go,
The prairie winds blow,
The tumbleweeds go.

[Third stanza all instrumental, with flute on the high tenor note.]

[Fourth stanza similar to first two.]

 **LISTENING GUIDE** 📼 & CD

LUDWIG VAN BEETHOVEN • *SYMPHONY NO. 5 IN C MINOR, OP. 67, MVT. 1, ALLEGRO CON BRIO (1807–1808)*

EXPOSITION

Theme A

A   Famous four-note motive, dot-dot-dot-dahhhh, then repeated and held.

        Sequential treatment of the four-note motive, which is then expanded into a six-note version by the French horns (sometimes called a "Bridge Theme") to give a feeling of finality before the B theme.

Theme B

B   Short, lyrical, folklike theme, accompanied by versions of the four-note motive. This theme is given little attention before the return of the more important and dramatic A theme after a full stop by the orchestra.

DEVELOPMENT

A   As at the beginning, except a slow oboe cadenza replaces the third held note.

B   As before, except in a new key. The Recapitulation stays very close to the original version in the Exposition.

CODA

Directly into the coda without stopping from the Recapitulation, with an altered version of the Bridge Theme and a new march-like tune, ending with a strong, rhythmic, defiant, fist-shaking conclusion.

AARON COPLAND • *FANFARE FOR THE COMMON MAN* (1942–1943)

0:00   Strong, explosive accents by the tympani and cymbals, sounding almost improvised

0:25   Three trumpets present the theme, which features a bugle-like three-note head motive, ending with three loud tympani strokes

0:56   High brass in two parts, interrupted by two tympani strokes

1:29   Explosive percussion, again sounding improvised

1:40   Three-note head motive in low brass, followed by the high brass, with the tympani imitating the head motive

2:06   Full chords, punctuated by the tympani

2:22   The main theme for full brass, punctuated by tympani explosions

FREDERIC CHOPIN • *SHERZO IN E MAJOR, OP. 54* (1843)

The word *scherzo* ("joke," or "game") is particularly apropos to this work. The entire eleven-minute composition has an impish, elflike flavor, with rapid changes of "altitude," as if a water sprite were flying from place to place on the piano. The melody and the connecting material is always very fast and unpredictable. Often it appears to be made up on the spot. There are five easily identified bits of musical material:

A	Opening four-note melody with a held chord
B	Altered, harmonized version of opening material
Chordal Arch	A fast, harmonized "arch" in the right hand
Slow Melodic Arch	Half melody, half harmonized
Fast Melodic Arch	Swirls of melody, usually in an arch form

The opening minute of the work uses the following outline:

0:00	**A**	melody (four notes with chord)
0:04	**B**	altered and harmonized melody
0:08	**Chordal arch**	
0:12	**Slow melodic arch**	
0:16	**A**	harmonized
0:20	**B**	as at the first
0:23	**Chordal arch**	
0:27	**Slow melodic arch**	
0:31	**Fast melodic arch**	
0:34	A version of the **slow melodic arch**	
0:38	**Fast melodic arch**	
0:42	Another version of the **slow melodic arch**	
0:47	**Fast melodic arch**, extended	
0:52	Chordal punctuation	
0:58	Fast melodic section, ending at . . .	
1:02	Strong chord, after which the work continues	

CHARLES IVES · "AT THE RIVER" (1916)

Ives's version, approx. 1:20 min.

original ending of "Shall We Gather at the River"

Piano introduction   Drifting, dreamlike harmonies.

1. Shall we gather at the river,   The traditional hymn melody, until
2. Where bright angel feet have "by the throne of God," where the
   trod, melody is altered.
3. With its crystal tide forever
4. Growing by the throne of God   The piano accompaniment is very independent.
5. . . . gather at the river?   The voice is meditative, remembering other times.
6. Yes, we'll gather at the river,   Traditional melody, with chiming
7. The beautiful, the beautiful river, sounds from the piano
8. Yes, we'll gather at the river accompaniment.
9. That flows by the throne of God   Line 9 similar to line 4.

Brief piano interlude

10. Shall we gather . . . shall we   Meditative, similar to line 5, as the
    gather at the river? sounds drift away.

APPENDIX

BRIEF BIOGRAPHICAL DATA ON THE MAJOR CULTURAL FIGURES OF WESTERN CIVILIZATION

Showing Differences in Class, Sex, and Religious Beliefs. Keyed to Matthews and Platt's The Western Humanities.

THE ANCIENT WORLD

Mesopotamia/Egypt [Chapter 1]

Few names of creative geniuses survive from Mesopotamia or Egypt; those that do, such as Enheduanna, the first known author in the world and composer of *The Exaltation of Inanna,* and Imhotep, the designer of Egypt's Step Pyramid, appear to be members of the ruling elite.

Greece [Chapters 2–4]

In Greece, the ruling elite was at first defined narrowly: Greek males living in a particular polis. By 500 B.C. citizenship had become more democratic, with the franchise opened up to new classes, so that all free Greek males, 18–21 years old or older, were given the vote—but only within a specific polis. After 334 B.C. another significant change occurred when the Greek world fell under Macedonia's sway; thereafter, in the Macedonian empire and the successor Hellenistic kingdoms, the self-governing polis came to an end, but society grew more diverse as Greeks intermingled with Orientals, Persians, Jews, Egyptians, and Celts.

Aeschylus (about 525–about 456 B.C.), an Athenian aristocrat; one of the founders of the literary genre tragedy.

Anaxagoras (about 500–428 B.C.), a citizen of the Greek polis of Clazomenae in Asia Minor; lived and taught philosophy in Athens until he was charged with impiety by city officials and forced into exile; an important philosopher who influenced Socrates.

Aristophanes (about 445–about 388 B.C.), probably a rich Athenian landowner; the founder of Old Comedy, the earliest type of stage comedy in the West.

Aristotle (384–322 B.C.), a Macedonian Greek, son of the court physician to the rough-living Macedonian court; tutor to Alexander, who later became ruler of the Macedonian empire; studied philosophy in Athens under Plato and eventually set up his own school; the founder of Aristotelianism; a second-class citizen in Athens.

Carneades (about 214–129 B.C.), a Greek philosopher in the Hellenistic Age; born in Cyrene, North Africa, of a wealthy family; driven from Rome because his critical perspective was deemed subversive; a founder of Skepticism.

Democritus (about 460 B.C.–?), a wealthy citizen of Thrace; made important contributions to the atomic theory of the universe.

Diogenes (about 412–about 323 B.C.), a Greek; a social rebel who chose to live as a beggar; the first and most famous Cynic.

Empedocles (about 484–about 424 B.C.), a Greek born in Sicily; an important pre-Socratic thinker who influenced Aristotle.

Epicurus (about 342–270 B.C.), a prosperous Athenian citizen who lived the first half (thirty-five years) of his life outside Athens; the founder of the Epicurean philosophy.

Euripides (about 480–406 B.C.), a social rebel who was indicted on a charge of impiety by his fellow Athenians; probably of middle-class origins; a playwright; one of the founders of the literary genre tragedy.

Galen (about A.D. 130–about 201), Greek anatomist, physiologist, and physician in Rome; author of about 500 books covering nearly all aspects of ancient medicine; works were preserved by Arab scholars; filled with information unknown to European doctors, Galen's works were accepted uncritically in the Middle Ages.

Heraclitus (about 545–about 485 B.C.), a prosperous citizen of the Greek polis of Ephesus in Asia Minor; one of the leading pre-Socratic thinkers and the author of the first dialectical type of reasoning.

Herodotus (about 484–about 430 B.C.), a prosperous citizen of the Greek polis of Halicarnassus in Asia Minor; lived in exile in Athens after a failed revolt forced him from his home city; the founder of the West's tradition of secular history.

Homer (about 800 B.C.), by tradition, a blind Greek poet; the author of the first books of Western literature, the *Iliad* and *Odyssey*.

Menander (about 343–about 291 B.C.), a rich Greek of upper-class family; a dramatist; the supreme poet of New Comedy, the last phase of Greek stage comedy.

Parmenides (about 515 B.C.–?), a citizen of Elea, a Greek polis in southern Italy; one of the important pre-Socratic thinkers.

Plato (about 427–347 B.C.), a member of a distinguished Athenian family; one of Greece's most important philosophers and the founder of Platonism.

Praxiteles (active in Athens from about 375 to 330 B.C.), a member of a family of Greek sculptors; the artist who sculpted *Hermes with the Infant Dionysus.*

Protagoras (about 481–411 B.C.), an Athenian thinker who won great fame and fortune as a teacher; forced into exile by the Athenian citizenry as a result of being convicted of impiety; the first Sophist.

Pythagoras (about 580–about 507 B.C.), a citizen of the Greek polis of Samos; settled in southern Italy, probably as a result of Samos's tyrannical government; an outstanding pre-Socratic philosopher; the founder of Pythagoreanism.

Sappho (about 600 B.C.), a female member of an aristocratic family on the Greek island of Lesbos; a poet; considered by ancient authorities to be one of the greatest lyric poets of Greece.

Socrates (about 470–399 B.C.), a citizen of Athens; though well born, he fell into poverty in his later years; condemned by his fellow Athenians for impiety and corrupting the youth by his teachings; a thinker who reoriented philosophy from the study of the natural world to a consideration of human nature.

Sophocles (about 496–406 B.C.), son of a well-placed Athenian family; one of Greece's important playwrights; the author of *Oedipus Rex* and *Antigone.*

Thales (about 585 B.C.), by tradition, a wealthy citizen of the Greek polis of Miletus in Asia Minor; the founder of European philosophy.

Theocritus (about 310–250 B.C.), a Greek from rural Sicily; flourished in Alexandria; founder of the literary genre known as the pastoral.

Thucydides (died about 401 B.C.), a member of a well-to-do Athenian family; a general during the Peloponnesian War; forced into a twenty-year exile when he failed to prevent a Spartan victory in battle; the founder of the tradition of scientific history.

Non-Christian Rome [Chapters 5 and 6]

Non-Christian Rome, during its 1,000-year history, was transformed from a tiny city-state governed by a narrowly defined elite, into a vast empire whose society was the most diverse of the ancient world. When Rome was founded, the patricians (nobles) constituted an exclusive ruling class; in 287 B.C., full citizenship was extended to the Roman plebeians, but still only to those within the small city-state. In about 80 B.C., citizenship was conferred on all free Italians up and down the Italian peninsula; and, under the Roman Empire, in A.D. 212, citizenship was given to virtually all free men throughout the vast Roman world.

Arrian (second century A.D.), a Greek noble, writer, and governor in the era of the Roman Empire; author of two manuals on Epictetus's teachings.

Catullus (about 84–about 57 B.C.), an aristocrat from northern Italy at a time when Italians enjoyed full Roman citizenship; his father was a friend of Julius Caesar; a poet.

Celsus (second century A.D.), probably a Greek aristocrat in the Roman Empire; a philosopher.

Cicero (106–43 B.C.), an Italian, i.e., a non-Roman; born before Italians were given full Roman rights; Rome's most prolific writer and the creator of the Latin language's philosophic vocabulary.

Epictetus (about A.D. 55–115), an ex-slave and freeman; physically lame as a result of an injury; a Stoic philosopher who founded a school in Asia Minor.

Horace (65–8 B.C.), the son of an ex-slave; an Italian plebeian; one of the outstanding poets of the Golden Age of Roman letters.

Juvenal (about A.D. 60–about 140), a member of a well-to-do family; forced into exile in Egypt for unknown reasons; impoverished for much of his life; returned to Rome and lived on grudging handouts from the rich; author of satirical poems.

Lucretius (about 94–about 55 B.C.), probably a Roman noble; author of *On the Nature of Things*, a poem based on Epicurean ideas.

Marcus Aurelius (A.D. 121–180), a Roman emperor who followed Stoic ideals; author of the *Meditations.*

Origen (about 185–about 254), an Egyptian Christian who was persecuted by Roman authorities; an extreme ascetic, he emasculated himself; after his death, the church condemned his writings as heretical; his works influenced later Christian writers, including Augustine and Erasmus.

Ovid (43 B.C.–about A.D. 17), an aristocrat who was forced into exile from Rome to Tomis on the Black Sea, because his poems were judged obscene by the ruler, Augustus; the finest poet of love themes in Roman letters.

Paul (about A.D. 5–about 65), an ex-Jew and a Christian during a period when both religions were persecuted in Rome; the first Christian theologian and the church's first outstanding missionary.

Plautus (about 254–184 B.C.), a plebeian and an Italian, i.e., a non-Roman; the founder of Roman Comedy.

Seneca (4 B.C.–A.D. 65), son of a teacher of rhetoric; descended from a wealthy family in Spain; the outstanding Roman intellectual of the mid–first century A.D.

Tacitus (A.D. 55?–117), a member of a family from Gaul, perhaps of Roman aristocratic background; a distinguished public career; the finest writer of history in the Latin language.

Terence (about 195–159 B.C.), a North African slave who was granted his freedom in Rome; one of Rome's two outstanding comic playwrights; his comic plays later influenced Shakespeare and Molière.

Tertullian (about 160–about 230), a Christian convert at a time when Christians were persecuted in Rome, and a North African, reflecting the growing prominence of North Africa in the third-century Roman Empire; a convert to the Christian heresy of Montanism made him anathema to orthodox Christians.

Judaism [Chapter 6]

Judaism originated outside of Greco-Roman civilization, although in the first century B.C. it passed under the hegemony of the Roman world. In early Judaism the key figures were simultaneously religious and political leaders, like Moses and David. After David and Solomon's unified Jewish state collapsed, the leading representatives of Judaism were prophets—charismatic figures whom later Jews regarded as divine emissaries. The prophets, by definition, were outsiders in Jewish society, since they condemned the wealthy and powerful and sided with the poor and downtrodden.

Christian Rome [Chapter 7]

In A.D. 311, after a decade-long attempt to stamp out Christianity had failed, then-emperor Constantine extended toleration to all Christians, thus inaugurating a new era in Roman history. By A.D. 400 the Christian religion was adopted as the official faith of the empire and the old polytheistic religions were legislated out of existence.

Ambrose (about 340–397), a Christian from Gaul; his career as bishop of Milan reflects the ethnic diversity of the late Roman world.

Antony (about 250–about 350), an Egyptian who was one of the first Christian monks.

Arius (about 250–about 336), a Greek priest in Alexandria; his teachings on the Trinity were condemned as heretical by the church in 325.

Athanasius (about 296–373), a Greek Christian who helped establish the church's doctrine of the Trinity.

Augustine (354–430), a North African; became a Christian in late pagan Rome; a church father.

Eusebius (about 260–about 340), a Greek Christian; lived through the Great Persecution; the founder of the literary genre of church history.

Jerome (about 340–420), a Christian writer from Dalmatia (modern Yugoslavia); his career reflects the ethnic diversity of late Rome; translator of the Greek Bible into Latin; a church father.

Pachomius (about 280–about 346), an Egyptian Christian; a founder of one of the first Christian monasteries.

Ulfilas (about 311–about 382), descended from Cappadocians who were captured by the Goths; converted to a heretical form of Christianity (Arianism); his translations of Christian scriptures into German (Gothic) were the first written works in the German language.

MEDIEVAL EUROPE

The Middle Ages [Chapters 8–10]

From the start of the Middle Ages until around 1400, European society was highly feudalized and was dominated by the feudal nobility and ecclesiastical leaders. Between 1400 and 1500 there were some changes, as feudal society began to decline and the earliest stage of commercial capitalism emerged. Untitled owners of large estates and prosperous merchants and businessmen in the larger cities now joined feudal lords and church leaders as members of the ruling elite. The status of skilled artisans and craftspeople, primarily in the arts, also improved, but their position in society remained below that of the dominant groups.

Abelard (1079–1142), son of a Breton knight; castrated for having seduced his female pupil Heloise; embraced monasticism; solved the problem of universals, the intellectual controversy that dominated thought in the early twelfth century.

Alcuin of York (735–804), lived fifty years in Yorkshire, England, where he headed the York cathedral school for many years; at Charlemagne's invitation settled in Aachen (modern Germany) as head of the palace school; the foremost scholar of the Carolingian Renaissance.

Thomas Aquinas (1226–1274), son of a noble Italian family; a Dominican friar; some of his ideas were condemned after his death; the dominant intellectual of the thirteenth century.

Roger Bacon (about 1220–1292), member of a wealthy English family; a Franciscan friar and university professor; near the end of his life he was imprisoned briefly at the command of his fellow friars who questioned some of his teachings; an early exponent of the experimental method in science.

Bede (673–735), an Anglo-Saxon monk; entered a monastery at age seven; the author of the earliest history of the English church.

Benedict of Nursia (480–543), born of a good Italian family; a monk and head of his monastery; the founder of the monastic rule that became the model used in Western monasticism.

Bernard of Clairvaux (1090–1153), son of Burgundian aristocrats; a monk; a central figure in Cistercian monasticism; the "uncrowned pope" of the twelfth century.

Giovanni Boccaccio (1313–1375), offspring of a Tuscan merchant who disapproved of his son's literary efforts; occasional periods of poverty throughout his life; helped to establish the modern short story.

Boethius (about 480–524), a member of a distinguished Roman family; served the Ostrogothic king Theodoric, who ruled Italy; a philosopher whose writings dominated intellectual life for much of the Middle Ages; executed in the aftermath of court intrigue.

Bonaventure (1221–1274), son of an Italian physician; a Franciscan monk and university professor; an important mystic.

Hieronymus Bosch (about 1450–1516), a painter who lived in the Dutch town of s'Hertogenbosch for his entire life; possibly acquainted with the heretical beliefs of the underground sect of Adamites; modern scholars generally rate him a stern moralist with a ferocious vision of human life.

Geoffrey Chaucer (about 1340–1400), son of a London wine merchant; courtier to English royalty; the first great writer in the English language.

Chrétien de Troyes (about 1148–about 1190), a frequenter of the court of Marie, countess of Champagne; the author of the first poetic version of the legends of Arthur and the Knights of the Round Table.

Cimabue (about 1240–1302), the last great artist in the Italo-Byzantine style.

Dante Alighieri (1265–1321), a member of the Florentine aristocracy; a government official in Florence; died in exile, having been forced from his native city-state by his political enemies; author of the outstanding literary work of the High Middle Ages.

Duns Scotus (about 1300–about 1349), a Franciscan friar; a Scottish thinker who lectured at Oxford, Paris, and Cologne universities; a major figure of the Late Middle Ages.

Meister Eckhart (about 1260–1328), a leader of the Dominican friars in Germany; some of his ideas were condemned as heretical by the pope in 1329; a great Christian mystic.

Einhard (about 770–840), of Frankish descent; a scholar and historian attached to Charlemagne's imperial court; author of the first medieval biography of a lay figure (Charlemagne).

Eleanor of Aquitaine (about 1122–1204), daughter of a distinguished family of Aquitainian nobility; queen first of France and then of England; a founder of the courtly love tradition.

Jan van Eyck (about 1370–about 1440), a Flemish painter; worked for various noble courts in northern Europe, notably that of the dukes of Burgundy; the outstanding painter in northern Europe in the early fifteenth century.

Hrotswitha (about 935–about 975), a German canoness (a nunlike vocation that did not require vows for life) at Gandersheim convent in Saxony; the first German playwright; educated in the Latin Classics.

Francis of Assisi (1182–1226), son of a wealthy Italian cloth merchant; renounced his material goods and led a life of extreme poverty; the founder of the Franciscan order of friars.

Giotto (about 1276–1337), a student of the painter Cimabue; an Italian painter; introduced a new era in Western painting.

Gregory the Great (pope 590–604), son of a distinguished Roman family; a brief career as a high-placed official; related by blood to earlier popes; one of the outstanding popes; standardized the use of music in worship services.

Gregory of Tours (about 538–593), a member of a distinguished Frankish family; a bishop and writer; the author of the only surviving contemporary history of the Merovingian kings.

Robert Grosseteste (about 1175–1253), a Franciscan friar and university professor; an English bishop; author of a scientific method that used mathematics and subjected hypotheses to repeated testings.

Guido of Arezzo (about 995–about 1050), an Italian monk; modernized music notation, an innovation that simplified the teaching of music.

Joan of Arc (1412–1431) French patriot; a peasant from Domremy, France, who helped liberate the city of Orleans in 1429, during the Hundred Years' War; she claimed to be acting with the aid of the Archangel Michael, St. Margaret, and St. Catherine; captured by the Burgundians in 1430, and sold to the English who brought her to trial on the charges of heresy and witchcraft; found guilty by the English and their French accomplices; burned at the stake; in 1456 the verdict was overturned by a papal commission and she was canonized. (See *The Western Humanities* for additional information.)

Johann Gutenberg (about 1400–about 1468), son of a patrician of Mainz; exiled to Strasbourg because of an economic dispute; rendered destitute in later years as a result of litigation; blind in old age; a German printer and inventor; the inventor of movable type.

Hildegard of Bingen (1098–1179), a German nun, from age eight, and founder and abbess, after 1136, of the Benedictine house of Rupertsberg, near Bingen; a leading figure of the High Middle Ages; corresponded with kings, emperors, popes, and other high church officials; visionary author of *Scivias*; learned in medicine, science, and poetry; composer of church music.

Jan Hus (about 1369–1415), born of poor parents in southern Bohemia (modern Czech Republic); a Czech theologian; founder of a Late Medieval heresy that foreshadowed Luther's ideas.

Thomas à Kempis (1380–1471), a member of the Congregation of Windesheim, a German monastic order; a religious reformer; author of *The Imitation of Christ*, one of the outstanding devotional works of the Middle Ages.

William Langland (about 1332–1400), an English writer, perhaps a cleric in minor orders in London; used his writings to condemn the social and economic system of his time; author of the greatest example of alliterative poetry in Middle English.

The Limbourg Brothers, Pol, Herman, and Jean (about 1385–1416), the sons of a Flemish sculptor; employed by the Duke of Burgundy; painters of the most famous illuminated manuscript of the Late Middle Ages.

Thomas Malory (flourished around 1470), an English knight and writer; author of the first prose account in English of the rise and fall of King Arthur and his court.

Marie de France (flourished about 1170), a poet from Brittany who lived most of her life in England; invented the lay, a literary genre based on Celtic legends and devoted to short tales on courtly love themes; active in post–Norman Conquest England among the French-speaking nobility, perhaps at the court of King Henry II and Eleanor of Aquitaine.

Mechthild of Magdeburg (about 1207–1282), German mystic; the author of *The Flowing Light of the Godhead*, an account of her heavenly visions; contributed to the lay piety movement of the High Middle Ages.

William of Ockham (about 1300–about 1349), an English Franciscan friar and theologian; excommunicated for his opposition to certain papal teachings; his style of reasoning dominated university theology from his day until 1600.

Francesco Petrarch (1304–1374), son of an Italian lay official at the papal court in Avignon; spent time at the papal court and various noble courts throughout Italy; a writer; helped revive the Classical forms of literature in the Late Middle Ages.

Giovanni Pisano (1245–1314), a member of a dynasty of Italian sculptors; his classically inspired works foreshadowed later developments in Renaissance sculpture.

Christine de Pizan (sometimes written as "de Pisan" or "of Pisa") (1364–about 1430), the first known Western woman to earn a living through her writings; worked in various genres of the day; the first Western writer to raise "the woman question," the modern term for the issue of women's rights in society and culture; daughter of an Italian courtier at the French court; married to a French court official; self-educated.

Claus Sluter (about 1350–1406), a Netherlandish sculptor who was chief sculptor to the Duke of Burgundy; his works epitomized the Late Gothic style.

Suger (about 1081–1151), son of peasant parents; a monk and abbot; adviser to French kings; regent of France during the absence of King Louis VII on crusade; originator of Gothic-style architecture.

William of Champeaux (about 1070–1121), a French bishop and theologian; one of the leading intellectuals of the early twelfth century.

John Wycliffe (1320–1384), educated at Oxford; recipient of royal patronage and adviser to the English king; denounced by the clergy for his heretical views; founder of a religious heresy that anticipated many of Luther's ideas.

THE EARLY MODERN PERIOD

The Early Modern Period, 1400–1700 [Chapters 11–15]

The changes under way in Late Medieval society intensified during the Early Modern period, although the feudal and ecclesiastical elite still occupied the upper rungs of the social ladder. Untitled owners of large estates continued to gain social and political power, as did prosperous businessmen. Skilled painters, sculptors, and architects, if their manners were courtly, often became part of the cultural elite. Other influential social groups outside the feudal and ecclesiastical order also appeared upon the scene, such as religious reformers and secular writers and thinkers.

Leone Battista Alberti (1404–1472), an illegitimate son of a wealthy merchant-banker family in Florence; born during his father's exile from the city; reared by his real father and became his heir; entered holy orders though this had little impact on his career and life; an architect; the leading theoretician of Early Renaissance art.

Fra Angelico (about 1400–1455), a Dominican friar in Italy; an artist; helped to establish the Early Renaissance style of painting.

Marguerite of Angoulême (better known as Marguerite of Navarre) (1492–1549), queen of Navarre and sister of King Francis I of France; probable author of the *Heptameron,* a collection of seventy frankly sexual tales in the style of Boccaccio's *Decameron;* she was a friend and protector of Rabelais, Protestant reformers, and other free spirits.

Sofonisba Anguissola (about 1532–1625), a female painter from Cremona in north Italy, who, along with El Greco, is credited with helping to introduce the Italian school of painting into Spanish culture; official court painter to the court of King Philip II of Spain, 1559–1579.

Johann Sebastian Bach (1685–1750), a member of a family of German musicians; parents died when he was ten years old; trained as a choirboy; court organist at Weimar and musician to the city of Leipzig; famous for his Baroque church music.

Francis Bacon (1561–1626), son of a powerful English court official who was a self-made man; educated at Cambridge; a high government official and scientist; impeached for abuse of office; instrumental in popularizing the new science.

Pierre Bayle (1647–1706), son of a Calvinist minister in the Netherlands; briefly a Roman Catholic; a professor at a Protestant academy; compiler and author of a famous dictionary that helped to inspire similar works during the Enlightenment.

Aphra Behn (1640–1689), an English writer who lived briefly in Surinam, South America, before coming to London where she married a man named Behn; one of the first European writers to exploit the New World in fiction, as in the short story *Oroonoko;* author of about twenty Restoration-style comedies; served as a British spy in Flanders; spent time in debtor's prison; England's first professional woman of letters.

Gianlorenzo Bernini (1598–1680), son of a Florentine sculptor; recipient of aristocratic and papal patronage; an architect; established the Florid Baroque style of architecture.

Bishop Bossuet (1627–1704), born into a family of French magistrates; educated by Jesuits; associated with the church from the age of ten onward; a high church official; author of a work that defended the divine right of kings.

Sandro Botticelli (1445–1510), an Italian painter; associated with the Medici court; famous for his chaste nudes.

Robert Boyle (1627–1691), born into an English family of wealth and influence; a physicist; his research laid the groundwork for modern chemistry.

Tycho Brahe (1546–1601), son of a Danish government official; abducted by a wealthy and childless uncle who reared him in his own castle and financed his university studies; trained as a lawyer; an astronomer; made copious observations of planetary movement that were used by Kepler in his research.

Donato Bramante (1444–1514), son of well-to-do peasants; received patronage from Milan's Sforza family and Rome's popes.

Pieter Bruegel the Elder (about 1525–1569), a Flemish painter and founder of a painting dynasty; noted for his Mannerist style and his scenes of peasant life.

Filippo Brunelleschi (1377–1446), son of a Florentine notary; trained as a goldsmith and sculptor; an architect; a founder of the Early Renaissance style.

Leonardo Bruni (1374–1444), a Florentine political leader and scholar; an exemplar of civic humanism.

John Calvin (1509–1564), son of middle-class parents, the father a lay administrator for the local bishop in Noyon, France; a religious reformer; established his Calvinist ideals in Geneva, Switzerland, his spiritual home and secular refuge.

Caravaggio (Michelangelo Merisi) (1573–1610), son of a steward and architect; orphaned at eleven years of age; apprenticed to a painter; a social rebel; an outstanding artist in the Florid Baroque style.

Baldassare Castiglione (1478–1529), son of an illustrious family; a humanist and a bishop; an embodiment of the ideal courtier; author of a popular book on court etiquette.

Nicolas Copernicus (1473–1543), son of a well-to-do Polish merchant; university educated; an astronomer; revived the heliocentric theory of the universe in modern times.

Pierre Corneille (1606–1684), born into a well-to-do, middle-class Norman family; educated in a Jesuit school; a legal official from 1628–1650; a playwright; author of *Le Cid*, one of the greatest dramas in the French language.

René Descartes (1596–1650), son of a wealthy French landowner; reared by a maternal grandmother when his mother died; a soldier and thinker; the founder of modern philosophy.

Donatello (1386–1466), son of a Florentine wool carder; trained as a sculptor; employed by the Medici and other nobles.

John Dunstable (1380–1453), served in the court of the Duke of Bedford who was regent of France from 1422 to 1435; an English composer; a key figure in the rise of Renaissance music.

Albrecht Dürer (1471–1528), son of a German goldsmith; apprenticed as a goldsmith to his father; famed for his engravings.

Desiderius Erasmus (about 1466–1536), illegitimate son of a Dutch priest; became a monk and a priest; active in English court and aristocratic circles; the outstanding Northern Humanist of the sixteenth century.

Marsilio Ficino (1433–1499), an Italian humanist and philosopher; protégé and tutor to the Medici family; directed the Florentine Academy.

Fontenelle (1657–1757), son of an impoverished nobleman; educated by Jesuits; composed libretti for operas; secretary of France's Academy of Science; a popularizer of the Scientific Revolution.

Galileo Galilei (1564–1642), son of an Italian musician; studied medicine at university; an astronomer; censured by the papacy for his scientific views; a key figure in the birth of modern science.

Artemisia Gentileschi (1593–1653), daughter of an important artist, Orazio Gentileschi, who instructed her in the art of painting; the only female follower of Caravaggio; worked in Florence, Venice, Naples, and Rome; famed for the female assertiveness in her paintings.

Lorenzo Ghiberti (about 1381–1455), unclear parentage because his mother, while married to Cione Ghiberti, lived as the common-law wife of a goldsmith (Bartolo di Michele), whom she later married after the death of Cione; trained as a goldsmith; the creator of "the Gates of Paradise," Michelangelo's term for the east doors of the Florentine Baptistery.

El Greco (Domenikos Theotokopoulos) (1541–1614), a Greek who spent most of his adult life in Italy and Spain; served various ecclesiastical and aristocratic patrons in Toledo, Spain, from 1577 to 1614; his art epitomized the Spanish Mannerist style.

Hugo Grotius (1583–1645), son of a civic and university official in the Netherlands; a child prodigy; university trained; the founder of the study of international law.

Matthias Grünewald (about 1460–1528), court painter and leading art official to the Archbishop of Mainz; numerous ecclesiastical commissions; famous for his *Isenheim Altarpiece.*

George Frederick Handel (1685–1759), son of a successful German surgeon and the daughter of a Lutheran clergyman; a composer; renowned for his Italian-style operas and the oratorio, *Messiah.*

Jules Hardouin-Mansart (1646–1708), a member of a family of distinguished French architects; official architect to King Louis XIV of France; one of the two architects who redesigned the Palace at Versailles.

William Harvey (1578–1657), son of a prosperous English businessman; university trained; a university professor at Padua, Italy; a scientist; proved that the blood circulated.

Henry VIII (1509–1547), king of England; founder of the Church of England.

Thomas Hobbes (1588–1679), son of an English priest who abandoned his family after a brawl outside his own church door; after the father's disappearance, the family was taken in by a well-to-do maker of gloves; educated at Oxford; a philosopher; author of *The Leviathan.*

Josquin des Prez (about 1440–1521), trained as a choirboy from an early age; a Burgundian; Europe's dominant composer in about 1500.

Johannes Kepler (1571–1630), son of a scruffy mercenary German soldier and the daughter of an innkeeper; a sickly child; university educated because of the generosity of the local dukes; served the Austrian emperor; an astronomer; originator of three laws of planetary motion; a key figure in the Scientific Revolution.

Thomas Kyd (about 1557–1595), son of a London notary; arrested for treasonable activity; a playwright; author of an early version of *Hamlet.*

Andre Le Nôtre (1613–1700), son of the master gardener to France's King Louis XIII at the Tuileries; succeeded to his father's career; designed the park at Versailles Palace.

Louis Le Vau (1612–1670), son of a stonemason; chief architect to Louis XIV of France; one of the two architects who redesigned Versailles Palace.

Leonardo da Vinci (1452–1519), illegitimate son of a Florentine notary and a peasant woman who lived on his father's estate; apprenticed to the sculptor Verrochio; the outstanding example of a Renaissance Man.

Judith Leyster (1609–1660), Dutch painter and art teacher; member of an artists' guild in Haarlem; skilled as a painter of genre scenes for the art market; after 1643, she abandoned her career to give support to her painter-husband's business and artistic interests.

John Locke (1632–1704), son of an English lawyer of modest means; university educated; received the patronage of aristocrats; a scholar; the founder of modern liberalism; author of *Essay Concerning the Human Understanding.*

Ignatius Loyola (about 1493–1556), youngest son of a noble and wealthy Spanish family; a religious reformer; founder of the Jesuit order.

Jean-Baptiste Lully (1632–1687), an Italian, brought to France at a young age; trained as a musician; a naturalized French citizen; court composer to Louis XIV; founded French opera.

Martin Luther (1483–1546), son of a wealthy miner; a monk and a priest; educated at university; a religious reformer; condemned as a heretic and saved by German nobles; founded Lutheranism, the first Protestant Christian religion.

Niccoló Machiavelli (1469–1527), son of a prominent though poor Florentine family; important government official, 1498–1513; forced into exile by his political enemies; the founder of modern political theory.

Carlo Maderno (1556–1629), member of a family of well-known architects; chief architect of St. Peter's; changed St. Peter's from a Greek cross shape to a Latin cross shape.

Christopher Marlowe (1564–1593), son of a middle-class tradesman, a shoemaker; violent and disreputable behavior often got him into trouble; a reputation for atheism; a playwright; the author of several important dramas, including *Dr. Faustus*, the first English stage version of the Faust legend.

Masaccio (1401–1428), son of an Italian notary and a daughter of an Italian innkeeper; trained as a painter; the first painter to master linear perspective in the Early Renaissance.

Maria Sibylla Merian (1647–1717), a painter and a scientist; German-born but lived in the Netherlands most of her life; earned fame with her precise illustrations of insects and animals for the book *Dissertation in Insect Generations and Metamorphoses in Surinam*; this work was based on her two-year stay in the South American Duth colony of Surinam.

Angela Merici, founder (1535) of the Company of St. Ursula, or the Ursulines, a Counter-Reformation order of laywomen, in Brescia, Italy; at first, the Ursulines did not take formal vows, but lived in their own homes, practiced chastity, served the sick and the poor, and taught the young; after 1540, they were cloistered and placed under male supervision.

Michelangelo Buonarroti (1475–1564), son of a minor government official who had come down in the world; apprenticed briefly to the painter Ghirlandaio; taken under the wing of the Medici ruler of Florence; a painter, sculptor, and architect; one of the towering figures of Western art.

John Milton (1608–1674), son of an English Protestant notary and moneylender; educated at Cambridge University; supported the Puritan cause in the English civil war; blind at forty-three years of age; a poet; author of *Paradise Lost.*

Molière (Jean Baptiste Poquelin) (1622–1673), son of a furnisher of the royal household of the French king; confined to debtor's prison; toured for years with a traveling theater troupe as author, actor, and manager; official entertainer to Louis XIV; certain of his plays were banned by the church; the founder of modern stage comedy in France.

Michel de Montaigne (1533–1592), son of a French noble; a governmental official and thinker; the originator of modern skepticism.

Claudio Monteverdi (1567–1643), son of a barber-surgeon and chemist; trained as a musician; received aristocratic patronage; one of the founders of opera.

Thomas More (1478–1535), son of an English lawyer and judge; a political leader and humanist; beheaded by the English king, Henry VIII, for his political views; author of *Utopia.*

Isaac Newton (1642–1727), son of an English farmer of modest means; a sickly child; father died before Isaac was born and his mother later remarried, leaving the baby to be reared by a grandmother; tension between son and stepfather; educated at Cambridge; a scholar; one of the originators of calculus; completed the revolution in astronomy begun by Copernicus.

Giovanni Pierluigi da Palestrina (about 1525–1594), trained from an early age as a choirboy; wrote music for the papal court; the chief composer of the Counter-Reformation.

Palladio (Andrea di Pietro) (1508–1580), son of a miller; trained as a sculptor and architect; his works and writings launched Palladianism, a highly influential architectural tradition.

Parmigianino (1503–1540), trained as a painter by his uncles; served various noble and ecclesiastical patrons; helped to establish the Mannerist style.

Blaise Pascal (1623–1662), son of a French judge and mathematician; a child prodigy; a mathematician and philosopher; a forerunner of modern Christian existentialism.

Pico della Mirandola (1463–1494), son of an Italian prince of a minor principality; a humanist; a leading exponent of Renaissance Neo-Platonism.

Piero della Francesca (about 1420–1492), son of a tanner and shoemaker; trained as a painter; a member of the town council in Sansepolcro; associated with the noble court of Montefeltro; an important painter in the Early Renaissance style.

Pius II (1458–1464), son of a noble Italian family of reduced circumstances; a papal official and later a pope; a leading humanist of the Early Renaissance.

Nicolas Poussin (1594–1665), son of poor peasants; awakened to artistic abilities late, at age eighteen; a painter-philosopher in later life; the outstanding painter in the French Baroque style.

Andrea Pozzo (1642–1709), a Jesuit lay brother; trained as a painter and architect; noted for his illusionistic ceiling paintings in the Florid Baroque style.

François Rabelais (about 1494–1553), son of a rich landowner and a prominent lawyer; a Franciscan friar; studied medicine; his works were condemned as indecent and obscene by the Council of Trent; author of satirical books; a leading Northern Humanist.

Jean Racine (1639–1699), son of a French family of modest means, excise or legal officials; orphaned and penniless at age three; educated at a convent where his grandmother had settled; a playwright; after success as a playwright, he withdrew and became a court official; the outstanding author of tragedy in the French language.

Raphael Santi (1483–1520), son of a minor Italian painter; served various aristocrats and several popes; famous for his images of sweet madonnas; one of the geniuses of the High Renaissance.

Rembrandt van Rijn (1609–1669), son of a prosperous Dutch miller and a baker's daughter; trained as a painter; one of the greatest artists in the Western tradition.

Peter Paul Rubens (1577–1640), son of a Protestant courtier and lawyer; well-educated; trained as a painter; lucrative commissions from aristocrats in Italy, Spain, and France; one of the outstanding painters in the Florid Baroque style.

Madame de Sévigné (born Marie de Rabutin-Chantal, 1626–1696), a French noblewoman wed at age eighteen to Henri, Marquis de Sévigné, and widowed seven years later; never remarried; a woman of letters, author of over 1,500 letters, mainly to her daughter; her letters constitute a portrait of late-seventeenth-century upper-class life.

William Shakespeare (1564–1616), son of an English tradesman and alderman of Stratford-upon-Avon; a playwright and poet; revived stage comedy and tragedy for English-speaking audiences; the outstanding playwright in the English language.

Elisabetta Sirani (1638–1665), daughter of the Bolognese painter Gian Andrea Sirani, although her father did not encourage her art; her artistic gifts were identified by Carlo Cesare Malvasia, a friend and a biographer of Bolognese artists; she was a virtuoso painter who worked quickly and easily, so that famous visitors (such as the Duke of Tuscany) came to observe her at work; her style was similar to that of Guido Reni, the leading Bolognese painter of the day, and she specialized in religoius and mythological and historical subjects; she died at twenty-seven, and her sudden death resulted in a murder trial but the accused servant was acquited; today, she is thought to have died of stomach ulcers brought on by overwork.

Gaspara Stampa (about 1524–1554), a Venetian courtesan, or kept woman; pioneered a type of sonnet that asserts the moral worth of the suffering (usually female) lover; transformed the male Petrarchan ideal into a female point of view.

Tintoretto (1518–1594), son of an Italian silk dyer; trained as a painter; a leading Venetian Mannerist.

Titian (about 1488–1576), son of a modest Italian official; trained as a painter; the supreme European painter around the middle of the sixteenth century.

Lorenzo Valla (1406–1457), son of a lawyer employed at the papal court in Rome; held heretical views but survived because of the protection of political and religious leaders, including the pope; proved that the Donation of Constantine was a forgery.

Anthony Van Dyck (1599–1641), son of a well-to-do Flemish silk merchant; trained as a painter; court painter in Italy and England; noted for his portraits of the English court.

Diego Velázquez (1599–1660), trained as a painter; official painter to the Spanish court; one of the masters of the Florid Baroque style.

Jan Vermeer (1632–1675), son of a tavern owner in Delft, where he lived for his entire life; a painter and art dealer; noted for his interior scenes, painted in the Protestant Baroque style.

Vesalius (1514–1564), a member of a family of physicians and pharmacists in Italy; a university professor; an important figure in establishing modern medicine.

Vittorini da Feltre (1378–1446), an Italian schoolmaster and humanist; one of the most significant educational reformers of the Early Renaissance.

Thomas Weelkes (about 1575–1623), an English composer; England's leading composer of madrigals; organist at Winchester College, then at Chichester cathedral, where he remained until his death; perhaps associated with the Chapel Royal.

Adrian Willaert (about 1490–1562), trained first as a lawyer, then as a musician; a Netherlandish composer who is considered the founder of the Venetian school of music.

Christopher Wren (1632–1723), son of a clergyman, later dean of Windsor; educated at Oxford; a university professor; an architect; rebuilt London's churches after the great fire of 1666; his masterpiece is St. Paul's Cathedral.

THE MODERN WORLD

The Modern World, 1700–1914 [Chapters 16–19]

In 1700 the nobility and church leaders still constituted a ruling elite, although the middle class was rapidly gaining ground. During the course of this period, between 1700 and 1914, the middle class overtook and passed its old rivals, to become the ruling class, thus completing a rise to political and social power that had begun in the High Middle Ages.

Robert Adam (1728–1792), son of a Scottish architect; trained as an architect; built houses for English nobles and wealthy businessmen; a founder of Neoclassical-style architecture.

Jane Austen (1775–1817), daughter of an English clergyman; a novelist; author of gently satirical novels that portray the middle-class world from which she sprang.

Honoré de Balzac (1799–1850), middle-class background; son of a French governmental official; his mother was the daughter of prosperous cloth merchants; a writer; author of *The Human Comedy*, a series of nearly one hundred novels that depict French society in the early nineteenth century.

Charles Barry (1795–1860), son of an English stationer; trained as an architect; codesigned with Pugin the British Houses of Parliament.

Aubrey Beardsley (1872–1898), son of an English worker of odd jobs; an illustrator; associated with the late-nineteenth-century Decadent movement.

Pierre Beaumarchais (1732–1799), son of a French clockmaker; an accomplished harpist; a playwright; author of the satirical play that inspired Mozart's opera *The Marriage of Figaro*.

Ludwig van Beethoven (1770–1827), son and grandson of German court musicians; the family name shows a distant Dutch background; trained as a musician; supported himself through concerts, lessons, and the sales of his music; deaf in his later years; a composer; one of the West's greatest musicians.

Jeremy Bentham (1748–1832), a member of a prosperous English family of landowners; a child prodigy; the founder of Utilitarianism.

Hector Berlioz (1803–1869), son of a French physician and a domestic servant; studied medicine and then music; a composer; a master of the Romantic style.

Umberto Boccioni (1882–1916), son of an Italian governmental employee; a sculptor; one of the Futurists.

Niels Bohr (1885–1962), son of an eminent Danish physiologist; a physicist; made major contributions to quantum theory.

Germain Boffrand (1667–1754), son of a minor French sculptor and architect; trained as an architect; designed the interior rooms of the Hotel de Soubise in Paris; worked in the Rococo style.

Rosa Bonheur (1822–1899), reared in a progressive family devoted to the enlightened ideas of the Utopian Socialist, St. Simon; famed for her Realist paintings of animal scenes; she often wore male attire; the sale of lithographs based on her paintings made her a celebrity in France, Britain, and the United States.

François Boucher (1703–1770), son of a French designer who kept an art shop near the Louvre; learned painting from his father; official painter to Louis XV; a master of the Rococo style.

Matthew Brady (about 1823–1896), of impoverished background; perhaps illiterate; blind in the prime of life; established a photographic studio in New York City when he was about twenty; died penniless; famed for his photographs of the American Civil War.

Johannes Brahms (1833–1897), son of a German musician; trained as a musician; a composer; the involuntary leader of the conservative anti-Wagner school in the late nineteenth century.

Georges Braque (1882–1963), son of a French painter and owner of a decorating business; a painter; with Picasso, a developer of Cubism.

Vera Brittain (1893–1970), daughter of an upper-middle-class family in Buxton, England; one of the first women graduates of Oxford University; nurse volunteer during World War I; socialist, political activist, novelist, and most famously, author of *Testament of Youth*, her autobiography, covering the years from her birth until about 1930.

Charlotte Brontë (1816–1855), daughter of an English clergyman; a member of a distinguished literary family; a novelist; author of *Wuthering Heights*, a masterpiece of Romantic fiction.

Emily Brontë (1818–1848), daughter of an English clergyman; a member of a distinguished literary family; a novelist; author of *Jane Eyre*, a masterpiece of Romantic fiction.

George Gordon, Lord Byron (1788–1824), a member of an impoverished noble family in England; physically handicapped; lived in the ruins of a castle inherited from his great uncle; a poet; in virtual exile from England because of his scandalous personal life; his behavior inspired Byronism, a nineteenth-century fashion that encouraged bohemian living; a master of Romanticism.

Mary Cassatt (1845–1967), daughter of an American banker; studied and lived in Paris; a painter; a leading Impressionist.

Paul Cezanne (1839–1906), son of a wealthy French banker and tradesman; a painter; a leading Post-Impressionist.

Anton Chekhov (1860–1904), son of a Russian former serf who became a struggling grocer; a playwright and short story writer; a major figure in Naturalism.

Kate Chopin (born Catherine O'Flaherty, 1851–1904), an American short story writer and novelist; a native of St. Louis; married for twelve years to a Creole planter and merchant in Louisiana; widowed, she supported herself and her family through her writings; a member of the Naturalist school, though she used local color, or regional details, especially about Creole and Cajun life in Louisiana; abruptly stopped writing when her novel *The Awakening* (1899), about a passionate woman's sexual awakening, was greeted with a firestorm of negative criticism.

Samuel Taylor Coleridge (1772–1834), son of an English priest and schoolmaster; a poet; coauthor with Wordsworth of *Lyrical Ballads,* the first work of Romantic literature in England.

John Constable (1776–1837), son of a wealthy English miller; a painter; a master of the Romantic style.

François Couperin (1668–1733), born into a French family of musicians; trained as a musician; a leading musician in the Rococo style.

Gustave Courbet (1819–1877), son of a prosperous French farmer; trained as a painter; helped to establish the Realist style.

Marie Sklodowska Curie (1867–1934), daughter of a Polish teacher; a governess and then a scientist; first person to win two Nobel Prizes in science.

Pierre Curie (1859–1906), son of a French doctor; working with his wife, Marie, he identified two new radioactive elements, radium and polonium.

Louis-Jacques-Mandé Daguerre (1787–1851), an unstable background; son of a French minor government official and designer of stage sets; trained as a stage designer; one of the inventors of the photographic technique.

John Dalton (1766–1844), son of an English weaver; a Quaker in Anglican England; a teacher; contributed to modern atomic theory.

Charles Darwin (1809–1882), son of a well-to-do English physician; his mother was a member of the wealthy Wedgwood family who manufactured china; a scholar; author of *Origin of Species* and *Descent of Man.*

Honoré Daumier (1808–1879), born into a French family of glaziers, a lower-middle-class occupation; a caricaturist and painter; an early Realist.

Jacques-Louis David (1748–1825), son of a small but prosperous French textile dealer; reared by uncles after the early death of the father; trained as a painter; the founder of Neoclassical painting.

Claude Debussy (1862–1918), born to an impoverished French family; a musician and composer; rescued by a wealthy Russian heiress who hired him to play duets with her and her children; helped to establish Impressionism.

Madame du Deffand (Marie de Marquise du Deffand, 1679–1780), French noblewoman; maintained a famous Parisian salon frequented by Voltaire and other leading *philosophes;* influenced the spread of ideas through her salon.

Edgar Degas (1834–1917), son of a wealthy French family who had banking and other business connections; trained as an artist; a painter; a leading painter associated with both Impressionism and Post-Impressionism.

Eugène Delacroix (1798–1863), middle-class background, his father a government official and his mother a member of a family of furniture-makers for the royal court; trained as a painter; a master of the Romantic style.

Charles Dickens (1812–1870), son of an English governmental clerk whose impecunious habits landed him in debtors' prison; a journalist and novelist; the most popular novelist of the nineteenth century; a Realist.

Denis Diderot (1713–1784), son of a French cutler who specialized in surgical instruments; a writer; editor of the *Encyclopédie,* the monumental project that stands as a summation of the Enlightenment.

Feodor Dostoevsky (1821–1881), son of a Russian army doctor and landowner who was later murdered by his serfs; educated at an army engineering college; forced into exile in Siberia because of his liberal values; a writer; author of *Crime and Punishment,* one of the outstanding novels of Western literature.

Albert Einstein (1879–1955), born into a family of German Jews; father owned a small electrical plant and engineering works; a physicist; one of the founders of modern physics.

George Eliot (Mary Ann Evans) (1819–1880), daughter of an English estates agent for a wealthy landowner; an outstanding Realist novelist.

Friedrich Engels (1820–1895), son of a family of German Jews; his father was a wealthy manufacturer; coauthor with Marx of *The Communist Manifesto.*

Johann Gottlieb Fichte (1762–1814), son of a German ribbon weaver; university educated; a philosopher and university professor; made important contributions to German idealism.

Henry Fielding (1707–1754), an upper-middle-class background; his father was a colonel in the army and his mother was the daughter of a judge; a novelist; author of *Tom Jones.*

Gustave Flaubert (1821–1880), a member of a French family of physicians; his father was a surgeon and his mother the daughter of a doctor; a novelist; an outstanding Realist.

Charles Fourier (1772–1837), inherited his mother's estate; a leading utopian socialist.

Jean Honoré Fragonard (1732–1806), son of a French haberdasher's assistant; apprenticed to a lawyer; trained as a painter; a master of the Rococo style.

Benjamin Franklin (1706–1790), son of a soap- and candlemaker in the North American British colonies; formal education ended at age twelve; apprenticed to his brother, a printer; a diplomat and hero of the American Revolutionary War.

Sigmund Freud (1856–1939), son of an Austrian Jewish wool merchant; a psychologist; the founder of psychoanalysis.

Caspar David Friedrich (1774–1840), son of a German candlemaker; trained as a painter; the outstanding German Romantic painter.

Elizabeth Gaskell (1810–1865), daughter of an English Unitarian minister; reared by a maternal aunt; a novelist; an outstanding Realist.

Paul Gauguin (1848–1903), son of a French father and a half-French, half-Peruvian Creole mother; father was a journalist; spent most of his childhood in Peru; a sailor for six years; a bank clerk and a painter who exhibited with the Impressionists; abandoned Europe for the French colony of Tahiti in the South Pacific; a leading Post-Impressionist.

Theodore Géricault (1791–1824), son of French well-to-do parents; trained as a painter; a master of the Romantic style.

Edward Gibbon (1737–1794), a member of a prosperous, upper-middle-class English family; a man of independent means; a scholar; author of *History of the Decline and Fall of the Roman Empire.*

Johann Wolfgang von Goethe (1749–1832), of middle-class German stock, the father was a lawyer and the mother a daughter of a civic official; a writer and thinker; the greatest figure in German literature.

Francisco Goya (1746–1828), son of poor Spanish parents; trained as a painter; official painter to the Spanish court; the most significant painter in Spanish art.

Franz Joseph Haydn (1732–1809), son of a German wagon maker and house painter; trained as a musician; musical director for aristocrats; a composer; a master of Classical music.

Georg Wilhelm Friedrich Hegel (1770–1831), son of a German revenue official; university trained; a university professor and thinker; a contributor to German idealism and one of the most important Western thinkers.

William Hogarth (1697–1764), son of an English schoolteacher and minor writer; trained as a silversmith; a painter; the first major artist to produce multiple copies (engravings) from his works.

Victor Hugo (1802–1885), son of a French general in Napoleon's army; a writer; author of *Les Misérables,* one of the leading Romantic novels.

David Hume (1711–1766), a member of a Scottish middle-class family; the father was lord of a small estate and the mother was the daughter of a judge; an important philosopher in the Enlightenment.

Joris-Karl Huysmans (1848–1907), son of a French father and a Dutch mother; a civil servant; a founder of the Decadent movement.

Henrik Ibsen (1828–1906), son of a Norwegian businessman who went bankrupt; spent much of his life abroad in Italy; a playwright in the Naturalist style; the outstanding playwright of the nineteenth century.

Jean-Auguste-Dominique Ingres (1780–1867), son of a minor French artist; trained as a painter; a master of Neoclassicism.

Scott Joplin (1868–1917), born into a musical family of African Americans; his parents were former slaves; a musician and composer; popularized ragtime music.

Carl Jung (1875–1961), son of a Swiss philologist and Protestant minister; a psychologist; the founder of Jungian therapy; famous for his theory of archetypes.

Franz Kafka (1883–1924), son of a Jewish merchant in Austria; overshadowed by a domineering father; a writer; author of *The Trial,* one of the classic works of Modernism.

Wassily Kandinsky (1866–1944), born into a well-to-do Russian family in Siberia; he was descended from Mongolian aristocrats; voluntary exile from his native Russia; a painter; founder of *Der Blaue Reiter (The Blue Rider)* school in Munich, Germany.

Immanuel Kant (1724–1804), son of a German saddler; university educated; a university professor and thinker; one of the most significant thinkers in the West.

Julie de Lespinassse (1732–1776), acting first as companion to Madame du Deffand and then as hostess of her own Parisian salon; a frequent guest in her salon was Jean d'Alembert, coeditor of *Encyclopédie;* influenced the spread of ideas through her salon.

Charles Lyell (1797–1875), descended from a Scottish family of aristocrats; his father was a naturalist; a geologist; his research on fossils proved that the earth was much older than Christians claimed.

Thomas Malthus (1766–1834), son of a prosperous English family; a clergyman; author of the groundbreaking essay *On Population.*

Edouard Manet (1832–1883), son of a high-placed French governmental official; a painter; his "art for art's sake" theory laid the groundwork for Modern art.

Karl Marx (1818–1883), a member of a German Jewish family who had converted to Christianity; his father was a successful lawyer; exiled from Germany because of his political views; coauthor with Engels of *The Communist Manifesto.*

Henri Matisse (1869–1954), son of a French grain merchant; became an artist at age twenty; a painter and sculptor; a founder of Fauvism.

Dmitri Mendeleev (1834–1907), son of a Russian schoolmaster; his mother operated a glass factory that she leased; a scientist; worked out the periodic table of elements based on atomic weights.

John Stuart Mill (1806–1873), son of a well-known Scottish intellectual; a child prodigy; a leading Utilitarian.

Jean-François Millet (1814–1875), son of French peasants; trained as a painter; a member of the Barbizon school.

Claude Monet (1840–1926), son of a successful French businessman in ship-chandlering and groceries; trained as an artist; a painter; a founder of Impressionism.

Lady Mary Wortley Montagu (1689–1762), a noblewoman; granddaughter of the famous diarist John Evelyn and a distant cousin of the novelist Henry Fielding; wife of Edward Wortley, ambassador extraordinary to the Turkish court; eventually separated from her husband and moved to Italy where she led a bohemian existence; largely self-taught, she was one of the best educated women of her day; author of one of the West's most famous collections of letters.

Baron de Montesquieu (1689–1755), a member of a French aristocratic family; a major figure of the Enlightenment; author of *Spirit of the Laws,* one of the works that represented the beginning of the social sciences.

Berthe Morisot (1841–1895), a member of a wealthy French family of artists; her grandfather was Fragonard and she married Manet's brother; trained as a painter; a leading Impressionist.

Wolfgang Amadeus Mozart (1756–1791), son of a successful musician; a child prodigy; trained as a musician; served various aristocratic courts; a master of Classical music and one of the West's greatest musical geniuses.

Edvard Munch (1863–1944), a member of a distinguished and wealthy Norwegian family; a painter; experienced a nervous collapse in 1908–1909; a major Expressionist.

Balthasar Neumann (1687–1753), son of a poor German weaver; trained as a canon and bell founder; studied architecture; designed the Residenz, the palace of the prince-bishop of Würzburg.

Friedrich Nietzsche (1844–1900), son and grandson of Lutheran ministers; after age five and the death of his father, reared in a household of women; university educated; abandoned a university career and lived abroad; suffered a nervous collapse in about 1890 from which he never recovered; a chief prophet of Modernism.

Robert Owen (1771–1858), son of an English saddler and ironmonger; trained as a clothier; a self-made man, he became a wealthy industrialist; a leading utopian socialist.

Louis Pasteur (1822–1895), born into a family of French tanners; a scientist; established the germ theory of disease; a national hero in nineteenth-century France.

Pablo Picasso (1881–1973), son of a Spanish art teacher; trained as an artist; dominated Western painting from about 1906 until his death.

Camille Pissaro (1830–1903), born in the West Indies, the son of a Portuguese-Jewish father and a Creole mother; a prosperous family; lived in Paris after the age of twelve; a painter; a major Impressionist.

Max Planck (1858–1947), son of a distinguished German professor of law; university educated; a physicist; established quantum theory.

Alexander Pope (1688–1744), son of an English linen merchant; a Roman Catholic in Protestant England; had severe physical disabilities; a poet; author of *Essay on Man.*

Marcel Proust (1871–1922), son of a wealthy French physician and a French Jewish mother; moved in the upper reaches of middle-class society; retreated to a cork-lined study to write; a novelist; a major figure in the Decadent movement.

A. W. N. Pugin (1812–1852), son of an English architect; trained as an architect; codesigned with Barry the British Houses of Parliament.

Jean-Philippe Rameau (1683–1764), son of a French church organist; trained as a musician; a master of the Rococo style.

Maurice Ravel (1875–1937), French composer, conductor, and pianist; loosely indebted to Debussy; composer of operas, ballet scores, orchestral works, songs, chamber music, and piano music; refused the Legion of Honor in 1920, for his work as a transport driver in World War I; final years marred by failing health caused by Pick's disease.

Auguste Renoir (1841–1919), son of a French tailor; worked in a china factory at age thirteen, painting porcelain plates; a painter; a major figure in Impressionism.

David Ricardo (1772–1823), a member of an English Protestant family of converted Jews; his father made a fortune on the London stock exchange; a thinker; author of "the iron law of wages," a key concept in classical economics.

Samuel Richardson (1689–1761), son of an English tradesman; a novelist; author of *Pamela,* one of the first novels.

Auguste Rodin (1840–1917), born into a poor French family; trained as a mason; a sculptor; the leading Western sculptor in the early twentieth century.

Wilhelm Conrad Roentgen (1845–1923), son of a prosperous German textile merchant; expelled from secondary school; university educated; a scientist; discovered X rays.

Jean-Jacques Rousseau (1712–1778), son of a Swiss master watchmaker and sometime dancing master; changed religion several times; an unstable personality; a writer and thinker; one of the outstanding figures of the Enlightenment.

Comte de Saint-Simon (1760–1825), a member of a family of impoverished French aristocrats; an officer in the army, served with the Americans in their war for independence; a leading utopian socialist.

George Sand (the pen name of Amandine Aurore-Lucie Dupin) (1804–1876); her father was descended from Polish royalty and her mother was the daughter of a Parisian birdseller; a supporter of progressive causes, such as female emancipaton and socialism; usually dressed in public in the garb of a typical bourgeois gentleman; the first woman to play an active role in a revolutionary government (the Paris uprising of 1848); the best-known woman novelist of the nineteenth century; author of about eighty novels and twenty plays.

Friedrich Wilhelm Joseph von Schelling (1775–1854), son of a German Lutheran minister and professor of Oriental languages; a child prodigy; a thinker; a major figure in German idealism.

Arnold Schoenberg (1874–1951), son of an Austrian owner of a small business; a composer; the originator of serial music.

Franz Schubert (1797–1828), son of an Austrian schoolmaster; trained as a musician; a composer; perfected the German art song.

Robert Schumann (1810–1856), German composer, pianist, and writer; composer of *lieder,* four symphonies, works for chorus, chamber works, and piano works; trained as a pianist but his right hand became crippled in 1832, probably as a result of disease; famed for his musical criticism; music director in Dusseldorf until forced to retire as a result of the onset of neurological illness; died in an insane asylum.

Georges Seurat (1859–1891), son of a French landowner of moderate means; a painter; a major Post-Impressionist.

Mary Shelley (1797–1851), outstanding English novelist; the daughter of the feminist writer Mary Wollstonecraft and the radical novelist William Godwin; eloped with the married poet Percy Bysshe Shelley whom she married after his first wife committed suicide; her first novel, *Frankenstein*, written before she was twenty-one, supplied two of the most pervasive figures in Western culture—Dr. Frankenstein and his manufactured monster.

Adam Smith (1723–1790), son of a Scottish governmental official; studied at Oxford; a thinker; the founder of laissez-faire economic theory.

Jacques Germain Soufflot (1713–1780), son of a French lawyer; an architect; designed the Panthéon in Paris; a master of Neoclassicism.

Madame de Stael (Germaine Necker) (1766–1817), daughter of a famous Swiss banker who served under King Louis XVI of France; helped popularize German culture and writers with her book *On Germany* (1810).

Igor Stravinsky (1882–1971), son of a distinguished Russian opera singer; trained as a musician; a composer; the head of the Neoclassical school of music after 1919.

August Strindberg (1849–1912), son of a Swedish aristocrat who had come down in the world, becoming a steamship agent; his mother was a former waitress; unstable childhood; a playwright; a leading figure of Expressionism.

Louis Sullivan (1856–1924), son of American immigrants, an Irish father and a Swiss mother; father was a dance instructor; university educated; an architect, the leader of the Chicago school.

William Henry Fox Talbot (1800–1877), born into an English middle-class family; university educated; one of the originators of the photographic process.

Giovanni Battista Tiepolo (1696–1770), son of a prosperous Venetian merchant; a painter; famous for his illusionistic ceiling paintings.

Leo Tolstoy (1828–1910), son of a Russian landowner; a military officer; a novelist; converted to fundamentalist Christianity; author of *War and Peace*; an outstanding Realist.

Joseph Mallord William Turner (1775–1851), son of an English barber; reared by an uncle after the age of ten; trained as a painter; a master of Romantic painting.

Vincent Van Gogh (1853–1890), son of a poor Dutch pastor; a failed career as a minister to the poor; a painter; emotionally unstable, he committed suicide; a major figure of Post-Impressionism.

Giuseppe Verdi (1813–1901), son of a poor Italian merchant and tavern owner; a composer; the greatest Italian composer of opera.

Louise-Elizabeth Vigée-Lebrun (1755–1842), daughter of a French painter; a portrait painter; court painter to Queen Marie Antoinette; a master of the Rococo style.

Voltaire (François-Marie Arouet) (1694–1778), son of a well-to-do French lawyer; educated by Jesuits; interned in the Bastille twice and exiled to England once; spent most of his career outside of Paris because of his unorthodox views; a writer and thinker; a major figure of the Enlightenment.

Richard Wagner (1813–1883), son of a German police chief; after the father's death, his mother wed an actor; university trained; a composer; composed *The Ring of the Nibelung*, the most famous cycle of operas in the repertory; the dominant musical figure at the end of the nineteenth century.

Jean-Antoine Watteau (1684–1721), son of a Flemish tiler; trained as a painter; a painter and decorator; founded the Rococo style.

John Wesley (1703–1791), a member of an English family of gentry and clergy; there were religious nonconformists in the family background; founded the Methodist religion.

Oscar Wilde (1854–1900), son of a wealthy Irish surgeon; university educated; imprisoned for homosexuality; author of *The Picture of Dorian Gray*; a major figure in the Decadent movement.

Mary Wollstonecraft (1759–1797), writer and early feminist; the daughter of a failed farmer who abandoned the family; a failure as a schoolteacher and a governess; author of *A Vindication of the Rights of Woman*, 1792; attempted suicide after the birth of an illegitimate child; later married the radical writer William Godwin, and died in childbirth, though her daughter survived and grew up to become Mary Godwin Shelley.

William Wordsworth (1770–1850), son of an English businessman and the daughter of a linen merchant; a poet; coauthor with Samuel Taylor Coleridge of *Lyrical Ballads*; founded English Romantic poetry.

Frank Lloyd Wright (1869–1959), born into a middle-class family that had a precarious existence; the father was an itinerant minister and the mother a schoolteacher; an architect; the designer of the prototype of the "ranch house," the type of domestic architecture that dominated American suburbia in the mid–twentieth century.

Émile Zola (1840–1902), son of an Italian father and a French mother; a writer; a major figure in Naturalism.